Nineteenth-Century Amer
A Critical 1

G000109906

In Memoriam

This collection is dedicated to the life and work of
Elaine Hedges (1927–1997),
model scholar, generous mentor,
and trailblazer in the recovery of nineteenth-century
American women's writing

Jayne Wood
December 2002
Leeds, England.

Nineteenth-Century American Women Writers:

A Critical Reader

Edited by

Karen L. Kilcup

BLACKWELL
Publishers

Copyright © Blackwell Publishers Ltd, 1998
Preface, introduction, and selection copyright © Karen L. Kilcup, 1998

First published 1998

2 4 6 8 10 9 7 5 3 1

Blackwell Publishers Inc.
350 Main Street
Malden, Massachusetts 02148
USA

Blackwell Publishers Ltd
108 Cowley Road
Oxford OX4 1JF
UK

All rights reserved. Except for the quotation of short passages for the purposes of criticism and review, no part of this publication may be reproduced, stored in a retrieval system, or transmitted, in any form or by any means, electronic, mechanical, photocopying, recording or otherwise, without the prior permission of the publisher.

Except in the United States of America, this book is sold subject to the condition that it shall not, by way of trade or otherwise, be lent, resold, hired out, or otherwise circulated without the publisher's prior consent in any form of binding or cover other than that in which it is published and without a similar condition including this condition being imposed on the subsequent purchaser.

Library of Congress Cataloging-in-Publication Data
Nineteenth-century American women writers: a critical reader/edited by Karen L. Kilcup.
p. cm.
Includes index.
ISBN 0–631–20053–3. – ISBN 0–631–20054–1 (pbk)
1. American literature – Women authors – History and criticism.   2. Women and literature – United States – History – 19th century.   3. American literature – 19th century – History and criticism.
I. Kilcup, Karen L.
PS217.W64N57   1998
810.9'9287'09034–dc21   97–45807

British Library Cataloguing in Publication Data
A CIP catalogue record for this book is available from the British Library.

Typeset in 10.5 on 12 pt Garamond 3
by Graphicraft Typesetters Ltd., Hong Kong
Printed in Great Britain by T.J. International, Padstow, Cornwall

This book is printed on acid-free paper

Contents

Contributors

Judith Fetterley is Professor of English and Women's Studies at the University at Albany, SUNY. A distinguished feminist scholar and award-winning teacher, she has published work that includes *The Resisting Reader: A Feminist Approach to American Fiction* (1978), *Provisions: A Reader from 19th Century American Women Writers* (1985), and (with Marjorie Pryse) *American Women Regionalists, 1850–1910* (1992).

Editor of *Western American Literature* and Past President of the Western Literature Association, Melody Graulich is Professor of English and Director of American Studies at Utah State University. In addition to *Western Trails: A Collection of Short Stories* (1987) and *Western Women Writers*, a special issue of *Legacy: A Journal of American Women Writers* (1989), her work includes *Exploring the Lost Borders: A Collection of Critical Essays on Mary Austin* (forthcoming, Nevada).

A US national Distinguished Teacher, Karen L. Kilcup is Associate Professor of English at The University of North Carolina at Greensboro. Recently the Dorothy M. Healy Visiting Professor of American Studies at Westbrook College, she has many publications in the field, including *Nineteenth-Century American Women Writers: An Anthology* (1997) and *Robert Frost and Feminine Literary Tradition* (1998).

Annette Kolodny is Professor of Comparative Cultural and Literary Studies at the University of Arizona. Known internationally for such work as *The Lay of the Land: Metaphor as Experience and History in American Life and Letters* (1975) and *The Land Before Her: Fantasy and Experience of the American Frontier, 1630–1860* (1984), she has recently published *Failing the Future: A Dean Looks at Higher Education in the Twenty-First Century* (1998).

Tiffany Ana López is Assistant Professor of English at the University of California, Riverside, where she teaches American drama, twentieth-century American literatures, Latina/o theater and children's literature. Her recent publications include "Performing Aztlán: The Female Body as Cultural Critique in the Teatro of Cherríe Moraga" (in *Nationalism in American Theater*, 1998) and "Beyond the Festival Latino: (Re)Defining Latina Drama for the Mainstage" (in *Women Playwrights of Diversity*, 1997). Her current book project explores representations of the body and the imagining of community in US Latina drama.

Barbara McCaskill is Assistant Professor of English at the University of Georgia. The editor of *Multicultural Literature and Literacies* (1993) and author of several articles, including "'Yours Very Truly': Ellen Craft – The Fugitive as Text and Artifact" (1994), she is completing a book on the representations of nineteenth-century African American women in the British and American abolitionist press.

A noted scholar of Rebecca Harding Davis, among others, **Jean Pfaelzer** is Professor of English and American Studies at the University of Delaware. Her recent publications include *The Rebecca Harding Davis Reader* (1995), *Parlor Radical: Rebecca Harding Davis and the Origins of American Social Realism* (1996), and an edition of Mary E. Lane's *Mizora* (forthcoming, Syracuse).

A. LaVonne Brown Ruoff is Professor of English (Emerita) at the University of Illinois, Chicago. An authority on Native American literatures and a leader in its recovery, she has recently published *Literatures of the American Indian* (1990), and editions of S. Alice Callahan's *Wynema: A Child of the Forest* (1997) and George Copway's *Life, Letters and Speeches* (1997).

Rosemarie Garland Thomson is Associate Professor of English at Howard University. Opening important connections between disability studies and literary studies, she has recently published *Freakery: Cultural Spectacles of the Extraordinary Body* (1995) and *Extraordinary Bodies: Figuring Physical Disability in American Culture and Literature* (1997).

Cheryl Walker is Richard Armour Professor of Modern Languages in the Department of English at Scripps College. Having published widely on nineteenth-century American women's poetry, including *American Women Poets of the Nineteenth Century: An Anthology* (1992), she has recently published *Indian Nation: Native American Literature and Nineteenth-Century Nationalisms* (1997).

A leader in the recovery and study of American women's humor and Southern women's writing, **Nancy A. Walker** is Professor of English at Vanderbilt University. Her publications include *A Very Serious Thing: Women's Humor and American Culture* (1988), *Redressing the Balance: American Women's Literary Humor from Colonial Times to the 1980s* (1988), and *The Disobedient Writer: Women and Narrative Tradition* (1995).

Joyce W. Warren, Associate Professor of English, Queens College, CUNY, has published widely on nineteenth-century American women's writing. Her books include *The American Narcissus: Individualism and Women in Nineteenth-Century American Fiction* (1984) and *Fanny Fern: An Independent Woman* (1992). She has also edited *Ruth Hall and Other Writings*, by Fanny Fern (1986), and *The (Other) American Traditions: Nineteenth-Century Women Writers* (1993).

Preface

Having lost both her parents by her mid-teens, the daughter of a Swedish clergyman and his wife goes to live with economically distressed relatives and is forced to earn a living as a seamstress. Residing in a seaside town, she meets and falls in love with a sailor who apparently deserts her, though he intends to marry on his return, but his ship sinks. The young woman discovers with dismay that she is pregnant, and a sympathetic older woman companion who is soon to return home to Norway agrees to adopt the infant, departing with it soon after its birth. Wrongly accused of infanticide when an unknown infant is found dead and her older woman friend cannot be located, the young woman is convicted and sentenced to death. Her sentence is commuted when a scientist proposes to freeze her for a hundred years. Waking from sleep, discouraged by her sad memories and lack of community, she decides to travel to Norway, where she falls in love with and agrees to marry a local youth, whom she ultimately discovers is her great-grandson.

Romantic fantasy? Sci-fi nightmare? Feminist reform fiction? Nineteenth-century soap opera? All of the above, and published as "Hilda Silfverling" by Lydia Maria Child in 1846.

Child's story is in one sense astonishingly contemporary. It raises questions about (among other things) free sexuality, cultural exclusion, scientific experimentation on women's bodies, female self-sufficiency, the constitution of community, and incest. It is both frightening and alluringly humorous. It confuses boundaries between "high" and "popular" art.[1] Not only does "Hilda Silfverling" embody the generic complexity of much nineteenth-century American women's writing, it also suggests a utopian motive. Many of the selections included in *Nineteenth-Century American Women Writers: An Anthology*, the companion volume to this one, reflect a similar vision or urge: whether we are speaking of Fanny

Fern's incisive criticism of the sexual double standard practiced by US husbands in "A Word on the Other Side," Frances Harper's exhilarating call for aesthetic democracy and national unity in "Songs for the People," Alice Cary's appeal for racial cooperation in the "children's" poem "Three Bugs," Ida Wells-Barnett's exposure of the horrors of lynching, or Pauline Johnson's affirmation of adoptive maternal love in "The Tenas Klootchman," the women of the nineteenth century frequently envisioned a better society, whether they expressed that vision through affirmation or through dystopian critique.[2]

To highlight this utopian impulse, however, is not to overlook the stunning complexity of forms, themes, perspectives, and goals embodied by that writing. Until fairly recently, portraits of nineteenth-century American women's writing have depicted it as a relatively homogeneous landscape: One or two mountains (Dickinson, sometimes Stowe), a few hills here and there (Jewett, Chopin, Gilman), dotted by many small, deep, and dangerous pools of water (*any* "sentimental" writing) that posed hazards to the wary traveler. Many university courses still reflect this earlier understanding in spite of the fact that this view of nineteenth-century American women's writing, formulated in the first half of this century, has been consistently challenged over the last twenty-five years. From such earlier texts as Emily Stipes Watts's *The Poetry of American Women from 1632 to 1943*, Nina Baym's *Woman's Fiction*, and Erlene Stetson's *Black Sister: Poetry by Black American Women, 1746–1980*, to more recent work by Elizabeth Ammons, Frances Smith Foster, Carolyn Karcher, Annette White-Parks, Carla Peterson, and many more, feminist scholars have transformed the field.[3]

In spite of this transformative work, a number of accounts continue to focus primarily on fiction – typically the novel, but less comprehensively the short story or sketch – or on one kind of poetry, the sentimental. If we study more closely the individuals who make up the literary landscape, however, we discover that we have often been myopic to nontraditional genres, and more importantly, to elements of those genres in fruitful (if sometimes confusing) combination. Thus, as I have already suggested, to say that "Hilda Silfverling" is short fiction is not only to miss the subtitle ("A Fantasy") but also to miss the complex blending of genres that the story embodies. Or to take other examples, Lucy Larcom's "Weaving" (sentimental poem, regionalist sketch, reform writing), Rebecca Cox Jackson's spiritual writing (parable, autobiography, gothic), Sarah Piatt's "The Black Princess" (sentimental poem, elegy, utopia), Alice Dunbar-Nelson's "A Carnival Jangle" (regionalist sketch, thriller, postmodernist "carnival"). Yet we have only recently begun to move beyond the notion of how such writing "fails" by traditional standards of "goodness" and to inquire about the internal standards set by each text, especially for shorter pieces.

Although the initial impetus for this collection emerged from a need to provide readers new ways of perceiving and understanding the diverse texts assembled in *Nineteenth-Century American Women's Writing: An Anthology*, it is aimed at a larger audience of scholars and students interested in nineteenth-century American women's literature and nineteenth-century literature more broadly. The essays collected here both address large conceptual issues and offer suggestive close readings of individual texts. Like the primary selections in the anthology, they often write across boundaries of race, genre, class, location, and gender. Indeed, although I originally set out to draw texts together in smaller groupings like "Contexts," "Genres," and "Places," I decided that to do so would limit the boundaries of the conversation that is taking place. The interconnection of concerns that the authors evince suggests that the ordering at which I have arrived is hardly the only one available, and I encourage readers to explore and ruminate on the many other connections that occur.

A word about citation practice will be useful here. Some of the writers in this collection refer readers to the original sources, which will be difficult for some to find. Thus, where the essays below quote primary materials also included in *Nineteenth-Century American Women Writers: An Anthology*, I have added the references for that collection (as *NCAWW*). Generally, if the piece is short and references easily located I have cited page range in order to keep footnotes to a minimum; where the piece is long, or where an author has chosen to cite only the anthology, I have given individual page references. Focusing on readings of the primary materials and offering a wide selection of secondary texts in the footnotes, the essays included here refer to biographical materials only when such materials are central to the critics' concerns, assuming that readers will turn to the wealth of sources currently available.[4]

In her autobiography of 1867, written at the end of a long and prominent career, Lydia Sigourney asserted that "Fame, as a ruling motive, has not stimulated me to literary effort. It has ever seemed too flimsy a wing for sustained and satisfactory flight. . . . the only adequate payment are the hope and belief that, by enforcing some salutary precept, or prompting some hallowed practice, good may have been done to our race." In writing about the sexual double standard, Fanny Fern observed more acerbically in "A Word on the Other Side" (1857), "These are bold words; but they are needed words – words whose full import I have considered, and from the responsibility of which I do not shrink."[5] Like Child's "Hilda Silfverling," some of the contributions included here look to "great-grandmothers" for inspiration or direction about cultural intervention. To *do* good as well as to *be* good – where "good" possesses very different inflections and meanings in these two phrases – represents one significant strand of the discussion – or, to borrow from Annette Kolodny's essay on Margaret Fuller, conversation – that proceeds below.

NOTES

1   For discussions of the relationship between "elite" and "popular" art forms, see Andreas Huyssen, *After the Great Divide: Modernism, Mass Culture, Postmodernism* (Bloomington: Indiana University Press, 1986); Suzanne Clark, *Sentimental Modernism: Women Writers and the Revolution of the Word* (Bloomington: Indiana University

Press, 1991); Lawrence Levine, *Highbrow/Lowbrow, The Emergence of Cultural Hierarchy in America* (Cambridge: Harvard University Press, 1988); David S. Reynolds, *Beneath the American Renaissance: The Subversive Imagination in the Age of Emerson and Melville* (Cambridge: Harvard University Press, 1988).

2 For a discussion of the utopia, see Carol Farley Kessler, Introduction to *Daring to Dream: Utopian Fiction by United States Women before 1950* (Syracuse: Syracuse University Press, 1995); Jean Pfaelzer, *The Utopian Novel in America, 1886–1896: The Politics of Form* (Pittsburgh: University of Pittsburgh Press, 1984).

3 A complete listing of such texts is impossible, but they might include: Emily Stipes Watts, *The Poetry of American Women from 1632 to 1943* (Austin: University of Texas Press, 1977); Nina Baym, *Woman's Fiction: A Guide to Novels by and about Women in America, 1820–1870* (Ithaca: Cornell University Press, 1978); Erlene Stetson, *Black Sister: Poetry by Black American Women, 1746–1980* (Bloomington: Indiana University Press, 1981); Cheryl Walker, *The Nightingale's Burden: Women Poets and American Culture before 1900* (Bloomington: Indiana University Press, 1982); Josephine Donovan, *New England Local Color Literature: A Women's Tradition* (New York: F. Ungar Pub. Co., 1983); Annette Kolodny, *The Land Before Her: Fantasy and Experience of the American Frontiers, 1630–1860* (Chapel Hill: University of North Carolina Press, 1984); Mary Kelley, *Private Woman, Public Stage: Literary Domesticity in Nineteenth-Century America* (New York: Oxford University Press, 1984); Jane Tompkins, *Sensational Designs: The Cultural Work of American Fiction 1790–1860* (New York: Oxford University Press, 1985); Nancy Walker, *A Very Serious Thing: Women's Humor and American Culture* (Minneapolis: University of Minneapolis Press, 1988); Susan K. Harris, *19th-Century American Women's Novels: Interpretative Strategies* (New York: Cambridge University Press, 1990); Elizabeth Ammons, *Conflicting Stories: American Women Writers at the Turn into the Twentieth Century* (New York: Oxford University Press, 1991); Frances Smith Foster, *Written by Herself: Literary Production by African American Women, 1746–1892* (Bloomington: Indiana University Press, 1993); Carolyn L. Karcher, *The First Woman in the Republic: A Cultural Biography of Lydia Maria Child* (Durham: Duke University Press, 1994); Annette White-Parks, *Sui Sin Far/ Edith Maude Eaton: A Literary Biography* (Urbana: University of Illinois Press, 1995); Carla L. Peterson, *"Doers of the Word": African-American Women Speakers and Writers in the North (1830–1880)* (New York: Oxford University Press, 1995).

4 See, for example, Denise Knight, ed., *Nineteenth-Century American Women Writers: A Bio-Bibliographical Critical Sourcebook* (Westport, CT: Greenwood Press, 1997); the *Dictionary of Literary Biography*; Edward T. James et al., eds, *Notable American Women, 1607–1950*, 3 vols (Cambridge, MA: Belknap-Harvard University Press, 1971); and Cathy N. Davidson and Linda Wagner-Martin, eds, *The Oxford Companion to Women's Writing in the United States* (New York: Oxford University Press, 1995).

5 *NCAWW*, 50, 124.

Acknowledgments

The assistance and advice provided by individuals and institutions acknowledged in *Nineteenth-Century American Women Writers: An Anthology* has in large measure also forwarded *Nineteenth-Century American Women Writers: A Critical Reader*. In my completing this collection, however, several individuals and institutions provided especially important support. I want to thank Westbrook College in Portland, Maine for honoring me with their research professorship for 1996; the Dorothy M. Healy Visiting Professorship in American Studies and Women's Studies enabled me to further the project significantly. The International Nineteenth-Century American Women Writers Research Group in the UK and EC, and the Northeast Nineteenth-Century American Women Writers Group in the USA, have offered ongoing support and feedback. To my department head at The University of North Carolina at Greensboro, Jim Evans, and my dean, Walter Beale, many warm thanks for their continuing support of my research. I am grateful to the students in my spring 1997 graduate seminar on nineteenth-century American women's writing (Beth Howells, Mary-Robyn Adams, Jewell Mayberry, Rich Gray, Dottie Burkhart, Essie McKoy, Chris Porter, and Sandra Foster), whose engagement with the anthology and comments on the introduction and advice essay were both encouraging and helpful. From reading drafts of the introduction to retyping onto disk contributions that proved recalcitrant, I am grateful for the assistance of UNCG English Department administrator, Lydia Howard; my research assistant, Greg Tredore; colleagues Alison Easton (Lancaster University, UK) and Jean Pfaelzer (University of Delaware). I much appreciate the support, patience, and hard work of my commissioning editor, Andrew McNeillie, and my desk editor, Brigitte Lee. As always, my husband, Chris, offered ongoing help and support, and my parents, Mary Gove Kilcup and Richard Kilcup, provided important encouragement.

The editor and publisher are also grateful for the right to reproduce the following copyrighted material:

Judith Fetterley, "'Not in the Least American': Nineteenth-Century Literary Regionalism as UnAmerican Literature"; originally published as "'Not in the Least American': Nineteenth-Century Literary Regionalism" in *College English* 56.8 (December 1994): 877–95. Copyright © 1994 by the National Council of Teachers of English. Reprinted with permission.

Annette Kolodny, "Inventing a Feminist Discourse: Rhetoric and Resistance in Margaret Fuller's *Woman in the Nineteenth Century*," *New Literary History: A Journal of Theory and Interpretation* 25.2 (1994): 355–82. Copyright © 1994 by Annette Kolodny. Reprinted with permission.

Introduction: A Conversation on Nineteenth-Century American Women's Writing

KAREN L. KILCUP

In 1846, Margaret Fuller reflected on the relationship between British and American literature, distinguishing forcefully between the two:

> What suits Great Britain, with her insular position and consequent need to concentrate and intensify her life, her limited monarchy, and spirit of trade, does not suit a mixed race, continually enriched with new blood from other stocks the most unlike that of our first descent, with ample field and verge enough to range in and leave every impulse free, and abundant opportunity to develope [sic] a genius, wide and full as our river, flowery, luxuriant and impassioned as our vast prairies, rooted in strength as the rocks on which the Puritan fathers landed.
>
> That such a genius is to rise and work in this hemisphere we are confident; equally so that scarce the first faint streaks of that day's dawn are visible. . . . That day will not rise till the fusion of races among us is more complete.[1]

Fuller's remarks foreground the racial and ethic mixing evident in American culture at the time that she wrote, and they forecast the productive meetings of individuals from different locations as well as identities on a space that the contemporary Chicana writer and critic Gloria Anzaldúa calls "the borderlands/ la frontera." Fuller's radical call for what many of her peers would have seen as miscegenation suggests that we need to look for evidence of the compound genius that was already well underway in American literature.[2]

The mixing that is everywhere apparent in this literature, from Lydia Sigourney's *Sketch of Connecticut, Forty Years Since* to Sarah Winnemucca's *Life Among the Piutes*, has been obscured by a literary critical history that privileges purity of all kinds, whether racial or aesthetic. In this connection, the contemporary Native American writer and critic Paula Gunn Allen observes that one of Western readers' preoccupations is "the purity of genre": "This rigid need for impermeable classificatory boundaries is reflected in turn in the existence of numerous institutional, psychological, and social barriers designed to prevent mixtures from occurring. Western literary and social traditionalists are deeply purist."[3] Conducting what Allen calls a form of "intellectual apartheid," Western literary critics have erased connections and interpenetrations that have existed virtually since the beginning of American literature. Both Sigourney's and Winnemucca's texts, for example, evince a generic mixing that parallels and sometimes even highlights ethnic blending: in the case of the former, with the inclusion of texts like Uncle Primus's "oral" slave narrative, and the latter, with the use of the stylistic conventions of the sentimental novel alongside traditional Native American oratory and myth. The opening myth itself bespeaks and indeed urges fruitful racial mixing, with Winnemucca's grandfather urging his people that "should I not live to welcome [the white people] myself, you will not hurt a hair on their heads, but welcome them as I tried to do."[4]

Contemporary reviewers of nineteenth-century American women's writing often insisted that these writers adhere to certain standards for both subject and form.[5] What happened to those who did not do so, who attempted to create their own new or hybrid forms, constitutes one of the subjects of this collection. Two examples are instructive at this moment. The first is the case of Sarah Pratt McLean (Greene), the writer of the novel *Cape Cod Folks*, which provoked the first libel suit for fiction in the United States. McLean was famous, even infamous, in her time; but like so many other women of this era, she disappeared from sight shortly after her death in 1935. Among the reasons for her disappearance were her use of humor (that is, she wasn't a "serious writer") and her participation in the tradition of literary regionalism. But an equally compelling reason for her obscurity resides in her use of multiple genres and "conflicting" styles. As one critic would put it in his review of *The Moral Imbeciles* (1898), "The novels of Mrs. Sarah Pratt McLean are quite unclassifiable. They violate the ordinary rules of fiction at every turn."[6]

A better known example of this phenomenon is Sarah Orne Jewett's *The Country of the Pointed Firs*. For a number of years the writer's detractors pointed out the shortcomings of this "novel," while sympathetic critics attempted to reconstruct it in ways that would allow the text to be recuperated into the tradition of the regionalist or realist novel.[7] The degree to which women writers themselves internalized this criticism of their work is apparent in Jewett's now-famous remark in a letter to Horace Scudder: "But I don't believe I could write a long story. . . . In the first place, I have no dramatic talent. The story would have no plot. I should have to fill it out with descriptions of character and meditations. It seems to me I can furnish the theatre, and show you the actors, and the scenery, and the audience, but there is never any play!"[8] Though to different degrees, both McLean and Jewett, like many of their contemporaries, have been relegated to "minor" or "obscure" status in part because of their structural innovation. In spite of twenty years' exploration by literary critics, many of them feminist, of the "impurity" of much American literature, this critical notion still possesses considerable power and authority. As Annette Kolodny's essay below suggests, even writers like Margaret Fuller, whose work is relatively well known today, have been marginalized on the basis of their "lack" of aesthetic "control."

Along with the historical privilege assigned to "pure" genres – and the arguments constructed to ensure this purity, such as rationalizations for the "odd" yet textually "coherent" "The Custom-House" chapter of Hawthorne's *The Scarlet Letter*, for example[9] – comes the academic hierarchization of genres that are more "literary": the novel and (nonsentimental) poetry, in particular. In recent years, even feminist criticism eager to recover women's writing from obscurity has focused more on these genres, and in particular, on the former, since among most academics, the assumption has been that the only woman poet worth mentioning in the nineteenth century was Emily Dickinson.[10] That this hierarchization continues is apparent in the strong sales of novels over collections of short fiction by individual authors, for example.[11] But just as we cannot make generalizations about nineteenth-century American women's writing – or, for that matter, about nineteenth-century American writing more broadly – based on the study of a few texts by northeastern, middle-class white women, so too we should be skeptical about generalizations based exclusively or even primarily on the study of the novel. "Small" is not necessarily "insignificant," for as Celia Thaxter observes in another context, "I marvelled much that so very small a head should contain such an amount of cunning."[12]

This collection of critical essays points to the generic complexity and diversity, especially of shorter texts, written by nineteenth-century American women, and it suggests the collective importance of these texts to American literature as a whole. After a long period of obscurity created in large measure beginning in the 1920s, when literary study became more masculinized and professionalized, moving from the parlor to the academy, American women writers have reappeared on the literary landscape in force and, in many senses of the phrase, for good.[13] Nevertheless, within this environment of renewed attention to their work, shorter pieces are often overlooked – or in a variation on the same theme, the same short pieces (such as Sarah Orne Jewett's "A White Heron," Mary Wilkins Freeman's "The Revolt of 'Mother,'" Rebecca Harding Davis's "Life in the Iron Mills," and Frances Harper's "The Two Offers") are taught or reprinted repeatedly and exclusively. We can speculate about some of the reasons why this situation has occurred.

Perhaps students will be surprised to learn that pragmatism is one immediately compelling response. University instructors are reluctant to insist that students purchase collections of short works by an individual author from which they will study only a few pieces. Not only are constraints of cost at work here, but also those of time, because a single short story or sketch can easily occupy an entire class period. With novels, students feel they are getting more for their money and instructors can justify the rapidly inflating costs of textbooks. However much either group would like to feel that texts are chosen on the basis of "quality" or "representativeness" alone, economic considerations intervene. The publishers of university level textbooks, responding to the demand for the novel, either refuse to reprint collections of shorter works by a single author, or allow to go out of print those that have already been reissued.

Another explanation for this situation is the relatively advanced development of standards of assessment and understanding for the novel. To the earlier conceptual frameworks of romanticism and realism, for example, critics have added those of sentimentalism and regionalism. Works like Jane Tompkins's *Sensational Designs* have taught us how to read for, in the subtitle's phrase, "the cultural work of American fiction." Susan K. Harris's work has mapped out an analysis of nineteenth-century American women's novels in terms of process, arguing that we need to understand these works "within the shifting currents of nineteenth-century American ideologies."[14] While many of the questions that Harris raises for the novel seem readily adaptable to shorter forms, we still do not have a broad theoretical account of both shorter texts as a whole or of the differences and interactions between different genres within this category (for example, "privileged" poetry in relation to journalism).[15]

One of the most compelling reasons for the continuing dominance of the novel in contemporary literary studies and university courses is the sense that in order to be more than "minor" a work not only has to express certain values, such as individualism, and fulfill certain structural norms, such as being conflict- or plot-driven, but also has to be "sustained" – that is, long.[16] There are at least three explanations for this obsession with length, one related to social class, another to historical gender roles, and a third to gender psychology. In the first instance, we can extend Carla Peterson's observations about the disparities between two groups of northern, urban, nineteenth-century black American women writers to encompass the period more generally. Peterson highlights a class difference within the group of black women who published; in this case, between a group of elite, educated women who would be more likely to write in the "mainstream" – and hence privileged – genres of fiction, poetry, and autobiography, and "the black subaltern class . . . composed primarily of unskilled laborers," that was "[l]ess literate . . . [and] rooted in oral and folk culture."[17]

As *Nineteenth-Century American Women Writers: An Anthology* indicates, the ramifications for this bifurcation extend beyond the antebellum northern black milieu. For example, although some working-class writers, like a number of the *Lowell Offering* women, were well educated and wrote in the more "literary" forms of poetry and fiction, many others, like domestic servant Lorenza Stevens Berbineau, often wrote texts of indeterminate, multiple, or marginalized genre – in Berbineau's case, the travel journal or diary – when they wrote at all. But even though we might wish to make such a generalization, we have to recognize its limitations, for while women like Rose Terry Cooke, Martha Wolfenstein, and Frances Harper wrote in these "mainstream" genres, all three frequently transformed those genres by undergirding them with the (nonliterary) orality and intimacy of good gossip or the bracing firmness of a strong sermon, as we see in their "How Celia Changed Her Mind," "Genendel the Pious," and "Aunt Chloe's Politics," respectively. In the context of canonical American literature, such texts assume a marginality because of their oral component; as early as 1854 Thoreau would, in the section of *Walden* entitled "Reading," pronounce the literate languages to be masculine and oral language feminine and even brutish: "there is a memorable interval between the spoken and the written language, the language heard and the language read. The one is commonly transitory, a sound, a tongue, a dialect merely, and we learn it unconsciously, like the brutes, of our mothers. The other is the maturity and experience of that; if that is our mother tongue, this is our father tongue, a reserved and select expression, too significant to be heard by the ear, which we must be born again in order to speak."[18] Yet when Frances Harper announces powerfully, "You white women here speak of rights. I speak of wrongs," in a speech urging these women to be responsible for the injustices of racism, the "mother tongue" takes on another meaning entirely.[19]

Historical gender roles have also played a part in women's participation in "literary" or "nonliterary" genres. Just as Ann Bradstreet had done much earlier, many nineteenth-century American women writers, from Alice Cary to Emma Lazarus, from Lorenza Stevens Berbineau to Charlotte Perkins Gilman, often felt the need to apologize for their authorial audacity or to mitigate, downplay, or conceal their actual participation in literary tradition.[20] Even that exception, Emily Dickinson, writing without the constraints of certain or necessary publication, often found it psychologically necessary or expeditious to deny her own authority, as when she told her putative mentor, Thomas Wentworth Higginson, that "I smile when you suggest that I delay 'to publish' – that being foreign to my thought, as Firmament to Fin."[21] Moreover, the genres in which women chose to write were as often dependent upon the shape and rhythms of their lives as any other factor. Even that prototypical "success story," Harriet Beecher Stowe, sometimes found it necessary (financially and personally) to write her "novels" in serial form, which suggests that each chapter has an internal coherence that we lose when we read and discuss *Uncle Tom's Cabin*, for example, as a whole. From this perspective, one task before us may be to deconstruct the "coherence" of the novel and attempt to understand how an accretive or composite formal structure parallels or diverges from that of short fiction or the sketch. For many women, then, it may have been more possible to write in journal, sketch, or poetic forms – all short, though not all equally valued in literary tradition – because of such constraints as child care and household management. Nevertheless, many women who could choose to do otherwise opted to write more often in the forms of the sketch or short fiction, perhaps because they valued intensity and compactness over expansiveness, or in the forms of the journalistic essay, because they assigned social activism priority over more "purely" aesthetic motives.

In this context, the example of Emily Dickinson is once again instructive. Paula Bennett has argued that Dickinson foregrounds in her work an affirmative smallness, figured in such objects as gems, berries, and buds. Describing the poet as working out of a tradition in which these images metaphorized (consciously or unconsciously) female sexuality, Bennett reminds us, with the poet herself, that bigger is not always or necessarily better. In some sense, then, we could regard the "smallness" of many texts by female writers as affirmations of female creative power; as Bennett points out, "To Dickinson and other nineteenth-century American women writers, the little could also be great."[22] We can extrapolate from this analysis to propose that genre may sometimes be determined by authorial preference for a form that mirrors female sexuality itself: the hidden, the intense, and the small, over the expansive, the extensive, and the large. Although this generalization, like so many others about the field of nineteenth-century American women's writing, is easily countered (by *Uncle Tom's Cabin* and Susan Warner's *The Wide, Wide World* in the domain of the novel, and Lydia Sigourney's *Traits of the Aborigines of America* and Lucy Larcom's *An Idyl of Work* in the realm of poetry), the fact that many women who could choose to write in longer – and often more financially rewarding – forms chose not to do so suggests the attraction of the "compact" over the "sustained." Finally, women, like their male counterparts, wrote in both "short" and "long" forms. It is the *readers* of those forms who have determined their relative value.[23]

A more complete history of nineteenth-century American literature might then set out to ask some of the following questions about shorter genres that the essays below begin to address: How do these texts use and "misuse" the conventions of their time to create new perspectives and voices? What is the work of nontraditional forms such as cookbook, advice, and children's writing? What are the connections between various kinds of texts, writers, genres? What have we missed because we have hierarchized long fiction? More specifically, how does Child's introduction to *The Frugal Housewife* anticipate some of the concerns of a writer like Thoreau ("Economy" in *Walden*, for example); how does Rose Terry Cooke's "Blue-Beard's Closet" alter our view or definition of romanticism; how do Emily Dickinson's letters influence our perspective on what constitutes a nineteenth-century poem; how do Maria Amparo Ruiz de Burton's novels indicate the spurious line between fiction, autobiography and nonfiction, between "made" and "lived" truths? What are the continuities between "masculine" and "feminine" traditions?

A number of issues recur within different forms and contexts in this collection, suggesting the metaphor of "conversation" for its structure and direction. Reflecting the important current debates about social class, the selections by Warren, Nancy Walker, Thomson, and McCaskill, for example, indicate the crucial situation of nineteenth-century American women in the economic structures and struggles that propelled so many of them to become writers in the first place. The body figures importantly in the contributions by Thomson, Pfaelzer, and López. Many essays, such as those by Kolodny, Fetterley, Cheryl

Walker, Kilcup, Pfaelzer, Thomson, and Graulich, concern themselves indirectly or directly with matters of categorization, whether related to aesthetic or cultural matters, to genre or social identity. López, Pfaelzer, and Cheryl Walker address the often-overlooked relationships between American women's and American men's writing, while Ruoff, López, Graulich, Nancy Walker, and McCaskill consider the relation of social identity to aesthetic or political perspective. Reading and readers, both nineteenth-century and contemporary, form another compelling set of concerns for the contributors to *Nineteenth-Century American Women Writers: A Critical Reader*. These scholars help us to understand interconnections and to recognize the artificiality of the intellectual boundaries that create "intellectual apartheid" not only in relation to primary texts, but in critical discussions of those texts as well.

Providing a broad context in which to begin discussion of nineteenth-century American women's writing, Judith Fetterley's essay reflects on issues that many of the others ponder, though sometimes less explicitly: what is an "American"? What is "American literature," and what is the proper role of women in it? What is the relationship between regionalism and nationalism? How do we find a place for women and girls, as well as men and boys, as *readers* of American literary texts? Explicitly political, propelling readers toward self-awareness, Fetterley issues a call for transformation that echoes the activism of many nineteenth-century American women writers, observing, "in regionalism I find a literature that models a subjectivity attained by standing up for others, not on them." In this context, "figuring one's critical stance as unAmerican provides a way of thinking about one's activity that does justice to its political intent and recognizes the dangers which attend it."

Arguing that nineteenth-century Southern women writers were in some sense "unAmerican" in the ways that Fetterley outlines, Nancy Walker situates their work both in a regional and national tradition, at the same time indicating the conflicts that emerge as a consequence of identity differences (black and white writers), class transformations (the "reduced circumstances" suffered by many white women after the Civil War), and varying locations (Georgia or Louisiana). "Difference," in this context, is not only difference *between* the South and "America," "Southern literature" and "American literature," but the difference *within* various depictions of the region. Describing the writers' attention to myth and reality, similarity and difference, tradition and progress, Walker's essay provides a fruitful approach to the study of other regional literatures, and their "place" in national literature as well.

Melody Graulich's essay investigates Fetterley's and Walker's concern with region and nation on Western terrain. Graulich points out that the definition of the "West" itself occupied shifting territory as the nineteenth century progressed. Indicating Western women's ambiguous and ambivalent relationship to place, she maps out the ways in which they hold ideal and real in creative tension. Independence, a key concept in national terms, occupies a large space in conceptualizing and living in the West; but access to independence, and declarations of its possession by individual women, were often mediated by the ethnic and economic differences that Walker observes about Southern women. Like the essays that precede it, Graulich's is also concerned with the stance of the observer; reflecting on her own critical history, Graulich offers a cooperative, multi-voiced performance that seeks to model the "Western biodiversity" that she locates in the array of primary texts with which she is concerned.[24]

This "biodiversity" includes the work of Western writers like Maria Amparo Ruiz de Burton and the transplanted Maria Cristina Mena. In seeking to situate the latter in larger literary historical and cultural contexts, Tiffany Ana López contests the view that these earlier Mexican American writers were invested in socially conservative white middle-class norms. While it reconnects Mena with her Mexican heritage, López's argument explicitly locates the writer in a lively, hybrid cultural discourse that discourages homogenizing or segregating her work, and by extension, that of any ethnic American writer, into an isolated cultural and aesthetic tradition. Possessing echoes of Nathaniel Hawthorne and Robert Browning as well as Mexican oral tradition, responding to its interstitial position between elite and popular (including the cultural discourse of whiteness embedded in *Century Magazine*'s advertisements), Mena's work mediates identity for a largely white audience while it creates a subversively polyvocal discourse that performs a "tolerance for contradictions."

LaVonne Brown Ruoff's overview of Native American women's writing indicates that many of these early writers engaged in a cultural mediation similar to that of Mena. Situating their work in the larger tradition of Native American writing, Ruoff's essay also concerns itself with the intersection of gender and ethnicity in a tradition of dazzling generic variety, including poetry, myth, autobiography, short fiction, essay, and oratory. Like López, Ruoff points out the affiliation of some of this writing with an elite, canonical, and aestheticized male tradition. At the same time, Ruoff's insistence on biographical details underscores the continuities between "literature," "everyday life," and social activism for many Native Americans; unlike some of their non-Indian counterparts, literature was a tool as well as a pleasure. These details also suggest the varying standards of behavior and of authority assigned to nineteenth-century Native American women, and the disjunctions as well as connections between them and their non-Indian counterparts.

While Ruoff's essay ruminates indirectly on the idea of national literature, Jean Pfaelzer's takes up the subject again explicitly. Pfaelzer maps out the subversive transformation by Rebecca Harding Davis of a male-authored captivity narrative into a tale of maternal power and authority. Depicting a Southern rather than a Western frontier – but one that is equally "wild" and menacing to white males – Davis affirms a continuity between women and Indians that promises a fruitful alliance yet simultaneously ensures the genocide of the Indians, as the women bond across ethnicity. Pfaelzer's carefully historicized discussion argues that the construction of this sentimental connection allows Davis's privileged postbellum readers, wittingly or unwittingly aligned with a brutal process of

Indian slaughter and dispossession, to discover "an image of national identity" that effectively eradicates and incorporates difference. Pfaelzer's argument resonates beyond discussion of Davis to suggest the caution with which we should approach apparently utopian images of the "other" in nineteenth-century American women's writing.

Also suspicious of sentiment, Rosemarie Thomson's essay converses with a number of the issues raised in the pieces that precede it, including matters of class, style, identity, and reader relations. Exploring the conjunction of sentimentalized reform fiction, the disabled body, and the female body, Thomson indicates how in some cases "economic exclusion is embodied as visible disability." Class disadvantage, she argues, is figured in the literal bodily "disadvantage" that the writer hopes will engender sympathy (and action toward reform) on the part of an engaged reader. Thomson proposes that the alliance between women, the church, and social reform movements emerged in women writers' deployment of a bodily discourse based in a spectacle of suffering embodied by Christ and appropriated for the purposes of reform of class- and gender-based disadvantage. As with other forms of contact between different individuals, this border crossing can be a precarious one for the disabled person, engendering erasure when the imperfect body – which figures the feminine self in American culture – refuses to be amenable to amelioration.

Taking on four writers who have become central to our understanding of the nineteenth century, Joyce Warren offers a broad view of women's advocacy for economic independence. Like other contributors, Warren situates her account carefully in historical contexts, underlining, for example, the potentially damaging association between that independence and (the culture's perception of) sexual promiscuity. Offering a comparative view of Fanny Fern, Frances Harper, Louisa May Alcott, and Charlotte Perkins Gilman, for each of whom, though in different ways, gender and class inevitably converged, Warren argues that each was forced to "fracture the concept of gender" in order to assert female economic independence, to which some assigned priority over political enfranchisement. Just as Fetterley's, Graulich's, and Thomson's pieces challenge readers to interrogate the constructed boundaries between "literature" and "life," Warren's account opens out into a compelling set of questions for today's readers.

Though she begins with a very different perspective, Barbara McCaskill's essay resonates with Warren's discussion of economics and class, as it takes on the difficult question of the relationship of spirituality to class in nineteenth-century African American women's literature. Affirming black women's transformation of a victim-oriented Christianity into a tool for radical social empowerment and change, McCaskill skillfully reveals how several important women writers, encoding African traditions within "American" ones, rewrite Christianity and the church in order to deploy them as tools of social, spiritual, and political reform – and unity – for African Americans and for America more broadly. McCaskill's essay invites us once again to consider the relationship between gender and genre, politics and aesthetics,[25] as well as between African American and "mainstream"

literary traditions. It also underscores the fractures within the black community
and women writers' willingness to critique the sources of these fractures.

My essay on advice writing seeks to illuminate the continuities between what
we might call the literature of advice and the advice of literature. Arguing for
an aesthetic view of advice writing and other forms of "domestic discourse," it
situates a range of nineteenth-century women's texts on a continuum of conformity and resistance, a continuum shaped by the norm of respectability for
white middle-class women. Working women, women of color, and ethnic women,
in particular, I suggest, offer critiques of the accessibility of this norm and its
standards; they often accomplish this critique via an astute manipulation of the
genre of advice writing. As in many other essays in this collection, the question
of aesthetics – its meaning, shape, and intentions – forms an important strand of
the discussion.

Representative of much larger issues of structure and perspective in feminist
criticism as well as in nineteenth-century primary works, Annette Kolodny's
essay on the structure of Margaret Fuller's *Woman in the Nineteenth Century* not
only provides us with a newly contextualized way of understanding that centrally important text, but also evokes a range of other nineteenth-century women's
writing that does not fit neatly into preestablished categories of analysis, modeling
for us the kind of critical work that still needs to be done. Kolodny's essay is
particularly useful in directing our attention to reader–audience relations and
the requirements that Fuller's form placed on her readers. Fuller's example of
written "conversation," which borrows from the voices of others, suggests an
approach route to the work of Ida Wells-Barnett, and closer in time to us,
Marianne Moore, both of whom represent different constructions and uses of the
composite text. It also points, Kolodny suggests, to a nonadversarial and "conversational" form of contemporary feminist literary criticism.

Returning us to the broad overview with which we began, Cheryl Walker
surveys the development of criticism on nineteenth-century American women's
poetry and elaborates a more complex way to envision that work. Organizing
the poetry into the four major categories of "the early nationals," "the American
romantics," "the realists," and "the moderns," Walker accomplishes the important work of reconnecting female writing with male writing, while she underscores the participation of many poets in more than one domain. At the same
time that she highlights some of the women poets whose work stands outside
of her classifications, such as Frances Harper and Pauline Johnson, she acknowledges the incompleteness of such categories and hence invites us toward yet
another reconceptualization of the field, acknowledging, as do all these essays,
the necessarily developmental, accretive, and cooperative nature of this critical
reconceptualization. Finally, she leads us out of the nineteenth century, crossing
yet another artificial boundary by offering links with modernist literature.

Taken individually and as a whole, these essays, and what they are *not* able to
encompass, along with the contents of *Nineteenth-Century American Women Writers:
An Anthology*, also suggest work, especially on shorter forms, that remains to be

done.[26] The reintegration of children's literature into the body of nineteenth-century American women's writing is one important task that could be accompanied by, for example, literary studies of the delineation of children across genres. Representations of physical and emotional violence against women and children deserve further study.[27] Another important area is the understanding of writing by and about working-class women; we have yet to formulate a widely accepted definition of the term or to contextualize its very different ambitions in the context of "mainstream" literature, however the latter is conceptualized.[28] Spirituality in literature by women other than African Americans remains a relatively unexplored area, along with temperance, ecofeminist, and peace literature.[29] Studies of the continuities between oral forms and written literature in African American and Native American literature could inform further examination of those continuities in white and middle-class literature.[30] Emotion (as opposed to sentimentality), and in particular, the representation or intimation of negatively charged emotions for women, such as anger, need exploration.[31] Finally, as my earlier remarks – and indeed, this collection as a whole – suggest, structural studies of nineteenth-century American women's writing are crucial to arriving at a broader and more accurate conceptualization of the field. With the development of these and other concerns, we can then move toward a reconceptualization of categories such as "romanticism," "realism," and "sentimentalism" that have so often served as exclusionary devices in relation to American women's writing.[32] These are just a few of the openings that nineteenth-century American women's writing, particularly in its more compact forms, offers.

Finally, short forms sometimes express more than they are saying. The almost conventional gesture of women writers, from well known to unknown in their time and our own, of underlining what is not and cannot be said, intimates a world of meaning. From Dickinson's poem "I cannot paint a picture," to Lorenza Stevens Berbineau's affirmation that "I am neither Painter nor Poet," to the "lies" told by the princess's servants in Sui Sin Far's "What About the Cat," what is hidden or unspoken but resonant in a story or sketch is sometimes as important as what is revealed, "told as no pen on earth can write it,"[33] in this "unAmerican" "American" literature.

NOTES

1 Margaret Fuller, "American Literature," *Papers on Literature and Art* (New York: Wiley & Putnam, 1846), 299–300.

2 Gloria Anzaldúa, *Borderlands/La Frontera: The New Mestiza* (San Francisco: Aunt Lute, 1989); see Annette Kolodny, "Letting Go Our Grand Obsessions: Notes Toward a New Literary History of the American Frontiers," *American Literature* 64 (1992): 1–18.

3 Paula Gunn Allen, Introduction to *Spider Woman's Granddaughters: Traditional Tales and Contemporary Writings by Native American Women* (Boston: Beacon Press, 1989),

2; see also Allen, *The Sacred Hoop: Recovering the Feminine in American Indian Traditions* (Boston: Beacon Press, 1986), 1–7. For a discussion of the effects of this policing of purity, see Karen [Kilcup] Oakes, "'We planted, tended and harvested our corn': Gender, Ethnicity, and Transculturation in *A Narrative of the Life of Mrs. Mary Jemison,*" *Women and Language* 18 (1995): 45–51.

4   *NCAWW*, 336.

5   See Nina Baym, *Novels, Readers, and Reviewers: Responses to Fiction in Antebellum America* (Ithaca: Cornell University Press, 1984).

6   *The Outlook* 3 (September 1898): 89. Another reviewer wrote, "*Flood-Tide* is more like a series of character sketches than a novel." *The Bookman* 14 (1901): 434. Such observations by reviewers were common. For a detailed discussion of Greene's life and work, see my "*Legacy* Profile: Sarah P. McLean Greene," *Legacy: A Journal of American Women Writers* 11 (1994): 55–64 (as Karen Oakes); "'I like a woman to be a woman': Theorizing Gender in Stowe and Greene," *Studies in American Humor* 4.3 (1996): 14–38; and "'Quite Unclassifiable': Crossing Genres, Crossing Genders in Twain and Greene," in *New Directions in American Humor Studies*, ed. David E. E. Sloane (Birmingham: University of Alabama Press, forthcoming).

7   For one important discussion of the structure of Jewett's "novel," see Elizabeth Ammons, "Going in Circles: The Female Geography of Jewett's *Country of the Pointed Firs,*" *Studies in the Literary Imagination* 16 (1983): 83–92.

8   Richard Cary, ed., *Sarah Orne Jewett Letters* (Waterville, ME: Colby College Press, 1967), 29.

9   For three discussions of the subject, see Nina Baym, "The Romantic *Malgré Lui*: Hawthorne in 'The Custom-House,'" *ESQ: A Journal of the American Renaissance* 19 (1973): 14–25; John Franzosa, "'The Custom-House,' *The Scarlet Letter*, and Hawthorne's Separation from Salem," *ESQ: A Journal of the American Renaissance* 24 (1978): 57–71; and Eric Savoy, "'Filial Duty': Reading the Patriarchal Body in 'The Custom-House,'" *Studies in the Novel* 25 (1993): 397–417.

10 The exceptions to this rule of the novel have been Joanne Dobson, Paula Bennett, Cheryl Walker, Annie Finch, and Nina Baym. See, for example, Joanne Dobson, "Sex, Wit, and Sentiment: The Poetry of Frances Osgood," *American Literature* 65 (1993): 631–50; Paula Bennett, "'The Descent of the Angel': Interrogating Domestic Ideology in American Women's Poetry, 1858–1890," *American Literary History* 7 (1995): 591–610; "Late Nineteenth-Century American Women's Nature Poetry and the Evolution of the Imagist Poem," *Legacy: A Journal of American Women Writers* 9 (1992): 89–103; Cheryl Walker, *The Nightingale's Burden: Women Poets and American Culture before 1900* (Bloomington: Indiana University Press, 1982); Annie Finch, "The Sentimental Poetess in the World: Metaphor and Subjectivity in Lydia Sigourney's Nature Poetry," *Legacy: A Journal of American Women Writers* 5 (1988): 3–15; and Nina Baym, "Reinventing Lydia Sigourney," *American Literature* 62 (1990): 385–404. Walker's and Bennett's anthologies have also made important contributions to this field; see Walker, ed., *American Women Poets of the Nineteenth Century, An Anthology* (New Brunswick: Rutgers University Press, 1992); and Bennett, ed., *Nineteenth-Century American Women Poets: An Anthology* (Oxford and Cambridge, MA: Blackwell Publishers, 1998).

11 At the spring 1996 meeting of the US Nineteenth-Century American Women Writers Study Group in Boston, Massachusetts, an announcement was made that in the successful Rutgers University Press American Women Writers Series, one

collection of short stories was about to go out of print and at least two others were selling poorly and endangered.

12   *NCAWW*, 281.

13   Paul Lauter, "Race and Gender in the Shaping of the American Literary Canon: A Case Study from the Twenties," *Feminist Studies* 9 (1983): 435–63; see Lauter, *Canons and Contexts* (New York: Oxford University Press, 1991).

14   Susan K. Harris, "'But is it any *good*'?: Evaluating Nineteenth-Century American Women's Fiction," *The (Other) American Traditions: Nineteenth-Century Women Writers*, ed. Joyce W. Warren (New Brunswick: Rutgers University Press, 1993), 263.

15   As I have suggested, the "privilege" of poetry is to a large degree a fiction, since the only woman poet who has been considered "good enough" to study has long been Emily Dickinson.

16   In addition to Lauter, *Canons and Contexts*, see for example Louis A. Renza, *"A White Heron" and the Question of Minor Literature* (Madison: University of Wisconsin, 1984); Judith Fetterley and Marjorie Pryse, "Introduction," in *American Women Regionalists, 1850–1910*, ed. Judith Fetterley and Marjorie Pryse (New York: Norton, 1992); Joyce W. Warren, "Introduction: Canons and Canon Fodder," *The (Other) American Traditions*, ed. Warren, 1–25; Joanne Dobson, "The American Renaissance Reenvisioned," in *The (Other) American Traditions*, ed. Warren, 164–82.

17   Carla L. Peterson in *The (Other) American Traditions*, ed. Warren, 186; see Peterson, *Doers of the Word: African-American Women Reformers in the North (1830–1879)* (New York: Oxford University Press, 1995).

18   Henry David Thoreau, "Reading," *Walden and Selected Essays* (1854; New York: Hendricks, 1973), 95.

19   *NCAWW*, 157.

20   Sandra M. Gilbert and Susan Gubar, *The Madwoman in the Attic: The Woman Writer and the Nineteenth-Century Literary Imagination* (New Haven: Yale University Press, 1979).

21   Emily Dickinson, *The Letters of Emily Dickinson*, ed. Thomas H. Johnson (Cambridge, MA: Belknap-Harvard University Press, 1957), 2: 408, L265.

22   Paula Bennett, "Critical Clitoridectomy: Female Sexual Imagery and Feminist Psychoanalytic Theory," *Signs: Journal of Women in Culture and Society* 18 (1993): 236; see also Bennett, "The Pea that Duty Locks: Lesbian and Feminist-Heterosexual Readings of Emily Dickinson's Poetry," in *Lesbian Texts and Contexts*, ed. Karla Jay and Joanne Glasgow (New York: New York University Press, 1990), 104–25.

23   Barbara H. Smith, *Contingencies of Value: Alternative Perspectives for Critical Theory* (Cambridge, MA: Harvard University Press, 1988).

24   Diane P. Freedman, Olivia Frey, and Frances Murphy Zauhar, eds, *The Intimate Critique, Autobiographical Literary Criticism* (Durham: Duke University Press, 1993).

25   Kilcup, Introduction to *NCAWW*, xlvii–l.

26   I pursue in detail one area explored by several of the contributors here – the connections between American women's and men's writing – in my *Robert Frost and Feminine Literary Tradition* (University of Michigan Press, 1998).

27   See Susan Koppelman, *Women in the Trees: U.S. Women's Short Stories about Battering and Resistance, 1839–1994* (Boston: Beacon, 1996).

28   See Laura Hapke, "Proletarians or True Women?: The Female Working-Class Experience and Nineteenth-Century U.S. Labor Authors," and Susan Alves, "Intruding Upon the Poet's Art: Considering the Poetic Production of Nineteenth-Century

Female Factory Workers," both in *Nineteenth-Century American Women's Culture*, ed. Karen L. Kilcup, special issue of *Over Here: A European Journal of American Culture* (1998), 5–28; 29–48.

29 Wendy Chmielewski, "'Mid the Din a Dove Appeared': Women's Writing in the Nineteenth-Century American Peace Movement," in *Nineteenth-Century American Women's Culture*, ed. Kilcup, 71–98.

30 See Shelley Fisher Fishkin, *Was Huck Black?: Mark Twain and African-American Voices* (New York: Oxford University Press, 1993).

31 Carolyn Heilbrun, *Writing a Woman's Life* (New York: W. W. Norton, 1988).

32 In addition to the studies by Baym, Tompkins, Dobson, and others cited above, see Joanna Russ, *How to Suppress Women's Writing* (Austin: University of Texas Press, 1983).

33 Elliott, "An Ex-Brigadier," *NCAWW*, 374.

1

"Not in the Least American": Nineteenth-Century Literary Regionalism as UnAmerican Literature

JUDITH FETTERLEY

My title comes from a book called *Deephaven* published in 1877 by a writer named Sarah Orne Jewett. In this book Jewett describes the experiences two young women have when they choose to spend the summer in a little town in Maine rather than remaining in Boston or traveling with friends or family. The summer in Deephaven becomes the occasion for a pause in the lives of Kate and Helen before the presumptively inevitable plunge into marriage and mother-hood, irreversible adulthood. Yet for one of the women, Helen (the narrator), the pause provides the opportunity to interrogate, however indirectly, conven-tional wisdom on the subjects of marriage and motherhood, the definition of adulthood, and the value of the characteristics associated with it. For Jewett, who chose not to marry, who chose in one crucial sense not to grow up as her culture defined this process for women, writing *Deephaven* may have helped her acknowledge and understand this difference and may have enabled her four years later to enter into a life-long relationship with Annie Adams Fields, widow of James T. Fields, the man who made the *Atlantic Monthly*, founded Ticknor and Fields, and for twenty years served as the arbiter of what would be called American literature. Was Jewett's choice unAmerican? Is her book unAmerican?

Deephaven, Jewett's narrator declares, "was not in the least American. There was no excitement about anything; there were no manufactories; nobody seemed in the least hurry. The only foreigners were a few standard sailors. I do not know when a house or a new building of any kind had been built."[1] I take this text as my starting point in proposing the term "unAmerican" as a way of thinking about a particular body of nineteenth-century texts and as a way of describing a particular critical stance, for when Jewett refers to the town of Deephaven as "not in the least American" I read her as thus marking the difference of her own text from what even in the 1870s could be considered American literature. In this context we might note the choice of another writer, Henry James, who appropriated the term "American" for the novel he published in 1877, the same year Jewett published *Deephaven*, and who thus signaled his ambition to write a specifically American novel, perhaps even "the great American novel."[2]

While the term "unAmerican," like all terms constructed in opposition, is problematic by virtue of its connection to the very thing it opposes, it has the advantage of foregrounding the degree to which the term "American" in the context of American literature has always referred to certain thematic content and to the values associated with that content – has, in this sense, always been political. Thinking of texts as unAmerican has the added advantage of moving the question of the canon beyond tokenism, for it suggests that the controversy over what we teach cannot be resolved by merely adding a woman and/or a minority male writer to our syllabi, since not all texts by women or minority males challenge the values currently associated with the term "American" in the context of American literature. Although adding texts by women and minority males to our courses and syllabi is necessary political work, it is not sufficient, for we may well ask how much has been gained if black men establish personhood through invoking sexism or if white women establish personhood through invoking racism. It is, for example, no accident that I have sought to recover the tradition of American literary regionalism as opposed to, say, the body of anti-Tom texts written by white Southern women in the years following the publication of *Uncle Tom's Cabin* and preceding the Civil War. For in the texts of literary regionalism I find the values that lead me to critique the canon in the first place; that is, in regionalism I find a literature that models a subjectivity attained by standing up for others, not on them. Invoking the concept of "unAmerican" thus helps focus attention on the significance of which texts by minority males and women we choose to include. Finally, figuring one's critical stance as unAmerican provides a way of thinking about one's activity that does justice to its political intent and recognizes the dangers which attend it.

In this essay, I wish to model what Paul Lauter has labeled canonical criticism, a criticism that focuses on "how we construct our syllabi and anthologies, on the roots of our systems of valuation, and on how we decide what is important for us to teach and for our students to learn," and specifically that form of canonical criticism which, in the words of Lillian Robinson, takes treason as its text.[3] Canon critique, a term I prefer to canonical criticism, which can perhaps be misread as traditional interpretation of the current canon, has been from the outset overtly political, concerned with issues of power and aligned with certain values. As an overtly political criticism, canon critique has sought to expose the political nature of the processes of canon formation and literary valuation, asking such questions as: by what specific historical processes have certain texts become canonical, what politics have informed these processes, and what politics inform the definitions of aesthetic value that accompany such processes? – questions given still greater urgency from a context of increasing pressure to "get back to basics" and to create a set body of texts that will define what is

American and who is literate. Indeed, as Paul Lauter comments, "it would not be too much to say that canonical criticism constitutes a part of a broader effort to reconstruct our society, and particularly our educational institutions, on a more democratic and equitable basis."[4]

In the field of American literature, canon critique has sought to expose how the term "American" has been used to create a literary canon so hegemonic in the privileging of certain subjectivities as to make the term unAmerican not simply politically useful but actually meaningful.[5] The equation of American literature with a handful of texts written by white men, primarily of Anglo-Saxon ethnicity and middle- or upper-middle-class backgrounds, with formal and thematic coherence sufficient to enable a theory of the "Americanness" of American literature, began in the early decades of the nineteenth century.[6] Paul Lauter, Nina Baym, and Elizabeth Renker, however, have focused our attention on the middle decades of the twentieth century, when American literature became fully institutionalized as a field of study in colleges and universities, as the period which produced the map of American literature still operative today. Nina Baym has aptly labeled the canon established during these decades "melodramas of beset manhood" and has demonstrated how this paradigm ensures "that stories about women could not contain the essence of American culture" and thus "that the matter of American experience is inherently male." Elizabeth Renker, in tracing how the First and Second World Wars created a context in which American literature could be read as engendering masculinity, has provided an additional context for understanding our current situation and in particular for understanding the connection between what we currently identify as American literature and certain formulations of our national interest.[7]

If the analyses of Baym, Lauter, and Renker are correct – that what we currently accept as American literature implicitly and explicitly defines as American only certain persons and only the stories that serve the interests of those persons – then those of us who challenge the value of those texts and seek to disrupt the hegemony of the canon by recovering texts with different definitions and different stories are engaging in a process that could itself be described as unAmerican. And if the fictions we recognize as American serve the interests of those who also represent the state, then the feminist critique of the American literary canon can be seen as a form of treason – a connection that explains the not-so-strange career of Lynne Cheney, perhaps the most politically motivated appointment in the history of the NEH, whose goal was to delegitimate, if she could not eradicate, the unAmerican activity of feminist canon critique. To put it another way, one can reasonably argue that American education at every level is currently organized to serve the needs of "boys" (here understood as a synecdoche for Baym's "beset manhood") and that through what is taught and how it is taught our educational system ratifies boys' sense of agency and primacy, their sense of themselves as subjects, particularly as defined against their sense of girls as objects. Thus those of us who seek to place the needs of girls first – in our classroom practices, in our determination of course content, in our criticism

– can be considered to be acting in an unAmerican, even treasonous fashion. For those of us who engage in feminist canon critique do so from a complex set of assumptions about the relation of identity to reading and writing practices. To put it simply, we assume a connection between the self-concept of a reader and the self imagined by and in a literary text. Thus, extrapolating again from Baym's argument and from my own argument in *The Resisting Reader*,[8] the classic tradition of American literature, by excluding women from the definition of American, constructs the girl reading this tradition as herself unAmerican. To the degree, then, that our literature cannot imagine the American as other than male, to that degree we who are women are already unAmerican, so indeed let treason be our text.

I wish to use as my example of the "unAmerican," and as my basis for exploring the political utility of this term, a body of texts produced in the United States primarily by women writing during the second half of the nineteenth century constituting what Marjorie Pryse and I call literary regionalism. (Pryse and I have gathered together works by fourteen such "unAmerican" writers in *American Women Regionalists, 1850–1910*. The obligatory use of the term "American" to describe this anthology for marketing purposes in itself provides a rich context for thinking about the difficulties and even contradictions of our enterprise.) While some of the writers in this tradition may be familiar to readers – Kate Chopin, Alice Dunbar-Nelson, Mary Wilkins Freeman, Sarah Orne Jewett – most are marginal to, if not absent from, current American literary history. Absent as well from that history is any concept of the tradition of nineteenth-century regionalist writing as we understand it. Though some of the writers and texts included in our anthology come into the field of American literature through the rubric of "regional realism" or "local color," understood as subsets of "realism,"[9] these categories derive from a history of American literature based on the writing of men, one which privileges their work as the source of its definitions. Indeed, certain recent texts have sought to establish the specifically masculinist nature of realism, the dominant term in virtually all writing about American literature after the Civil War.[10] Although in the case of Michael Bell in *The Problem of American Realism* this identification has the effect of allowing him to ask "what Jewett made of American realism," and thus of positioning Jewett as a potential alternative to the values of realism, he reads her only within the context of her entanglement with what he calls "realist thinking." Thus he concludes, not surprisingly, that the ambitious Nan Prince of *A Country Doctor* (1884) is "free" to defy tradition only by embracing it and that once Jewett left behind the ambition projected into the story of Nan Prince "she would appear to have left herself with no clear rationale or counter-rationale to put in its place and after *The Country of the Pointed Firs* there was no obvious direction for her career to go."[11] Hence the fall in 1902 which effectively ended her life as a writer was for Bell "fortunate." Bell fails to recognize that Jewett's work derives from a tradition of women's writing that goes back at least as far as the end of the eighteenth century and Maria Edgeworth, a tradition

developed through the first half of the nineteenth century by writers such as
Mary Russell Mitford, Harriet Beecher Stowe, Alice Cary, and Rose Terry Cooke,
and practiced by Jewett's contemporaries and acquaintances such as Celia Thaxter,
Mary Noialles Murfree, and Mary Wilkins Freeman. In Bell's version of American
literary history Jewett appears as an isolated individual struggling to create an
alternative to oppose to the dominant discourse of realism and failing precisely
because of her isolation and because realism is finally the only game in town. In
a different version of American literary history, but perhaps not called that,
Jewett might appear as a particularly talented practitioner of a long-established
tradition, seeking to critique the self-consciously masculine "new" realism from
a larger historical perspective.

The elegiac tone Michael Bell adopts for his discussion of Jewett finds an echo
in Eric Sundquist's chapter in the *Columbia Literary History of the United States*.
Sundquist subsumes regionalism under the rubric of local color and identifies
it as "a literature of memory," a memory, he observes, "often lodged in the
vestiges of a world of female domesticity."[12] This reading bears an uncanny
resemblance to the process Laura Romero has analyzed in "Vanishing Americans:
Gender, Empire, and New Historicism," a process in which the elegiac mode of
cultural and literary history performs the "historical sleight of hand" of representing "the disappearance of the native as not just natural but as having already
happened."[13] Both Michael Bell in *The Problem of American Realism* and Richard
Brodhead in *Cultures of Letters* position their reading of Jewett in relation to
what they see as an overtly feminist effort to recuperate Jewett for contemporary
readers,[14] and both participate in a process I call the "re-vanishing" of Jewett –
Brodhead by seeking to dismantle the conceptual framework which has led to
her recuperation and Bell by suggesting that she cannot finally be distinguished
from the masculinist enterprise of realism. In Sundquist's chapter the palpable
politics of the discourse over Jewett is itself "vanished" to reemerge as a description of her disappearance as "having already happened."

While Marjorie Pryse and I retain the term "regional" for this tradition, in
part to focus attention on the significance of place to the production, reception,
and content of these texts, and in part to avail ourselves of whatever recognition
currently obtains from its present usage, we seek primarily through this term to
create a category parallel to and thus potentially of equal importance to the category of realism. And we seek as well to create a framework that will enable us
to see connections, origins, and aims that remain obscure if we continue to subsume the work of regionalist writers under the category of realism. In creating
the category of regionalism, then, we seek to model the effect on our understanding of "American" literature of deriving our map of American literary history
from an analysis of the work of women. That this constitutes an unAmerican
activity may be inferred from the fact that presentation of our work invariably
leads to the question, "Weren't there any men writing regionalist fiction between
1850 and 1910?" – a question which barely contains the anxiety that men might
be excluded from an American tradition or that certain male writers (for example,

Charles Chesnutt) might best be understood in a context created by the work of women and subsumed within a category primarily female.

In asking readers to engage with the tradition of regionalist writing and in identifying the stakes of this engagement, I seek to provide you with a context within which the concepts of "unAmerican" and "treason" have meaning. For one can perhaps understand the intent of the effort to write Jewett out of history before she is even in, to "re-vanish" her, if one considers the effect of choosing Jewett's *The Country of the Pointed Firs* as *the* required American text for an eighth-grade English class or a freshman introduction to literature course; or of organizing an entire course in American literature around the issues it raises; or even of introducing it in an American literature survey. As my students like to point out, "This isn't an American book. It has no story and it is all about old women and a few old men. There isn't an American in it." Or consider the effect of defining Sylvy, the protagonist of "A White Heron," as an American cultural hero, a girl who comes to understand (hetero)sexuality as sexual harassment, the great red-faced boy who used to chase and frighten her in town reappearing in the form of the "nice" boy with a gun who seeks to kill and stuff "the very birds he seemed to like so much";[15] a girl who chooses to renounce the world, her chance of being an "American," perhaps even nationality itself, in favor of a bird's life. My students can't understand why she doesn't promise to marry the hunter when she grows up, and so we talk about domestic violence and why so much romance should end in so much battering.

My use of the term "unAmerican" presents one final question which I wish to raise here. In introducing literature currently considered unAmerican, is our goal to redefine the meaning of "American," to make it possible for girls to be Americans too? Or is the goal to replace the term "American" entirely? Can significant change be accomplished without renaming the field or has the term "American" become so profoundly associated with certain values that in order to introduce literature with different values into the field we will need to do nothing less than to cease using the term "American" and develop instead an alternative term, for example, "Writing in the US," as Gregory Jay has suggested in "The End of 'American' Literature"?[16] To put the matter another way, can the term "American" be recuperated for a different set of values, or does its energy, its power, its eroticism derive from the values currently associated with it and from its association with these values? Yet if we abandon the term are we not complicit in the very pattern we protest, and, by leaving all that power in the "wrong" hands, have we not made a major political error? Yet can we have the power without a price? And is it possible that our very attachment to the term "American" derives precisely from those values which have precluded the participation of all but a few persons in the literary and cultural definition of the term in the first place? By playing with the terms "American" and "unAmerican," I seek thus to join the effort to identify the naming of the field of "American literature" as itself a site of contestation, not so much because I care what name we give it as because I care what values we promote through it. In seeking to gain readers for these texts, I seek nothing less than the creation of a citizenry committed to the values of inclusion, empathy, diversity, and community, and the cultural change which would follow upon the creation of such a citizenry. And in bringing attention to texts which have historically been excluded from the canon of American literature, I seek to model the process of inclusion and the change which it can accomplish, whether the end result be a redefined American literature or a new name for our enterprise.

If Huckleberry Finn, white boy on the run from the "sivilization" of women, provides the paradigm for how "our" literature has constructed the American, a story like Mary Wilkins Freeman's "On the Walpole Road," which opens with a description of a woman "who might have been seventy" with "a double brist-ling chin," driving slowly along a road in company with another woman who was "younger – forty perhaps,"[17] marks a difference, just as in *The Country of the Pointed Firs* Mrs. Todd, a woman of sixty-seven, and Mrs. Blackett, a woman in her eighties, pass on their knowledge to the younger generation, defined as a woman in her forties, "perhaps." A literature which foregrounds old women rather than boys hardly seems American; it is as if the Widow Douglas were to take the story away from Huck.

But when we consider more closely that "bristling" chin, we realize that regionalism's understanding of story must be as different as its understanding of character, for women with bristling chins are not capable of generating those stories we have come to think of as American, nor even those other fictions not quite so American, those novels whose business it is to negotiate the marriage of girls. Indeed, I would argue that literary regionalism occurs primarily in the form of the sketch or short story because this form made it possible to tell stories about elderly women with bristling chins, about women for whom the eventful means something other than marriage, about women in relation to each other, about women who take care of themselves. In "A New England Nun," one of the few regionalist texts that might be considered well known, Freeman makes this feature of regionalist writing the subject of the fiction itself, for in this story Louisa Ellis comes to realize that her meaningful event is not the marriage she has awaited for fourteen years but the ritualized and sacramental life she has created during those years, feeding herself "with as much grace as if she had been a veritable guest to her own self."[18] Similarly, Jewett's "A White Heron," one of the few regionalist texts to feature a young girl as its protagon-ist, dramatizes Sylvy's instinctive swerve away from the seemingly inevitable heterosexual plot, her choice of her own life over the hunter's need. In that pause which halts the headlong rush, in that Deephaven time-out, regionalism creates its own "world elsewhere" which has yet to be recognized as American – no doubt in part because our current understanding of "American" cannot encompass the privileging of women's relations to themselves or other women over their relation to men. Indeed, since the literature we call American romanticizes the relation of boy to boy and man to man while it denies, if it does not vilify, the love of women for women and presents women primarily as rivals for the attention of boys and men, *Deephaven* deserves the accolade "unAmerican" for its devotion to inscribing romantic love between women and the "deephaven" of female friendship.[19]

If the sketch provided the form which made it possible to talk about unAmerican women – women with bristling chins, women who love other women, women who love themselves, women who choose birds over boys – it did so precisely because such fictions could not be candidates for the accolade "great American novel." Indeed, the vexed relation of the form of regionalist writing to the definition of great American literature can best be demonstrated by *The Country of the Pointed Firs*. This text, which Jewett herself referred to as "papers," has defied efforts to define it as a novel and puzzled readers who have previously tried to label it. In concluding her preface to the edition of *The Country of the Pointed Firs* published in 1925, Willa Cather writes: "If I were asked to name three American books which have the possibility of a long, long life, I would say at once, 'The Scarlet Letter,' 'Huckleberry Finn,' and 'The Country of the Pointed Firs.' "[20] If Jewett recognized that she had to write a novel-length book in order to have a chance at the "immortality" predicted by Cather, she nevertheless refused in so doing to relinquish the essential identity of the sketch, no doubt one reason why her text has not in fact had the kind of life Cather predicted for it. And while Jewett's genius enabled her to find a way to write a novel-length regionalist text and thus to seek for regionalist fiction the status associated with length, the very fact that she needed to do this underscores the marginal status of the sketch in American literature. Yet if the marginal status of the sketch form was the price that had to be paid to gain the discursive freedom of regionalism, and if to gain that discursive freedom literary regionalists sold their birthright to be considered great American writers, they too, like Louisa Ellis, could be said not to "know it, that taste of the pottage was so delicious."[21] For, as Freeman suggests, to persons excluded from rights and required to cook, pottage may be preferable.

In Rose Terry Cooke's "Miss Beulah's Bonnet," first published in 1880 in *Harper's*, an elderly woman, having opened her house to her niece and her niece's children, Sarah, Janey, and Jack, finds herself "free to say I never did like boys. I suppose divine Providence ordained 'em to some good end; but it takes a sight o'grace to believe it: and of all the boys that ever was sent into this world for any purpose, I do believe [Jack] is the hatefulest."[22] Published four years after Mark Twain's *The Adventures of Tom Sawyer*, "Miss Beulah's Bonnet" can be read as an item in a dialogue about boys as a privileged subject of American literature and culture, and Miss Beulah's "free to say I never did like boys" can be read as Cooke's articulation of her desire to be free to write about women with "bristling" chins. Though Miss Beulah's "boy" refers to an actual Jack, we feel free to read "boys" as referring to a cluster of values associated with that word and we see regionalism as originating in part in the desire to participate in a dialogue which challenges those values by doing something other than "liking boys."

Regionalist writers were themselves aware of the difficulties they faced in trying to create a space in American literature for stories asserting that bonnets matter more than boys, and they both addressed these difficulties in their fiction and developed strategies for circumventing them. For regionalist writers to be able to tell stories about bonnets rather than boys, they had to imagine audiences capable of hearing and reading such stories. In "Miss Beulah's Bonnet," Miss Beulah finds herself unable to attend church because her new bonnet, hidden under the cushion of a chair by that Jack, gets smashed when the "stout" Mrs. Blake unwittingly sits on it during a visit. When the deacons come to interrogate Miss Beulah about her absence from church, they are confounded by her explanation:

> "Well, if you must know, I hain't got no bunnit."
> The deacons stared mutually; and Deacon Morse, . . . curious as men naturally are, asked abruptly, "Why not?"
> "Cause Miss Blake sot on it."
> The two men looked at each other in blank amazement, and shook their heads. Here was a pitfall. Was it proper, dignified, possible to investigate this truly feminine tangle? They were dying to enter into particulars, but ashamed to do so; nothing was left but retreat.[23]

Because the culture associated with the church defines Miss Beulah's story as a trivial feminine tangle, hers is not a story that can be told or heard in church; and since the deacons are there in their official capacity as churchmen who must report back to their congregation, they cannot hear her story because they cannot imagine telling it. Indeed, within Cooke's fiction Miss Beulah's story only gets told by a woman to other women, within the separate sphere of the sewing circle, though we may suppose that the women go home and tell their husbands. In describing the deacons as dying to enter into particulars but ashamed to do so, Cooke herself constructs men as a rich potential audience for her story, just as she suggests that "girls'" stories may not get fully heard until men can imagine themselves telling them. In writing *her* story for a readership obviously comprised of men as well as women, she proposes that men in the privacy of reading can satisfy their desire to enter a truly feminine tangle without the loss of status that would attend a public acknowledgment of their curiosity. Yet such a proposition reveals men to be boys, governed primarily by the peer pressures of male bonding formalized in such institutions as the church. In this context, male bonding, that holiest of holies in American culture (as witness the rituals of Superbowl Sunday), takes on a negative cast as Cooke challenges men to commit the treason of admitting publicly in front of other men their interest in and connection to women's lives. In a culture obsessed with the question of why *Johnny* can't read and insistent on providing boys' stories to lure Johnny into literacy, since, as one elementary school teacher put it to me, girls will read stories about boys but boys won't read stories about girls, to ask men to hear and tell women's stories may indeed be unAmerican. Yet, as Cooke implies, what's truly shameful is a construction of masculinity which makes boys ashamed to read girls' stories.

For those of us interested in the unAmerican act of getting Janey to read, regionalism not only provides "girls'" stories but models as well the importance for women of having and telling their stories. In the figure of her own Janey, Cooke presents the situation of woman and story in a world of boys. Jack preserves the letter of his own honesty by making his little sister hide Miss Beulah's bonnet; he then terrifies her into silence with "wild threats of bears and guns"[24] and quickly distracts her so that she soon forgets what she has done. In creating women who come to recognize that they have a story and who become empowered to tell their story, regionalist fiction seeks to construct women as storyful rather than storyless and to connect having and telling stories to their sanity and survival. In "Sister Liddy," Freeman identifies having a story to tell as the one thing that maintains the sanity and dignity of the old women who are inmates of the county poorhouse. Polly Moss, whose physical deformity adds another dimension to her struggle, temporarily comes into her own in this strife-ridden community when she makes up and tells a series of stories about her imaginary sister, Liddy. Similarly, in "The Praline Woman," Alice Dunbar-Nelson shows the significance of story to a working-class woman of color who is determined to share her stories with her customers and who exercises considerable ingenuity to find openings in the chatter of commerce for such an exchange. Of Jewett we could say that the entire art of *The Country of the Pointed Firs* lies in creating a written text that can identify women as a rich source of story and as storytellers, through characters such as Mrs. Todd and, more importantly still, through the narrator herself, who must find the way to write them down.

In seeking to empower persons made silent or vacant through terror to tell stories which the dominant culture labels trivial, regionalism seeks to change our perspective and thus to destabilize the meaning of margin and center. For including the story of one previously silenced and marginalized inevitably affects the definition of margin and center and calls into question the values that have produced such definitions. In *Deephaven* Jewett specifically associates this process with the category of the American, seeking thus to unsettle and destabilize our understanding of that term. In a chapter entitled "The Circus at Denby," Kate and Helen attend a circus. At the end of the day, their companion, Mrs. Kew, declares an interest in the side shows and they enter the tent containing the Kentucky Giantess, for, as Mrs. Kew says, "she never heard of such a thing as a woman's weighing six hundred and fifty pounds."[25] When Kate and Helen return from looking at the monkeys, an added attraction of this side show, they find Mrs. Kew engaged in conversation with the giantess, who turns out to be someone Mrs. Kew used to know. In a quiet but momentous revolution, the freak turns out to be a neighbor with a story and a secret and feelings, and as we experience this revolution we are forced to question definitions of center and margin, norm and freak, national and regional. Positioned as a spectacle, the fat lady is not herself meant to speak. By placing cages of monkeys on the same platform as the giantess, the entrepreneur running the show seeks to rationalize the category of freak as somehow not really human and as therefore available for profit and use to exhibitor and viewer alike. Thus when the fat lady does in fact speak and the "freak" becomes "somebody's neighbor," the title Cooke gave to her 1881 collection of regionalist fiction, the rationalization collapses and the category it has sustained no longer seems inherent. Once revealed as constructed, it can then be deconstructed.

In the second half of the chapter, Kate and Helen attend an evening lecture on "The Elements of True Manhood." Evoking here the Emersonian doctrine of self-reliance, Jewett associates this event with the issue of who is and is not included in the term "American." The young white man who comes to Deephaven to deliver this lecture assumes that in talking of and to himself he addresses everyone. His use of the stage as a place from which to speak at an audience expected to remain silent – so different from the arrangements of the fat lady – confirms his assumption of his own centrality. The lecture would seem to contrast with the circus, yet in Jewett's hands it comes to seem far more of a "show" than the circus itself. "You would have thought," observes Helen, "the man was addressing an enthusiastic Young Men's Christian Association. He exhorted with fervor upon our duties as citizens and as voters, and told us a great deal about George Washington and Benjamin Franklin, whom he urged us to choose as our examples." And she continues, "If the lecture had been upon any other subject it would not have been so hard for Kate and me to keep sober faces; but it was directed entirely toward young men, and there was not a young man there."[26] As the lecture drones on, we come to see the lecturer himself as crazy for delivering a talk on the elements of true manhood to an audience composed entirely of old men, women, and children. Yet his failure to recognize his audience, and the arrogant solipsism implicit in this failure, reflects a larger cultural madness. For young men do not represent the majority of the population in Deephaven or anywhere else, and a culture that devotes itself entirely to the feeding of boys, as if they constituted the whole human race, and has nothing to say to old men, women, and children, is crazy, if not malicious. After they have laughed long and hard, Kate and Helen come to see "the pitiful side of it all" and send a contribution to the lecturer to help pay his expenses. Later they learn that he will repeat his lecture the following evening and, as Helen observes, "I have no doubt there were a good many women able to be out, and that he harvested enough ten-cent pieces to pay his expenses without our help."[27] Although the chapter ends in anger, however subdued, we should memorialize Kate and Helen's laughter, their inability to keep sober during the lecture, as an instance of treason *in* the text and as a model of unAmerican activity.

Challenging and destabilizing the meaning of margin and center serves as a paradigm for regionalism's efforts to dismantle and deconstruct hierarchies based on the categories of gender, race, class, age, and region. Although certainly not free itself of the infection of these hierarchies, regionalist fiction works toward dismantling the binary oppositions and the concomitant privileging of one item over the other that structure a culture dedicated to the elements of true manhood. Regionalist texts are astonishingly free of the dialect of gender that dominates most of nineteenth-century American writing by both men and women, for while regionalist fiction acknowledges gender differences, it recognizes these differences as the product of privilege, not biology. Jack is not so much born a nuisance as made one by the fact of living in a world run by deacons. And a story like Freeman's "A Church Mouse," which opens with the line, "I never heard of a woman's bein' saxton," develops the position that such failures to hear exist not because of "nature" but because they help men maintain the privilege of not having to share the church with a "mouse," the world with women. Hetty Fifield, old, poor, and homeless, fights for her own survival through pressing the revolutionary question, "I dun know what difference that makes."[28]

Writing of a world inhabited by old men and women, Jewett creates a space to experiment with breaking down the rigid gender identities associated in her mind with the Emersonian definition of "American." No figure in *The Country of the Pointed Firs* is more pathetic than Captain Littlepage, landlocked in the trivial feminine tangle of Dunnet Landing while longing for a world of high art and obsessed by the memory of another man's last voyage to the "end" of the world, the ultimately masculine adventure. Yet, ironically, those discoveries he has promised to pass on of "a kind of waiting place between this world an' the next"[29] are emblems of mediation, dissolution, blending – as if Jewett means to say, go as far as possible toward one pole and you will arrive at a space that dissolves the idea of pole. For at the end of the world there seems to be a middle ground, a meeting place of this world and the next, emblematic of the dissolution of oppositional polarities. This space both obsesses and horrifies Captain Littlepage, but for other characters and perhaps for Jewett herself it functions as a desired goal. Thus Elijah Tilley places stakes in his fields to indicate, like buoys, the presence of rocks, declaring that "one trade helps another," and in the absence of his wife has become himself a careful housekeeper. And thus Mrs. Blackett declares that "William as been son an' daughter both."[30] Regionalism's intention to dismantle race and gender differences finds succinct expression in Alice Dunbar-Nelson's "The Praline Woman." Here a praline-colored woman speaks a dialect which renders such distinctions temporarily inoperative: "Ah, he's fine gal, is Didele."[31] If this were American language, maybe we might not have a problem with gays in the military.

In regionalist fiction, the impulse to dissolve binary oppositions and destabilize the definition of margin and center through shifting our perspective begins with a feeling that can best be described as empathy, as the capacity to imagine how someone else might feel, and we see regionalism as a fiction characterized, indeed inspired, by empathy. Regionalism's commitment to empathy serves to distinguish it from the post-Civil War local color movement under which regionalist writers are often subsumed. In local color writing, genteel narrators present regional characters to urban readers as instances of the quaint or queer. Such characters form a literary circus which serves to ratify readers' sense of their own normalcy and normativeness. Despite the gesture toward the local, then, local color writing in effect ratifies the hegemony of the "national" as a standard against which the local can be measured and found wanting. Regionalism, however, as we have seen from the instance of *Deephaven* and "The Circus at Denby," deconstructs the "national," revealing its presumed universality to be in fact the position of a certain, albeit privileged, group of locals.

In valuing empathy, regionalism proposes alternative behaviors to those which characterize the world of boys; to the extent that boys are equated with the national, regionalism models behaviors not in the national interest. In "Miss Beulah's Bonnet," Jack gets the reputation of a nuisance for his harassment of the hens, the cat, Nanny Starks, and even Miss Beulah herself, all creatures relatively defenseless against him. While empathy can obtain in a context of peers – as witness the impassioned defense of Beulah Larkin by Mary Jane Beers, the milliner who made her bonnet – regionalist fiction presents empathy primarily as a model for the relationships of "persons" with differing amounts of cultural power. By modeling an alternative mode of relating to that evinced by the "boy," regionalist fiction seeks as well to convert the boy and by such conversion to redistribute cultural power. When Sylvy, in "A White Heron," refuses to "tell the heron's secret and give its life away,"[32] we are left to wonder how different her life might have been had the boy looked at her the way she looks at the bird. A further instance of this phenomenon can be found in Stowe's *The Pearl of Orr's Island*, a text which Jewett identified as the origin of her own career as a writer of regionalist fiction.

In this story, Stowe describes a boy and a girl, Moses and Mara, growing up together in early nineteenth-century New England, and analyzes the social structures which lead the boy to view the girl as an inferior being and to treat her with contempt. Mara, watching Moses prepare for his first fishing voyage, protests, however faintly, her own exclusion from the event:

> "How I do wish I were going with you!" she says [*sic*]. "I could do something, couldn't I – take care of your hooks, or something?"
> "Pooh!" said Moses, sublimely regarding her while he settled the collar of his shirt, "you're a girl – and what can girls do at sea? you never like to catch fish – it always makes you cry to see 'em flop."[33]

Moses reads empathy as disqualifying Mara for life – Mara will later literally die for lack of the air and exercise such a voyage might give her – and as justifying his contempt for her, but Stowe reads Moses's lack of empathy as a far more serious disqualification. In Moses we recognize a version of Tom Sawyer, the American bad boy who can do no wrong in the nation's eyes, despite the cries of tormented cats and aunts. Thus when we realize that Stowe's text intends to convert this boy into a "girl," to bring him to the point of feeling pain when a girl gasps and thus to be more like her, we have a context for reflecting on the unAmericanness of empathy.

Empathy can characterize narrator as well as character; in creating empathic narrators, regionalist writers propose a different model of storytelling from that "American" tradition begun by Washington Irving and developed in the genre of the tall tale, in particular by the humorists of the old Southwest. In "In the Name of Wonder: The Emergence of Tall Narrative in American Writing," Henry B. Wonham provides evidence of the gendered nature of "American" in this explicitly American genre, and not simply through the masculinist content of the tales or the masculine identity of the teller. More significantly, Wonham notes, the audience for such tales is composed of "boys," the action involves the humiliation of a naive outsider frequently figured as female, and "her victimization becomes a patriotic victory for American wit."[34] In "The Legend of Sleepy Hollow," Irving poses the question of who will be given possession of Sleepy Hollow, that imaginative space which inspires our stories, and who will be driven out. Irving identifies the masculine Brom Bones as the decisive victor, the effeminate Ichabod Crane as the figure to be driven out, and the tall tale as the best way to tell a story about winning and losing because its very telling enacts a similar drama. Indeed, in his postscript to this story Irving suggests that the quintessential American story will be a tall tale circulated among men for the purpose of establishing dominance. The good reader is the one who gets the joke; the bad reader is the one who doesn't get it or refuses to find it funny, perhaps because the joke is on her or him; and telling stories about winning and losing becomes itself an act of winning and losing, of inclusion and exclusion, with character, teller, and listener all invited to identify with one another and against someone else, everyone becoming a Brom Bones getting rid of an Ichabod Crane. As Wonham puts it, the tall tale serves an audience of "cultural insiders" whose enjoyment depends upon the exclusionary practices of a narrative form appropriately characterized as "a sort of inside joke."[35]

Regionalist writers provide a different model of storytelling. Constructing women as storytellers, they also present storytelling as an activity designed to include rather than exclude, to heal rather than harm. In *The Country of the Pointed Firs*, the long anticipated visit of Susan Fosdick creates the occasion for an evening of storytelling. The narrator has invited Mrs. Todd and Susan Fosdick to her room, and as storytelling follows from this invitation Jewett suggests the connection between storytelling and hospitality, just as she connects storytelling and healing through references to the season as the "time of syrups and cordials."[36] Telling the story of Joanna serves as a way of keeping Joanna, the one "driven" out, connected in some way to her community and of easing the pain of those who feel they have lost her. Indeed, it continues the efforts Dunnet Landing folk made to stay connected with Joanna while she was still alive as "one after another ventured to make occasion to put somethin' ashore for her if they went that way." Storytelling as one mode of staying connected thus participates in creating the community of Dunnet Landing as one in which far islands

and scattered farms are linked together through "constant interest and inter-
course . . . into a golden chain of love and dependence." Moreover, in elaborating Joanna as a symbol of that place "in the life of each of us . . . remote
and islanded, and given to endless regret or secret happiness,"[37] the narrator
indicates that in hearing this story she has come not simply to empathize with
but to identify with the exile.

In her last published story, entitled "The Foreigner," however, Jewett chose
to critique the limits of regionalist empathy and in so doing to complicate still
further the question of the American and the unAmerican, a gesture appropriate to a tradition which takes the critique of cultural values as its particular
province. Yet it would be a mistake, I think, to read Jewett's critique as in fact
arguing for a recuperation of the American, for the question her final story
asks – how could Mrs. Todd have missed the foreigner and her story? – suggests
that such losses occur through creating the category of the foreigner, a category
which has meaning only in the context of the American and not American.
Indeed, anticipating the arguments Virginia Woolf would make in *Three Guineas*
against the value of nationalism for women, Jewett's regionalist fiction implies
that the ancient knowledge women need to learn and inherit, and the stories we
all need to hear, can be unfolded only in a space which refuses to participate in
the masculinist notion of nation. Thus I would like to conclude this essay with
a brief meditation on Jewett's "The Foreigner," a story which helps me think
about the value of the term "American" in the global context of the twenty-
first century. Deephaven, Jewett tells us, was not in the least American in part
because "the only foreigners there were a few standard sailors." Here Jewett
identifies Deephaven, and by extension the Dunnet Landing of her later work, as
ethnically and racially homogeneous, an observation which prepares us for a story
that seeks to extend the range of empathy to include those constructed as foreign.

"The Foreigner" tells the story of a woman, French by birth and Jamaican by
residence, rescued from poverty and sexual harassment through marriage to a
Captain Tolland, who brings her home to Dunnet Landing – a community as
unable to hear her story as the deacons to hear Miss Beulah's, and lacking their
curiosity. As Mrs. Todd recounts to the narrator her story of Mrs. Tolland's life
in Dunnet Landing and of the circumstances of her death, she reveals as well the
limits of her own empathy, her failure to extend herself to include this woman
in her definition of community.

Jewett's critique of the limits of Mrs. Todd's empathy becomes even more
pointed when we consider how she has constructed the foreigner whom Mrs.
Todd belatedly accepts. In creating her foreigner, Jewett hints at dimensions of
otherness that might have made it impossible for Mrs. Captain Tolland to live
in Dunnet Landing at all. She comes to Dunnet Landing by way of the West
Indies, yet she herself is white and French, not colored or even native to those
foreign islands. In this severely Protestant community, she seems foreign in her
Catholicism, but she is neither Jewish nor atheist nor a practitioner of voodoo.
Though the captains rescue her from a bar full of drunken men, she has not been

raped and is not a prostitute, nor does she arrive either pregnant or with an illegitimate child. If Dunnet Landing cannot extend itself to include a white French Catholic who, duly married, still loves to sing and dance, what, Jewett makes us wonder, would they do to a black unwed mother who practiced voodoo?

Belatedly, Mrs. Todd finds common ground with the foreigner. Through her love for her own mother, Mrs. Todd can "see" the foreigner's mother and assure her that her mother is indeed present in the room where she lies dying. While we are all familiar with the cliché "as American as motherhood and apple pie," nothing is in fact more foreign to our literature than "seeing" mother or listening to her story. To return for a moment to Freeman's "On the Walpole Road" and the woman with the "bristling chin," we might equally locate this story's unAmericanness in its celebration of the resurrection of "mother," for when Mis' Green discovers that the funeral she has been called to attend is not for Aunt Rebecca, the woman who has been like a mother to her, but for Uncle Enos, she becomes "kinder highstericky" and laughs "till the tears was runnin' down my cheeks, an' it was all I could do to breathe." "I thought you was dead," she explains to Aunt Rebecca, "an' there you was a-settin.'"[38]

Throughout this essay I have used the term "unAmerican" to refer to a body of literature that challenges the values currently understood as "American" in order to provide reflection about what we are doing when we teach American literature. For, to me, the question of values constitutes the "to what end" of rethinking American literature, the title I gave to the 1993 NCTE Summer Institute for Teachers of Literature, where this paper was first presented. We suffer today from a national narrative that valorizes violence, that defines masculinity as the production of violence and defines the feminine and the foreign as legitimate recipients of such violence. We need different narratives and different identities, whether we locate these in a field named "American literature" or "writing in the US" or "the literatures of America" – or "the Americas" – or "postcolonial writing." It is my argument here that we can find such narratives and such identities in certain texts, of which the work of nineteenth-century literary regionalists serves as one instance, that have been systematically excluded from the definition of American literature precisely because they do not reproduce the national narrative of violence or the definitions of masculine and feminine, American and foreign, which such a narrative presents as our national interest. It is time, then, to take treason as our text and to begin reading "unAmerican" literature.

NOTES

1 Sarah Orne Jewett, *Deephaven* (1877; reprint, New Haven: College and University Press, 1966), 84.

2 William C. Spengemann, *A Mirror for Americanists: Reflections on the Idea of American Literature* (Hanover: University Press of New England, 1989), 98–114.

3   Paul Lauter, *Canons and Contexts* (New York: Oxford University Press, 1991), 134; Lillian S. Robinson, "Treason Our Text: Feminist Challenges to the Literary Canon," *Tulsa Studies in Women's Literature* 2 (1983): 83–98. Reprinted in *Feminisms*, ed. Robyn Warhol and Diane Price Herndl (New Brunswick: Rutgers University Press, 1991), 212–26.

4   Lauter, *Canons*, 144–5.

5   For readers interested in exploring this claim further, I suggest the following references which, in the aggregate, provide evidence of a fairly continuous equation since the mid-nineteenth century of American literature with a very limited number of texts: Nina Baym, "Early Histories of American Literature: A Chapter in the Institution of New England," *American Literary History* 1 (1989): 459–88; "Melodramas of Beset Manhood: How Theories of American Fiction Exclude Women Authors," *American Quarterly* 33 (1981): 123–39; Ezra Greenspan, "Evert Duyckinck and the History of Wiley and Putnam's Library of American Books, 1845–1847," *American Literature* 64 (1992): 677–93; Lauter, *Canons*, 22–47; Lawrence Oliver, "Theodore Roosevelt, Brander Matthews, and the Campaign for Literary Americanism," *American Quarterly* 41 (1989): 93–111; Elizabeth Renker, "Resistance and Change: The Rise of American Literature Studies," *American Literature* 64 (1992): 347–65; Jane Tompkins, "Susanna Rowson, Father of the American Novel," in *The (Other) American Traditions: Nineteenth-Century Women Writers*, ed. Joyce Warren (New Brunswick: Rutgers University Press, 1993), 29–38. In addition, in *A Mirror for Americanists*, William Spengemann, though by no means inspired by the politics of feminist canon critique, does an excellent job of laying out the difficulties that historically have beset the definition of American literature and the writing of American literary history. His work thus provides an important context for understanding the hegemony I refer to, for one can see such hegemony as one "obvious" solution to the problems posed by the term "American literature."

6   See Baym, "Early Histories of American Literature"; Richard Brodhead, *The School of Hawthorne* (New York: Oxford University Press, 1986), 48–66.

7   Baym, "Melodramas of Beset Manhood," 130; Renker, "Resistance and Change."

8   Judith Fetterley, *The Resisting Reader: A Feminist Approach to American Literature* (Bloomington: Indiana University Press, 1978).

9   Warner Berthoff, *The Ferment of American Realism: American Literature 1884–1919* (1965; reprint, Cambridge: Cambridge University Press, 1981), 90–102; Eric J. Sundquist, "Realism and Regionalism," *Columbia Literary History of the United States*, ed. Emory Elliot (New York: Columbia University Press, 1988), 501–24.

10 See, for example, Alfred Habegger, *Gender, Fantasy, and Realism in American Literature* (New York: Columbia University Press, 1982); Michael Bell, *The Problem of American Realism: Studies in the Cultural History of a Literary Idea* (Chicago: University of Chicago Press, 1993).

11 Bell, *Problem*, 179, 204.

12 Sundquist, "Realism and Regionalism," 508, 509.

13 Laura Romero, "Vanishing Americans: Gender, Empire, and New Historicism," *American Literature* 63 (1991): 385.

14 Bell, *Problem*, 197ff.; Richard H. Brodhead, *Cultures of Letters: Scenes of Reading and Writing in Nineteenth-Century America* (Chicago: University of Chicago Press, 1993), 142–4.

15 Judith Fetterley and Marjorie Pryse, eds, *American Women Regionalists, 1850–1910* (New York: W. W. Norton, 1992), 201. Cited below as *AWR*.

16   Gregory Jay, "The End of 'American' Literature: Toward a Multicultural Practice," *College English* 53 (1991): 264–81.

17   Fetterley and Pryse, *AWR*, 306.

18   Ibid., 356.

19   Marjorie Pryse, "Archives of Female Friendship and the 'Way' Jewett Wrote," *New England Quarterly* 66 (1993): 47–66; Judith Fetterley, "Reading *Deephaven* as a Lesbian Text," *Sexual Practice, Textual Theory: Lesbian Cultural Criticism*, ed. Susan J. Wolfe and Julia Penelope (Oxford: Blackwell Publishers, 1993), 164–83.

20   Willa Cather, "Preface," *The Country of the Pointed Firs and Other Stories* (Boston: Houghton Mifflin, 1925), n.p.

21   Fetterley and Pryse, *AWR*, 365.

22   Ibid., 130; also in Kilcup, *NCAWW*, 186.

23   Fetterley and Pryse, *AWR*, 135; *NCAWW*, 189–90.

24   Fetterley and Pryse, *AWR*, 126; *NCAWW*, 183.

25   Jewett, *Deephaven*, 106.

26   Ibid., 110.

27   Ibid., 111.

28   Fetterley and Pryse, *AWR*, 344.

29   Sarah Orne Jewett, *The Country of the Pointed Firs*, ed. Marjorie Pryse (1896; reprint, New York: Norton, 1981), 26.

30   Ibid., 120, 41.

31   Fetterley and Pryse, *AWR*, 481.

32   Ibid., 205.

33   Harriet Beecher Stowe, *The Pearl of Orr's Island* (1862; reprint, Hartford: Stowe-Day Foundation, 1979), 136.

34   Henry B. Wonham, "In the Name of Wonder: The Emergence of Tall Narrative in American Writing," *American Quarterly* 41 (1989): 303, 297.

35   Ibid., 288, 305.

36   See Ann Romines, *The Home Plot: Women, Writing and Domestic Ritual* (Amherst: University of Massachusetts Press, 1992), 63.

37   Jewett, *Country*, 77, 90, 82.

38   Fetterley and Pryse, *AWR*, 310.

2

Living With Difference: Nineteenth-Century Southern Women Writers

NANCY A. WALKER

The nineteenth-century poet Emma Lazarus, best known today as the author of the inscription on the base of the Statue of Liberty, never lived in the American South. Indeed, the inspiration for her poetry and her writings on behalf of the downtrodden was of European rather than American origin: first the German poets Schiller and Heine, and later the persecution of the Jews in Russia and elsewhere. Thus it is interesting to look closely at her characterization of the Southern United States in her 1889 poem "The South." Given Lazarus's passionate commitment to oppressed peoples, we might expect her to focus on the experience of slavery, as Harriet Beecher Stowe had done in *Uncle Tom's Cabin*. Instead, the poem includes no direct reference to the enslavement of one race by another, and Lazarus seems oddly sympathetic to a region she might well have castigated for its sins against humanity. The "Spirit" of the South presented in the poem is a languid woman, a "creole" described in lush, sensual images as she reposes in a tropical night. The only sinister note in this idyllic scene is the "dark visions" that "haunt" the female figure, and that these visions might have to do with the Civil War is suggested only by the "soldier's wooden cross" in the sixth stanza. By the end of the poem, the soldier's grave and all that it represents seem relegated firmly to the past as dawn breaks and the woman "leaps from dreams to hail the coming day."[1]

Lazarus's optimism about the future of the South – if, indeed, this is the way one reads the poem – is remarkably similar to that of another woman from the North: a woman who shared Lazarus's reforming zeal, but who in other respects could hardly have been more different. Charlotte Forten Grimké, born into a prominent free black family in Philadelphia in 1837 – twelve years before Lazarus was born in New York City – foresaw in 1864 a "higher, holier, and happier life" for the freed slaves she taught on the Georgia Sea Islands even

before the Civil War was over. While Lazarus imagined the South as an almost
mythic figure arising from troubled sleep to the promise of a new dawn, Grimké's
vision arose from the specificity of the individual former slaves among whom
she lived and worked, members of a "long-abused race" with whom she had
deep personal sympathy.

Despite the great differences between these two women – differences that
include race, degrees of involvement with the South as a region, and the genres in
which they wrote – I would suggest that they share, as both women and writers,
the condition of being "unAmerican" in somewhat the same sense that Judith
Fetterley uses the term in the previous essay, "'Not in the Least American.'"
Fetterley points to the ways in which Sarah Orne Jewett, in both the choices she
made about her personal life and the themes of many of her stories, remained
apart from the norms established for American womanhood and American literature in the latter half of the nineteenth century. Yet as a white, Protestant
New Englander, Jewett had ties to "mainstream" America that the Jewish
Lazarus and the black Grimké lacked. Each of the latter women, in fact, identified herself closely with a group accorded minority status or worse in American culture: as waves of Jewish immigrants arrived in the United States in the
1880s, Lazarus became one of the early advocates of establishing a Jewish home-
land in Palestine, and Grimké devoted herself to "changing the condition of
my oppressed and suffering people."[2] As outsiders to the South, yet acutely
conscious of the human drama of oppression and bloodshed at the core of its
existence as a region, Lazarus and Grimké were uniquely positioned to enter it
imaginatively and see both its tragedy and its potential.

Women writers who did inhabit the South during the nineteenth century,
insofar as they regarded themselves as living in a distinct region, could be considered "unAmerican" in a more literary sense. The center of literary taste and
publication had long been located in the Northeast, where Emma Lazarus's
poetry was championed by Ralph Waldo Emerson, and Charlotte Grimké was
a friend of John Greenleaf Whittier. The editor of *The Living Female Writers of
the South* (1872) lamented the fact that although Southern literature had "a
bloom of youthful vigor and glowing enthusiasm," the Southern literary enterprise suffered from "dilettanteism [sic] – the treating literature as if it were the
amusement of an idle hour, instead of a most grave and serious pursuit, on
the right following of which, to a great extent, our people's intellectual life
depends."[3] Even at the end of the century, it mattered less that the St Louis
Post-Dispatch praised the work of Kate Chopin than that the Northeastern press
castigated it, relegating *The Awakening* to the status of "forgotten novel" until
the 1950s. This is not to suggest that the South lacked a flourishing literary
culture, but rather to point to the fact that it was a long way from Savannah to
Boston, where repeated calls for the establishment of a "national" literature were
both issued and answered. The political divisiveness over the issue of slavery
eventually, if briefly, created two nations out of one, and left the South historically as well as literarily marked as "different." As late as the 1920s, on the eve

of what some have termed the "Renaissance" of Southern literature, journalist and pundit H. L. Mencken declared the South barren of artistic vitality.

While Mencken was in many ways wrong about Southern culture after the turn of the twentieth century, few Southern writers – Edgar Allan Poe and Augustus Baldwin Longstreet are exceptions – drew national attention until well after the Civil War. Education was not readily available to those outside the small planter class, and within it the production of literary works was largely considered one of the accouterments of gentility rather than a vocation – especially so for women. As Clara Childs Mackenzie points out in her study of the South Carolina-born author Sarah Barnwell Elliott, the fact that Elliott was the first writer in her family to achieve national prominence had much to do with the fact that she came to maturity in the years following the war, when cultural and economic disruption broke down the former class system at just the time when interest in regional literature was gaining momentum in the 1870s and 1880s.[4]

Just as Jewett's "unAmerican" qualities provide her fiction with depth and vigor, so the peculiar history, geography, and culture of the South intensified and prolonged its distinct regional identity, both on the part of its own inhabitants and in the perceptions of observers elsewhere in the country. For Emma Lazarus, writing in 1889, the South was distinctive – even exotic – for its everglades, bayous, mockingbirds, alligators, and cypress trees as well as its "dark visions." Rebecca Harding Davis, in both her story "A Faded Leaf" and her 1904 autobiography *Bits of Gossip*, similarly describes the "far South" in which she spent part of her youth in exotic terms; in the latter, her time there resembles "an uneasy dream": the "semi-tropical forests" and "mile-long hedges of roses" are home to poisonous snakes, while both "birds like jewels" and annoying insects inhabit the air.[5] Davis's and Lazarus's use of such features of the Southern landscape might have been inspired by the regional literature sometimes known as "local color" fiction,[6] which used the speech, dress, and customs of an area as well as features of the physical landscape to make the sense of place an important element of the story. Kate Chopin, Alice Dunbar-Nelson, and Grace King were particularly successful at capturing and presenting to a national readership the flavor and customs of South Louisiana culture; Mary Noialles Murfree, writing as Charles Egbert Craddock, set her stories and novels in the mountains of Tennessee; Ruth McEnery Stuart brought to life the dialect of the Arkansas hill country. Decades before Ellen Glasgow chronicled successive generations of life in Virginia and William Faulkner created Yoknapatawpha County, Mississippi, women writers of the South recognized and made use of precisely those features of their region that set it apart from the rest of the country.[7]

Like their New England counterparts, such as Mary Wilkins Freeman, Rose Terry Cooke, and Sarah Orne Jewett, most Southern women writers of regional short fiction made the lives of women central to their stories. Grace King not only dedicates her 1893 collection *Balcony Stories* to her mother, "whose balcony stories were the delight of my childhood," she also devotes her prefatory essay, "The Balcony," to setting up the premise that the stories to follow emanated from the conversations of women sitting on balconies on summer nights, while their children sleep indoors. That these are experiences that only women share is made plain by King's curt statement that "men are not balcony sitters"; that women are best suited to tell the stories of women is made explicit in the next paragraph:

> Experiences, reminiscences, episodes, picked up as only women know how to pick them up from other women's lives — or other women's destinies, as they prefer to call them, — and told as only women know how to relate them; what God has done or is doing with some other woman whom they have known — that is what interests women once embarked on their own lives, — the embarkation takes place at marriage, or after the marriageable time, — or, rather, that is what interests the women who sit of summer nights on balconies.[8]

Of interest to the women on the balcony are not only stories of women like themselves, whom the reader assumes to be relatively privileged white women, dressed in "vague, loose, white garments," but stories of women in various social classes, black women as well as white women, who have in common dignity and the ability to adapt to changing circumstances. In "A Crippled Hope," a slave woman made lame by an injury in infancy is initially considered unsaleable by the slave trader who owns her, but from childhood she is so effective at nursing the slaves who pass through his auction-house that she earns the name "little Mammy," and he refuses to sell her. When the slaves are liberated by the Union army, she wanders the region caring for the white women whom the war has desolated. By thus bringing together black and white women in equally desperate circumstances, the war has a curious leveling effect.

Many of the women in *Balcony Stories* must cope with what were euphemistically called "reduced circumstances" — brought on not only by the Civil War, but also by faithless men, business losses, or death in the family. In "Anne Marie and Jeanne Marie," the seventy-five-year-old twins of the title have lived together in slowly increasing poverty during the fifty years since Jeanne Marie's husband and three children died in a fever epidemic. Jeanne Marie considers herself the "lucky one" of the pair: she had, however briefly, the marriage that Anne Marie did not, and she is still healthy, while Anne Marie is bedridden with rheumatism. The sisters' one indulgence is the purchase of a weekly lottery ticket apiece, and when the "lucky" sister's ticket wins the magnificent sum of forty dollars, she tells Anne Marie that it was her ticket that has brought them the windfall. Jeanne Marie is shocked and saddened to observe Anne Marie hiding the money from her. As the story ends, Jeanne Marie thinks, "it seemed to her that she had never known her twin sister at all."[9] The concept of unknowability also infuses "The Old Lady's Restoration," in which the unnamed title character falls — for reasons not revealed — from a position of great wealth to poverty. Her decline is gradual, and at each stage she calls into question the "truths" her mother had imparted to her about the requisites for respectability. She discovers – and declares – that a box at the opera is not necessary to life, and that one can, with dignity, rent rather than own a residence, drink tea instead of coffee, and do without gloves. When word circulates in New Orleans that the woman's fortune has been restored, the friends who had dropped away seek her out in her rented room, only to find her expressing satisfaction with her current circumstances. Is she demented, or "imbecile," as the visitors decide? Or has she adopted a new set of values that her fair-weather friends cannot understand?

The New Orleans that the old lady inhabits at the end of King's story, with its "washing, ironing, sewing women, . . . cobbling, chair-making, carpentering men, [and] screaming, laughing, crying, quarreling, swarming children,"[10] is as far from her former fashionable residence as South from North. Contrary to the visions of a monolithic plantation culture in popular mythology, differences in social class and race made even a single city such as New Orleans a complex, many-layered culture, and it was this complexity that interested writers such as King, Chopin, and Dunbar-Nelson. Although one might expect the fictional perspectives of the white, St Louis-born Chopin and the nominally African American (although quite light-skinned) New Orleans-born Dunbar-Nelson to be very different, they are in fact remarkably similar: both writers make clear their fascination with the rich cultural mix of the city, and like Grace King's balcony women they are observers of life in its streets, adept at singling out characters who in their very eccentricity seem somehow representative of the city's vitality and its simultaneous penchant for harboring isolation and secrets.

In her introduction to Dunbar-Nelson's collected work, Gloria T. Hull writes that in order to escape the "odious expectations" of the "plantation and minstrel stereotypes" on the part of the reading public, Dunbar-Nelson wrote "charming, *aracial*, Creole sketches that solidified her in the then-popular 'female-suitable' local color mode."[11] While it is true that Dunbar-Nelson's stories do not consistently depict black characters, and that her fiction does not argue overtly for racial justice or harmony, as does Lydia Maria Child's 1842 story "The Quadroons" or *Uncle Tom's Cabin*, they are not "aracial." Indeed, as Hull correctly points out, one of the writer's most consistent themes is "difference,"[12] and one of the differences she deals with, however subtly, is race. In the title story of Dunbar-Nelson's best-known collection, *The Goodness of Saint Rocque* (1899), the dark-skinned Manuela visits a voodoo woman for assistance (which is effective, as the title would suggest) in winning back her beloved Theophile, who has been paying too much attention to the "blonde and petite" Claralie, who wears "dainty white skirts" while Manuela wears "a cool, pale yellow gown."[13] All three young people are Creoles of the same social set, but Dunbar-Nelson makes clear that even in this context, colors of hair, eyes, and skin were markers of difference derived from racial inheritance.

"The Goodness of Saint Rocque" is a lighthearted story; racial divisions are depicted more grimly in "Mr. Baptiste" and "Sister Josepha," also published in the 1899 collection. Mr. Baptiste, a harmless, elderly Creole man who subsists on handouts of fruit from ships that have brought it from South America to the port at New Orleans, becomes the innocent victim of a dispute between a group of predominantly Irish longshoremen, who have gone on strike because they refuse to work alongside blacks, and a group of blacks brought in to load cotton in their stead. When Mr. Baptiste makes the mistake of cheering on the black combatants, one of the white longshoremen throws a brick that kills him instantly. In "Sister Josepha," violence takes the more subtle form of sexual threat. The eighteen-year-old nun now known as Sister Josepha had been brought to the orphanage of the Sacred Heart convent as a black-eyed three-year-old about whom nothing was known except her first name, Camille. When Camille is fifteen, a "glorious tropical beauty," a couple wants to adopt her, but Camille's intuition picks up on the "pronounced leers and admiration of her physical charms which gleamed in the man's face," and she refuses, choosing instead to join the Sacred Heart sisters. Although she is quickly bored by life in the convent, she is aware that making her way outside it would be difficult because she has "no name but Camille, . . . no nationality."[14] A more tragic fate befalls the young girl in Dunbar-Nelson's very short story "A Carnival Jungle," in which Flo, costumed as a young male troubadour for Mardi Gras, is mistaken for the enemy of another reveler and stabbed in the back. Her innocent act of cross-dressing plunges her into a nightmarish world where identity is unknowable; appearing to be a boy, she is killed by a man dressed as an Indian, so that both gender and racial categories are unstable. At the end of the story, Flo's mother mourns the death of "a horrible something that lay across the bed."[15]

Dunbar-Nelson's contributions to American fiction have been eclipsed by several factors. They stand, first of all, at the beginning of a multifaceted career during which she was, by turns, a poet, an educator, a journalist, and a political activist on behalf of black women. In addition, her brief (four-year) marriage to poet Paul Lawrence Dunbar and her longer one to journalist Robert J. Nelson relegated her to a "wife of" footnote in literary and political history. Finally, the importance of the Harlem Renaissance of the 1920s has overshadowed earlier artistic production by African Americans. Most of Dunbar-Nelson's later fiction remained unpublished until the Schomburg Library edition of her work was issued in 1988, and one of these pieces, a novelette titled "A Modern Undine," written just after the turn of the century, makes one wonder whether Dunbar-Nelson had read and been influenced by Kate Chopin's 1899 novel *The Awakening*. Its central character, a white woman named Marion, is entranced by the power of the sea in a manner similar to Chopin's character Edna, and when, at the end of the extant draft of the story, Marion's son dies, she requests that he be buried at sea, so that "perhaps it will sing to him the same songs it has sung to me."[16]

The Awakening was for Chopin, who died in 1904, a late work, following more than a decade of short fiction that can be described as "local color" in its evocation of place, but which, like the short fiction of Dunbar-Nelson and most other women fiction writers of the late nineteenth century, transcends the limitations often associated with that genre in presenting human dramas that often deal with the problem of personal identity in a culture marked by difference and fluidity. "The Story of an Hour" (1894), in fact, could take place anywhere. In this very short story, Mrs. Mallard, known to have "a heart trouble,"[17] is informed gently of the news of her husband's death in a train wreck. We soon realize that "heart trouble" is meant in two senses, for almost immediately after receiving the news, she has a realization of freedom and possibility that is in sharp contrast to the previous day's dread of a long married life. Thus, when her husband, unharmed after all, enters the house, it is the shock of disappointment that kills her, not, as the doctors assume, an excess of joy. Another Chopin story that challenges the Victorian notion of woman's complete fulfillment in marriage is set firmly in the Cajun counties of rural south Louisiana. "The Storm" is commonly published – and can be read – as a free-standing story, but its regional qualities are best understood if it is read as a sequel to "At the 'Cadian Ball," which provides the history leading to Calixta's and Alcée's passionate though curiously innocent encounter in "The Storm" and which makes clear certain class differences within Cajun culture. Alcée Laballière is a wealthy landowner whose flirtations with the not-quite-respectable Calixta infuriate Bobinêt, who wants to marry her. On the night of the Acadian Ball, Bobinêt and Calixta become engaged, as does Alcée to Clarisse, who comes to retrieve him from what she perceives as "slumming." At the end of the first story, then, the social class lines have been maintained, but "The Storm" momentarily disrupts them when Alcée finds Calixta home alone during a thunderstorm. Their sexual encounter does not threaten either marriage, but "The Storm" does suggest that happiness results from greater personal freedom than conventional marriage allows. When Alcée writes – perhaps with an ulterior motive – to Clarisse in Biloxi, suggesting that she extend her visit there, Clarisse is enjoying "the pleasant liberty of her maiden days." Chopin concludes: "So the storm passed and every one was happy."[18]

Sensuality and questions of identity are also themes in Chopin's less-well-known story "Lilacs," in which Adrienne, a successful, unmarried, Parisian actress, makes an annual spring pilgrimage to the convent where she had lived as a child, lured by the memory of the scent of lilacs blooming there. For four years she has been welcomed with affection by the nuns of the convent – and with cool tolerance by the Mother Superior – for her two-week visit. Chopin sets worldliness against piety in this story, favoring neither, but suggesting in her conclusion that Adrienne cannot continue to live both lives – cannot, specifically, bring her Parisian sensuality into the cloistered world of the convent. The nuns believe Adrienne to be a young widow for whom music is merely an avocation; therefore, the expensive gifts she brings are assumed to represent a sacrifice on her part. But the extravagance of an ivory crucifix or an embroidered altar cloth is not nearly so dangerous as the affection she brings to Sister Agathe, with whom she exchanges "ardent kisses" when she arrives at the convent at the beginning of the story; such is the opinion of the Mother Superior, who refuses to let Adrienne into the convent the following spring, returning the gifts she has brought over the years. After Adrienne has left, having read (as readers of the story do not) the Mother Superior's letter, Sister Agathe cries softly in her room as a lay sister sweeps Adrienne's lilacs, and the sensuality they represent, from the portico.[19]

Stories by King, Dunbar-Nelson, and Chopin testify to fluidity among socio-economic classes and acknowledge women's sexuality in the late nineteenth-century South, but women's fiction also provides evidence that race was a vexed issue. That both forced and willing miscegenation were facts of Southern life is attested in the work of a number of writers; Child's "The Quadroons," set in Georgia, is one of the earliest to sound the "tragic mulatto" theme. Chopin's "Désirée's Baby" is one of the most stark treatments of racial prejudice published in the 1890s, in part because the suspicion of racial "taint" is sufficient to destroy a marriage and two lives. Like Dunbar-Nelson's Sister Josepha, Désirée is a foundling of unknown parentage; thus, when the child that is born to her and her husband Armand begins to display his African heritage, everyone assumes that the problem lies in Désirée's ancestry, and Armand sends her and the child away. Only after Désirée's suicide does Armand discover that his own mother had belonged to "the race that is cursed with the brand of slavery."[20]

If racial difference is always perceived as volatile in the work of late-nineteenth-century Southern women writers, and often as threatening or tragic, another kind of difference – place – is the source of comfort and stability. As many critics have observed, one of the hallmarks of Southern literature well into the twentieth century is its sense of being rooted in a locale so distinctive as to become a character in the narrative. One thinks of Glasgow's Virginia, the Mississippi of Faulkner and Eudora Welty, and even Anne Tyler's Baltimore. Although the second half of the nineteenth century is most closely associated with regional literature, a Southern preoccupation with place can be traced back to Longstreet's *Georgia Scenes* in the 1830s (and, earlier still, the writings of William Byrd of Virginia), and persists in such works as Dorothy Allison's 1992 novel *Bastard Out of Carolina*. One reason for this insistence on geographical setting is the fact that there is no single "South." When Emma Lazarus imagined "the South" in her 1889 poem, she chose a coastal setting far removed from the mountains of Tennessee and North Carolina or the pine forests of northern Louisiana. Differences in terrain are accompanied by differences in dialect, customs, and political ideologies, and writers have been eager to record and preserve these differences as if to counter perceptions of a monolithic South.

The work of two writers whose careers extended from the 1870s until after the turn of the century illustrates how a sense of place served different modes of Southern regional literature. There are a number of parallels between the lives of Mary Noialles Murfree (1850–1922) and Sarah Barnwell Elliott (1848–1928). In addition to their nearly identical lifespans, both women were born into upper-class Southern families. Murfree was born on a plantation near a town – Murfreesboro,

Tennessee – named for her great-grandfather, who had fought in the Revolutionary War. Elliott could claim an equally distinguished heritage: several of her ancestors had served as Governor or Lieutenant Governor of her home state of South Carolina, and her father was an Episcopalian Bishop. The Elliott family moved to Tennessee following the Civil War, and both she and Murfree received honorary degrees from the University of the South at Sewanee, Tennessee, late in their lives. Neither woman married; both retained strong ties to their immediate families. Despite their backgrounds, neither writer glorified the antebellum South in her fiction; Murfree wrote about the people of the Tennessee hill country, and Elliott depicted the problems of the Reconstruction South, setting her work in South Carolina, Georgia, Tennessee, and Texas.

Murfree's fascination with the landscape of the mountainous regions of Tennessee at least equals her interest in their inhabitants. A reviewer of the 1970 reprint edition of her 1884 collection of stories, *In the Tennessee Mountains*, notes that she has provided "a setting so geographically unique as to provide for actions . . . which seemingly could occur nowhere else." In "The Star in the Valley," the death of a frail young woman is made to seem of a piece with "many things that suffer unheeded in those mountains: the birds that freeze on the trees; the wounded deer that leaves its cruel kind to die alone."[21] The stories are filled both with the beauties of spring flowers, blue mountain hazes, and waterfalls, and the dangers of steep precipices, falling boulders, and sudden storms. In "Over on the T'other Mountain," two parallel mountain ranges are in a sense the protagonists of the story: the lower range is benign and hospitable, while the higher one is forbidding and thought to be the source of bad luck. The major role these mountainous areas play in the lives of their inhabitants is to isolate them from the outside world, so that with their dialect, superstitions, and lawlessness they are as exotic as the New Orleans eccentrics depicted by Chopin and Dunbar-Nelson.

Judith Fetterley and Marjorie Pryse have argued that one difference between Murfree and the regional writers of New England is that whereas the latter assumed that "character and narrator are more alike than different," Murfree "did not assume that all Tennesseans or all southerners were potentially alike."[22] In a story such as "The Star in the Valley," Murfree underscores this difference by making her narrator, Reginald Chevis, a visitor who has come to the mountains to hunt, and who assumes that his mountain companions are "incapable of appreciating and comprehending his delicate and dainty musings."[23] Such an elitist sentiment may point to Murfree's own distance from her subjects, and Allison Ensor has stated that Murfree, "as a genteel daughter of an aristocratic, Episcopalian Murfreesboro family, would always be an outsider to the mountain people she sought to depict for the rest of the country."[24] Indeed, many of Murfree's characters rely heavily on stereotypes of mountain people as lazy, heavy drinkers resistant to law and order. But in the creation of some of her female characters, Murfree drops her narrative distance and – while still seeing them as "different" – shows empathy for their limited lives. In "The 'Harnt'

That Walks Chilhowee," the briefly sketched Mrs. Giles is a reminder of the premature aging of backwoods women: at forty-five, she is "anxious . . . to assume the prerogatives of advanced years"[25] and sit by the fireplace with her pipe, leaving the household chores to her daughter, Clarsie. Clarsie, in turn, is a kind-hearted girl who has little control over her own fate. Believing her mother's chance remark that widowers have the power to "witch" young girls into marrying them, Clarsie believes that she is destined to marry old Simon Burney, especially when the sign from nature that she superstitiously invokes seems to confirm this.

While Murfree's interest in people and situations she had observed but not experienced causes the "local color" elements in her fiction to predominate, Elliott's stories are more realistic in both depth of character development and the social issues with which they deal. She writes, for the most part unsentimentally, about postwar conditions in the deep South, and does so out of her own family's experience: the Elliotts fled Savannah in 1864, just ahead of Sherman's army, and lived with family and friends for several years before settling in Sewanee, where Sarah's father had been instrumental in founding the University of the South. In many of Elliott's stories, place achieves its resonance through the fact of *displacement*, as white Southern families leave their plantations – and the sense of family history they represent – to find makeshift housing elsewhere. Several of the stories in the 1981 reprint edition of Elliott's stories, *Some Data*, feature the town of Kingshaven (Beaufort, South Carolina), described as "almost Arcadian . . . where the soft wind swayed the long, gray moss, and the slow tides rose and fell."[26] It is this idyllic place that Miss Maria Cathcart, who figures in several of the stories, must leave during the Civil War, clutching family valuables and accompanied by several faithful black servants, in the 1896 story "Faith and Faithfulness." The story turns on the relationship between Maria and Kizzy, the black woman who alone does not desert Maria as she sinks into poverty. Both women struggle to preserve their dignity and their accustomed roles from the old days, sometimes to comic effect, but Kizzy must finally work as a clergyman's housekeeper in order to support herself and her mistress.

Such a plot could easily lead to stereotypes of the helpless white Southern woman and the faithful black servant, but Elliott achieves a depth of character that goes beyond the surface. Nor, despite her obvious sympathy with those whose lives were disrupted by war and Reconstruction, does she programmatically defend the Southern cause. The "victory" in the story "Jim's Victory," for example, is that he does finally swear the oath of allegiance to the Union so that his brother's horse will not be confiscated. In "A Speculation in Futures," which constitutes an interesting companion piece to Chopin's "Désirée's Baby," a young Southern man who argues for abolition with his slaveowning father, and who frees and then marries a mulatto woman, nonetheless commits suicide when his son is born black. Rather than vindicating slavery or condemning miscegenation, the story points to the gulf which can exist between ideological avowal and the realities of one's personal life.

Elliott's interest in place and displacement went beyond the immediate effects of the Civil War to encompass the conflict between agrarian values and technological and mercantile "progress" that marked the emergence of the "New South" in the late nineteenth and early twentieth centuries. While authors in other parts of the country also perceived and depicted the tension between rural and urban, the land and the factory, this tension had particular resonance for Southerners, whose defense of slavery was in large part the defense of a life dependent upon agriculture, and whose loss of that life was linked to defeat on the battlefield. In ways that anticipate the agrarian manifesto *I'll Take My Stand* in 1930, several of Elliott's stories investigate the trade-offs in quality of life, morality, manners, and definitions of prosperity inherent in a shift from a rural, agricultural culture to one based on urban growth, the spread of railroads, and mercantilism. Perhaps because they are largely removed from the Civil War itself and overt racial tensions – and thus removed from subjects likely to provoke stereotype or sentimentality – stories such as "An Ex-Brigadier" and "Progress" are among Elliott's most realistic. Although in these stories her sympathies tend to lie with the way of life that is being displaced by "progress," she does not give way to nostalgia, but instead is concerned with analyzing the choices people must make when faced with fundamental change.

"An Ex-Brigadier," first published in *Harper's* in 1888, brings together elements of "Old South" and "New South" in the persons of the former Civil War General Billy Stamper, living in the faded grandeur of his old mansion after many postwar adventures, and John Kemper Willoughby, a young civil engineer sent from New York to study the possibilities for rail expansion in tiny Booker City. But Elliott complicates the simple identifications of the two characters: Willoughby was born in the South, where Stamper had known his father, and maintains the demeanor of the old-fashioned gentleman, whereas Stamper is realistic about the changes the South faces. Stamper deplores the new emphasis on money rather than family position – "We are learning to be avaricious, for now in the south position is coming to depend on money; so all grind along together; and I hate it" – but is willing to sell his land for the development of Booker City. When Willoughby expresses concern that his own position as disinterested scout for the railroad company is compromised by his family's friendship with Stamper, the General characterizes his reservation as a 'befo'-de-wah' sensitiveness which we cannot afford now."[27] The story "Progress," published eleven years later in *McClure's*, serves almost as a sequel to "An Ex-Brigadier." Sam Long, formerly owner of a large farm, has lent his name to "Longville," which developed after the railroad came by his property and one person after another has bought a piece of his farm to develop a business. Even Sam Long has turned businessman when encouraged to open a general store, but he remains at heart a farmer, not a merchant, and loses money rather than making it. Similarly, Sam's wife, running a boardinghouse, cannot bear to charge their friends for meals, so they are on the verge of having to sell their property. When the plans for the railroad were being made ten years before, Sam had felt that "the whole South was making tremendous strides; that a grand new era of prosperity was dawning; that progress, with an enormous capital P, was pushing and pulling every creature in the poor, old belated South into a financial paradise." Now he utters the word "progress" with scorn; and his lawyer concurs, recalling "all the time before that we just lived along comfortable and easy." At the end of the story, the Longs are preparing to return to the agrarian life by building a house on some land "back in the hills"[28] that Sam's mother owns, and the lawyer muses that perhaps the next generation will know how to deal with "progress."

As various kinds of progress did in fact radically alter the way Southerners related to place, money, family, and race, the habit of retrospective mythologizing that reached its apotheosis in Margaret Mitchell's *Gone With the Wind* created a South defined in terms of an agrarian aristocracy to which few could ever have laid claim. Women who lived and wrote in the nineteenth-century South, on the other hand, celebrated above all the diversity of the region. Whether writing about urban areas such as New Orleans or the countryside of Georgia or Tennessee, they were astute observers who entered with quick sympathy the lives of those both like and unlike themselves. Not only do they present to us the variety of attitudes and values to be found in the region, but they also seem particularly attuned to the inevitability of change – change in social status, geography, relationships, and expectations. Perhaps as women they were conscious of being particularly vulnerable to such alterations; whatever the reason, this body of late nineteenth-century fiction bears witness to the mutability of Southern culture.

NOTES

1   Emma Lazarus, *The Poems of Emma Lazarus* (Boston: Houghton Mifflin, 1889), 1: 178–80; see Kilcup, *NCAWW*, 379.

2   Brenda Stevenson, ed., *The Journals of Charlotte Forten Grimké* (New York: Oxford University Press, 1988), 67.

3   Mary T. Tardy, ed., *The Living Female Writers of the South* (Philadelphia: Claxton, Remsen & Haffelfinger, 1872), 1.

4   Clara Childs Mackenzie, *Sarah Barnwell Elliott* (Boston: Twayne, 1980), 15–29.

5   Rebecca Harding Davis, *Bits of Gossip* (Boston: Houghton Mifflin, 1904), 69.

6   For much of the twentieth century, the term "local color" was used to designate the short fiction of the post-Civil War decades that was set in specific regions of the United States – most notably, New England, the South, and the frontier West. Recently, however, scholars have begun to prefer the term "regional fiction." The term "local color" suggests that the story's main purpose is to capture the peculiarities of a setting, while thematic concerns are secondary; and the dismissive connotations of the term have been a barrier to serious consideration of the work of the women writers who so frequently wrote regional fiction. For a range of discussions on these matters, see Ann Douglas, *The Feminization of American Culture* (New York:

Knopf, 1977); Josephine Donovan, *New England Local Color Literature: A Women's Tradition* (New York: Frederick Ungar, 1983); Louis Renza, *"A White Heron" and the Question of Minor Literature* (Madison: University of Wisconsin Press, 1984); Caroline Gebhard, "The Spinster in the House of American Criticism," *Tulsa Studies in Women's Literature* 10.1 (1991): 79–91; Judith Fetterley and Marjorie Pryse, eds, *American Women Regionalists, 1850–1910* (New York: W. W. Norton, 1992), xi–xx; David Jordan, ed., *Regionalism Reconsidered: New Approaches to the Field* (New York: Garland, 1994).

7 Most works on nineteenth-century Southern women have tended to concentrate on the more familiar writers like Kate Chopin and Grace King. A small sampling of texts which focus on the period or include some materials on nineteenth-century women writers would include: Richard Cary, *Mary N. Murfree* (New York: Twayne, 1967); Per Seyersted, *Kate Chopin: A Critical Biography* (Baton Rouge: Louisiana State University Press, 1969); Nina Baym, *Woman's Fiction: A Guide to Novels by and about Women in America, 1820–1870* (Ithaca: Cornell University Press, 1978); Louise Daniel Hutchinson, *Anna Julia Cooper: A Voice from the South* (Washington, DC: Smithsonian Institution Press, 1981); Ann Goodwyn Jones, *Tomorrow is Another Day: The Woman Writer in the South, 1859–1936* (Baton Rouge: Louisiana State University Press, 1981); Barbara C. Ewell, *Kate Chopin* (New York: Frederick Ungar, 1986); Robert Bush, *Grace King: A Southern Destiny* (Baton Rouge: Louisiana State University Press, 1989); Anna Shannon Elfenbein, *Women on the Color Line: Evolving Stereotypes and the Writings of George Washington Cable, Grace King, Kate Chopin* (Charlottesville: University of Virginia Press, 1989); Helen Taylor, *Gender, Race, and Region in the Writings of Grace King, Ruth McEnery Stuart, and Kate Chopin* (Baton Rouge: Louisiana State University Press, 1989); Emily Toth, *Kate Chopin* (New York: William Morrow, 1990); Elizabeth Ammons, *Conflicting Stories: American Women Writers at the Turn into the Twentieth Century* (New York: Oxford University Press, 1991); Dorothy H. Brown and Barbara C. Ewell, eds, *Louisiana Women Writers: New Essays and a Comprehensive Bibliography* (Baton Rouge: Louisiana State University Press, 1992); Carol S. Manning, ed., *The Female Tradition in Southern Literature* (Urbana: University of Illinois Press, 1993).

8 Grace King, *Balcony Stories* (New York: The Century Co., 1893), 1–3; *NCAWW,* 429.

9 King, *Balcony Stories,* 101; *NCAWW,* 436.

10 King, *Balcony Stories,* 189–90; *NCAWW,* 433.

11 Gloria T. Hull, "Introduction," in Alice Dunbar-Nelson, *The Works of Alice Dunbar-Nelson* (New York: Oxford University Press, 1988), 1: xxxii (emphasis mine). Abbreviated below as *Works.*

12 Dunbar-Nelson, *Works,* 1: xxxiii.

13 Dunbar-Nelson, *Works,* 1: 5, 14.

14 Dunbar-Nelson, *Works,* 1: 158–9, 170; *NCAWW,* 567–8, 570.

15 Dunbar-Nelson, *Works,* 1: 134; *NCAWW,* 566.

16 Dunbar-Nelson, *Works,* 2: 71.

17 Kate Chopin, *The Awakening and Selected Stories* (1899; New York: Penguin, 1984), 213 (abbreviated below as *TASS*); *NCAWW,* 397.

18 Chopin, *TASS,* 286; *NCAWW,* 409.

19 *NCAWW,* 399, 406.

20 Chopin, *TASS,* 194.

21 Harry R. Warfel, "Local Color and Literary Artistry: Mary Noailles Murfree's *In the Tennessee Mountains," The Southern Literary Journal* 3 (1970): 154–5; see also Fetterley and Pryse, *American Women Regionalists*, 270.

22 Fetterley and Pryse, *American Women Regionalists*, 255.

23 Mary Noailles Murfree, *In the Tennessee Mountains* (Boston: Houghton Mifflin, 1885), 122.

24 Allison Ensor, "The Geography of Mary Noailles Murfree's *In the Tennessee Mountains," The Mississippi Quarterly* 31 (1978): 199; see 191–9.

25 Fetterley and Pryse, *American Women Regionalists*, 290.

26 Sarah Barnwell Elliott, *Some Data and Other Stories of Southern Life* (Bratenahl, OH: Seaforth Publications, 1981), 37.

27 Elliott, *Some Data*, 176–7; *NCAWW*, 374.

28 Elliott, *Some Data*, 95, 97, 102.

3

Western Biodiversity: Rereading Nineteenth-Century American Women's Writing

MELODY GRAULICH

How much does that expression ["the West"] mean to include? I never have been able to discover its limits.

> Caroline Kirkland, *A New Home, Who'll Follow? or,*
> *Glimpses of Western Life* (1839)[1]

In 1898, Paul Wilstach designed and published in *The Bookman* "A Map which is a Literary Map" of the United States. Numerous names crowd the land east of the Mississippi River. The western two-thirds of the continent is empty space, barely marked with tiny names: a minuscule "Longfellow" in Minnesota (which the poet never visited), a teeny "Garland" in South Dakota, Wister and Remington delicately criss-crossing each other across Arizona and New Mexico, Bret Harte and Joaquin Miller perched in the Sierras. Larger "Unclaimed's" march across three or four states at a time, land apparently available for the planting of the imperialist pen.[2]

On one level, Wilstach's map, surveying the literary production of the nineteenth century, seems a precursor of the famous *New Yorker* cover of a truncated continental map including only New York and California, which, depending on one's point of view, reveals or mocks Eastern cultural hegemony. As Caroline Kirkland's question suggests, the definition of what we mean by "West" is always problematic, ever retreating westward throughout the nineteenth century. Yet the plains and far West *were* storied lands by the turn of the century. And the literary West was not the "Hisland" Wilstach implies, to borrow a pun from historian Susan Armitage:

> There is a region of America that I have come to call Hisland. In a magnificent Western landscape, under perpetually cloudless Western skies, a cast of heroic characters engages in dramatic combat, sometimes with nature,

sometimes with each other. Occupationally, these heroes are diverse: they are mountain men, cowboys, Indians, soldiers, farmers, miners, and desperadoes, but they share one distinguishing characteristic – they are all men. It seems that all rational demography has ended at the Mississippi River: all the land West of it is occupied only by men. This mythical land is America's most enduring contribution to folklore: the legendary Wild West.

When Charlotte Perkins Gilman wrote a utopian novel about an all-female world called Herland, she knew that she was writing a fantasy. The problem with hisland is that many people believe it is history, and some of those people are historians.[3]

Armitage's comment suggests that even in 1987 Wilstach's map was still guiding Western scholars. So "the legendary Wild West" needs a new survey. In place of Wilstach's "Unclaimed" across Idaho, Colorado, and California, let's write in Mary Hallock Foote, with her fifteen novels and short story collections. In Texas, we can mark a wandering Mary Austin Holley and poet/journalist Sara Estela Ramirez crossing the Rio Grande. Across the prairies troop Eliza Farnham, Kate McPhelim Cleary, Zitkala-Ša, Mary Catherwood, Eleanor Gates. Crossing the borders of the Pacific Northwest, Ella Higginson and Pauline Johnson write both poetry and stories. Abigail Scott Duniway launches *The New Northwest* in Oregon and writes many of its articles in support of women's rights, as well as an autobiography, *Path Breaking*, and little known novels. Eliza Snow and Josephine Spencer claim Utah for Mormonism, while years in retrospect Annie Clark Tanner will explore turn-of-the-century polygamous marriages in *A Mormon Mother*. Sharlott Hall writes poetry in mining camps in Arizona, where Gwendolen Overton is raised in army forts and sets her story about Apache uprisings in the 1870s volume, *The Heritage of Unrest* (1901). Sarah Winnemucca describes a Nevada girlhood and the dispossession of her people, while Ida Meacham Strobridge chronicles desert ranch life in Nevada in *In the Loom of the Desert* (1907) and *The Land of Purple Shadows* (1909). Shortly after Wilstach drew his map, in Wyoming Elinore Pruitt Stewart writes *The Letters of a Woman Homesteader* to a friend in Colorado, and in Montana, B.(ertha) M.(uzzy) Bowers begins to write popular formula Westerns with a feminist slant. And California shows the kind of cultural and racial diversity which still characterizes it: María Amparo Ruiz de Burton writes political and Yda Addis gothic stories about the conquered Mexican Californios, a group which also draws the attention of the prolific Gertrude Atherton; Helen Hunt Jackson writes with sympathy if not always full understanding about the native tribes of California, as does Mary Austin, with far more knowledge; Sui Sin Far brings her readers into the various West coast Chinatowns, exposing racial stereotypes; the poet Ina Coolbrith edits the influential *Overland Monthly*; Margaret Collier Graham, Atherton, Austin, and Gilman publish fiction about women who, as Austin says, "want to live lives of their own."

In claiming a place on the Western map, women like Austin claimed for themselves the free will and independence that the legendary West has always seemed to promise to men. In 1893 Frederick Jackson Turner suggested at the Chicago World's Fair that the presence of free undeveloped land determined American history, and his influential "Frontier Thesis" expanded upon the popular nineteenth-century theme that the frontier's freedom from authority and tradition helped to shape the American character. Austin and many other writers certainly believed that the West offered them opportunities to live freer lives than those dictated by social conventions in more settled regions, a persistent theme in their work. (And, in fact, Western states generally passed women's suffrage laws earlier than Eastern states, though there are conflicting readings of the reasons for such votes.) In her autobiographical writings, Austin suggested that the arid spaces of the West gave her "the courage to shear off what is not worthwhile"; there she learned to cast off conventional definitions of what she called "young ladihood," making the "revolutionary discovery" that her life was her own, to live fully and freely:[4] "[T]here was something you could do about unsatisfactory conditions besides being heroic or a martyr to them, something more satisfactory than enduring or complaining, and that was getting out to hunt for the remedy. This, for young ladies in the eighteen-eighties, was a revolutionary discovery to have made."[5]

The narrators of the two Austin stories included in Karen Kilcup's *Nineteenth-Century American Women Writers*, "The Basket Maker" and "The Walking Woman," "get out" to search actively for the meaning in their lives. As Austin did in her own life, they discover new trails from native women and "outliers" like the Walking Woman, who had "walked off all sense of society-made values, and, knowing the best when the best came to her, was able to take it."[6]

But if the West offered some women opportunities for independence and rebellion, Turner's thesis certainly cannot describe the lives of other Western women. "Society's" very definition of "ladihood" denies some women the choice to reject it by denying them access to it; like Frances Harper and other African American women writers, ethnic Western writers like Ruiz de Burton, Winnemucca, and Sui Sin Far often insist upon their heroines' acceptance of propriety and sexual conformity as a way of countering racial stereotypes about "primitive" others. Their rebellion against the roles assigned them is far different from Austin's or Gilman's. And writers like Abigail Scott Duniway, Kate McPhelim Cleary, Nannie Alderson, and a number of diarists remind us that many women, especially first generation white settlers, saw their Western lives as circumscribed and isolated, cutting them off from the now famous female world of love and ritual, often turning them into victims of abusive husbands.[7] The West turned them into captives of their husbands' dreams, "married," as Foote said, "irretrievably into the West."[8]

Indeed, one way of reading Mary Hallock Foote's "The Fate of a Voice" (1886) is as a captivity narrative; the heroine, Madeline, an opera singer, finds that in the West her "voice was lost," her life story confined within her husband's

version of it. Yet Foote herself is a paradoxical Westerner, claiming when she
first went West, "I never felt so *free* in my life"; and the ending of "The Fate of
a Voice" yields multiple readings: liberated from the dominance of elitist Eastern and European culture, Madeline develops a democratic voice in the West.[9]
In fact, the West gave Foote her subject matter as a writer, as it did Caroline
Kirkland, another reluctant pioneer, who said she "little thought of becoming
an author before [she] lived in the wilderness. . . ."[10] Austin and others insisted
they *found* their voices in the West. As Austin wrote in her third-person autobiography, *Earth Horizon*:

> [Mary] was never much taken with the wish of many girls of her acquaint-
> ance that they had been boys. She thought there might be a great deal to
> be got out of being a woman; but she definitely meant neither to chirrup
> nor twitter. She meant not to remit a single flash of wit, anger or imagina-
> tion. She had no idea of what, in her time, such a determination would
> entail. She was but dimly aware of something within herself, competent,
> self-directive; she meant to trust it.[11]

But let us further complicate the subject of voice.[12] With few models to guide
her, Austin turned to American Indian women and found her voice in conversation with them, as her stories reveal. Did she appropriate their stories to her
own needs? Assume she could speak for them? How did the Anglo settlement
of the West, both Spanish and American, affect the voices of American Indian
women? Zitkala-Ša, Sarah Winnemucca, Alice Callahan, and Pauline Johnson
wrote in English largely for white audiences and for political purposes; in a
narrow sense, their "literacy" is the product of their contact with whites, used to
advance their peoples' causes. Yet as the "Native American Myths about Women"
section of Kilcup's *Nineteenth-Century American Women Writers* shows, and the recent
work of Leslie Silko or Paula Gunn Allen attests, the stories from their tribal
oral traditions about mythic figures like Thought Woman, or Spider Grandmother, and Changing Woman provide enabling models of female creativity,
power, and self-expression, in contrast to the handicapping stereotypical stories
they had to struggle against. Indeed, the stories told *about* American Indians
throughout American literary history might best (if ironically) be termed "captivity narratives," for American Indian lives and voices were captive within
them. As Nez Perce leader Yellow Wolf said, "The Whites told only one side.
Told it to please themselves. Told much that is not true. Only his own best
deeds, only the worst deeds of the Indians, has the white man told."[13]

Who gets to tell what Western story about whom? Many Western stories,
such as Sui Sin Far's "Its Wavering Image" or Cleary's "Feet of Clay" or any of
innumerable Austin stories, explore this very question. Wilstach's story of the
West, told in his map, leaves women out entirely; more often literary historians
have presented women heading West as cultural baggage carted into Hisland,
burdening the lives of men, or as repressive agents of civilization. But as I've

suggested by the questions I've raised above about recurring Western themes – liberation, isolation, cultural conventions, race, class, and voice – any story is only part of the story, often leaving out, distorting, or even silencing other stories.

Critics like Annette Kolodny, Vera Norwood, Lois Rudnick, Paula Gunn Allen, Tey Diana Rebolledo, and myself have found recurrent themes in Western women's literature, but we have done so by narrowing our focus to a particular region, a specific period, a single race – that is, by telling only part of the story.[14] However defined, the West is a vast, diverse, rapidly changing region. Even the most commonly accepted geopolitical definition today, that the West is defined by aridity, cannot encompass the whole region; what of the Pacific Northwest and, hence, the seaside stories and poems by Higginson and Johnson? We associate the legendary West with vast, empty spaces, and indeed the strong and abiding relationship between land and human character is a major theme in much Western literature. Yet by the late nineteenth century most Westerners lived in cities, many of them containing Chinatowns like those described by Sui Sin Far. The legendary West is populated by American Indians who live in the tepees of the nomadic Sioux, but the agricultural pueblo peoples of the Southwest lived in cities themselves. Even generalizations about American Indian presence and culture in the West ultimately confront cultural diversity and must recognize tribal differences.

Historical changes further complicate our definition. Are the various "frontiers" of the eighteenth and nineteenth centuries the "West"? Caroline Kirkland, writing about soggy Michigan mudholes, certainly believed she was writing about the West in 1837, as did Alice Cary, as her subtitle to *Clovernook*, a series of Ohio stories, indicates: *Recollections of Our Neighborhood in the West* (1852). As Ruiz de Burton ironically suggests in *The Squatter and the Don* (1885), Western history is commonly told from an Eastern perspective of Manifest Destiny; *her* West was settled not from the East but from the South, from Mexico. Yet while she self-consciously explores historical changes and imperialistic power, contrasting life in California under Mexican and United States rule and exposing racist attitudes in government policies toward "Californios," she grants the "original Spanish" settlers the right to have taken California lands from the real *original* settlers, the Native peoples who came from the North. Her "Mexicans" are really transplanted Europeans, and like the Eastern perspective she critiques, her historical time begins with white settlement.

In exploring American Indian literature, "historical" time often comes to mean the post-contact period. Sarah Winnemucca's *Life Among the Piutes* (1883) begins with a chapter called "First Meeting of Piutes and Whites," as if history, told as a tragedy, begins with that meeting, which yields a very different life story than, for example, Maria Chona's as-told-to autobiography, *The Autobiography of a Papago Woman* (1936), which chronicles tribal life with very little contact with whites. Definitions of historical periods also overdetermine our readings of the literature of American Indians; at 1900, with the Western tribes "conquered" and gathered on reservations, ten years after Wounded Knee, the Dawes Act just passed, the "Dream was Ended," as Black Elk said. But if we read on into the twentieth century, to Humishima, Ella DeLoria, and more contemporary writers, we are forced to realize that the dream only *seemed* ended, that American Indians cannot be contained in the frames of Western movies, as antagonists or tragic albeit heroic victims, but they have a significant ongoing presence in American culture. Nowhere is their cultural influence clearer than in the Southwest.

Like its historical borders, the West's national and cultural borders are also permeable, despite all political efforts to patrol and control and place "keep out" signs along the Rio Grande and to segregate Asian communities in China- or Korea-towns. Responding to Gloria Anzaldúa's immensely influential *Borderlands/ La Frontera* (1987), recent critics have begun to expand American literature by crossing all kinds of borders, particularly in the West. So we return to Kirkland's question of where "the West" begins and ends.

Twenty years ago, when I wrote my dissertation on nineteenth-century Western writers (all male!), my director, the historian David Levin, pestered me with a recurrent marginal comment, "But what about x, or y, or z," whenever I attempted a generalization. David, it seemed to me, had changed Thoreau's famous "Simplify, simplify, simplify" into "Qualify, qualify, qualify!" and I often felt thwarted. While in the intervening years I have ventured many generalizations about Western women, David's voice has, I hope, helped me present my generalizations as postulations or, as the postmoderns would say, as constructed knowledge, as stories. But as I write today, David's warning voice echoes, and all generalizations about Western literature seem partial, slippery. In fact, writers and then scholars of Western writing have struggled with the prevailing assumptions – some might call them legends – about The West. For the rest of this essay, I'd like to look at some of the inherited dilemmas scholars of Western women's writings have faced in the past fifteen or so years, dilemmas that have informed readings of Western writings and thereby constituted meanings, leading to partial stories. Among them are the pervasive influence of the never-dying Turner's thesis and the ongoing fascination with the frontier's fabled freedom and liberation; the mythic West's stranglehold on the scholarly and popular imagination; the ongoing sense that the West is male territory; and the focus on gender differences in the West. Then I will move into the borderlands to discuss some recent approaches which offer us new possibilities and new metaphors.

In the new wave of feminist recovery in the late 1970s through the 1980s, historians and literary critics ambivalently confronted not only the ongoing influence of Turner's thesis and its echoing hoofbeats in American Studies scholarship, but also their own desires to discover and claim feminist heroines. Turning to private documents of ordinary women – diaries, letters, journals, memoirs – a host of historians began to write about Western women's lives. Like Susan Armitage, who in 1981 described the "central question" in Western women's history as whether or not the frontier liberated women, they initially attempted to evaluate women's experience in relation to male patterns, which often led to the conclusion that the frontier's fabled freedom was not offered to women, that women went West reluctantly and were often unhappy there.[15] Julie Roy Jeffrey describes her response in *Frontier Women: The Trans-Mississippi West, 1840–1880*:

> During the course of doing the research for this book and writing it, my attitude toward my subject shifted, and I think it is important to explain this shift. My original perspective was feminist; I hoped to find that pioneer women used the frontier as a means of liberating themselves from stereotypes and behaviors which I found constricting and sexist. I discovered that they did not. More importantly, I discovered why they did not.[16]

There is considerable support in primary documents for this view of pioneer women's lives, and fiction like Kate McPhelim Cleary's "Feet of Clay," Hamlin Garland's many stories about Plains women, and Dorothy Scarborough's *The Wind* (1925) stress the sense of isolation, the hardship and struggle, the brutal landscape and weather of rural Western life. Accepting, at least on some level, that the West *had* offered men new opportunities, these historians somewhat reluctantly concluded, as did Armitage, that "there were two Wests: a female and a male one." While earlier critics had challenged fictional portrayals of women as civilizers who fail to respond to the grandeur of the Western landscape and its egalitarian nature, the dialectical view of men's and women's response to the West, initially attacked as stereotyping, gained legitimacy. Ironically, this viewpoint seems to echo one of the progenitors of the legendary West, Owen Wister's Virginian, who says, "'There's cert'nly a right smart o' difference between men and women.'"[17]

The "difference" between how men and women respond to the West and what the West offers them is a recurrent theme in both Western literature and scholarship. For instance, in his influential *Regeneration through Violence*, Richard Slotkin has demonstrated how the male hero of the mythic Western often proves his manhood through acts of violence. In my own work on violence against women in Western literature, I built on the insights of the Western women's historians to explore crucial differences in how Western women focus on violence, writing a series of essays about texts in which daughters write openly and graphically about their mothers' victimization at the hands of fathers. Resisting their mothers' circumscribed lives and their roles as apparently powerless victims, early twentieth-century daughters like Agnes Smedley, Mari Sandoz, and others often identified with their storytelling fathers and sometimes seemed to reject their own womanhood.[18] They became what I think of as "Annie Oakley feminists," declaring "Anything you can do I can do better." Popular Western literature is filled with such heroines. Even the Virginian's fiancée, Molly Wood, recognizes the different opportunities apparently available to men in the West and proclaims, "'I've always wanted to be a man.'"[19]

Like the daughters I discussed in my violence essay, many critics have challenged or rejected the role of the long-suffering pioneer woman, as did Dawn Lander in writing about her Western childhood:

I did not identify myself with houses, churches, and fences. I loved to be outdoors. I loved the space, energy, and passion of the landscape. Repeatedly, however, I could find no place for myself and for my pleasure in the wilderness in the traditionally recorded images of women on the frontier. Tradition gives us the figure of a woman, strong, brave, and often heroic, whose endurance and perseverance are legendary. It may seem strange that I find it difficult to identify with this much praised figure, but I can almost hear her teeth grinding behind her tight-set lips; her stiff spine makes me tired and her clenched fists sad. Victimization and martyrdom are the bone and muscle of every statue, picture, and word portrait of a frontier woman. She is celebrated because she stoically transcended a situation she never would have freely chosen. She submits to the wilderness just as – supposedly – she submits to sex. But she needn't enjoy it, and her whole posture is in rigid opposition to the wilderness experience: to the land, to the Indians. Her glory, we are told, is that she carried the family, religion, fences, the warmth of the hearth and steaming washtubs, inviolate to the West.[20]

Lander's honest exploration of her reaction to her inherited literary tradition is a particularly effective early example of feminist "personal voice" criticism, yet her response points to another problem in early Western studies, a variant of the "Annie Oakley syndrome": tomboy feminism, where the desire to have access to male privilege sometimes leads to a further stereotyping of women's roles. While Lander, unlike Molly Wood, certainly doesn't want to be a man, I find myself unnerved by her phrase "the warmth of the hearth," which inevitably recalls for me the female body, with its capacity for nurturance. In her effort to claim male freedom and power Lander, like Sandoz and Smedley, seems to reject traditional women's roles and values. As early as 1932, Mary Austin suggested that the Western feminist's revolt must be built upon an understanding of the influence and power of the "happenings of the hearth." In her autobiography, she reflected on her pioneer foremothers' influence:

Whatever in Mary makes her worth so much writing about has its roots in the saga of Polly [McAdams] and Hannah and Susanna Saville, in the nurture of which she grew up. . . . It is to the things that the Polly McAdamses discovered in their Westward trek that Mary's generation owed the success of their revolt against the traditional estimate of women. . . . Chief of the discoveries of the Polly McAdamses, as it was told to Mary, was the predominance of the happenings of the hearth, as against what happens on the battlefield and in the market-place, as the determinant of events. What they found out was that the hope of America . . . depended precisely on the capacity of the Polly McAdamses to coordinate society, to establish a civilization, to cause a culture to eventuate out of their own wit and the work of their hands, out of what they could carry with them into the wilderness.[21]

Throughout her career, Austin tried to merge the "space, energy, and passion of the landscape" with the "warmth of the hearth," as did Mary Hallock Foote, Pauline Johnson, and other Western writers. She provides a trail recent scholars have also tracked.

Instead of attempting to appropriate male territory, freedom, and patterns of heroism for women characters – and for themselves – feminist literary critics began in the 1980s to map a female territory and tradition, as did Annette Kolodny in *The Land Before Her: Fantasy and Experience of the American Frontiers, 1630–1860*. Kolodny explores how women writers like Kirkland, Cary, Fuller, and others "escape the psychology of captivity" to envision the West as a feminized Eden, a "potential sanctuary for an idealized domesticity," where "women reveal themselves healed, renewed, revitalized – even psychically reborn."[22] Like the male hero, these women find psychic health in the West, yet they do so not by leaving behind civilization and domesticity but by creating through them. Accepting essential differences between how women and men write about the West, Kolodny seems to follow the trail that Gerda Lerner suggests women's culture often maps: to turn subordination into complementarity and then redefine it in positive ways.[23] Thus, Kolodny's description of the female fantasy of "idealized domesticity" in some ways resembles the role women are assigned in the legendary mythic West, the role Lander rejected, seen from a healing, renewing vantage point.

I made this same move myself in some of my earlier work.[24] Like the historians, I began with a theoretical model based on male writers, exploring the ways in which women writers have responded to the pervasive mythology of the American West, as revealed in literary and cultural traditions. In a satiric line, "O Beautiful for Spacious Guys," Jean Stafford suggests that America's fruited plains and majestic mountains are the domain of "spacious guys" and mocks the most cherished myth in American Studies: the tale of the independent male who escapes civilization and heads West to find freedom. This classic American story offers boys heroism and "space" in return for rebellion and nonconformity, but in canonized American literature and literary criticism, I suggested, the West's legendary freedom is not promised to girls. In fact, the "false" values of society, with its constrictions, obligations, and capitulations, are assigned to white women, the representatives of civilization, the hypocritical Miss Watsons who force Huck to wear shoes and go to school, the Molly Woods who learn in the West to acknowledge their desires for dominant men, or the "Victorian gentlewomen" who are unable to respond to the West's egalitarian grandeur. Adventure, independence, and freedom belong to male characters, while women "endure," as does the long-suffering pioneer helpmate who tries to recreate "home" in the West. Thus, as Nina Baym has suggested in an influential essay, "Melodramas of Beset Manhood," what has come to be the quintessential American plot not only denies women the hero's role but defines them as obstacles to the male hero's freedom, as antagonists to the implicit values of the story.[25]

In this earlier work, I adapted Judith Fetterley's description of the woman reader's response to such plots: disallowed identification with the hero and presented with repressive facades of womanhood, she becomes a "resisting reader" to avoid being forced to reject herself.[26] Women writers, too, resist this powerful cultural tradition. Seeking ways to write about their own and other women's experiences in the West, they question the dichotomized gender roles and the values associated with them. Often aspiring to rebellion and escape, to nonconformity and adventure, they create women whose imaginations do respond to the West's limitlessness, but they also acknowledge and seek to understand the real restrictions in women's lives, to redefine the ways in which we understand such concepts as "individualism" and "freedom."

Women writers thus try to liberate Western literary traditions for themselves, I argued, by claiming male territory as their own *and* by reclaiming the significance of traditional women's values. In Adrienne Rich's term, they "re-vision" this dominant cultural tradition, with its rigid definitions of masculine and feminine roles: "We need to know the writing of the past," she argues, "and know it differently than we have ever known it, not to pass on a tradition but to break its hold over us."[27] My theoretical model caused me to turn to texts like Mary Austin's "The Return of Mr. Wills," in which she challenges the assumptions of one of the patriarchs of the rebellious male/civilizing female tradition, for her little known story revises from a woman's point of view that classic story of escape into the wilderness, "Rip Van Winkle."

Austin focuses on how the actions of the wandering male affect his wife's character. Like Rip, Mr. Wills is initially a likeable enough fellow, a dreamer who becomes obsessed with searching for lost mines, but his obsession, the female narrator tells us, becomes "the baldest of excuses to be out and away from everything that savored of definiteness and responsibility." Meanwhile his family, like Rip's, suffers; his actions "struck" at them, and his wife becomes "hopeless." Finally, like Rip, he disappears. The story stays with Mrs. Wills instead of following her husband into the wilderness. Having "lived so long with the tradition that a husband is a natural provider," she at first feels abandoned. But she and the children realize they can support themselves, with "a little over." She realizes that "she not only did not need Mr. Wills, but got on better without him" and finds a "new sense of independence and power." Unfortunately, Mr. Wills does not stay away for twenty years but returns to the home his family has built and settles on them "like a blight," announcing "'There's no place like home' . . . or something to that effect."[28] But the story ends with Mrs. Wills's happy realization that her husband will inevitably wander off again, probably forever, and she and her family will be rid of him.

And yet as Austin's story implies, resist as she might, no writer, no critic, can ultimately be rid of her cultural traditions: in mocking them or challenging them, she reaffirms their centrality to her way of understanding the West and women's experience there. Although many women writers readily make fun of the West's spacious guys, they are less certain about how to claim for women a *sweet* land of liberty, and their writings show a good deal of ambivalence about how to wed the West's liberating spirit and individualism with traditional women's values of connection and care.

My conclusion to this earlier work once again presumed difference, as I argued that the overlap in the two traditions of Western literature, male and female, will suggest that just as the male fantasies of freedom and self-determination are universal human, not exclusively male, dreams, so are the female concerns with human interdependence and obligation universal human needs that have been undervalued or overlooked. At about this same time, as I was struggling to unite, to marry, male and female traditions, Jane Tompkins published *West of Everything: The Inner Life of Westerns*, in which she saw popular Westerns as engaged in a power struggle for cultural "hegemony" with the domestic novels written by nineteenth-century women like Susan Warner, Harriet Beecher Stowe, and Maria Cummins, particularly in their rejection of evangelical Christianity.[29] In Tompkins's brilliant readings of male writers and Western films, men and women seem perpetually at odds, and no woman has a powerful voice in interpreting the West.

While much writing about Western literature and history has struggled to escape the fascination with the past and the mythic West captured in little Joey Starrett's plaintive cry to the vanishing gunman hero at the end of Jack Shaeffer's *Shane* ("Come back, Shane, come back"), recent Western critics have struggled to replace the old clichés of Turnerian free will, imperialistic Manifest Destiny, and headdress-adorned Indian enemies with new metaphors. The finest treatment of Western women's writing, *The Desert Is No Lady: Southwestern Landscapes in Women's Writing and Art*, challenges the age-old stereotype that women resisted the Western landscape, exploring "how women have come to value the landscapes of the Southwest [and] also how their connections to the place shaped their artistic voices." Focusing on how women created art and artistic traditions out of their responses to the desert landscape, the editors collected essays that convey differences between the evolving traditions of transplanted Anglo writers and "the already well established traditions of Hispanic, Mexican-American, and American Indian women" and that shared feelings of wonder and self-renewal.[30] The collection's success stems partially from its multiple viewpoints; a diversity of critical voices, approaches, and foci allows the volume to represent the diversity of the region.[31] Read in the context of this collection, Mary Hallock Foote's writings and career reveal a woman substantially changed by her relationship to the Western landscape, a woman whose focus on water and water metaphors presents a subtle reading of the West.

More recently, Western historians like Patricia Limerick, Richard White, and William Cronin have been "rethinking America's western past," as a subtitle to an influential book suggests, by looking at processes of change, at how the interactions between peoples and between humans and land modified both. Influenced by these "New" Western historians and postcolonial theory, literary critics have moved in the same direction. In an award-winning essay, "Letting Go Our Grand Obsessions: Notes toward a New Literary History of the American Frontiers," Annette Kolodny offers the trope of borderland studies, where the West, which she sees as a series of frontiers, is defined by encounters with "others":

> [The West is] a physical terrain that, for at least one group of participants,
> is newly encountered and is undergoing change because of that encounter;
> a currently indigenous population and at least one group of newcomers or
> "intruders"; and the collisions and negotiations of distinct cultural groups.
> . . . Thus, the literature of the frontiers may be identified by its encoding
> of some specifiable first moment in the evolving dialogue between differ-
> ent cultures and languages and their engagement with one another and
> with the physical terrain.[32]

As well as for other nineteenth-century writings, Kolodny's model works effectively for many of the pieces included in Kilcup's *Nineteenth-Century American
Women Writers*. Kirkland's "One Class of Settlers" from *A New Home* presents the
"negotiations" between an educated middle-class woman and her less privileged
working-class neighbors, while Foote's "The Fate of a Voice" implies in its ending that Madeline begins to communicate with ordinary working-class people
in the West. Austin's stories explore the conversations and mutual influence
between a white newcomer to the West and American Indian women. Other
works like Sarah Winnemucca's *Life Among the Piutes*, Ruiz de Burton's *The
Squatter and the Don*, and Pauline Johnson's "As It Was in the Beginning" focus
on cultural collision between groups, while works by Sui Sin Far and Zitkala-Ša
reveal the internalized struggles within women.

As critics turn to regionalism as a way of understanding the complex make-
up of our national identity, the study of Western literature will take on greater
importance precisely because of the region's cultural complexity. Responding to
metaphors and critical paradigms that focus on "cultural resistance" and collisions, Michael Kowaleski has offered a new way of thinking about the fierce
cooperation that Patricia Limerick suggests characterized the West: "The most
fruitful recognition of cultural diversity in the West will be one that complicates our conception of both mainstream *and* marginal cultures – questioning
along the way the usefulness of thinking about centers and margins in Western
writing rather than about interdependence, hybridity, and overlap."[33]

Kowaleski's model of "interdependence, hybridity, and overlap" offers us a
sustaining model for the future to think about issues of race and gender in
the West. (It may not work so effectively in terms of class.) While our critical
models have often been imperialistic, dedicated to destroying what came before,
I like to see my work not as individualistic but as cooperative; and to conclude
this survey of Western women's literature I offer another metaphor for thinking
about Western literature which extends from Kowaleski's. Mary Austin recognized early the importance of interrelationships and mutual interdependence in
the landscape of the West, writing, "The sagebrush and other things that grow
all of one kind together are called social shrubs. Each one of them has its own
kind of herbs growing up in its shade"; and she extended this understanding of
the natural world to the interrelationships among various cultures of the West.[34]
From Austin, from Aldo Leopold, from contemporary ecocritics, we might borrow

an ecological metaphor. Instead of focusing on a past series of mistakes, a lost Eden and a lost wilderness, we might think about how we can nurture and sustain the biodiversity of the region, replanting and rebuilding in an effort to allow space for everyone in community with each other.

NOTES

1 Caroline Kirkland, *A New Home, Who'll Follow?*, ed. Sandra Zagarell (1839; New Brunswick: Rutgers University Press, 1990), 5.

2 Paul Wilstach, "A Map which is a Literary Map of the United States," *The Bookman: An Illustrated Literary Journal* 7 (1898): 469. My thanks to Stephen Tatum for this reference.

3 Susan Armitage, "Through Women's Eyes: A New View of the West," in *The Women's West*, ed. Susan Armitage and Elizabeth Jameson (Norman: University of Oklahoma Press, 1987), 9.

4 Mary Austin, *The Land of Little Rain* (Albuquerque: University of New Mexico Press, 1974), 91.

5 Mary Austin, *Earth Horizon* (Albuquerque: University of New Mexico Press, 1991), 195.

6 Mary Austin, *Western Trails: A Collection of Stories by Mary Austin*, ed. Melody Graulich (Reno: University of Nevada Press, 1987), 97; Kilcup, *NCAWW*, 552.

7 Christiane Fisher points out differences in Western writing between the first generation mothers who left behind relationships and landscapes that defined their identities and their daughters, born and raised in a Western landscape they often loved. Fisher, *Let Them Speak for Themselves: Women in the American West 1849–1900*, (New York: Dutton, 1977), 13, 19–20.

8 Quoted in Lee-Ann Johnson, *Mary Hallock Foote* (Boston: Twayne Publishers, 1980), 152.

9 Letter, Foote to Helena De Kay Gilder, July 18, 1876, Mary Hallock Foote collection, Stanford University Library.

10 Kirkland, quoted in "Introduction," *A New Home*, ed. Zagarell, xv.

11 Austin, *Earth Horizon*, 157–8.

12 And yet another complication: in *Articulate Silences* (Ithaca: Cornell University Press, 1993), King-Kok Cheung explores the work of contemporary Asian American writers Hisaye Yamamoto, Maxine Hong Kingston, and Joy Kogowa, all writing about the West, and suggests that feminist critics have too readily assumed that having or gaining a voice is a measure of strength, self-awareness, or power, and that Asian women recognize the value of and speak through silence.

13 Quoted in Dee Brown, *Bury My Heart at Wounded Knee: An Indian History of the American West* (New York: Bantam Books, 1970), 300.

14 See Annette Kolodny, *The Land Before Her: Fantasy and Experience of the American Frontiers, 1630–1860* (Chapel Hill: University of North Carolina Press, 1984); Vera Norwood, "Crazy Quilt Lives: Frontier Sources for Southwestern Women's Literature," in *The Desert Is No Lady: Southwestern Landscapes in Women's Writing and Art*, ed. Vera Norwood and Janice Monk (New Haven: Yale University Press, 1987); Lois Rudnick, "Re-Naming the Land: Anglo Expatriate Women in the Southwest,"

in *The Desert Is No Lady*, ed. Norwood and Monk; Paula Gunn Allen, *The Sacred Hoop: Recovering the Feminine in American Indian Traditions* (Boston: Beacon Press, 1987); Tey Diana Rebolledo, *Women Singing in the Snow: A Cultural Analysis of Chicana Literature* (Albuquerque: University of Arizona Press, 1995); Melody Graulich, "'O Beautiful for Spacious Guys': An Essay on 'the Legitimate Inclinations of the Sexes,'" in *The Frontier Experience and the American Dream*, ed. David Mogen, Paul Bryant, and Mark Busby (College Station: Texas A & M Press, 1989), 186–201; and "Violence against Women in Literature of the Western Family," *Frontiers* 7 (1984): 14–20 (reprinted in *The Women's West*, ed. Armitage and Jameson).

15 Susan Armitage, "Western Women's History: A Review Essay," *Frontiers* 5 (1980): 71–3. Arguing that what she calls the "frontier process" possesses universal appeal but that the "frontier myth" has been shaped by preoccupations with courage, honor, violence, and individualism, Armitage later suggested that attention to women's lives would provide historians with the basis for a major reinterpretation of Western history, an assertion borne out in works by the so-called "new" Western historians.

16 Julie Roy Jeffrey, *Frontier Women: The Trans-Mississippi West, 1840–1880* (New York: Hill and Wang, 1979), xv–xvi.

17 Owen Wister, *The Virginian* (1902; New York: Signet, 1979), 284.

18 See Graulich, "Violence against Women in Literature of the Western Family," and "Somebody Must Say These Things," *Women's Studies Quarterly* 13 (1985): 2–8, reprinted in *The Intimate Critique: Autobiographical Literary Criticism*, ed. Olivia Frey, Diane Freedman, and Frances Zauhar (Durham: Duke University Press, 1992).

Readers will notice that all of my texts are by white working-class women. Cross-cultural treatment of an explosive topic like women abuse is indeed a minefield, one I was unwilling to enter. Contemporary American Indian women writers like Louise Erdrich who explore violence against women or Chicana writers who challenge their culture's fascination with "machismo" are often attacked as promoting cultural stereotypes. Some feminist American Indian scholars have suggested that the abuse of women did not exist in the Americas before contact with whites.

19 Wister, *The Virginian*, 83.

20 Dawn Lander, "Eve among the Indians," in *The Authority of Experience: Essays in Feminist Criticism*, ed. Arlyn Diamond and Lee R. Edwards (Amherst: University of Massachusetts Press, 1977), 195–6.

21 Austin, *Earth Horizon*, 14–15.

22 Kolodny, *The Land Before Her*, 6, xxi, 8.

23 See, for instance, Gerda Lerner, "The Challenge of Women's History," in *The Majority Finds Its Past* (New York: Oxford University Press, 1981), 168–80.

24 See, for instance, my essay, "'O Beautiful for Spacious Guys.'"

25 Nina Baym, "Melodramas of Beset Manhood: How Theories of American Fiction Exclude Women Writers," *American Quarterly* 33 (1981): 123–9.

26 Judith Fetterley, *The Resisting Reader: A Feminist Approach to American Literature* (Bloomington: Indiana University Press, 1978).

27 Adrienne Rich, "When We Dead Awaken: Writing as Re-Vision," in *On Lies, Secrets and Silences* (New York: W. W. Norton, 1979), 35.

28 Mary Austin, "The Return of Mr. Wills," in *Western Trails*, 54, 55, 56.

29 Jane Tompkins, *West of Everything: The Inner Life of Westerns* (New York: Oxford University Press, 1992).

30 Vera Norwood and Janice Monk, "Introduction," in *The Desert Is No Lady*, ed. Norwood and Monk, 2, 8.

31 Perhaps the diversity of the West is best captured in collections by multiple authors rather than in thesis-driven books. In a special issue of *Legacy: A Journal of Nineteenth-Century American Women Writers* published in Spring 1989 (Vol. 6, No. 1), I attempted as a guest editor to offer a "new" reading of the West by including essays on American Indian, Chicana, Chinese American, and Anglo women writing at the turn of the century.

32 Annette Kolodny, "Letting Go Our Grand Obsessions: Notes toward a New Literary History of the American Frontiers," *American Literature* 64 (1992): 5.

33 Michael Kowaleski, ed., *Reading the West: New Essays on the Literature of the American West* (New York: Cambridge University Press, 1996), 11.

34 The quotation is from Austin's Tejon notebook, contained in The Huntington Library's Austin collection.

4

"A Tolerance for Contradictions": The Short Stories of María Cristina Mena

TIFFANY ANA LÓPEZ

This would seem to be a good place for "local color," but the writer resists that fatal allurement.

María Cristina Mena, "Julian Carillo"[1]

Recent recovery work of Mexican American writing, such as that being performed by Arte Publico Press's series on Recovering the US Hispanic Literary Heritage, tends to spotlight authors whose writings are clearly and primarily grounded in the culture of the Southwest. Discussions usually focus on the consistency of themes and images, emphasizing a coherent definition of a writer's work and, in turn, a Mexican American literary tradition. Focusing first on some biographical and cultural contexts, and then on particular pieces of her short fiction, this essay looks at a Mexican American woman writer, María Cristina Mena, who defies such categorizations. Furthermore, it explores the exceptions and contradictions in Mena's work for what they can tell readers about the evolution of her writing within its own distinct tradition and the larger tradition of American literature.

Translating Cultures: Mena and *Century Magazine*

María Cristina Mena was born in Mexico City, April 3, 1893, the daughter of a Spanish mother and Yucatan father of European descent. Her father worked as a politically powerful and socially prominent businessman during the last two decades of the rule of Porfirio Diaz. Raised privileged and upper class, educated at the convent and later an English boarding school, Mena began writing poetry at the age of ten. Her family sent her at age fourteen to live with family friends in New York City due to the escalating political tensions in Mexico preceding the revolution that would begin in 1910. In New York she continued her studies and writing, which culminated in the publication of her first two short stories in November of 1913, "John of God, The Water-Carrier" (*Century Magazine*) and "The Gold Vanity Set" (*American Magazine*).²

In 1916, Mena married the Australian playwright and journalist Henry Kellett Chambers. Both moved in social circles that included prominent writers such as D. H. Lawrence and Aldous Huxley. After the year of her marriage, Mena published only one other short story, "A Son of the Tropics" (*Household Magazine*, January 1931). Her husband died in 1935 and she is said to have become a "virtual shut in."³ When she did leave her home, it was to participate in regular meetings of the Catholic Library Association and the Authors Guild of New York, which enabled her to maintain contact with a literary community. Like many other writers of her time, Mena wrote children's literature; between 1942 and 1953, she published five books for children, additionally working to translate them into Braille.⁴ Mena died in Brooklyn on August 3, 1965.

One of the first Mexican American women to write fiction in English and be featured in a national, mainstream popular literary publication, María Cristina Mena is a distinct figure in that she migrated from Mexico to New York, wrote almost exclusively in English (though Spanish was her first language), and drew on an impressively disparate array of literary influences, from Hawthorne to Huitzilopotchli. Mena wrote about Mexican culture and people during a period of American history in which there were heated political tensions between the US and Mexico. Always focused on current cultural, political, and social debates, *Century Magazine* contracted Mena to produce a series of short stories specifically on Mexican life. These appeared every three or four months for about five years, with the majority of her writing produced from 1913 to 1916.

Mena's work tends to portray Mexicans either as noble, struggling, and impoverished "inditos" – familiar representational cousins to characters in Helen Hunt Jackson's novel *Ramona* (1884) – or as members of a highly cultured, notably light-skinned, "Spanish" ruling class with the potential to assimilate easily into the dominant culture of the United States. Though somewhat limited in scope, Mena's character portraits present Mexicans as complex and human subjects rather than the abject "greaser" stereotypes found elsewhere at the time, including other *Century Magazine* stories.⁵ Those commentators most critical of Mena's work describe her stories as "trivial," "condescending," and politically unaware and read Mena as an author who simply capitulated to the desires of the white audiences and editors who determined the content of *Century Magazine*. Raymund Paredes, for example, describes Mena as a writer who "knew what Americans liked to read about Mexico, so she gave it to them. . . . a braver, more perceptive writer would have confronted the life of her culture more forcefully."⁶ Yet, according to literary historians Luis Leal and Pepe Barrón, the kind of narrative confrontation called for by Paredes did not occur until after 1943.⁷

By attending primarily to matters of race, critics have obscured a reading of Mena's work on its own terms as it sought to address other issues, most notably those of gender and class. *Century Magazine*, in deliberately commissioning a Mexican-born author to write about Mexican life for an American audience, literally placed Mena in the role of the cultural translator. Yet Mena continually redefined this role and grew to embody the position of transculturation that Gloria Anzaldúa describes in *Borderlands* as "the new *mestiza*":

> [She] copes by developing a tolerance for contradictions, a tolerance for ambiguity. She learns to be Indian in Mexican culture, to be Mexican from an Anglo point of view. She learns to juggle cultures. She has a plural personality, she operates in a pluralistic mode – nothing is thrust out, the good, the bad and the ugly, nothing rejected, nothing abandoned. Not only does she sustain contradictions, she turns the ambivalence into something else.[8]

Though Mena was not the first short story writer in *Century Magazine* to publish work about Mexican life, she was the first Mexican American writer to do so. And not only was she Mexican American, she was also a woman. As such, her work is critically instructive for what it can tell readers about the ways in which early women writers and ethnic American authors grappled with issues of self-representation in their effort to define a place for themselves within a distinctly American literary tradition.

In order to grasp the full scope of the political interventions Mena attempted with her stories, one must place her work within the larger context of *Century Magazine*: the fiction, advertisements, and sociopolitical essays that bracketed her literary endeavors. My readings here thus focus on the ways in which Mena drew on elite, popular, and her own Mexican cultural traditions. Doing so illuminates the critical role she played as a Mexican American woman writer (re)constructing a narrative tradition that makes historically marginalized subjects central to cultural critique. While other critics have read her attempts at cultural translation as ambivalent at best, I want to argue that it is precisely the contradictions within Mena's writing that most meaningfully distinguish her as a writer strategically forging a Mexican American literary tradition.[9]

Century promoted itself as a cosmopolitan magazine devoted to disseminating the best of American culture through in-depth essays on current cultural and political events, editorials, literary stories, and upscale advertisements. Narratives of romance and travel predominate, with writers speaking authoritatively about their visits to foreign countries and their encounters with customs and predicaments worlds apart from those of *Century*'s readers. For example, Adachi Kinnosuke's "Kiao-chau, and its Meaning" (February 1915) reports on Japan's interest in the Pacific islands "from a Japanese point of view." In most cases, however, the cultural insider was not a "native informant," but rather a Westerner who had traveled and lived abroad to the extent that he or she returned an "expert." An advertisement for the book "The Harim and the Purdah: Studies of Oriental Women" situates its author, Elizabeth Cooper, in just this way: "Mrs.

Cooper, who has spent many years in China, Japan, Burmah, India, and Egypt, has come into the closest contact with Eastern women of every race, class, and type. With the intimacy of a familiar guest she knows their home life, their social life, their customs with regard to marriage, divorce, and polygamy, how they feel and think and act."[10] As this example indicates, prior to the period in which Mena was writing for *Century*, it was primarily white authors who wrote about ethnic people. However, their point of identification was not always empathetic.

For example, one of the first published works in *Century* to address US–Mexico relations, Stephen Crane's "A Man and Some Others" uses the genre of the adventure story about moving westward (a subgenre of the travel narrative) to focus on Mexicans as a group of lawless savages that terrorize a lone white male protagonist. The title itself – "Some *Others*" – enforces a clear separation between Mexican and American identity. Crane's story depicts the encounter between Mexican and American settlers as hostile and fierce with no possibility for cultural negotiation. The historical circumstances of land invasion documented by the Treaty of Guadalupe Hidalgo (1848) not only drop out but are completely reversed. Crane portrays Mexicans as "mystic and sinister," "greasers," "black things that moved like monster lizards" with no reason to be angry over land disputes. A lone American plains settler defends himself against this pack of serape- and sombrero-wearing Mexicans out to murder him without any clear provocation: "We no like you here. Un'erstan? Too mooch. You mus' geet out. We no like. Un'erstan'?"[11] The dialogue accurately reflects the anti-Mexican sentiment of the time but it also serves a pernicious narrative function: it renders Mexican outrage about dispossession cartoonish and thus of no historical or political significance whatsoever. The Mexican characters are stereotypes whose sole purpose is to confirm – rather than highlight, problematize, or contest – American fears about Mexican presence in the United States.

While the magazine progresses in later years toward less overtly racist stories, the illustrations nevertheless continue to emphasize a divide between Anglos and racialized others. The drawing that accompanies Marie Conway Oemler's "The One with the Eye" (February 1915) depicts a gentlemanly Anglo male dressed in colonial garb standing many feet taller than the small "natives" who greet him. The underlying caption reads: "Soame was known as the One with the Eye. Gentry with receding chins and protruding lips laid before him gifts of fruit and flowers and meal cakes and yams; also they brought him unpleasant live things."[12] At the same time that these images convey an interest in ethnic people, within the overall context of *Century Magazine* they also serve the purpose of bolstering a reading of "American" identity as "white" and "not-foreign." Additionally, as is the case here, most often the foreigner is feminized and placed under the complete control of an Anglo male gaze.

The advertisements that intermingle with these stories and illustrations further delimit *Century*'s audience as a distinctly upper-middle to wealthy-elite class of American readers by promoting luxurious, high-end items, such as

Columbia records and phonographs, Kodak cameras, Arco wand vacuum clean-
ers, Reed and Barton silver, Hart Schaffner and Marx men's garments, White
House Brand coffee and teas, and Western Electric inter-phones – whose tag-
line most clearly addresses the ideal *Century* reader: "Nowadays to strain one's
voice by undignified loud calling to the maid is entirely unnecessary. So is the
tedious stair climbing when the maid can't hear."[13] The images that accompany
the stories make clear who are the implied servants.

The pictures that accompany *Century*'s advertisements never feature anyone in
the foreground who isn't clearly visually codified as Anglo, a fact further under-
scored by the narrative obsession with whiteness – be it of soap, flour, hand-
cream, or paint. The advertisements construct whiteness as the assumed universal
to be envied by all others, especially the female members of the target audience.
Bath and kitchen products most often emphasize whiteness as the signifier of
domestic success – in the immediacy of the family (Ivory Soap, Occident Flour)
and, by extension, the larger nation (White House Brand coffee and teas). Additionally, the narratives of these advertisements racialize the social hierarchy.
Those, such as women of color, who cannot "naturally" access the whiteness
promised by the flour, soap, toothpaste, cream, etc., are constructed as looking
up to that which remains fundamentally unobtainable. The ads also actively
play into class anxieties as whiteness gets coupled with economic security: one
must have the financial means necessary to purchase the product.

When non-white people do appear in the ads, they are definitively placed
in the background. For example, Hart Schaffner and Marx's ad for men's garments pictures an Anglo man and woman sharing a meal. In the background, a
Chinese waiter – complete with clogs and braid – holds out to the couple a bowl
of rice, chopsticks carefully poised as he serves the dish.[14] Similarly, when the
woman of color appears in *Century* advertisements and stories contemporary to
Mena's writing, she is placed under both a colonial and a male gaze. Though the
focus of Hugh Johnson's "Race" on an interracial marriage between a US soldier
and a Filipino woman might initially be read as politically progressive, a closer
reading quickly reveals a retrograde colonialist fantasy:

> He was standing there one morning when something softly pressed aside
> two elephant-ear palm-leaves on the water's-edge, as a butler pushes aside
> portieres, and through the aperture silently slipped a black prow. Stand-
> ing, one bare foot on the gunwale, head thrown back, hair flowing free,
> was what might have been a Naiad of the marshland, if Naiads wore print
> trade-cloth skirts. . . . the Naiad looked at him thoughtfully and spoke. . . .
> You are most magnificently wet, Señor.[15]

Both female *and* racialized, the woman's body becomes the vehicle for a colonialist
fantasy which views the woman of color as part of the landscape and, like the
resources, there at the soldier's service. The explicit sexual imagery – her sexually aggressive look, her penetrating gaze – completely inverts the reality of

those striving against colonization, much in the same way that Stephen Crane's "A Man and Some Others" distorts the historical experiences of Mexicans struggling with land disputes in the Southwest.

To complicate matters, next to such stories might be placed the kind of social critique offered by George Jean Nathan in "The Drama's Advertising Page," one installment of his parodic column "In Lighter Vein," which exemplifies the magazine's more conscious attention to changing social attitudes about issues of race: "Old Negro wants situation in Civil-War play in which he will not have to wear white cotton hair above his ears and assuage the Southern heroine in Act II with, 'It's a' right, Missy; it's a 'right, it's a' right Miss Vohginia. Massa 'il come back safe t' yoh,' thereupon hobbling off the stage shaking his head in melancholy doubt." The illustration accompanying this piece – which, quite tellingly, appears in the form of a mock advertisement for the drama pages – presents this "negro" male in full caricature, risking replication of the very thing the piece critiques.[16]

These examples demonstrate that *Century* is a magazine fraught with contradictions concerning people of color. On one hand, it published news articles and stories about the oppression of ethnic peoples related to the large influx of European and Mexican immigrants that characterized the historical moment; on the other, its visual images consistently consigned those very people to the role of servants to an Anglo population. The magazine's identity crisis carried into the years Mena wrote for *Century*, and the inclusion of Mena's work played a distinct role during this period, but not one without controversy.

The editors' response to Mena's writing illustrates the magazine's ambivalence as it worked to address issues of representing cultural difference. While *Century* commissioned Mena specifically to write about Mexican life, the editors also wanted her to do so in as conformist a manner as possible. In a letter to one editor defending her portrait of the struggling inditos in "John of God," Mena describes her feelings in an attempt to make the editors see the compromised position in which they had placed her: "I felt as if I had foisted a white elephant upon an amiable friend who now begged my permission to make the creature more conformable by amputating its legs, trunk and tail – not forgetting its ears."[17] To compound matters, *Century* often bracketed Mena's stories with racist and anti-Mexican political tracts, like W. Morgan Shuster's "The Mexican Menace" or Edward Alsworth Ross's series on immigrant groups in America.[18]

Undoubtedly Mena's goal as a writer was to see her work published and shared with as broad an audience as possible. Importantly, her stories and letters to the editor indicate that as the first Mexican American author commissioned for the express purpose to write about Mexican life for a magazine with a history of negative portrayals of Mexicans, Mena aimed to produce work that would visibly and proudly revise previous representations. Understanding the multiple contradictions that permeate the images of people of color in *Century Magazine* leads to a more complex reading of Mena's work, one which allows for a better understanding of Mena as a writer producing a literature of compromise as part of the process of creating a distinctly new Mexican American literary tradition.

Transforming Traditions

To themselves, people made peripheral by the dominant society are not "marginal," "other." But to counter the narratives of their alterity produced by the dominant society, they must tell other stories that chart their exclusions, affirm their agency (however complicit and circumscribed), and continually (re)construct their identities.

> Susan Stanford Friedman, "Craving Stories"[19]

Mena's *Century* stories follow a clear trajectory, beginning with colorful narratives about a very pious, devoted, and hard-working Mexican people and then developing into works that can be read as allegories for the period's political tensions. Throughout these stories, Mena provides a rich context that explains her characters' behavior and details their lives, from personal economic struggles to national revolution. Her early narratives introduce readers to images of Mexicans that, while politically charged, are not particularly threatening. None of Mena's stories are about Mexicans in the United States, and all take place in Mexico with many featuring visiting American tourists; thus, while her works ask US readers to confront the behavior of Americans in Mexico, they do not force them to confront directly the racialized social practices of Americans living with Mexicans in the US.

Significantly, Mena drew upon those narrative forms such as romance and travel stories already familiar to the *Century* audience in order to win readers over and then push them toward a position of cultural critique, similar to the way that Bertolt Brecht used popular stories to illuminate contradictions in society for his audiences. For example, "John of God, The Water-Carrier" (*Century*, November 1913)[20] depicts humble, low-class inditos struggling to come closer to God through their work; "The Emotions of María Concepción" (*Century*, January 1914) revolves around a young señorita's crush on a bullfighter; "The Education of Popo" (*Century*, March 1914) focuses on a gregarious, handsome young Mexican male in love with an Anglo woman tourist. At times, Mena's representations do not appear to be entirely different from the stereotypes of the quaint, dark-skinned primitive and the elegant Spaniard whose affable light-skinned ways win him a place with Americans. However, she distinguishes her stories by humanizing her characters, giving them dignity, and portraying them in complex ways rather than as merely one-dimensional caricatures.

Perhaps more significantly, Mena's stories directly engage the space of cultural negotiation refused by those *Century* writers, such as Stephen Crane, who preceded her. In her writing, Anglo Americans demonstrate a wide range of behaviors, from insensitive tourists merely out for their own entertainment ("The Education of Popo") to sincere participants in cultural exchange ("The Gold Vanity Set"). Furthermore, Mena's portraits attempt to map truthfully the ways in which people negotiate relationships when unfamiliar with the customs of another. "The Gold Vanity Set" (*American Magazine*, November 1913) best illustrates this point. In this story, the young Mexican female protagonist steals an American tourist's gold make-up compact so that she may offer it to the Virgin de Guadalupe in prayer that her husband will remain sober and stop beating her. At first, the American tourist is upset about the loss of her compact. However, when she discovers the villagers' customs about property and, more importantly, the uses to which the vanity set is put, she gladly parts with the object: "Well, if it saves that nice girl from ever getting another beating, the saint is perfectly welcome to my vanity set." Though the two women are separated by class and race, Mena's story binds them together through their mutual desire to see an end to spousal abuse.[21]

Mena follows María Amparo Ruiz de Burton (1832–95) in beginning a tradition of Mexican American writing. Both came from comfortable families, married outside of their ethnicity, wrote predominantly in English, and drew on the popular narrative conventions of their time.[22] Like Mena's short stories, Ruiz de Burton's two novels, *Who Would Have Thought It?* (1872) and *The Squatter and the Don* (1885), explore the volatile and unavoidable cultural negotiations that take place in the wake of the Treaty of Guadalupe Hidalgo. Ruiz de Burton often uses humor to broach the subject of Northern racism toward Mexican Americans. The comedic sketches she draws in her chapter, "The Little Black Girl" (from *Who Would Have Thought It?*), provide scathing social commentary on the hypocrisy of Mrs. Norval, a woman who professes to be an abolitionist yet refuses to accept into her home the Mexican girl her husband adopts. Ruiz de Burton underscores the absurdity of Mrs. Norval's racism by depicting her inability to see the girl as anything other than black: "'How black she is!' uttered Mrs. Norval with a slight shiver of disgust. . . . 'Drop her hand, Mattie! You don't know what disease she might have'. . . . 'How old is she? Her face is so black that truly, it baffles all my efforts to guess her age.'" Her daughter Mattie's more credible description of the young girl clarifies for the reader just how hysterical a reaction is Mrs. Norval's: "'I don't think she is so black,' said Mattie, taking one of the child's hands and turning it to see the palm of it. 'See, the palm of her hand is as white as mine – and a prettier white; for it has such a pretty pink shade to it.'"[23]

Both Ruiz de Burton and Mena are keenly aware of the complexities of racism, and both make use of humorous meetings across cultures to unpack and critique it. While Ruiz de Burton often focused on such matters as political and economic corruption, like Mena she addressed such issues as class struggle and social identity. Mena was also attuned to such "mainstream" concerns as temperance and domestic violence, nevertheless maintaining their specificity to Mexican culture. Paralleling one strategy that her predecessor employed in *The Squatter and the Don*, Mena provided images of Mexicans that frequently cultivated identification through imagined mutual suffering. "The Education of Popo," for example, focuses on a Mexican boy who has his first crush on an English woman eleven years his senior, an adolescent relationship in which the white subjects of the story can be read positively while at the same time sympathy is evoked for the adolescent Mexican male through the universal emotion of love.

The by-line to Mena's stories – "Author of 'John of God,' 'The Education of Popo,' etc." – reveals that she quickly gained a following. Once she established her audience, she drew more directly upon Mexican folklore, offering readers a literary synthesis of American and Mexican cultural influences. The stories of this period reveal the provocative ways in which Mena affirms Mexican culture and history by asserting Mexican female characters as powerful figures in the community, as matriarchs, heroines, and – most significantly – storytellers. "The Birth of the God of War" best illustrates Mena's use of Mexican folklore to signify the integral relationship between storytelling and cultural survival. The tale begins with the narrator describing her *mamagrande*'s store of "Aztec mythology," recounting in detail her grandmother's version of the story of Huitzilopochtli ("Weet-zee-lo-potch-tlee"), the god of war, an alternative creation myth. *Mamagrande*, however, is more than just a storyteller. The grandmother also occupies the role of the narrator's first history teacher, as she indirectly comments on the colonization of indigenous people in Mexico by telling how the church that the two of them attend is built upon an Aztec temple. Mena further valorizes women as storytellers by emphasizing the significance of Coatlicue, Huitzilopochtli's mother, even though the story initially focuses on the survival (and power) of the male god: "'Mother fear not! I will save thee!' How it thrilled the voice of *mamagrande* as she repeated the first words of the god! And how it thrilled the little heart of the never-wearied listener!"[24] The intergenerational exchange between the women excites the heart of the granddaughter as much as, if not more than, the story itself.

"The Birth of the God of War" is also significant in its turning to indigenous female figures as role models of resistance and endurance in the face of colonization – "Once I voiced the infantile view that the fate of Coatlicue was much more charming than that of the Virgin Mary, who had remained on this sad earth as the wife of a carpenter"[25] – a narrative strategy well before its time. Not until the 1960s did Chicano cultural nationalists embrace their indigenous past and turn to Aztec mythology for new symbols of resistance, celebrating *mestizaje* (signified by a distinctively brown body) as the powerful and permanent blending of cultural forces.[26] Also similar to the Chicana/o writers she predates, Mena employs Spanish words and phrases – *cuentos, mamagrande, macana, papacíto, chiquita* – to communicate the cultural specificity of the story. The narrator explains this strategy explicitly: "'*Ruge éste por la vez postrera*,' as it rolled out in my grandmother's voice, the *éste* signifying that ill-fated cub, for which I always wept. I render the construction literally because it seems to carry more of the perfume that came with those phrases as I heard them by the blue-tiled fountain."[27] Mena translates only when necessary and leaves untranslated those words easily understood in context or strategically needed to convey a sense of cultural exclusion. But perhaps most significant here is that Mena's prescient cultural critique stems from an understated but cogent feminist analysis. The young narrator prefers Coatlicue over the Virgin Mary because the indigenous figure possesses power in her own right and not just as "the wife" of a man. Furthermore, it is the female subjects who *create* the story – by giving birth to the male protagonist and by delivering the story to the next generation – who are most celebrated.

"The Birth of the God of War" exemplifies the more overt ways in which Mena incorporated Mexican mythology into her *Century* stories. Yet she also drew on erudite Anglo-based literary traditions in order to comment on women's cultural roles as they have been defined by and in such contexts. Clearly influenced by both Hawthorne's "The Birth-mark" (1846) and Robert Browning's "My Last Duchess" (1842), Mena's "The Vine-Leaf" (1914) addresses the central roles that male ideals of beauty and appropriate feminine behavior play in the maintenance of patriarchal control over women and their bodies.[28]

In Hawthorne's story, an eminent "man of science" named Aylmer becomes obsessed with creating an elixir to remove the small hand-shaped birthmark he views as blemishing the otherwise perfect body of his wife, Georgiana. As explained by the narrator, his desire to alter her appearance only surfaces after his marriage: "he thought little or nothing of the matter before." Prior to the marriage, Georgiana had also viewed her birthmark differently, as a source of attraction to her male suitors: "Georgiana's lovers were wont to say that some fairy at her birth hour had laid her tiny hand upon the infant's cheek, and left this impress there in token of the magic endowments that were to give her such sway over all hearts." Aylmer's sense of control over the birthmark – and more explicitly, over Georgiana's body and spirit – grows stronger as he torments her into internalizing his gaze to the point where she becomes self-loathing: "Not even Aylmer now hated it so much as she." Eventually, she risks her life for Aylmer's love and acceptance, which he gives when he is finally able to remove the birthmark. Only at the hour of her death does he fully accept Georgiana. Hawthorne's closing lines cast judgment on Aylmer not for his scientific ambitions but for his reckless need to employ them in order to gain control of the woman who would have brought him eternal happiness: "he failed to look beyond the shadowy scope of time, and, living once for all in eternity, to find the perfect future in the present."[29]

Browning's poem allows a similar reading of patriarchy through his use of dark parody and dramatic monologue. The poem's speaker, the Duke of Ferrara, addresses the agent arranging his marriage to the niece of a nearby count. The opening lines – "That's my last Duchess painted on the wall, / Looking as if she were alive" – begin the Duke's sinister and detailed description of the painting he commissioned of his former wife before her death, which he hints came at his own behest. In telling the agent of his careful interpretations of her behavior – "She thanked men – good! but thanked / Somehow – I know not how – as if she ranked / My gift of a nine-hundred-years-old-name / With anybody's gift" – the Duke pronounces his requirements for a wife unlike the previous Duchess, one who will eagerly and gladly submit to his authority. The poem ends with the Duke turning to the agent for a last time to reiterate his power to control a woman, a final warning designed to guarantee the compliant behavior of the future Duchess: "Oh sir, she smiled, no doubt, / Whene'er I passed her; but who passed without / Much the same smile? This grew; I gave commands; / Then all smiles stopped together." With the murder of the Duchess, the Duke is finally able to assert his complete control: "There she stands / As if alive. Will 't please you rise? We'll meet / The company below, then. . . ."[30]

Responding to texts like Hawthorne's "The Birth-mark" and Browning's "My Last Duchess," Mena's "The Vine-Leaf" offers a new twist on stories in the mainstream literary tradition about the interconnectedness of physical manipulation of a woman's body and the lurking shadow of male power and authority. Mena's narrator is a surgeon who tells his current female client a story about a former female patient who has trusted him with her life and made him vow that he would never reveal her identity nor the secret of the services she asked him to perform, the removal of a vine-leaf-shaped birthmark. Ironically, the doctor relates the story as a way to convince his client of his ability to keep a woman's secret.

Mena uses this narrative frame to plot a mystery about a large canvas painting of a beautiful woman who is looking into a mirror, her back to the viewer. The intrigue surrounding the portrait concerns the obliterated face of the woman looking in the mirror and the hastily added identificatory vine-leaf birthmark on the back of the female subject – presumably the same woman of the doctor's story. The artist is said to have been murdered while finishing the piece. The *marqués*, a man of great social and economic power, finds the artist's murdered body and takes the painting away with the explanation that he had been negotiating for it with the artist, Andrade, so that he could give the picture as a "betrothal gift." The story points to one reading that indicates the woman murders the painter of her portrait. Before the artist dies, he implicates her in the murder by placing an image of the birthmark onto the canvas in order to identify the murderer. If the police were to discover the woman as the assailant, she would have been delivered to the "hands of the public executioner."[31]

The narrative, however, opens out into a second and more sinister reading. The *marqués*, the woman's husband, is the one who discovers the murdered artist and who takes the painting to add to his collection: "I wished to make it a betrothal gift to the beautiful Señorita Lisarda Monte Alegre, who had then accepted the offer of my hand, and who is now the *marquesa*. When I have a desire, Doctor, it bites me, and I make it bite others. That poor Andrade, I gave him no peace."[32] Like Browning in "My Last Duchess," Mena attributes to her powerful male subtle turns of phrases ("when I have a desire . . . it bites me, and I make it bite others"). In this way, she emphasizes the intimacy of storytelling between men as a disturbing homosocial triangle in which the control of women's bodies becomes the currency of male bonding.[33] Here, the narrative suggests that the *marqués* killed the artist and painted the incriminatory vine-leaf on the body of the canvas to mark Alegre's body as suspect. In keeping with this reading, it could be deduced that she was possibly having an affair with the artist and was in love with him; the jealous and possessive *marqués* discovered this, killed her lover, and painted the birthmark in order to blackmail her into marrying him.

The ending of the story brings these readings together, as the doctor tells his auditor-client:

> With one look from her beautiful and devout eyes she thanked me for [my] prudence [in keeping her secret] . . . and then she sighed and said:
> "Can you blame me for not loving this questionable lady of the vine-leaf, of whom my husband is such a gallant accomplice?"
> "Not for a moment," I replied, "for I am persuaded, *Marquesa*, that a lady of rare qualities may have power to bewitch an unfortunate man without showing him the light of her face."[34]

If we read the doctor's words with a critical eye, we see that the *marquesa* actually refuses ever to look at the painting. She does "not" love the portrait and, in fact, finds it "questionable." However, the doctor's male point of view interprets the *marquesa*'s sighs as indicative of jealous feelings. Yet the verbal twists and turns of Mena's story underscore the ways in which the interpretive frame is always that of a male gaze.[35] Both the Duke of Ferrera of Browning's poem and the *marqués* of Mena's story capture their female subjects in the image of a painting. Similarly, Hawthorne's man of science preserves his sense of control over his wife by turning her into a carefully logged experiment in his handwritten journal. Repeatedly, Mena's words emphasize "the lady of the vine-leaf" as something created and possessed by men, from artist, to husband, to narrator. She scrupulously plots the doctor's storytelling as a performative act in which he shifts the spotlight away from women's life experiences and toward his own interpretations. In the end, the doctor "lifts" his female patient's story, just as he removes the vine-leaf birthmark from the woman's back.

While "The Vine-Leaf" obviously resonates thematically with Hawthorne's "The Birth-mark," Mena's story also differs in that the *marquesa*'s birthmark is not represented as detracting from beauty nor is it something that men want to see removed. Indeed, Mena's doctor describes it as "bewitching" to the "unfortunate" man who falls under the inexplicably powerful spell of the female body, while the *marqués* wants to control the female subject by *maintaining* the presence of the birthmark, the "stigma" that illuminates the power invested in female beauty. In Hawthorne's story, the woman dies when the birthmark is finally erased; in Mena's, the survival of the female subject depends upon her own removal of the mark. By demanding the physical eradication of the birthmark, the woman refuses both the painter's and the doctor's gaze, as well as the interpretation of her identity imposed by the imprint on the canvas and/or the ink on the page. As Elizabeth Ammons describes it, "The Vine-Leaf" shows "a woman outdoing men at their own game of violence and sexual control."[36]

Significantly, the illustration that accompanies Mena's story in *Century* shows a nude female figure with her back to the viewer, looking at herself in a small hand-mirror, presumably gazing at the birthmark on her back. At the beginning of the story, the wine-colored vine-leaf birthmark gets read as beautiful for the contrast it brings to the whiteness of the woman's back. Throughout "The Vine-Leaf" Mena emphasizes this whiteness. The natural blood-red naevus marks Alegre as Woman and sexual outlaw. Notably, it attracts the male gaze to her body; as the doctor observes to Alegre when she reveals it, "But it seems to me a blessed stigma . . . With permission, I should say that the god of Bacchus himself painted it here in the arch of this chaste back, where only the eyes of Cupid could find it." The doctor has little conversation with her and never sees her face, yet he falls in love with her after viewing her white back and then removing the infamous birthmark that only he and a few others, notably men, have seen. More pointedly, Mena's descriptions indicate that the *marqués* and the doctor are in love with an ideal, significantly one created by male gods. When the surgeon views her back, he remarks on, "this delicate, wine-red vine-leaf, staining a surface as pure as the petal of any magnolia."[37] This mark threatens to "stain" – as in physically defile and morally corrupt – the otherwise unblemished whiteness of her back.

Read within the larger context of Mena's portraits of fair-skinned Mexicanos in her other stories, the issue of racial marking has much larger significance. Consistently, Mena's stories in *Century* indicate a great effort on her part to remove cultural stigmas concerning Mexicanness as the marked status of an undesirable Other. As racial and gender hierarchies converge in "The Vine-Leaf," Mena's commentary on the symbolic value of whiteness extends to critique the broader systems of images in *Century* that repeatedly equate people of color with servitude. Undoubtedly, Mena was also working against those culturally ingrained images in Mexico that equate light skin with elevated class status.

Though Mena's stories are not always about race in terms of skin color and cultural differences, they always directly address the sharp class differences embedded in US–Mexico relations. One of Mena's last stories to appear in *Century*, "Marriage by Miracle" (March 1916), explores the North's technological export of plastic surgery to Mexico City. Typically in the literature Mena was drawing from, a woman undergoes the risks of surgery in order to gain a man's love, as in Hawthorne's "The Birth-mark." Mena's "The Vine-Leaf" recasts this narrative tradition by introducing the element of a woman who manipulates her body to save herself from the threats and abuses of a man. With "Marriage by Miracle" Mena further disrupts the conventional story of a woman willing to alter her appearance by featuring a woman who undergoes plastic surgery not for the love of a man, but for the love of a woman, her sister.

The story takes place in the wake of the Mexican revolution and focuses on the attempts of Doña Rosalia de Ramos Blancos to raise her two adult daughters in as socially respectable a manner as possible. The war has left her family bereft of a father and without the financial resources to maintain the standard of living traditionally associated with the family name of Ramos Blancos – which, significantly, translates to English as White Ramos. Ignoring the reality of the political and economic crisis in Mexico, Doña Rosalia obsesses with keeping up the appearance of an elevated class status: "the elaborate daily dinner ostentatiously served by the *nana*, clattering along the gallery from kitchen to dining-hall with course after course of covered dishes, was largely a symbolic rite by which the Ramos Blancos deceived their neighbors, and, I think, even their stomachs, so sincerely was it performed." Doña Rosalia's obsession with appearances also includes her daughters. The eldest, Ernestina, is viewed as "hopelessly disfavored, with her nose of ridicule, her eyes like two fleas, and her bony figure, which looked, as her mother often lamented, as if St. Joseph had passed the plane over it." In contrast, Clarita is described as "eighteen and surprisingly plump, considering her diet, and who had long, gray eyes which always appeared half closed."[38] The Doña's greatest concern in relation to her daughters is the preservation, at any cost, of the Ramos Blancos name. Mena's story shows the folly of such concerns, particularly given the historical moment.

In time, Clarita is pursued by a suitor, Luis Maldonado, whom her mother almost immediately dismisses as unworthy of the family name: "she announced confidently that he was of no family whatever. Of he being comely, honest-looking, and excellently dressed, she made no mention, as those attributes did not enter into her point of view." Rather than turn him away and risk forever alienating her youngest daughter, she promises that they can marry – but only after the eldest daughter is married. Everyone in the house knows what this means, including Ernestina: "Ernestina's eyes filled with tears, and her unfortunate nose grew pink when she learned that Clarita's happiness must wait upon her own marriage. 'Then for thee is no hope, *pobrecita!*' she cried." Ten years go by as Clarita and Luis wait for Ernestina's husband to materialize. Eventually they surrender to the fact that "nothing less than a miracle could unite them until after the death of Doña Rosalia," until one day Luis comes across a brochure that he believes will answer their problem: "a surgeon of beauty from the United States had set himself up in the City of Mexico and was anxious, for a consideration, to improve the faces of its inhabitants. . . . [T]his admirable surgeon of beauty was already beginning to achieve brilliant results in the newly rich, Americanized society of the Mexican capital."[39] As in her other stories, Mena offers insightful cultural critique on the matters of class and the ongoing climate of colonization that continue to characterize US–Mexico relations, especially with respect to their effects on the treatment of women. Yet such critical moments are never purely polemic but instead purposefully and artfully advance her stories' drama.

Out of love for her sister, Ernestina begins the series of operations necessary for her transformation under the guise that she has "promised God a retreat of six weeks." This allows her to remain heavily veiled without any suspicion by her mother. At the end of the six weeks, the doctor removes the veil to reveal a dramatically altered visage:

> *En nombre de todos los santos*! Not only had every wrinkle and blemish disappeared, not only had a nose of ridicule become a nose of dignity, not only had the sagging redundancies of jaw and neck given place to the

precise contours of youth, but the eyes, once like two fleas, now actually represented eyes, and the whole face, by some new trick in the angle of brows, had acquired a look of noble spirituality which would be highly creditable to a virgin martyr.

However, this beauty does not come without a disturbing side effect: Ernestina can no longer smile due to the incredible pain that ensues. The surgeon, however, assures her "that an expression of English immobility was in the latest mode cultivated by the most fashionable señoras." And Ernestina unquestioningly accepts this limitation as a small cost for the immediate attention she receives for her transformation. Ernestina becomes famous as a "saint whose piety had been rewarded with a visible, unequivocal signet of divine favor."[40]

Throughout "Marriage by Miracle," Mena unveils layer upon layer of irony, and with each turn she casts an increasingly darker vision. Shortly after the completion of the surgery, Ernestina no longer desires a husband; "from the rarefied heights on which she now dwelt a descent to the banality of marriage was out of the question." Clarita is, of course, left completely heartbroken. Doña Rosalia, though totally enamored with her miraculously transformed daughter, refuses to change her stipulations. Yet, eventually, Ernestina influences Doña Rosalia to allow Clarita to marry Don Luis. Mena's final closing lines bring this humorous – yet dark and ironic – story full circle: "if you had known Clarita in the past and could see her now with her three lovely children, I believe you would consider her transfiguration just as wonderful as that of the saintly Ernestina."[41]

As in Mena's other works, there is always more than one way to interpret the story. "Marriage by Miracle" offers perhaps the harshest of Mena's critiques concerning the limited scope of women's social roles. One could read her closing words as indicative of a utopian, fairy-tale ending, that both sisters find complete happiness in union with a male figure (God and mortal man). But this reading presumes that one accepts plastic surgery and its results as an uncomplicated and good thing. A contrasting reading allies being a perfect wife, mother, and saintly martyr with a kind of disfigurement. This dual edge to the ending of "Marriage by Miracle" only further attests to the complex nature of Mena's storytelling and to her commitment throughout her career to explore cultural contradictions, especially those concerning women's assigned social roles.

While Mexican American women and Chicanas have been the principal purveyors of oral storytelling traditions, only recently have they been formally recognized as narrators of culture. Historically, these cultural groups discouraged women from a fully active engagement in storytelling that would risk "making a spectacle." Those women, like Doña Marina (La Malinche), who dared to cast themselves as directors of the cultural script, were depicted as deceitful, unruly, transgressive, and otherwise disruptive of the patriarchal social order. While Eve is said to have brought on the downfall of man by eating an apple, Doña Marina is credited with having brought on the downfall of the indigenous people by sleeping with a white man. According to Mexican folklore, Doña Marina slept with Hernán Cortés, the Spanish conqueror of Mexico, begot his children and, as a direct result, contributed to the eventual demise of the indigenous people. She is said to be a traitor to her race for having been a translator between Cortés and the indigenous people. Mother of the first mestizos, Mexico's first mixed-blood children, she is known in folklore as La Malinche, the fucked one, a figure of horror within Mexicano/Chicano mythology.[42] While La Malinche narratives instruct about colonial oppression, to the horrific female figure *alone* gets attributed the responsibility of bringing about the downfall of the family and, by extension, the entire culture. The exclusion of the feminine thus becomes the very basis for the social contract, with cultural negotiation taking place through the sacrifice of women. From such tales women are supposed to learn the limits of their behavior: for example, the danger of talking too much and of taking too much power into their own hands.

In contrast, Mena depicts women as sexually assertive and communally productive – rather than destructive – individuals. They have a particular insight as to how power works that allows them to triumph as active and vital participants in cultural and political change. Furthermore, the keen quality of their vision comes as a direct result of their subject position as women in patriarchal societies. Mena works out of (in both senses) tradition in order to revise culturally ingrained representations of women and Mexicans and, by extension, to influence society's actual treatment of the members of these groups.

Mena drew from all of the resources at her disposal to illustrate the ways in which the stories a culture tells itself have the ability to impact inter- and intracultural relations. She wrote well before the emergence of identity politics and, as a result, her stories embrace a more contradictory and fluid sense of identities. It is this uneven quality to her work that speaks the greatest truth. Mena's constantly shifting point of view – from impoverished to erudite, from confrontation to conformity, from the US to Mexico – underscores the existence of the borderlands as a terrible and wonderful space where cultures clash and clasp in an ongoing performance of negotiating identities.

NOTES

This essay is dedicated to Karen Kilcup, whose ongoing patience, support, and thoughtful comments made possible the completion of this piece. I am also indebted to Elizabeth Ammons for introducing me to Mena's work and for continuing to actively support minority literatures in American literary studies. Amy Doherty has compiled, edited, and introduced an impressive collection of Mena's work, forthcoming in Arte Publico Press's Recovering the US Hispanic Literary Heritage Series, and I am grateful for her willingness to let me read the draft of this manuscript and quote from it in this essay, including Mena's letters to her editors at *Century Magazine*.

1   María Cristina Mena, "Julian Carillo," *Century* 89 (March 1915): 753–9.

2   For what little biographical information that exists about Mena in readily accessible
    sources, see Matthew Hoehn, ed., *Catholic Authors* (Newark, NJ: St Mary's Abbey,
    1948), 118–19, and Edward Simmen, ed., *North of the Rio Grande: The Mexican-
    American Experience in Short Fiction* (New York: Penguin, 1992), 39–40. Both stories
    are reprinted in Simmen's anthology.

3   Simmen, *North of the Rio Grande*, 40.

4   Beverly Lyon Clark provides a provocative discussion of the vital cultural role
    occupied by children's literature during the nineteenth century. Cited within this
    work, Henry Steele Commager writes, it was a time when "almost every major
    writer . . . wrote for children as well as adults, and . . . for over a century the line
    between juvenile and adult literature was all but invisible." Clark, "Kiddie Lit in
    Academe," *Profession 1996*, 149; 149–57. Mena's books were: *The Water-Carrier's
    Secrets* (1942), *The Two Eagles* (1943), *The Bullfighter's Son* (1944), *The Three Kings*
    (1946), all published by Oxford University Press; and *Boy Heroes of Chapultepec, A
    Story of the Mexican War* (Philadelphia: John C. Winston Company, 1953).

5   See Arnold de Leon's *They Called Them Greasers: Anglo Attitudes Toward Mexicans
    in Texas 1821–1900* (Austin: University of Texas Press, 1983). Edward Simmen's
    edited anthology, *The Chicano: From Caricature to Self-Portrait* (New York: Plume
    Books, 1971), offers a sense of the evolution in American literature from literary
    portraits by non-Mexican/Chicano writers which depict Mexicans and Mexican Amer-
    icans as "greasers" to the more affirmative self-portraits produced by Chicano writers
    following the late 1960s–1970s movements in cultural nationalism emphasizing
    the critical importance of self-representation.

6   Raymund Paredes, "The Evolution of Chicano Literature," in *Three American Liter-
    atures: Essays in Chicano, Native American, and Asian American Literature for Teachers
    of American Literature*, ed. Houston A. Baker (New York: The Modern Language
    Association of America, 1982), 50; 33–79.

7   In "Chicano Literature: An Overview" Leal and Barrón describe the emergence of
    Chicano literary forms as moving through four distinct stages: (1) Pre-Chicano liter-
    ature (to 1848): a period that produced mostly romances, corridos, folktales, and
    religious plays, "writings of a historical or semihistorical nature and descriptions of
    the regions visited by explorers to the Southwest where most Chicanos now live";
    (2) Literature of Transition (1848–1910): a period of response to the Treaty of
    Guadalupe Hidalgo in which Mexicans in the US had to decide whether to return
    to Mexico or stay in the US as citizens; (3) The Emergence of a Group Conscious-
    ness (1910–43): the beginning of a collective historical consciousness and active com-
    munity building due to the influx of Mexican immigrants following the Mexican
    Revolution; (4) A Literature of Confrontation: following the aftermath of the 1943
    Zoot Suit Riots, a time when writers distinguish themselves as Mexican Americans
    struggling against oppressive forces within the borders of the United States. In
    Three American Literatures, ed. Baker, 9–32.

8   Gloria Anzaldúa, *Borderlands/La Frontera* (San Francisco: Spinsters/aunt lute, 1987),
    79.

9   See my own earlier essay, "María Cristina Mena: Turn-of-the-Century La Malinche,
    and Other Tales of Cultural (Re)Construction," in Elizabeth Ammons and Annette
    White-Parks, eds, *Tricksterism in Turn-of-the-Century American Literature* (Hanover:
    University Press of New England, 1994), 21–45. See also Amy Doherty's critical
    introduction to her collection of Mena's work, which provides crucial details about

the writer's life and the historical context surrounding the production of her work (forthcoming, Houston: Arte Publico Press). This introduction offers sophisticated close readings of Mena's stories that scrutinize what others have dismissed as assimilationist or otherwise compromised narrative practices.

10 *Century* 89 (April 1915): 26.

11 Stephen Crane, "A Man and Some Others," *Century* 53 (February 1897): 601–7; Crane's story has been recently republished in Simmen, *North of the Rio Grande*, 12–26.

12 *Century* 89 (February 1915): 520–1.

13 The Western Electric ad appears in *Century* 89 (April 1915): 46. These examples are by no means exceptional. For additional readings of similar essays and advertisements in *Century*, see "Turn-of-the-Century La Malinche," cited above.

14 *Century* 89 (April 1915): 75.

15 Hugh Johnson, "Race," *Century* 88 (August 1914): 618.

16 George Jean Nathan, "The Drama's Advertising Page," *Century* 89 (March 1915): 799.

17 Letter cited in Doherty's edition of the collected works and letters of María Cristina Mena, Arte Publico Press (forthcoming).

18 Ross's titles include "The Old World in the New: Economic Consequences of Immigration" (November 1913); "Immigrants in Politics: The Political Consequences of Immigration" (January 1914); "Racial Consequences of Immigration" (February 1914); "Origins of the American People" (March 1914); "The Native Races" (January 1915). For a detailed discussion of these articles and their relationship to Mena's work, see "Turn-of-the-Century La Malinche."

19 Susan Stanford Friedman, "Craving Stories: Narrative and Lyric in Contemporary Theory and Women's Long Poems," *Feminist Measures: Soundings in Poetry and Theory*, ed. Lynn Keller and Cristanne Miller (Ann Arbor: University of Michigan Press, 1994), 17.

20 According to Doherty, "John of God" was chosen for inclusion in an anthology of the best stories of 1928 following its reprinting in *The Monthly Criterion*, edited by T. S. Eliot. Edward J. O'Brien, ed., *The Best Short Stories of 1928 and the Yearbook of the American Short Story* (New York: Dodd, Mead, and Company, 1928), 77–93. *The Monthly Criterion: A Literary Review* 6 (1927): 312–30.

21 "The Gold Vanity Set," in Susan Koppelman, *Women in the Trees: U.S. Women's Short Stories About Battering and Resistance, 1839–1994* (Boston: Beacon Press, 1996), 75. In her introduction Koppelman discusses the hopeful approach to the issue of spousal abuse taken by the author: "María Cristina Mena shows us the batterer in 'The Gold Vanity Set' as a man enacting conventions he can be turned away from with the right influence or intervention" (xx).

22 Ruiz de Burton is said to be the first Mexican woman to write fiction in English. Like Mena, she was married to an Anglo, a military man, and eventually went to the East. See the introductions in Rosaura Sánchez and Beatrice Pita, eds, *The Squatter and the Don* (Houston: Arte Publico Press, 1992) and Rosaura Sánchez and Beatrice Pita, eds, *Who Would Have Thought It?* (Houston: Arte Publico Press, 1995).

23 Kilcup, *NCAWW*, 261.

24 "The Birth of the God of War," *Century* 88 (May 1914): 45–9; *NCAWW*, 594.

25 *NCAWW*, 594.

26   For a discussion of the roles that symbolism and mythology have played on the
     development of Chicano nationalism, see Rudolfo Anaya and Francisco Lomelí, eds,
     Aztlán: Essays on the Chicano Homeland, (Albuquerque: El Norte Publications, 1989).

27   *NCAWW*, 592.

28   In *Conflicting Stories: American Women Writers at the Turn of the Twentieth Century*
     (New York: Oxford University Press, 1991), Elizabeth Ammons discusses "The
     Vine-Leaf" as addressing the issues of "fear and anger about male control of female
     sexuality and creativity" shared by other female writers of the period, such as Edith
     Wharton and Jessie Redmond Fauset. She writes: "The period from the 1890s to
     the late 1920s saw women in the United States from every major racial and ethnic
     group publish fiction. Not only were white women and black women able to build
     on predecessors' success in extraordinary ways, but also women from racial and eth-
     nic groups that before had been completely or almost completely silenced in the
     world of published literature in English were able to begin careers as authors. Sui
     Sin Far, Onoto Watanna, Humishuma, Zitkala-Ša, Anzia Yezierska, and Mary Antin
     all began publishing in the late nineteenth or early twentieth century. Added to
     this group of pathbreakers was María Cristina Mena, whose most powerful story,
     'The Vine-Leaf,' published in the *Century Magazine* in 1914, clearly shares her peers'
     concern with issues of silencing, sexual violation, violence, and male control of art
     in the modern west" (146).

29   Nathaniel Hawthorne, "The Birth-mark," *The Centenary Edition of the Works of
     Nathaniel Hawthorne*, ed. William Charvat et al., Vol. 10 (Columbus: Ohio State
     University Press, 1962), 36–56. Specific references to the story are to pages 38, 48,
     56.

30   Robert Browning, "My Last Duchess," *The Norton Anthology of English Literature*,
     ed. M. H. Abrams et al., 5th edn, Vol. 2 (New York: Norton, 1987), 1238.

31   Mena, "The Vine-Leaf," *Century* 89 (December 1914): 289–92; *NCAWW*, 598.

32   *NCAWW*, 597.

33   See Eve Kosofsky Sedgwick, *Between Men: English Literature and Male Homosocial
     Desire* (New York: Columbia University Press, 1985).

34   *NCAWW*, 598.

35   On this interpretive frame, see Laura Mulvey, *Visual and Other Pleasures* (Bloomington:
     University of Indiana Press, 1989).

36   Ammons, *Conflicting Stories*, 146.

37   *NCAWW*, 596.

38   Mena, "Marriage by Miracle," *Century* 91 (March 1916): 727, 728.

39   Ibid., 730, 731, 732.

40   Ibid., 732–3, 734.

41   Ibid., 734.

42   For further readings, see Octavio Paz, "The Sons of La Malinche," in *The Labyrinth
     of Solitude and Other Writings* (New York: Grove, 1985), 65–88; Norma Alarcón,
     "Traddutora, Traditora: A Paradigmatic Figure of Chicana Feminism," *Cultural
     Critique* (Fall 1989): 57–87; Sandra Messinger Cypress, *La Malinche in Mexican
     Literature* (Austin: University of Texas, 1991); and Monica Palacios, "La Llorona
     Loca: The Other Side," in *Chicana Lesbians: The Girls Our Mothers Warned Us About*,
     ed. Carla Trujillo (Berkeley: Third Woman Press, 1991), 49–51.

5

Early Native American Women Authors: Jane Johnston Schoolcraft, Sarah Winnemucca, S. Alice Callahan, E. Pauline Johnson, and Zitkala-Ša

A. LaVonne Brown Ruoff

Although contemporary Native American women authors have achieved wide-spread popularity and critical acclaim, their predecessors' contributions to Native American and American literatures have received far less attention. In the nineteenth and early twentieth centuries, five Native American women writers emerged whose lives and works illustrate the varieties of Indian experience in that period: Jane Johnston Schoolcraft (Ojibwe, 1800–41), Sarah Winnemucca Hopkins (Paiute, c. 1844–91), S. Alice Callahan (Muscogee, 1868–93), E. Pauline Johnson (Mohawk, 1861–1913), and Zitkala-Ša [Gertrude Simmons Bonnin] (Dakota Sioux, 1876–1938). Although the public perceived them primarily as emblems of Native American assimilation and survivalism, these authors wrote creative and ethnohistorical works that educated their audiences about Indian cultures and issues. In their works, these authors blend Native traditions and Western European literary genres. They also use multiple-voiced discourse that reflects Indian and non-Indian as well as male and female perspectives.[1]

The history of Native American literature written in English begins with the publication of the *Sermon on the Execution of Moses Paul, an Indian* (1772) by Samson Occom (Mohegan, 1723–92), which became the first Indian bestseller and was even translated into Welsh. Two other male Native American authors published in the early nineteenth century: William Apess (Pequot, b. 1798), and George Copway (Ojibwe, 1818–60).[2] Apess, a forceful protest writer, is best known for his *A Son of the Forest* (1829), the first published autobiography written by an Indian, and his *Eulogy on King Philip* (1836), an eloquent criticism of the Pilgrims' inhumane treatment of the Indians. Copway achieved literary fame with his *The Life, History, and Travels of Kah-ge-ga-gah-bowh* (1847), which went through six editions in a single year and appeared in a revised edition under two titles: *Life, Letters and Speeches* (1850) in the United States and *Reflections of a Forest Life* (1850) in Great Britain. All three of these writers were missionaries.

The first Native American woman to publish was Jane Schoolcraft. Though a contemporary of Apess and Copway, she is known less as an author than as the wife of Henry Rowe Schoolcraft (1793–1864), Indian agent and writer about Native American culture. Her life and brief literary career illustrate Joyce W. Warren's comment that in nineteenth-century America, "women in all walks of life were seen not as individuals but as secondary characters in the drama of the American individualist."[3] Born in Sault Ste Marie, Michigan, Jane Schoolcraft (Bame-wa-wa-ge-zhik-a-quay, Woman of the Stars) was the daughter of John Johnston, a Scots-Irish fur trader with great influence in the Lake Superior region, and Susan Johnston (Ozha-guscoday-way-quay, Green Meadow Woman). Her maternal grandfather was the famous chief Waub Ojeeg (White Fisher). Schoolcraft's mother, who understood English but spoke only her native language, educated her eight children in the Ojibwe language and culture as well as in the exploits of their grandfather and great grandfather, Ma Mongazida (Loon's Foot). A pious man devoted to his Ojibwe wife and family, Johnston was an avid reader and amateur poet who tutored his children, using his sizable library of books on religion, the classics, and English literature and history. As his favorite daughter, Schoolcraft often accompanied her father on trips to Detroit, Montreal, and Quebec. In 1809, Johnston took her to Ireland, where she briefly attended school. Unhappy and ill for most of her stay, Schoolcraft returned home with her father in 1810.

In 1822, Henry Schoolcraft, Indian agent for the Upper Great Lakes, arrived in Sault Ste Marie, where he roomed with the Johnstons. The next year, Jane and Henry married. The couple had four children: William Henry (b. 1824; d. 1826), a stillborn child (1825), Jane Susan Anne (Janee, b. 1826), and John Johnston (b. 1829). The Schoolcrafts lived at Elmwood, the elegant Agency house and the center of social life at Sault Ste Marie; later they wintered in Detroit so that the children could attend school. Gradually Schoolcraft and Henry became estranged. Henry, who attributed William's death to idolizing the boy over God, wrote Jane in November 1830 that the family would follow Christ and urged his wife to cleave to him rather than her family. He reminded her that she had been brought up in a remote place "without a regular education" and "the salutary influence of society to form your mind, without a mother, in many things to direct & with an over kind father who saw everything in the fairest light. . . ."[4] Henry's comment about Susan Johnston, who was highly respected by Sault Ste Marie Indians, undoubtedly reflects his increasing disaffection with his wife's Ojibwe heritage. As a traditional Ojibwe, Susan reared her children according to tribal values and parenting styles, which emphasized close family relationships and teaching by example rather than by stern reprimands or harsh discipline. Because of a series of illnesses and her loneliness during her husband's long business trips, the despondent Schoolcraft gradually became addicted to laudanum, prescribed as medication. In 1838, the couple moved East, and Henry sent the children to private schools, a separation almost unbearable for Schoolcraft. After settling his family in New York City in 1841, Henry traveled alone to England. Jane Schoolcraft died shortly after his arrival there.

Until her death, Schoolcraft collaborated with Henry on his Ojibwe research. Schoolcraft interpreted and translated stories and ethnographic information that her mother and relatives gave to Henry.[5] For him and for those who visited the couple, Jane exemplified the best of both the Ojibwe and non-Indian worlds. After her marriage, she was seen as the "northern Pocahontas" and was sought out wherever she traveled. Thomas McKenny, later Commissioner of Indian Affairs, and such writers as Anna Brownell Jameson and Harriet Martineau made special trips to the Schoolcraft home to meet her, praising Schoolcraft's delicacy of manner, polish, and tasteful appearance. In *Summer on the Lakes* (1843), Margaret Fuller alludes to Schoolcraft's comments on Indian women.

Schoolcraft, who began writing as a young girl, exchanged poems with Henry during their courtship. In the winter of 1826–7, Henry established a reading society at Sault Ste Marie, which, with Jane's help, published *The Literary Voyager or Muzzeniegun*, a literary magazine that included poems and essays mainly on Indian culture. The fifteen issues appearing from December 1826 to April 1827 were read both in Sault Ste Marie and Detroit. Under her Ojibwe name or under the pseudonyms of "Leelinau" and "Rose," Schoolcraft contributed several interpretations of Ojibwe stories and poems. Henry's statements about his wife's contributions to *The Literary Voyager* depict her as an emblem of assimilation and as a liaison between Indians and non-Indians more than as a writer and intellectual. At the end of her "The Origin of the Robin, an Oral Allegory," Henry comments that "a descendent herself, by European parentage, and of the race whose manners and customs, she depicts, in these legends, they derive additional interest from her familiar knowledge of the Indian legendary mind, and the position she occupies between the European and aboriginal races."[6] He both praises her Indian contributions for the "simplicity and artlessness of her details of Indian life and opinions" and contrasts her literary achievements with her background: "When to these positive recommendations of her poetic attempts, we add the limited opportunities of her early life, and the scenes of seclusion [in] which so much of her time had been passed, we think there is still greater cause to appreciate and admire."[7]

Schoolcraft's best work is her retelling of Ojibwe myths, several of which deal with transformation. "The Origin of the Robin: An Oral Allegory" describes how a son, whose father ignores his pleas to stop fasting, transforms himself into a red robin. "Moowis: The Indian Coquette" relates how a young man gets revenge on a young flirt by making a dirt man with whom the young woman falls in love. She leaves her family to follow him, only to be left alone. "The Forsaken Brother" describes how a young brother deserted by his siblings becomes transformed into a wolf. Later, when he meets his brother, he transforms that sibling as well. A more complex transformation story is "Mishosa, or the Magician and His Daughters," the account of two abandoned brothers who defeat an evil magician determined to kill them and who save his daughters. "The Origin of Miscodeed or the Maid of Taquimenon" tells how Miscodeed's guardian spirit, a white bird, turns her into a white flower to save her from the Dakotas, who killed her family.[8] Schoolcraft's traditional stories demonstrate a clear, direct, engaging voice, often combining a forthright narrative style with poetic diction. Schoolcraft also expresses her commitment to her Ojibwe heritage in two poems about her grandfather, Waub Ojeeg. Her angry "Invocation to My Maternal Grandfather on Hearing His Descent from Chippewa Ancestors Misrepresented," a monostrophic ode, defends her grandfather against the charge that he was born a Sioux. She defiantly urges him to "Resume thy lance, / And wield again thy warlike spear! / The foes of thy line, / With coward design, / Have dar'd, with black envy, to garble the truth." Her "Otagamiad," which reveals the influence of James McPhearson's poems written under the name of Ossian, pays tribute to her grandfather as a respected leader urging his council to battle: "war or slavery is our only choice."[9]

　Most of Schoolcraft's poems in *The Literary Voyager* reflect a love of nature, gentle piety, and fondness for English pre-Romantic and Romantic poetry. Her "Lines Written to a Friend Asleep," which urges the friend to wake up to observe the beauty of nature, evokes Wordsworth's "Expostulation and Reply." Her descriptive-reflective "To Sisters on a Walk in the Garden, After a Shower" uses the delicate beauty of the garden after the rain to exemplify the lesson that pain and care, like showers, are supplanted by the bright calm of faith. Several poems focus on stoic faith, grief, and suffering; for example, "Resignation" and "Lines Written under Severe Pain and Sickness" no doubt reflect her piety and fortitude during her many illnesses. Most poignant are those expressing Schoolcraft's despair over the death of young William in 1826, which include "Woman's Tears" and "Lines Written under Affliction." Her deep love for her son is most fully expressed in "To My Ever Beloved and Lamented Son": " 'Who was it nestled on my breast, And on my cheek sweet kisses prest' / And in whose smile I felt so blest? / Sweet Willy."[10]

　If Jane Schoolcraft was seen as a literary Pocahontas who combined a dedication to tribal traditions and a love of *belles lettres*, Sarah Winnemucca (Thocmetony or Shell Flower, Paiute, *c*.1844–91) was seen as a controversial fighter for her people and for her own reputation. Far less educated than Schoolcraft, Winnemucca authored the first ethnoautobiography by an Indian woman: *Life Among the Piutes* (1883). It differs from earlier nineteenth-century Native American autobiographies by William Apess and George Copway, which were patterned on spiritual confessions and missionary reminiscences. Like Copway and other traditionally raised Native American autobiographers, however, Winnemucca combines myth, history, and contemporary events with tribal ethnohistory and personal experience. American Indian autobiographers adopted this mixed form because they were accustomed to viewing their lives within the history of their tribe or band, clan, and family, as Julie Cruikshank makes clear in her introduction to *Life Lived*

Like a Story. Compiling the personal narratives of three Athabaskan women from the Yukon, Cruikshank observed that the women responded to her questions about secular events by telling traditional stories. These women "talk about their lives using an oral tradition grounded in local idiom and a mutually shared body of knowledge." Arnold Krupat argues that Native American autobiography consists of individually written autobiographies by Indians and compositely produced Indian autobiographies. Representing the encounter between a narrator and an editor (and sometimes a translator) and between two cultures, these autobiographical texts are dialogic rather than monologic.[11] Winnemucca's ethnoautobiography reflects these traditions. In its emphasis on the political issues of legal rights and race, *Life Among the Piutes* has more in common with the life histories written by women of color and of the working class and with the post-Civil War autobiographies by African Americans than with those by mainstream middle-class women, which usually do not broach these topics.[12]

Although marginalized within the dominant society because of her racial heritage, Winnemucca played a central role in her tribe. Born near the sink of the Humboldt River in Nevada, she was the granddaughter of Truckee, who, Winnemucca claimed, was chief of all the Paiutes, and the daughter of Old Winnemucca, who succeeded his father as chief. In her life and in her public performances, Winnemucca presented a complex image which sometimes reflected both her audiences' expectations and her genuine commitment to helping her people. As the granddaughter and daughter of chiefs, Winnemucca was often perceived by non-Indian audiences as Indian royalty and described by the press as a "princess."[13] Before she began lecturing about her people, Winnemucca appeared on stage with Old Winnemucca and her sister in performances that Gae Whitney Canfield says "bore little relationship to the true life of the Paiutes" but did "fulfill the public's notion of a good stage show."[14] In 1864 the family's appearance in Virginia City, Nevada, was a sensation. In October of that year, the chief, his daughters, and eight braves also appeared in a series of "Tableaux Vivants Illustrative of Indian Life" in San Francisco.

Throughout her life, Winnemucca was a controversial figure. Some of the gossip about her resulted from her complicated marital history, but the controversy surrounding her life was not limited to her marriages. Though she drank on occasion, Winnemucca deplored the effect of alcohol on her people. She also gambled, a popular pastime among the Paiutes. On two occasions in 1873, she physically attacked a woman and a man who impugned her honor. Commenting on Winnemucca's volatile nature, Canfield calls her "an object of admiration or contempt, depending on the viewer's attitude toward race and the role of women. As an Indian she had no legal protection of her person or property."[15]

Because she and her family followed Truckee's policy of peaceful coexistence with whites, Winnemucca spent much of her life as a liaison between Paiutes and whites. As such she became a courageous and eloquent spokeswoman for her people, pleading the Paiute cause before government officials and the general public. Disillusioned by federal Indian policy and angry at its venial agents,

Winnemucca took the Paiute cause to the public. Her first lecture in San
Francisco in 1879 was so successful that she then toured the East, where she
delivered more than three hundred speeches. In Boston, she was befriended by
Elizabeth Palmer Peabody, a well-known supporter of kindergarten education,
and by her sister Mary Tyler Mann, widow of Horace. Through their influence,
Winnemucca spoke in the homes of Ralph Waldo Emerson, John Greenleaf
Whittier, and Senator Henry L. Dawes. Enthusiastic response to her lectures
and support from Mary Mann convinced Winnemucca to write *Life Among the
Piutes*, which, with an article on Paiute ethnography appearing in *The Califor-
nian* (1882), "The Pah-Utes," was Winnemucca's only publication. Both in her
lectures and in her book, Winnemucca staunchly supported the General Allotment Act, sponsored by Senator Dawes, under which Indians would be allotted
tribal lands in severalty.[16] In 1884, she returned to her brother Nachez's farm
near Lovelock, Nevada, to establish a school for Paiute children. Three years
later, ill, despondent over her marriage to Lewis Hopkins, and in need of money,
she abandoned the school. Winnemucca died in 1891.

Winnemucca's role as advocate made her the Paiutes' mightiest word warrior.
In *American Indian Autobiography*, Brumble convincingly argues that *Life Among the
Piutes* is a kind of coup tale in which Winnemucca records her deeds in order to
establish how she ought to be regarded, as have such Indian men as Two Leggings
and White Bull. Kathleen Mullen Sands concludes that Winnemucca portrays
herself in opposing roles in her autobiography: male and female, private and public:
"She not only presents herself as a warrior for Indian justice, but she also develops
a portrait of a child terrified by white power who, toward the end of her narrative, has become a dedicated teacher of Indian pupils – a version of motherhood."[17]

Cheryl Walker calls Winnemucca a "sacrificial intermediary, and advocate of
both-and rather than *either-or*." Taking on both male and female roles, Winnemucca
advocated cooperation between red and white, and tried to position the Paiute
nation "as a viable entity in the heart of America."[18] Winnemucca is both the
personification of her own Indian nation and the quintessentially American
underdog. Walker also perceptively argues that much of Winnemucca's use of
the language of the subjugated can be understood with reference to the culture
of sentiment. As Shirley Samuels points out, the culture of sentiment "is literally at the heart of nineteenth-century American culture."[19] Emphasizing that
nineteenth-century feminism played a major role in the culture of sentiment,
Walker suggests that "through Mary Mann and Elizabeth Peabody, Sarah became
aware of its force."[20]

Life Among the Piutes covers the period from Winnemucca's birth to 1883,
from the first contacts between the settlers and Paiutes, through their many
conflicts with settlers, resettlements, and negotiations to receive justice from the
federal government. Winnemucca combines the authenticating devices and narrative techniques of earlier Indian autobiographies with dramatic re-creations
of episodes from her own and her family's personal experiences, a combination
that makes the book one of the most colorful personal and tribal histories of the

nineteenth century. Winnemucca carefully validates her narrative. Mary Mann emphatically states in the "Editor's Preface" that her own "editing has consisted in copying the original manuscript in correct orthography and punctuation, with occasional emendations by the author."[21] To establish her credibility as some-one capable of writing her own life history and to counteract her enemies' attacks on her morality, Peabody and Mann added an appendix containing documents attesting to Winnemucca's high moral character as well as to her services as an interpreter and intermediary for the government.[22] Brumble correctly links her use of these documents to the oral traditions of self-vindication in American Indian personal narratives, while Brigitte Georgi-Findlay perceptively comments that Winnemucca writes against those who "disclaim her authority as a political spokeswoman by disclaiming her respectability as a woman, by exposing the woman who speaks and acts in public as a 'public woman.'"[23]

In part one, a single chapter, Winnemucca describes the background of her family and the impact of white migration on Paiute life after 1844, when she was born. In part two, also one chapter, she portrays the domestic and social moralities of the Paiutes and provides ethnographic information about the tribe. The six chapters of part three depict the conflicts between the Paiutes and settlers from 1860 to 1863, when the Indians, struggling to retain their native land, were moved from one reservation to another as they attempted to gain allotments on the Malheur Agency in Oregon. A central theme is Paiute–settler relations. Like other early Native American autobiographers, Winnemucca strongly attacks the settlers' and government's hypocrisy. Chronicling the tribe's relations with non-Indians in the 1860s and 1870s, Winnemucca charges that Indian agents got rich by starting their own stores and then bringing in cattlemen to pay them a dollar a head to graze their cattle on reservation land.

The description of the impact of white migration into Paiute territory pro-vides a dramatic backdrop for Winnemucca's discussions of tribal beliefs and customs, which reflect the oral tradition of linking personal narrative to a fam-ily, clan, and tribal context. Her depiction of the Paiute councils reminds her readers that Indian women in traditional cultures had political power that was denied to white women in the "civilized" society: "The women know as much as the men do and their advice is often asked. We have a republic as well as you. The council-tent is our Congress, and anybody can speak who has anything to say, women and all . . . If women would go into your Congress, I think justice would soon be done to the Indians." She also stresses that Paiute girls are never forced to marry against their wishes and that after the birth of a child, the husband assumes all his wife's house work for twenty-five days: "If he does not do his part in the care of the child, he is considered an outcast."[24] Because nineteenth- and early twentieth-century autobiographies and ethnographies gave little information about female roles in Native American culture, Winnemucca's detailed accounts of their roles in the Paiute tribe are especially significant.

In addition to the themes of Indian/non-Indian relations and Paiute culture, Winnemucca also emphasizes what Georgi-Findlay calls "the outrageous issues of sexual violence and miscegenation revealed in the violation of native women's bodies by white men."[25] Winnemucca learned this danger as a child when settlers came into her family's camp asking that her mother give one of her daughters to them. Later the author describes how white men kidnapped two twelve-year-old Paiute girls and how, during the Bannock War of 1878, male settlers lassoed Paiute women and did "fearful" things to them. On one occasion, when Winnemucca and Mattie shared a room with eight cowboys, a man touched her during the night. Winnemucca punched the offender in the face and warned: "Go away, or I will cut you to pieces, you mean man!"[26] Through her depiction of the sexual violence that Indian women suffered at the hands of male settlers, Winnemucca, like many nineteenth-century slave narrators, reminds whites of their own brutality, particularly toward women. Such narratives emphasize how the conquest of Indians, like the slave system, destroyed the morality of the whites. Throughout her book, Winnemucca portrays herself as a proper Paiute woman whose morals correspond to the code of conduct of mainstream women in the nineteenth century.

Life Among the Piutes is more personalized and reveals far more about the author's adult personality than do the autobiographies of such early Native American male writers as Apess, Copway, and Charles Eastman. It contains a detailed account of Winnemucca's childhood, stressing her strong attachment to her grandfather, Truckee, and her intense fear of white men, who reminded her of owls. It does not, however, reveal much about her adolescence. Her selective account of her adult life depicts a complex but positive persona of an Indian woman who possesses the sensitivity, compassion, and virtue expected of heroines and the strength, courage, and aggressiveness expected of heroes. Winnemucca demonstrates her compassion and toughness in a description of her anguish when she must tell the Paiutes that they will be forced to move in midwinter to the Yakima Agency — despite government assurances at the end of the Bannock War that the tribe would not be relocated. She strongly criticizes the president who forced the weakened Paiutes to travel through freezing cold and deep snows to Yakima: "Oh what can the President be thinking about? Oh, tell me, what is he? Is he man or beast? Yes, he must be a beast; if he has no feeling for my people, surely he ought to have some for the soldiers."[27]

In her description of her role as a liaison between her people and the army or the federal government, Winnemucca depicts herself as a Paiute woman warrior. Her exploits during the Bannock War rival those of the Western adventure tales of the popular press and would remind her readers of the harrowing experiences of the heroines of captivity and slave narratives.[28] Between June 13 and 15, 1878, Winnemucca rode 223 miles, on horseback and by wagon, between the Indian and army lines, in danger both from the warring Bannocks and from whites eager to kill her for helping the Paiutes. In her accounts of this war, she also portrays herself as more courageous and civilized than the male settlers. During a battle between the Bannocks and the troops of General Oliver O. Howard, she is disgusted by the frightened volunteers, who, though always ready to exterminate her people, cowered behind the army's lines. To demonstrate the army's barbarism, she includes the incident in which Captain Reuben Bernard presents her with a scalp captured from the Bannocks. Winnemucca, who had never seen one before, leaves the unwanted item behind. In addition, the author endured the enmity of both men and women settlers who wanted her dead. Describing how one white woman hoped Winnemucca would be killed, she comments that Western white women were always ready to condemn her. Her remark contrasts sharply with accounts of sisterly solidarity given by many white women writers who were her contemporaries.

Life Among the Piutes is the most interesting of nineteenth-century Native American autobiographies, primarily because the author effectively dramatizes key episodes. Carolyn S. Fowler suggests that Winnemucca's re-creation of dialogue derives from the quotative style of Northern Paiute narratives.[29] Dramatizing scenes and reproducing dialogue enable Winnemucca to strengthen her attacks against her adversaries by including the testimony of witnesses. The technique emphasizes, as well, the influence of the performance aspects of storytelling in native oral traditions. Examples of her narrative skill occur in the re-creation of the scene in which her grandfather calls his people together to retell the Paiute origin myth and in her dramatization of Truckee's death, in 1859, in which she weaves together the threads of autobiography, ethnography, and Indian–white relations that dominate the book. Truckee's final speeches express his love for his family, his wish that his granddaughters be sent to a convent school, and his concern for good relations between Paiutes and whites. The author eloquently describes her grief at his passing: "I could not speak. I felt the world growing cold; everything seemed dark. The great light had gone out. I had father, mother, brothers, and sisters; it seemed I would rather lose all of them than my poor grandpa."[30] Her grief was shared by the Paiutes, who gathered from near and far for his death watch and funeral. As Sands perceptively comments, Winnemucca's use of lengthy speeches and dialogues suggests "a considerable use of poetic license, recollections edited with political as well as artistic intent in mind, other voices played through the voice of the narrator, noticeably in the narrator's narrative style." Sands concludes that Winnemucca's dialogues with military officers, settlers, family, and others "enhance her own stature and her case for justice toward the Paiutes."[31] Also significant is Winnemucca's use of different voices in varying sections of her narrative, moving from writing in a child's voice in the account of her childhood, to the young woman's voice as she becomes a liaison for her tribe, and finally to the confident tribal representative of the last section on Paiute–government relations.

Winnemucca's skill as an orator is exemplified in her final exhortation in *Life Among the Piutes*:

For shame! for shame! You dare to cry out Liberty, when you hold us in places against our will, driving us from place to place as if we were beasts. Ah, there is one thing you cannot say of the Indian. You call him savage, and everything that is bad, but one; but, thanks be to God, I am so proud to say that my people have never outraged your women, or have even insulted them by looks or words. . . . Oh, my dear readers, talk for us, and if the white people will treat us like human beings, we will behave like a people; but if we are treated by white savages as if we are savages, we are relentless and desperate; yet no more so than any other badly treated people. Oh, dear friends, I am pleading for God and for humanity.[32]

Although *Life Among the Piutes* was the only book-length autobiography published by an Indian woman in the nineteenth century, Native American women began to publish creative writing at the turn of the century. Two writers were mixed-bloods from acculturated families: S.[ophia] Alice Callahan, whose *Wynema* (1891) is probably the first novel by a woman author of American Indian descent,[33] and E. Pauline Johnson, who was the most widely read Indian woman writer in the nineteenth and early twentieth centuries. Undoubtedly, these authors and Zitkala-Ša (Gertrude Bonnin), who wrote fiction and nonfiction in the early twentieth century, were stirred to write by events and issues that affected Indians in that period. Indian hopes to resist white domination through force of arms or the messianic Ghost Dance religion ended with the failure of Louis Riel's second rebellion of 1885 to establish a Métis government in Canada, the surrender of Geronimo's band of Apaches in 1886, and the massacre in 1890 of Big Foot's Band of Ghost Dancers at Wounded Knee on the Pine Ridge Reservation. In the 1890s and the early twentieth century, native peoples struggled to survive drastic changes in traditional lifestyles and to gain justice from the governments of Canada and the United States, which were more committed to policies of acculturation than to protection of Indian rights. During this period, women increased their efforts to gain recognition of their rights, including suffrage. Not until 1918 in Canada and 1920 in the United States did women achieve the right to vote in national elections.[34] Although Callahan addresses more specifically the issues of women's rights than do Johnson and Zitkala-Ša, all three deal with the role of women. Moreover, their writing reveals how Indian women authors used and departed from literary trends present in women's literature of the nineteenth century.

Like their predecessors Schoolcraft and Winnemucca, Callahan, Johnson, and Zitkala-Ša were both part of and separate from the Indian peoples, cultures, and issues they discuss. This dual status emerged from life experiences. Callahan's parents were Samuel Benton Callahan, who was one-eighth Muscogee (Creek), and Sarah Elizabeth Thornberg McCallester Callahan, both of whom grew up in Sulphur Springs, Texas, near Dallas. A farmer and rancher near Okmulgee, in present-day eastern Oklahoma, Samuel served his tribe as a translator and liaison, edited the *Indian Journal*, and was superintendent of the Wealaka Boarding School for Muscogee children. When marauders raided the family's ranch and trading post during the Civil War, Sarah took her children to Sulphur Springs, Texas. They remained there until 1885, when the family joined Samuel, moving first to Okmulgee and then to Muskogee. Little is known about the life of Alice, born in Sulphur Springs in 1868. She spent ten months at the Wesleyan Female Institute in Staunton, Virginia, from which she returned in June 1888. When *Wynema*, her only book, was published, she was teaching at Muskogee's Harrell International Institute, a Methodist high school. In 1892 and 1893, Callahan taught at the Wealaka School. By late 1893, she had moved back to Harrell. Callahan planned to return to the Female Institute in 1894 to complete her studies so that she could open her own school. Before she could fulfill her plans, she was stricken with pleurisy shortly after Christmas 1893, and died on January 7, 1894.[35]

Callahan dedicates her book to the Indian Tribes of North America "who have felt the wrongs and oppression of their pale-faced brothers," and she prays that "it may serve to open the eyes and heart of the world to our afflictions" and usher in "an era of good feeling and just dealing with our more oppressed brothers." The plot focuses on the acculturation and romances of two heroines, Genevieve Weir, a non-Indian Methodist teacher from a genteel Southern family, and Wynema Harjo, a full-blood Creek child who becomes her best student and dear friend.[36]

The first section of the novel chronicles Genevieve's adjustments to life as a Methodist teacher in the Creek Nation. Wynema and Gerald Keithly, a Methodist missionary, help her to understand Creek culture. Parts one and two also describe the "civilizing" of Wynema. Callahan introduces a reverse acculturation theme in section two when Genevieve takes Wynema on a visit to the Weirs' home, where the heroines must adjust or readjust to Southern lifestyles. Genevieve, who has turned down Gerald's proposal because she has an "understanding" with Maurice Mauran, a childhood friend, breaks off the relationship when she realizes how prejudiced this Southern gentleman is against Indians and women. She then accepts Gerald's proposal. In the meantime, Wynema and Robin Weir, Genevieve's sensitive and enlightened brother, fall in love. Both women return to the Creek Nation, where they subsequently marry their fiancées. Two other romances involving Genevieve's younger sisters are briefly introduced but not developed. The last section tests our "willing suspension of disbelief" as Carl (a Methodist missionary to the Muscogees and former missionary to the Sioux) and Robin rush off to the Sioux Nation during the hostilities of late 1890 that led to the massacre at Wounded Knee on December 29.

Callahan's own bicultural background, years in Staunton, experiences as a teacher at Methodist mission school for Muscogees, and staunch support for women's rights and suffrage inform the novel. She uses a plot formula that Nina Baym indicates was common in America from 1820 to 1870: women fiction writers chronicled the "trials and triumph" of a "heroine, who, beset with hardships, finds within herself the qualities of intelligence, will, resourcefulness, and courage sufficient to overcome them."[37] Genevieve's adventures fit that criteria. Though "physically unfit to bear the hardships of Life Among the Indians," the intelligent and pretty Genevieve has great "moral courage and endurance." Raised amid the "luxuries of a Southern home," Genevieve possesses "the graces of heart and head."[38] At a time when few women, especially Southern women, left home on their own before marriage, Genevieve's decision reveals considerable independence.[39] However, by providing Genevieve with a husband who more than equals her in kindness and dedication, Callahan keeps her heroine within the boundaries that Larzer Ziff points out in *The American 1890s* as characteristic of that decade. Many a determined daughter in this period sought economic independence, "not just to show that she could compete equally with men, but to protect the sanctity of her inner nature. Her dream was to enter into marriage or other relations with men as an equal party whose demands were respected every bit as much as the demands the male's nature made upon him."[40]

Callahan's blending of domestic romance with discussions of women's and Indians' rights is consistent with the traditions of sentimental fiction, which Jane Tompkins describes in *Sensational Designs* as a move toward a greater scope and democratization that was profoundly a "political enterprise, halfway between sermon and social theory, that both codifies and attempts to mold the values of its time." Lauren Berlant states that nineteenth-century sentimental activists charged themselves "and their sister women with the dual aim of social amelioration and change." According to Peggy Pasco, a growing body of evidence suggests that Victorian female reformers fought against male privilege even as they defended the Christian home "centered around the moral authority of the wife rather than the patriarchal control of the husband." For them, "female 'submission' was no longer a mark of true womanhood"; they saw that female emancipation was the logical outcome of Christianization.[41] This concept of home is especially relevant to the plot of *Wynema*, in which Callahan emphasizes that a successful marriage requires that the partners share values and respect one another's independent views.

While Callahan's heroines and heroes possess the characteristics traditional to domestic romance, they also represent strong-hearted women of ideas and gentle men sensitive to Indians' and women's issues. Genevieve's nurturing, maternal side is revealed in her relationship with Wynema. However, she is also a complex domestic heroine – at once a shy romantic who longs for love and a strong-minded, independent woman wary of marriage. To portray what Callahan obviously feels is the ideal love that grows out of mutual respect between intelligent men and women, the author provides Genevieve with two lovers who behave very differently toward women: Gerald Keithly, a Methodist missionary, is a gentle, quiet, sympathetic man, while Maurice Mauran is a bullying bigot equally prejudiced against Indians and self-sufficient women. Another domestic romance between a woman of ideas and sensitive man is that between Wynema and Robin Weir, Genevieve's younger brother. An exceptionally bright and determined child, Wynema exemplifies the possibilities of acculturating Indians through education. By the time she visits Genevieve's home in the South, Wynema has become a cultured, refined young lady who speaks fluent English and whose personal qualities endear her to the Weir family. The relationship between Wynema and Robin exemplifies the true, respectful love that can be achieved both between educated and right-thinking adults and between an Indian woman and white man. In the section of the novel devoted to hostilities in the Sioux Nation, Callahan includes an idealized portrait of traditional Indian marriage between Wildfire, a defiant, proud warrior, and Miscona, his devoted wife. Wildfire and Miscona die in battle, locked in each others' arms. Callahan's portrait of a loving Indian marriage humanizes the impact of the conflict on the Sioux.

A central theme in the first section of the novel is traditional Muscogee culture. After opening the novel with a description of the Creeks' Edenic life in a virgin landscape, Callahan focuses on accounts of Muscogee customs and the theme of cross-acculturation. While Genevieve teaches Wynema about the culture of the dominant society, the little girl and Gerald Keithly instruct the teacher about the culture of the Muscogees. Undoubtedly, Callahan made Gerald her major spokesperson on Muscogee ethnohistory because he would be more convincing to non-Indian audiences than a Muscogee child just learning English. If Genevieve represents the possibility of how educated whites can learn to understand and love Creek people, Wynema exemplifies the extent to which full-bloods can become acculturated while retaining their commitment to their people. Although careful to defend the tribe's tastes and customs, Callahan may occasionally reveal her own ambivalence in her depictions of Genevieve's reputation. One such example is Genevieve's reaction to "sofky," a favorite Creek dish made from dried hominy, which Callahan describes as palatable when fresh but is preferred by Indians "after it has soured and smells more like a swill-barrel than anything else." The author pits Gerald's sympathy for Muscogee customs against Genevieve's "white is right" attitude during their discussion of the tribal "busk" or Green Corn Dance. He humorously defends the "busk" as more civilized than the galas held by whites on the grounds that Indians choose more sensible places for their dances than do whites, their "squaws" dress more modestly, and they dance only a few times a year, unlike whites who dance every night during "the season."[42]

Callahan also includes discussions of Indian issues. Genevieve's and Wynema's spirited debate on allotment of Creek land under the General Allotment or Dawes Act of 1887 illustrates their knowledge of Creek issues and their intellectual prowess. Though at first Wynema staunchly advocates allotment of Creek land, she finally acknowledges the validity of Genevieve's argument that allotment will be "the ruin of the poor, ignorant savage."[43] Callahan also includes discussions of Muscogee political corruption and the sale of alcohol to Indians in violation of federal laws.

Indian–white relations is the topic of the last third of the novel, devoted to Lakota Sioux hostilities, the murder of Sitting Bull, and a massacre that corresponds to what happened at Wounded Knee. This abrupt departure from the earlier romance plot was probably added to an almost completed novel. Accompanied by Robin, Carl rejoins the Sioux and becomes an intermediary between them and the army. Although Chief Wildfire realizes that resistance will have disastrous consequences for the Sioux, he and his young warriors choose to die rather than surrender: "is it right for the nation who have been trampled upon, whose land, whose property, whose liberty, whose everything but life have been taken away, to meekly submit and still bow their heads for the yoke?"[44] Inevitably, Wildfire, his wife, and followers die in a battle. Through the stories of Chikena, a surviving widow, Callahan tells of how the Sioux were starved by Indian agents and massacred by the army. Appalled by the events of late 1890 and early 1891 and by newspaper coverage of them, Callahan sarcastically proclaims that it is not her province to "show how brave it was for a great, strong nation to quell a riot caused by the dancing of a few 'bucks' – for *civilized* soldiers to slaughter indiscriminately, Indian women and children. . . . Will history term the treatment of the Indians by the United States Government, right and honorable?"[45]

Although Callahan devotes most of the novel to Indian issues, she also includes some strong statements by Genevieve, Wynema, and Robin about equality for women, reflecting her strong support of the movement to achieve equality for women that gained strength in the 1890s. Wynema is convinced that one day, "'the inferior of man,' the 'weaker vessel' shall stand grandly by the side of that 'noble lord of creation,' his equal in *every* respect." While she confesses that Creek women have no voice in the councils and do not speak in any public gathering or in churches, Wynema proclaims that "we are waiting for our more civilized white sisters to gain their liberty, and thus set us an example which we shall not be slow to follow."[46] Robin expresses his whole-hearted support. Genevieve's ideas on equality are expressed in her dialogue with the narrow-minded Maurice, in which she angrily rejects his ideas that women's rights are immodest and unwomanly: "The idea of a woman being unwomanly and immodest because she happens to be thoughtful and to have 'two ideas above an oyster,' to know a little beyond and above house and dress is perfectly absurd and untrue."[47]

Like Callahan's, Pauline Johnson's writing vividly expresses her anger at the injustices experienced by Indians and women. Though a loyal Canadian, Johnson both performed and published in the United States. Born in 1861 on the Grand River Reserve of the Six Nations, near Brantford, Ontario, Johnson was the daughter of George Henry Martin Johnson, a Mohawk chief, and Emily Susanna Howells, an English-born cousin of the American writer, William Dean Howells. After their marriage, George built his bride an impressive house called Chiefswood, which became a gathering place for Indian and white visitors; the pair established a reputation as gracious hosts for their many famous guests. Johnson and her siblings were primarily educated at home by their mother, who stimulated her children's love of literature by reading them the English Romantics. A strong influence on Johnson was her grandfather, Smoke (Sakayengwaraton or "Disappearing Mist") Johnson, a hero of the War of 1812 and renowned orator in the Iroquois councils. A gifted orator in his own right, her father frequently made speeches on behalf of his people and served as a liaison between whites and his people.

From ages fourteen through sixteen, Johnson attended the Brantford Collegiate Institute, where she particularly enjoyed performing in plays and pageants. In 1877 she returned to Chiefswood, where she devoted the next two years to visiting friends and writing poetry, little of which has survived. Not all of Johnson's childhood was idyllic. Because of his efforts to eradicate illegal alcohol and timber traffic on the reserve, George was severely beaten on three occasions, during one of which he was shot as well. Despite these attacks, he redoubled his efforts to curb lawlessness on the reserve.

After her father's death in 1884, Johnson, her mother, and sister moved to nearby Brantford in 1885. Johnson then returned to writing poems, several of which were published in the *Week*, a Toronto journal. Her public career began in 1892, when her recitation of her poem "A Cry from an Indian Wife" electrified her audience. To earn money to go to Great Britain to arrange for the publication of her poetry, Johnson toured for the next two years, performing her works to enthusiastic audiences in Ontario and along the East Coast of the United States. Often billed as "The Mohawk Princess," Johnson performed the Indian portion of her program in a fringed buckskin dress of her own design and the remainder of the program in an evening gown. In 1894, she traveled to London, where she became popular with society and arranged for the publication of her first volume of poetry, *The White Wampum* (1895).

For most of her adult life, performing was Johnson's major source of income. Following her return from London, she expanded her tours to midwestern and western Canada and Michigan, making Winnipeg her home after the death of her mother in 1898. At this time she became engaged to Charles Robert Lumbley Drayton, whose parents strongly opposed their son's marriage to a mixed-blooded, older woman and stage performer. He broke the engagement in 1900 in order to marry someone else. Vulnerable after her broken engagement and the loss of her mother, she may have become romantically involved with her unscrupulous manager, Charles Wuerz.[48] Johnson may allude to the tragic love affair in three of her best poems published after her death: "Morrow Land," "Heidelburgh," and "Song." In 1901, Walter McRaye became her partner and manager.

Johnson's second book of poems, *Canadian Born* (1903), disappointed her critics because it included many poems written years earlier and because the new ones lacked the fresh voice of the earlier volume. Nevertheless, she received rave reviews for her performances in London in 1906. After returning to Canada, Johnson and McRaye embarked in 1907 on an American tour. From 1907 to 1912, she frequently contributed stories and articles to *Boy's World* and the *Mother's Magazine*, both published by the Cook Publishing Company of Elgin, Illinois, near Chicago; the latter was a widely read journal with a circulation in 1910 of 600,000. Her small income from writing enabled Johnson to retire from performing in 1908 and settle permanently in Vancouver. During this period, she began her collaboration with Joe Capilano, the Squamish chief she met in London in 1906. Her imaginative and dramatic re-creations of his Chinook stories, which originally appeared in the *Vancouver Province* in 1910 and 1911,

were published as *The Legends of Vancouver* (1911). One of her best works, the
volume also contained some Iroquois tales. In 1912, Johnson published the
poetry collection *Flint and Feather*, including poems from her two earlier volumes as well as additional work. She died of cancer in Vancouver in 1913. Two
collections of her prose were published posthumously that year: *The Shagganappi*,
her adventure stories for boys, and *The Moccasin Maker*, which assembled her
women's stories and her essay "A Pagan in St. Paul's Cathedral."

Until recently, Johnson has been known primarily for her poetry. Published
simultaneously in Toronto and Boston, *The White Wampum* (1895), containing
thirty-six poems, established her as a Native writer of talent and sensibility.
Canadian Born (1903) contains thirty-one poems. Critics particularly praised her
lyrics in *The White Wampum*. Her most famous poem is "The Song My Paddle
Sings," which generations of Canadian schoolchildren memorized. Another favorite is her descriptive-reflective "Shadow River, Muskoka," a delicate lyric in
which she depicts her reactions as she floats on the river. "In the Shadows,"
which recalls Tennyson's "Soft and Low," captures the author's sensuous response
to nature while canoeing languorously on the river. Her nature lyrics reflect her
reading of Thomson, Shelley, and Swinburne. The best of her nature poems in
Canadian Born is "Crows' Nest Pass," undoubtedly influenced by Shelley's "Mont
Blanc." Among her finest lyrics are "Morrow Land," written at Easter 1900;
"Heidelburgh" (originally titled "To C. W."); and "Song" – all unpublished in
her lifetime. While "Heidelburgh" reveals powerful and bitter emotions not
present in Johnson's earlier work, "Song" demonstrates her mature lyricism:

> The night-long shadows faded into gray,
> Then silvered into glad and gold sunlight,
> Because you came to me, like a new day
> Born of the beauty of an autumn night.[49]

Both volumes included poems devoted to Native American subjects; most of the
eight such poems in *The White Wampum* are dramatic monologues or narratives.
The destructiveness of intertribal warfare is the theme of several. In "As Red
Men Die," Johnson vividly, if melodramatically, portrays the bravery of her
Mohawk ancestor taken captive by the Hurons. He defies his torturers, choosing to walk to his death on a bed of fire rather than be a slave. Two poems deal
with the bravery of Indian women. "Ojistoh" is a sexually complex monologue
that depicts a Mohawk wife's struggle to outwit her Huron kidnappers. Riding
behind one of her captors, Ojistoh seduces her enemy into loosening her bonds
and then kills him with his own knife. George W. Lyon gives a somewhat over-
wrought interpretation: Ojistoh, having "lulled her Huron captor into careless-
ness with his own stereotype of sexuality, asserts her right to power and equality
by murdering him, metaphorically, with his own phallus." He is on firmer
ground in his comment that when violence occurs in her work, Johnson often
attempts to demonstrate that "whites need not fear Indians."[50] Another example

of this attitude is the moving "Cattle Thief," in which a Cree woman's powerful protest speech about how hostile whites have destroyed Indians dissuades a group of white vigilantes from mutilating the fearless Brave Eagle, whom they have just murdered for stealing cattle to feed his people. *Canadian Born* contains two poems on Indian women. "The Quill Worker" portrays the daughter of a Sioux chief, while one of her most poignant, "The Corn Husker," depicts an old Indian woman who remembers a time before injustice banished her people from their lands; now they are unheeded "like the dead husks that rustle through her hands."[51]

The encroachment of settlers on Indian life is another theme in Johnson's Indian poems in *White Wampum*. "A Cry from an Indian Wife" expresses a wife's anguish as she alternates between her grief at knowing her husband will probably die if he goes to war against the settlers, and her courageous commitment to fighting their depredations against her people. "Wolverine," a dramatic monologue told in dialect by a settler, chronicles whites' unjust treatment of an Indian brave who tries to help them. The tragic-but-loyal love between a settler and an Indian woman is the focus of "The Pilot of the Plains," while the inevitable displacement of Indians by settlers is the theme of "The Happy Hunting Grounds" and "Joe," the portrait of a nine-year-old "semi-savage" settler.

From the beginning of her career, Johnson wrote as a mediator between the Indian – particularly the Iroquois – and non-Indian worlds. She explained Iroquois history, culture, and customs in such articles as "A'bram" (1891); "Indian Medicine Men and Their Magic" (1892); "The Iroquois of the Grand River" (1894); "Iroquois Women of Canada" (1909), a reworked version of "Mothers of a Great Red Race" (1908); and "The Great New Year White Dog: Sacrifice of the Onondagas" (1911).[52] Several of these have not been reprinted. Johnson's criticism of how Indian women were portrayed in literature by non-Indians is expressed in "A Strong Race Opinion on the Indian Girl in Modern Fiction" (1892), most of which is reprinted in Betty Keller's biography, *Pauline*. Here the writer strongly attacks white authors for denying Indian girls spontaneity, originality, and specific tribal background while depicting them as suicidal and as victims of doomed love affairs.

After 1907, Johnson turned her energies to prose. Like many heroines in nineteenth-century women's fiction, those in Johnson's stories inevitably triumph over great difficulty. Both they and their heroes recognize that genuine love between men and women reflects shared values. Like Callahan, Johnson combines the domestic romance with protest literature, expressing her anger at the injustices experienced by women and Native Americans. "A Red Girl's Reasoning" and "As It Was in the Beginning," two of the best stories in *The Moccasin Maker,* emphasize these themes. In both, Johnson combines the plot of mixed-blood women betrayed by weak white lovers with a forceful attack on white religious hypocrisy. "A Red Girl's Reasoning," awarded the 1892 prize for fiction by *Dominion Magazine*, was one of the most popular works in Johnson's performance repertory. The story focuses on non-Indian refusal to accept the sanctity of the tribal marriage ceremonies of settlers to Indian women and on the independence of women. Johnson presents these issues through the plot of domestic romance in which the heroine, Christine Robinson, gains her goal of marriage to Jimmy Robinson. The author departs from this pattern by having Christine leave Jimmy in order to maintain her sense of virtue and self-worth as a mixed-blood and as a woman. Just as Winnemucca employs a strategy of multiple perspectives and voices, so does Johnson. In Christine's defense of Indian marriage and insistence on independence, Johnson uses the voices of Native Americans and women, while in her characterization of Christine, the author uses the voice of an outsider with inside knowledge. This bicultural perspective is exemplified in her comment on Christine's love of velvet: "No woman in Canada, has she but the faintest dash of native blood in her veins, but loves velvets and silks."[53]

In "As It Was in the Beginning," Esther, who is Cree and French, takes physical and verbal revenge against her unfaithful white lover, Lawrence. Here Johnson uses first-person narration to intensify the heroine's reactions. Father Paul takes young Esther from her family and places her in a mission school. Denied permission to return to her parents for even a day, Esther is desperately lonely for her family, language, and culture. Johnson combines the plot of victimization with the domestic romance of the scorned woman. Though Lawrence, her childhood playmate and the priest's nephew, vows his love, Esther later overhears Father Paul dissuade him from marrying her because of her "uncertain blood." Enraged by their treachery, Esther poisons Lawrence in his sleep, thereby destroying the person the priest loves most. Although those who suspect her of the murder attribute it to the fact that she is a "Redskin," Esther reminds the reader that "they seem to have forgotten I am a woman."[54] Throughout the story, Esther is essentially silent in the presence of whites because English is the weapon they have used to eradicate her Cree heritage and to betray her. Although Elizabeth Looseley complains that the depiction of the white missionary is difficult to accept, "even with due allowance for Victorian melodrama," the missionary displays the prejudice against mixed-bloods common in American literature of the period.[55]

"The Legend of Lillooet Falls," "The Tenas Klootchman," and "Catharine of the 'Crow's Nest'" depict the deep love Indian women feel for their birth and adopted children, as well as the roles they play as guardians of tribal traditions. Mother love is also a powerful force in Johnson's stories about frontier women. Several of the plots of her stories about white wives and mothers are based on true stories that the writer heard. "Mother o' the Men," "Nest Builder," and "Envoy Extraordinary" all portray these women as loyal helpmeets who exhibit both courage and resourcefulness in caring for their families. Johnson stresses the isolation a wife can feel if she follows her husband into the wilderness or when a quarrel separates family members. The fullest description of the ideal wife and mother appears in "My Mother," a fictional account of the courtship and marriage of her parents that emphasizes that their relationship was based on mutual love, respect, and interests. In "A Pagan in St. Paul's Cathedral," Johnson draws parallels between Indian and white religions, concluding that there are no real differences. Finally, in *Legends of Vancouver* (1911), she describes in poetic detail the places alluded to in these Indian stories. Framing them with descriptions of the circumstances of the storytelling, she concludes with a return to the setting, storyteller, and listener. Here she uses a far more conversational style than she does in her fiction and poetry.

Another Native American woman who began publishing at the turn of the century is Zitkala-Ša. Like Winnemucca, Zitkala-Ša became a powerful spokesperson on Indian issues. Born Gertrude Simmons on the Yankton Reservation in 1876, she was the daughter of Ellen Simmons (Tate I Yohin Win or Reaches for the Wind, Dakota Sioux) and a white trader named Felker, who left before her birth. Although Ellen Simmons gave her daughter the last name of the second of her three white husbands, she reared Gertrude as a traditional Dakota and instilled in her a deep distrust of non-Indians.[56] As an adult, Gertrude gave herself the Lakota name "Zitkala-Ša" (Red Bird).[57] Her life as a traditional Dakota ended in 1884, when, lured by missionaries' promises of all the apples she could eat and a train ride, the eight-year-old girl convinced her mother to allow her to attend White's Manual Labor Institute, a Quaker boarding school for Indians in Wabash, Indiana. After finishing six years at the White's Institute in 1895, Zitkala-Ša defied her mother's wishes by entering Earlham College in Richmond, Indiana. Increasingly estranged from her mother and her people, in 1898 Zitkala-Ša accepted Colonel Richard H. Pratt's offer to teach at Carlisle Indian Industrial School in Carlisle, Pennsylvania. Disillusioned by the boarding school system, she left Carlisle to study at the New England Conservatory in Boston during 1900 and 1901. There the author met artists and intellectuals who encouraged her literary career. Using the name Zitkala-Ša, she published autobiographical articles in the *Atlantic Monthly* (1900, 1902), *Harper's Magazine* (1901), and *Everybody's Magazine* (1901),[58] which were later republished in *American Indian Stories* (1921). She returned to Yankton to collect material for *Old Indian Legends* (1901).

In March 1901 Zitkala-Ša became engaged to Carlos Montezuma (Yavapai), a Chicago physician and activist who strongly advocated assimilation. She broke off the engagement in August because she refused to move to Chicago to become a physician's wife and he would not move to Yankton. In May 1902, Zitkala-Ša married Raymond Talefease Bonnin, a Yankton Sioux employed by the Indian Service (predecessor of the Bureau of Indian Affairs). Later that year, the Bonnins moved to the Uintah Ouraye Ute Agency in Duchesne, Utah, where he had been assigned, remaining until 1916. Their only child, Raymond Ohiya, was born in 1903. Zitkala-Ša's marriage and move to Utah essentially ended her literary career, although in 1913 she collaborated with William Hanson on *The Sun Dance*, an Indian opera performed by the New York Light Opera Guild as the American opera of the year in 1937. Restless and unhappy, she taught, clerked, gave lectures, and volunteered in the Indian community.

The author's political career began in 1914, when she became a member of the advisory board of the Society for the American Indian (SAI), founded in 1911. After being elected secretary in 1916, Zitkala-Ša moved with her family to Washington, DC. From 1918 to 1919 she edited SAI's *American Indian Magazine*. Zitkala-Ša became an active and effective lobbyist for such causes as banning peyote use, Indian policy reform, and citizenship for American Indians.[59] A popular lecturer, she often delivered her talks in traditional dress. Conflicts within the SAI led to its demise in 1920, and during the 1920s, Zitkala-Ša worked with the Indian Welfare Committee of the General Federation of Women's Clubs and the American Indian Defense Association. In 1924, when Native Americans were finally given citizenship, she was appointed by the Indian Rights Association to investigate allegations that the federal government abused Oklahoma Indians. Two years later, the Bonnins formed the National Congress of American Indians (NCAI), with Raymond as secretary and, until her death, Zitkala-Ša as president. They effectively lobbied Congress and the Bureau of Indian Affairs on behalf of individual claimants and various Indian causes. After her death in 1938, Zitkala-Ša was buried in Arlington Cemetery.

Zitkala-Ša's most important book is her *American Indian Stories* (1921), which contains her autobiographical narratives, essays, and short stories. Particularly significant are her three autobiographical essays, "Impressions of an Indian Childhood," "The School Days of an Indian Girl," and "An Indian Teacher Among Indians." In her foreword to the 1979 edition, Dexter Fisher writes that these narratives represent "one of the first attempts by a Native American woman to write her own story without the aid of an editor, an interpreter, or an ethnographer." Fisher describes these essays as "emblems of the experience of many Indians living in transition between two worlds – the remembered past and the alien present, tradition and change."[60] In "Zitkala-Ša: The Evolution of a Writer," Fisher concludes that the author "struggled toward a vision of wholeness in which the conflicting parts of her existence could be reconciled. That she did not fully succeed is evident in her work, which is a model of ambivalences, of oscillations between two diametrically opposed worlds, but is also a model of retrieved possibilities. . . ."[61]

Fisher's binary perspective, however, does not address the issue of the personal, cultural borderland that the author creates for herself – one that is neither Dakota nor white but rather contains elements of both cultures. The author's struggles exemplify those by other traditionally raised Native Americans, particularly those separated from their families and sent to boarding schools. Too often Native Americans engaged in this struggle are depicted as "caught between the two worlds," and their failure to choose one over the other is portrayed as leaving them in limbo. What Zitkala-Ša and other Native American autobiographers reveal is their effort to establish their own identities in a cultural borderland, in which they are influenced by the world views of both their Native American heritage and the dominant society. Martha J. Cutter argues that Zitkala-Ša's failure to create a unified self is not a flaw because the author crafts a work "which calls generic standards of autobiography into question by refusing to conform to them." To Cutter the autobiographical essays reveal that the author is struggling "with the predominant (European, male) paradigm of autobiography, creating a narrative which in both form and content rejects the notion of a unified, coherent, transcendent identity achieved through linguistic self-authentication."[62]

Zitkala-Ša uses a variety of voices in her three autobiographical essays. In her analysis of the influence of the sentimental tradition on Zitkala-Ša, Laura Wexler considerably overstates the case when she argues that by the time the author wrote these essays her "self-conception had been so effectively ensnared within the codes of sentiment that there was no Indian in them that was left untouched by Western codes." Such a conclusion ignores the power of Zitkala-Ša's Dakota heritage and voice. In "Impressions of an Indian Childhood," Zitkala-Ša adopts the voice of a young Dakota child to depict what Cutter calls an "Edenic" life lived in harmony with nature, family, and tribe.[63] Here the writer stresses the importance to Dakota education of oral tradition, highlighting both the stories that stimulated her imagination and taught her about her tribe, and the verbal instruction that she received from her mother, aunt, and tribespeople on how to be a good Dakota. The scene in which she lies with her head in her mother's lap listening to the stories told by the elders exemplifies the warm, loving family life of this traditional world. Zitkala-Ša emphasizes that this culture is under attack from non-Indians, who have taken tribal land, force marched the Yanktons to their present reservation, and are greedy for more land. Another threat is posed by the missionaries, who, like Satan in the Garden of Eden, lure eight-year-old Gertrude away from her Dakota "paradise" with promises of red apples and a train ride to the East. Zitkala-Ša vividly depicts her mother's pain at losing her daughter, despite her realization that the child "will need an education when she is grown, for then there will be fewer real Dakotas, and many more palefaces." Prophetically, her mother predicts that her "daughter must suffer keenly in this experiment."[64] Wexler writes that Zitkala-Ša uses her own reactions to portray her mother's state of mind as the carriage carries the young child away. As the child sees "the lonely figure of my mother vanish in the distance," she feels "suddenly weak, as if I might fall limp to the ground. I was in the hands of strangers whom my mother did not fully trust. I no longer felt free to be myself, or to voice my own feelings."[65]

"The School Days of an Indian Girl" powerfully portrays the author's traumatic transition from traditional Yankton childhood to the harsh world of the White Manual Labor Institute, depicted as a cultural fall from a Dakota Eden into a hellish non-Indian school that neither nurtured the Indian children nor respected their cultures.[66] For Margo Lukens, Zitkala-Ša's narration of this cultural conflict is a "warrior's struggle" because she recognizes the system of white education to be part of the violent destruction of her people and their culture. Zitkala-Ša loses her spirit when after hiding to escape her tormentors, she is tied to a chair and has her hair cut in a style only cowards wore: "In my anguish I moaned for my mother, but no one came to comfort me. Not a soul reasoned quietly with me, as my own mother used to do; for now I was only one of many little animals driven by the herder."[67] In the course of this essay the child moves from being a terrified victim to an active rebel who, when instructed to mash turnips, pounds them so hard that she breaks the bottom of the bowl and who scratches out the eyes of Satan's pictures in *The Stories of the Bible*.

"The School Days of an Indian Girl" also describes Zitkala-Ša's estrangement from her mother and her former life when, after an absence of three years, she returns home for a visit. Disconsolate because she does not have the proper clothes to go to a reservation dance, she becomes enraged when her mother tries to mollify her by giving her an Indian Bible, which gave the teenager no help and was a "perfect delusion" to her mother.[68] Her decision to attend Earlham College in Richmond, Indiana, further alienates the author from both her mother, who strongly disapproved of her decision, and her people. Zitkala-Ša's acculturation and achievements as an award-winning college orator did not protect her from the prejudice she would encounter. During her speech at the state oratory contest, "college rowdies" displayed a large white flag with a "forlorn Indian girl" and words ridiculing the college for being represented by a "squaw." The "little taste of victory" that she received did not satisfy the hunger in her heart as she remembered her mother, "holding a charge" against her.[69]

"An Indian Teacher Among Indians" is written in the voice of a mature young woman who has completed her education and embarks on her first endeavor to help Indian people. Forced by illness to leave school, Zitkala-Ša is overcome by a "leaden weakness when she reports to her teaching position."[70] Sent off to the Sioux reservation to recruit students, she finds her reservation at the mercy of unscrupulous whites and her family in severe financial difficulty because her brother, David (Dawée) Simmons, was fired from his government job after trying to get justice for his tribe. The author is bitterly disillusioned by an Indian educational system in which incompetent and substance-abusing white teachers show little sensitivity to their students' needs. Her personal journey concludes with her decision to leave her teaching job to study music in Boston. According to Wexler, in this act Zitkala-Ša literally forsakes "the pseudoliteracy of 'the white man's papers'" and rebels against her years of "sentimental indoctrination." Zitkala-Ša's departure from Carlisle indicates that the author ceases to "apply the ill-fitting model of domestication" and begins to seek "another, sterner tongue."[71] Zitkala-Ša ends the essay with an attack on those whites who have visited Indian schools, boasting of their charity to Indians, but who did not pause "to question whether real life or long-lasting death lies beneath this semblance of civilization."[72] Her conclusion makes clear that although at this point she feels the need to gain more education to chart her own path, she will be an eloquent spokesperson for her people. This role enables her to live in a cultural borderland. There she achieves her greatest success, though at the painful cost of separation from family and tribe.

In 1902, Ginn published Zitkala-Ša's *Old Indian Legends*, fourteen *ohunkan* or fictional tales told in the evenings. Angel De Cora, a renowned Hochunk artist, illustrated the volume. Six of the stories deal with the adventures of the Sioux Trickster, Iktomi or Unktomi (Spider), whose appetites and tricks often get him into trouble. Jeanne Smith comments that Zitkala-Ša aligns the trickster with cultural threat in her legends. In her interpretation of the traditional "Dance in Buffalo Skull" story, Zitkala-Ša drops the comic ending of the tale, in which the trickster gets his head caught in a skull after seeing mice dancing there, and tells it from the view of the terrified field mice, who flee. Other stories about traditional figures in Sioux mythology focus on Iya or Eya, the glutton with magic powers that enable him to deceive people so that he can eat them; Anuk-ite or Old Double Face, an evil giant who likes to kidnap and torture children; and The Blood Clot Boy, a culture hero. Some deal with animals. Smith points out that the author connects traditional legend with contemporary issues in "The Badger and the Bear," "The Tree Bound," and "Shooting the Red Eagle." These "tales have special resonance in the context of their 1901 publication, when the allotment act and the mission boarding schools were gigantically, indifferently swallowing up Lakota lands and culture."[73] Zitkala-Ša's stories belong in a larger tradition, for many Sioux authors have published collections of tribal stories, including Charles Eastman (1858–1939), Marie McLaughlin (b. 1842), Luther Standing Bear (1868–1939), and Ella Deloria (1889–1971). Like most of the Indian and non-Indian interpreters of Native American stories during this period, Zitkala-Ša omits the ribald humor often present in the unexpurgated versions of traditional stories. She uses an easily accessible but descriptive, romantic style in retelling the stories she had heard since childhood.

Zitkala-Ša was also an accomplished fiction writer. "A Warrior's Daughter," one of her most interesting stories, portrays the courage and determination of Tusee, a beautiful daughter of a chief. Disguised as an old woman, Tusee sneaks into the enemy camp to rescue her lover. Though such heroic exploits are more commonly associated with Sioux warriors, Beatrice Medicine (Lakota) writes that women warriors in Dakota and Lakota society participated in war for "glory as well as revenge, and some even led war expeditions."[74] "The Trial Path," originally published in *Harper's Magazine* (March 1901), is a complex story of Dakota justice, in which a grandmother tells her granddaughter about how her husband, when he was young, killed his closest friend and rival for the grandmother's hand. The victim's father decrees that the murderer can live if he rides a wild pony to the center of a circle. After the warrior succeeds, the family of his victim accept him as their son and harmony is maintained within the camp circle.

As in "The School Days of an Indian Girl," Zitkala-Ša's disillusionment with missionary schools informs "The Soft Hearted Sioux," first published in *Harper's Magazine* (October 1901). Patricia Okker argues that the melodramatic elements in the story "suggest its affinity to late nineteenth-century American naturalism."[75] Told in the first person, the story describes the cultural conflict faced by a young Sioux who has returned to his tribe after years at a mission

school. Determined to convert his people to Christianity, he sends away the
medicine man, whose ministrations his dying father cannot live without, and
vainly tries to save the old man with his Christian prayers. Urged by his parents
to hunt for meat lest they starve, the young man kills a cow and then murders
the white man who catches him. He subsequently turns himself in and accepts
his death sentence. Okker perceptively comments that in the story, Zitkala-Ša
uses the language of Christianity to demonstrate the narrator's ultimate rejection
of Christianity and its "soft heart." The author portrays the narrator's emotional
detachment from his own fate as a sign of cultural displacement.[76] The story
vividly portrays the sense of alienation experienced by boarding school children
separated from their families and culture.

Zitkala-Ša also wrote essays and editorials on Indian issues. "America's Indian
Problem" is included in *American Indian Stories*. Here she reminds her readers
that Indian hospitality saved the early settlers from starvation. Pointing out all
the injustices Indians have suffered and that they are still wards rather than
citizens, she argues that "now the time is at hand when the American Indian
shall have his day in court through the help of the women of America." Sum-
ming up her contributions to the fight for Indian rights, David L. Johnson and
Raymond Wilson conclude that she "challenged American Indians and the
people of the United States to recognize the potential and ability of the American
Indian to contribute to American society."[77]

All five of these writers made significant contributions to the development of
a history of Native American literature written in English. Though they were
raised to a varying extent within the traditions of their tribes, they strove to
educate their largely mainstream audiences about Indian cultures and to fight
for justice for native peoples. These authors also emphasize women's roles, a
topic ignored by male writers in the nineteenth and early twentieth centuries.
Most of these Native American women wrote within the sentimental tradition
of the age which they and other women authors used to achieve political goals.
Like the works by many African American and popular women authors of the
period, their writing lacks the sophistication of *belles lettres*. Nevertheless, they
offer powerful statements about the significance of Native American cultures
and about how Native Americans and women fought for justice, equality, and
independence. The indomitable spirits of these Native American women writers
is summed up in Zitkala-Ša's words about herself: "I raise both hands to the
great blue overhead, and my spirit revels in a freedom no less than the vast
concave! I am free! I am proud! I am chosen!"[78]

NOTES

This essay incorporates revised portions of the following: "Three American Indian Auto-
biographers," *Redefining American Literary History*, ed. A. LaVonne Brown Ruoff and Jerry
W. Ward, Jr (New York: Modern Language Association, 1990), 251–69; "E. Pauline
Johnson," *Native American Writers of the United States*, vol. 175 of *Dictionary of Literary*

Biography, ed. Kenneth M. Roemer (Detroit: Brucolli Clark Layman/Gale Research, 1997), 131–6; and "Introduction," in S. Alice Callahan, *Wynema: A Child of the Forest*, ed. A. LaVonne Brown Ruoff (1891; reprint, Lincoln: University of Nebraska Press, 1997), xiii–xlvii.

1   Mikhail M. Bakhtin describes "heteroglossia" as serving two speakers at the same time and expressing simultaneously the direct intention of the character who is speaking the refracted intention of the author. Bakhtin, *The Dialogic Imagination: Four Essays*, trans. Caryl Emerson and Michael Holquist (Austin: University of Texas Press, 1981), 324.

2   The spellings and designations of tribal names in this essay are those in current use: Ojibwe rather than Ojibwa or Chippewa, Paiute rather than Piute, Hochunk rather than Winnebago.

3   Joyce Warren, *The American Narcissus: Individualism and Women in Nineteenth-Century American Fiction* (New Brunswick: Rutgers University Press, 1989), 8.

4   Quoted in Richard G. Bremer, *Indian Agent and Wilderness Scholar: The Life of Henry Rowe Schoolcraft* (Mount Pleasant: Clark Historical Library, Central Michigan University Press, 1987), 111.

5   As Henry acknowledged in his journal on July 28, 1822, "I have in fact stumbled, as it were, on the only family in Northwest America who could in Indian lore have acted as my guide, philosopher, and friend." Quoted in Philip P. Mason, "Introduction," in Henry Schoolcraft, *The Literary Voyager or Muzzeniegun* (1962; reprint, Westport, CT: Greenwood Press, 1974), xxv. Subsequent references to this source will be abbreviated *LV*. Though he published twenty volumes and hundreds of articles describing his explorations and Indian culture, Henry is best known today for his six-volume *Historical and Statistical Information Respecting the History, Condition, and Prospects of the Indian Tribes of the United States* (1851–7), his two-volume *Algic Researches* (1839), and *The Red Race of America* (1847).

6   H. Schoolcraft, *LV*, 38–9.

7   H. Schoolcraft, "To Our Correspondent, Leelinau" (December 1, 1826) and "To Correspondents" (February 7, 1827), cited in *LV*, 5, 84.

8   "The Origin of the Robin: An Oral Allegory," *LV* No. 3 (January 1827); "Moowis: The Indian Coquette," *LV* No. 4 (January 12, 1827); "The Forsaken Brother," *LV* No. 8 (February 13, 1827); "Mishosa, or the Magician and His Daughters," *LV* No. 5 (January 1827); "The Origin of Miscodeed or the Maid of Taquimenon," *LV* No. 11 (February 1827).

9   No. 13 (March 10, 1827), stanza 1, lines 3–6; cited in *LV*, 142–3; No. 13 (March 10, 1837), line 32, cited in *LV*, 139.

10   No. 14 [March 28, 1827], stanza 1, cited in *LV*, 157.

11   Julie Cruikshank et al., *Life Lived Like a Story: Life Stories of Three Yukon Elders*, American Indian Lives Series (Lincoln: University of Nebraska Press, 1990), 2; Arnold Krupat, *The Voice in the Margin: Native American Literature and the Canon* (Berkeley: University of California Press, 1989), 133.

12   According to Sidonie Smith, conventional women's autobiographies "engage the fictions of selfhood that constitute the idea of woman and specify the parameters of female subjectivity." Smith writes that in the autobiographies by women of color and the working class, the "identities of race and gender, sometimes even of nationality, intersect and confound those of gender." She concludes that a woman autobiographer from these grounds finds herself "resident on the margins of discourse,

always removed from the center of power within the culture she inhabits." Smith, *A Poetics of Women's Autobiography: Marginality and the Fictions of Self-Representation* (Bloomington: Indiana University Press, 1987), 50, 51. Nellie Y. McKay stresses that for the black female, in the search for self "issues of gender are equally important as those of race," a matter that black men usually overlooked. McKay, "Nineteenth-Century Black Women's Spiritual Autobiographies: Religious Faith and Self-Empowerment," in *Interpreting Women's Lives: Feminist Theory and Personal Narratives*, ed. the Personal Narratives Group (Bloomington: Indiana University Press, 1989), 142.

According to Bella Brodzki and Celeste Schenck, "autobiography localizes the very program of much feminist theory – the reclaiming of the female subject – even as it foregrounds the central issue of contemporary critical thought – the problematic status of the self." Brodzki and Schenck, *Life/Lines: Theorizing Women's Autobiography* (Ithaca: Cornell University Press, 1988), 1–2. For a discussion of Native American women's autobiography, see Gretchen M. Bataille and Kathleen Mullen Sands, *American Indian Women: Telling Their Lives* (Lincoln: University of Nebraska Press, 1984).

13 Reviewing the Winnemucca family's performance at the Metropolitan Theatre on October 22, 1864, *The Daily Alta California* (October 22, 1864) sarcastically referred to them as "The Royal Family." Quoted in Gae Whitney Canfield, *Sarah Winnemucca of the Northern Piutes* (Norman: University of Oklahoma Press, 1983), 39. According to Canfield, the press often referred to Sarah as the "Piute Princess" or "Princess Sarah" (92, 162). In 1885, when Winnemucca appeared in San Francisco, *The Morning Call* enthused "In the history of the Indians she and Pocahontas will be the principal female characters . . ." (quoted in Canfield, *Sarah Winnemucca*, 222).

14 Canfield, *Sarah Winnemucca*, 39.

15 Ibid., 191, 77, 78.

16 The General Allotment Act of 1887 was designed to end the reservation system. Under the act, supported by both reformers and opportunists, Indians who took their land in severalty became citizens of the United States and were subject to all its obligations. Although the act was passed to enable Native Americans to become prosperous landowners, the measure instead ushered in an era in which Indians lost their land by fraud and force. By 1934, 60 percent of the land owned by Indians in 1887 had passed from their control. See Wilcomb E. Washburn, *The Indian in America* (New York: Harper and Row, 1975), 242–3. For an Indian view of the impact of allotment, see D'Arcy McNickle (Cree-Salish), *Native American Tribalism: Indian Survival and Renewals* (New York: Oxford University Press, 1973), 80–5, 91–2; this volume is an excellent source for the history of Indian–white relations in the twentieth century.

17 H. David Brumble, III, *American Indian Autobiography* (Berkeley: University of California Press, 1988), 65–6; Kathleen Mullen Sands, "Indian Women's Personal Narrative: Voices Past and Present," in *American Women's Autobiography: Fea(s)ts of Memory*, ed. Margo Culley (Madison: University of Wisconsin Press, 1992), 277.

18 Cheryl Walker, *Indian Nation: Native American Literature and Nineteenth-Century Nationalisms* (Durham: Duke University Press, 1997) 151.

19 Quoted in ibid.; see Shirley Samuels, ed., *The Culture of Sentiment: Race, Gender, and Sentimentality in Nineteenth-Century America* (New York: Oxford University Press, 1992).

20 Walker, *Indian Nation*, 152.

21 Mary Mann, "Editor's Preface," in Sarah Winnemucca, *Life Among the Piutes: Their Wrongs and Claims* (1883; reprint, Reno: University of Nevada Press, 1994), 3. Mary Mann wrote Eleanor Lewis on April 25, 1883 that "I don't think the English language ever got such a treatment before. I have to recur to her sometimes to know what a word is, as spelling is an unknown quantity to her. . . . but the story is heart-breaking, and told with a simplicity & eloquence that cannot be described . . ." (quoted in Canfield, *Sarah Winnemucca*, 203).

22 Canfield, *Sarah Winnemucca*, 204.

23 Brumble, *Autobiography*, 69; Brigitte Georgi-Findlay, "The Frontiers of Native American Women's Writing: Sarah Winnemucca's *Life Among the Piutes*," in *New Voices in Native American Literary Criticism*, ed. Arnold Krupat (Washington: Smithsonian Institution, 1993), 229.

24 Winnemucca, *Life Among the Piutes*, 53, 50; see Kilcup, *NCAWW*, 334–41.

25 Georgi-Findlay, "The Frontiers of Native American Women's Writing," 229.

26 Winnemucca, *Life Among the Piutes*, 228, 231.

27 Ibid., 205.

28 I do not suggest that *Life Among the Piutes* was influenced by captivity or slave narratives, as Brumble implies. Basing his comments on an early draft I sent him of my "Three Nineteenth-Century American Autobiographies," Brumble says that "we should not simply *assume* the degree of literacy and breadth of reading which Ruoff's argument would require of Winnemucca" (*American Indian Autobiography*, 61, 63, 69; Brumble's italics). My argument is simply that her autobiography is a complex blend of influences, Native American oral traditions, and popular literary forms. We do not know how much she read. The parallels may well reflect other influences. A skilled performer, she may have structured her narrative to reflect a storytelling style she had learned was effective on stage. She may also have incorporated suggestions from her audiences, spouse, friends, and editors. Thus, the parallels may mirror the taste of the age rather than the literary background of the narrator. In an otherwise fine essay, Georgi-Findlay inexplicably bases her responses to my discussions of Winnemucca on my "Western American Indian Writers, 1854–1960," [in *The Literary History of the American West*, ed. Thomas J. Lyon (Fort Worth: Texas Christian University Press, 1987), 1038–58] and on Brumble's interpretation of my argument, rather than on the published version of the latter.

29 Carolyn S. Fowler, "Sarah Winnemucca, Northern Paiute, ca. 1844–1891," in *American Indian Intellectuals*, ed. Margot Liberty, 1976 Proceedings of the American Ethnological Society (St Paul: West Publishing, 1978), 40.

30 Winnemucca, *Life Among the Piutes*, 69.

31 Sands, "Indian Women's Personal Narrative," 278.

32 Winnemucca, *Life Among the Piutes*, 243–4.

33 The author's name is listed on the title page as "S. Alice Callahan"; references to her in the *Indian Journal* and *Muskogee Phoenix* use the name "Alice." The title *Wynema* is probably derived from Winema, a woman subchief of the Modocs who saved the Indian Commissioner, A. B. Meacham, from death in 1872 during the fight at the Lava Beds. Meacham paid tribute to her in *Wi-ne-ma {The Woman Chief} and Her People* (1876). Carolyn Thomas Foreman indicates that the name was a favorite among the Indians. The Creek journalist and writer Alexander Lawrence Posey (1873–1907) named his daughter "Wynema." Foreman, "S. Alice Callahan:

Author of *Wynema: A Child of the Forest*," *Chronicles of Oklahoma* 33 (1955): 307, n. 3. The idea for the title may also have been suggested by the Choctaw writer who signed her columns in the *Muskogee Phoenix* as "Wa-min-ne" and "Winema." Information provided by Daniel F. Littlefield, Jr.

34 For histories of women's rights movements in Canada and the United States, see Catherine Lyle Cleverdon, *The Woman Suffrage Movement in Canada* (Toronto: University of Toronto Press, 1950); and Eleanor Flexner, *Century of Struggle: The Woman's Rights Movement in the United States* (Cambridge, MA: Harvard University Press, 1950, 1970).

35 The most important biographical source is Foreman's "S. Alice Callahan: Author of *Wynema, A Child of the Forest*," 306–15, 549; "Samuel Benton Callahan," an appendix to the article on Alice, contains a biography of her father. For the dates of the writer's attendance at the Wesleyan Female Institute, see the *Indian Journal*, June 21, 1988, p. 5, col. 1. Grant Foreman describes the origins of Harrell International Institute in *Muskogee: The Biography of an Oklahoma Town* (St Louis: privately printed, 1945), 52–4.

36 Ceremonial titles like Harjo, Fixico, and Emarthla, which Callahan uses in her novel, became family surnames. Several unrelated families took the Harjo name. Alexander Posey's maternal grandfather was Pahosa Harjo from Tuskegee. Chitto Harjo (Crazy Snake), who led the Muscogee opposition to allotment of tribal lands, came from another family. Information provided by Alan Cook, historic preservation consultant, Muscogee (Creek) Nation; and Daniel F. Littlefield, Jr. See Angie Debo, *The Road to Disappearance: A History of the Creek Indians* (Norman: University of Oklahoma Press, 1941), 293–4.

37 Nina Baym, *Women's Fiction: A Guide to Novels by and about Women in America, 1820–1870* (Ithaca: Cornell University Press, 1978), 17. Elaine Showalter indicates that novels by British women follow a similar pattern; see *A Literature of Their Own: British Women Novelists from Brontë to Lessing* (Princeton: Princeton University Press, 1977), 28–9. In depicting Genevieve's adjustment to life in the Creek Nation, Callahan does not, as did many other women authors of frontier novels in the nineteenth century, emphasize her heroine's response to an unfamiliar, hostile landscape, which the heroines of novels by women often labored to transform into gardens that reminded them of the homes they had left. See Annette Kolodny, *The Land Before Her: Fantasy and Experience of the American Frontiers, 1630–1860* (Chapel Hill: University of North Carolina Press, 1984), 8–9.

38 Callahan, *Wynema*, 4; see *NCAWW*, 553–6.

39 Teaching was one of the few acceptable occupations open to unmarried women on the frontier. See Robert Griswold, "Anglo Women and Domestic Ideology in the American West in the Nineteenth and Early Twentieth Centuries," in *Western Women: Their Land, Their Lives*, ed. Lillian Schlissel et al. (Albuquerque: University of New Mexico Press, 1988), 20.

40 Larzer Ziff, *The American 1890s: Life and Times of a Lost Generation* (1966; reprint, Lincoln: University of Nebraska Press, 1979), 278.

41 Jane Tompkins, *Sensational Designs: The Cultural Work of American Fiction, 1790–1860* (New York: Oxford University Press, 1985), 123, 126; Lauren Berlant, "The Female Woman: Fanny Fern and the Form of Sentiment," in *The Culture of Sentiment*, ed. Samuels, 269; Peggy Pasco, *Relations of Rescue: The Search for Female Moral Authority in the American West, 1888–1912* (New York: Oxford University Press,

1990), 36, 40, 44; see also Ann Douglas, *The Feminization of American Culture* (New York: Knopf, 1977).

42 Callahan, *Wynema*, 11, 22.

43 Ibid., 52. Muscogees strongly opposed the allotment of their lands, which was finally authorized by Congress in the Curtis Act of 1897 (see Debo, *The Road to Disappearance*, 373). The arguments and language used by Wynema and Genevieve can be found in letters and articles in local newspapers such as the *Muskogee Phoenix* and the *Indian Journal*. For example, a correspondent named "Wing," who strongly opposed allotment, writes in the November 14, 1889 issue of the latter that these doctrines are ruinous to the last degree to the Indian: "The Indian is not ready for this radical change, and we can not see any promise of his being so ready for many generations to come" (p. 8, col. 1). Both "Wing" and Callahan imply that allotment can only be successful if the Muscogees abandon their tribal culture and traditional way of life. Their arguments ignore the fact that the strength of the Muscogee Nation had always come from its traditional social, religious, and cultural institutions, which remained strong among the traditionals during the allotment period.

44 Callahan, *Wynema*, 85.

45 Ibid., 92–3.

46 Ibid., 45, 80. Callahan does not, however, point out the powerful roles held by women in traditional Muscogee culture, in which clan membership was inherited though the mother. A married woman owned the family home. The children, whom she supervised, belonged to her as well. See Debo, *The Road to Disappearance*, 15.

47 Callahan, *Wynema*, 48.

48 Although Betty Keller spells his name as "Wurz," it was actually spelled "Wuerz." All biographical information has been taken from Keller, *Pauline: A Biography of Pauline Johnson* (Vancouver: Douglas & McIntyre, 1981).

49 Quoted in ibid., 159.

50 George W. Lyon, "Pauline Johnson: A Reconsideration," *Studies in Canadian Literature* 15 (1990): 141–2.

51 Johnson, *Flint and Feather*, 159; *NCAWW*, 502.

52 Johnson, "A'bram," *Brantford Expositor* December 25, 1891: 13, 16; "Indian Medicine Men and Their Magic," *Dominion Illustrated* 1 (April 1892): 140–3; "The Iroquois of the Grand River," *Harper's Weekly* 38 (June 23, 1894): 587–9; "Mothers of a Great Red Race," *Mother's Magazine* 3 (January 1908): 5, 14 (revised as "Iroquois Women of Canada," *Halifax Herald* [1909]); and "The Great New Year White Dog: Sacrifice of the Onondagas," *Daily Province Magazine*, weekly supplement (January 14, 1911): 16.

53 Johnson, *The Moccasin Maker*, 106.

54 Ibid., 152, 156; see *NCAWW*, 508–13.

55 Elizabeth Looseley, "Pauline Johnson, 1861–1913," in *The Clear Spirit: Twenty Canadian Women and Their Times*, ed. Mary Quale Innis (Toronto: Toronto University Press, 1966), 84–5. William J. Scheick notes that, because of Anglo-American revulsion at intermarriage between whites and Indians, "observations on the halfblood convey covert attacks on the French, the French-Canadians (particularly in the Midwest and Far West) and the Spanish or Mexicans (particularly in the Southwest)." Scheick, *The Half-Blood: A Cultural Symbol in Nineteenth-Century American Fiction* (Lexington: University of Kentucky Press, 1979), 5. The portrayal may also

represent Johnson's bitterness over the opposition to her parents' marriage by her uncle, the Reverend Robert Vashon Rogers, an Anglican minister. See the author's fictional version of this incident in "My Mother," *The Moccasin Maker*, 49–52.

56   Although Agnes M. Picotte (Lakota) describes the author as a Yankton-Nakota, Beatrice Medicine states that the Yanktons are Dakotas. Picotte, "Foreword," in Zitkala-Ša, *Old Indian Legends* (1901; reprint, Lincoln: University of Nebraska Press, 1985), xiiff.; telephone conversation with Medicine, March 13, 1997.

57   Zitkala-Ša to Carlos Montezuma, June 1901, quoted in Dexter Fisher, "Foreword," in Zitkala-Ša, *American Indian Stories* (1921; Lincoln: University of Nebraska Press, 1979), x.

58   Patricia Okker notes that Zitkala-Ša's *Atlantic* essays were published with the work of such established writers as Edith Wharton, Henry James, William Dean Howells, and Jack London, and that her pieces in *Harper's* in 1901 appeared with the writing of Thomas Hardy, Mark Twain, Bret Harte, Edith Wharton, Grace King, and Mary Wilkins Freeman. Okker, "Native American Literatures and the Canon: The Case of Zitkala-Ša," in *American Realism and the Canon*, ed. Tom Quirk and Gary Scharnhorst (Newark: University of Delaware Press), 90.

59   For an analysis of Zitkala-Ša's efforts to ban peyote, see William Willard, "The First Amendment, Anglo-Conformity and American Indian Religious Freedom," *Wicazo Sa Review* 7.1 (1991): 25–41.

60   Fisher, "Foreword," vi.

61   Dexter Fisher, "Zitkala-Ša: The Evolution of a Writer," *American Indian Quarterly* 5.3 (1979): 237.

62   Martha J. Cutter, "Zitkala-Ša's Autobiographical Writings: The Problems of a Canonical Search for Language and Identity," *MELUS* 19 (1994): 33.

63   Laura Wexler, "Tender Violence: Literary Eavesdropping, Domestic Fiction, and Educational Reform," in *The Culture of Sentiment*, ed. Samuels, 32; Cutter, "Zitkala-Ša's Autobiographical Writings," 34.

64   Zitkala-Ša, "Impressions of an Indian Childhood," *American Indian Stories*, 44.

65   Wexler, "Tender Violence," 31; Zitkala-Ša, "Impressions of an Indian Childhood," 44–5.

66   Other autobiographies describing the boarding school experience include Charles Eastman (Dakota), *From the Deep Woods to Civilization: Chapters in the Autobiography of an Indian* (1916); Luther Standing Bear (Lakota), *My People the Sioux* (1928); and Polingaysi Qoyawayma (Elizabeth White; Hopi), *No Turning Back* (1964). For critical discussions of this subject, see Paul Prucha, *Churches and the Indian Schools, 1888–1912* (Lincoln: University of Nebraska Press, 1979); Margaret Szasz, *Education and the American Indian: The Road to Self Determination, 1928–1973* (Albuquerque: University of New Mexico Press, 1974); and Tsianina Lomawaima (Creek), *They Called It Prairie Light: The Story of the Chilocco Indian School* (Lincoln: University of Nebraska Press, 1993).

67   Margo Lukens, "Zitkala-Ša (Gertrude Simmons Bonnin)," *Native American Writers of the United States*, 334; Zitkala-Ša, "The School Days of an Indian Girl," *American Indian Stories*, 56; see *NCAWW*, 581–90.

68   Zitkala-Ša, "The School Days of an Indian Girl," 73.

69   Ibid., 79, 80.

70   Zitkala-Ša, "An Indian Teacher Among Indians," *American Indian Stories*, 84.

71   Wexler, "Tender Violence," 34.

72 Zitkala-Ša, "An Indian Teacher Among Indians," 99.

73 Jeanne Smith, "'A Second Tongue': The Trickster's Voice in the Works of Zitkala-Ša," in *Tricksterism in Turn-of-the Century Literature*, ed. Elizabeth Ammons and Annette White-Parks (Hanover: Tufts University Press/University Press of New England, 1994), 49–50, 50.

74 Beatrice Medicine, "'Warrior Women': Sex Role Alternatives for Plains Indian Women," in *The Hidden Half: Studies of Plains Indian Women*, ed. Patricia Alberts and Beatrice Medicine (Washington, DC: University Press of America, 1983), 266–7.

75 Okker, "Native American Literatures and the Canon," 92.

76 Ibid., 93, 94.

77 Zitkala-Ša, "American's Indian Problem," *American Indian Stories*, 186; David L. Johnson and Raymond Wilson, "Gertrude Simmons Bonnin, 1876–1938: 'Americanize the First American,'" *American Indian Quarterly* 12 (1988): 37. Zitkala-Ša wrote a number of other important pieces. For example, she describes her belief in her Sioux religion in "The Great Spirit," originally published in the *Atlantic Monthly* (1902), in which she emphasizes how the natural harmony of the universe and the myths of her people are intertwined with aspects of nature. Though her mother and some of her tribespeople have converted to "the new superstition," the author prefers to Christian dogma her "excursions into the natural gardens, where the voice of the Great Spirit is heard in the twittering of birds, the rippling of mighty waters, and the sweet breathing of flowers" (*American Indian Stories*, 106, 107). "The Widespread Enigma Concerning Blue-Star Woman," which focuses on the corruption and disintegration of traditional Sioux customs after allotment, reflects the author's own experience in dealing with land claims. It is based on the case of Ellen C. Bluestone, who petitioned for a Yankton allotment and whose background was similar to that of Blue-Star Woman. Zitkala-Ša successfully fought the woman's petition. See Deborah Sue Welch, "Zitkala-Ša: An American Indian Leader, 1876–1938" (Ph.D. dissertation, University of Wyoming, 1985), 174–5.

78 Letter to Carlos Montezuma, March 1901, quoted in Johnson and Wilson, "Gertrude Simmons Bonnin, 1876–1938," 39.

6

Nature, Nurture, and Nationalism: "A Faded Leaf of History"

JEAN PFAELZER

In the decade following the Civil War, women, nature, and Native American Indians appeared in fiction and visual arts as interchangeable metonyms for reunion, conquest, and expansion.[1] That is to say, women, nature, and Native American Indians appeared incomplete; they mutually anticipated and required civilization. Although the American landscape, James Fenimore Cooper had observed, lacked "that wild sublimity which ordinarily belongs to a granite formation" (that is, the rock-hard masculinity of the Alps) it could be made attractive when "the peculiar blending of what may be termed the agricultural and the savage unite to produce landscapes of extraordinary beauty and grace." Thus Cooper likened the quality of American nature to the promise of American nationhood and to the immanence of American women and Indians. Cooper, however, did not confuse civilization with domesticity: "A fence that looks as if it were covered with clothes hung out to dry does very little toward aiding the picturesque."[2] Thus, the civilized feminine – not to be confused with wet laundry – resides in the rational presence and control of autonomous white masculinity. In the 1860s and 1870s, representations of women, nature, African Americans, and Native American Indians would mutually participate in the tempting, if dangerous, wildness of the female eros, cohabiting in a marginal territory of immaturity analogous to but not equal to the American home. The discourse of domesticity would subsume the discourse of race in the new promise of postbellum nationalism.

By the 1870s pressures toward an ideology of nationhood prompted elegiac and wishful representations of American unity in such forms as plantation novels, regionalist fiction, domestic novels, pastoral utopias, idealized tales of colonial revival, and stories about the inevitable eradication of Native American Indians. To confront emerging concepts of nationhood as white, male, and industrial, Rebecca Harding Davis recuperated an eroticized and politicized image of domesticity within nature. Her fiction of this period insistently questions the self-congratulatory tone of popular images of nationhood and suggests, instead, the profound national anxiety that accompanied the collapse of Reconstruction, the rise of immigration, pressures for women's suffrage, and the genocide of the Native American Indian.

In "A Faded Leaf of History" (1873) Davis rewrote Jonathan Dickinson's *God's Protecting Providence Man's Surest Help and Defence In the times of the greatest difficulty and most Imminent danger*, a well-known seventeenth-century captivity narrative. Written from a woman's perspective, "Faded Leaf" is in effect a palimpsest of Dickinson's tale of "Remarkable Deliverance of divers [*sic*] persons, From the Devouring Waves of the Sea, amongst which they Suffered Shipwreck, and Also From the more cruelly devouring jawes [*sic*] of the inhumane Cannibals of Florida." In this popular narrative, which was reprinted fifteen times between 1700 and 1868,[3] Dickinson wrote from his stance as a wealthy slaveholder and Quaker en route from his plantations in Port Royal, Jamaica, to Philadelphia, where he planned to pursue a career in international trade and local politics. Davis embeds her political critique in an ambivalent dialogue with sentimentalism, rewriting Dickinson's story of the wreck at sea, "capture" by the Jobese Indians, and the party's trek northward over 500 miles of swamps and barren coastline.[4] In her version, Dickinson's views about the conquest of nature, woman, and Indian derive from his nativist assumptions about cultures, optimistic assumptions about Providential nature, imperialist assumptions about expansion, and masculine assumptions about individualism and family. In Davis's "A Faded Leaf of History" Dickinson's views of nature, women, and Indian emerge as interchangeable symbols for the justification of Manifest Destiny.

From a woman's point of view, Davis retells the colonial Quaker's "testimony" of how God protected a group of travelers, from their departure from Port Royal, Jamaica on the barkentine *Reformation* on August 23, 1696, to the weeks when they were lost at sea, shipwrecked on a barrier reef just off the Florida coast and captured by two Indian tribes, as they undertook a dangerous trek northward over 500 miles of swamps and barren coastline. The Dickinson party reached Charles Town, South Carolina, the day after Christmas, where they spent the winter, finally sailing into Philadelphia in March, 1697, seven months after their departure from Jamaica. With Jonathan Dickinson were his wife, Mary, and their six-month-old son, John, as well as a frail Quaker missionary returning home after years of unsuccessful work in the Caribbean islands, the ship captain, and ten of Dickinson's slaves, including one Indian woman named Venus who would die of seizures the first month at sea.

Although the Native American was an unusual topic for fiction in the *Atlantic Monthly*, during the decade following the Civil War Indians appeared frequently in the dime novel as tropes for primitivism and social anarchy, dangers that would recede before the vanguard of white society.[5] If Jonathan Dickinson's narrative, first published in 1699, was written for a growing Quaker community

committed to economic expansion and Indian conversion, Davis's tale addressed
an expansionist nation attempting to eliminate the "Indian problem" through
the eradication and removal of tribal people.[6] By the 1830s most Eastern tribes
had been removed to land beyond the Mississippi, but the opening of Western
lands after the Treaty of Guadalupe Hidalgo of 1848 brought another wave of
struggle over tribal land, which endured throughout the Civil War. By the time
of "Faded Leaf," Native Americans were engaged in armed resistance to policies
which forced them to live, travel, and hunt inside the boundaries of reservations,
and which required thousands of Indian children to attend Christian boarding
schools, learn manual skills, and spend summers with white families – a cultural
trauma painfully described by the Sioux author Zitkala-Ša (Gertrude Bonnin)
in "The School Days of an Indian Girl" (1900). Caught between the forced
migrations of other tribes, the advance of the mining frontier, and the expro-
priation of their land under Homestead Acts, Plains Indians began their "last
stand." But peace came to the plains less from the military victories of the army
and more from the ravages of the advancing railroad, the presence of new dis-
eases, and General William Sherman's and General Philip Sheridan's deliberate
destruction of buffalo herds between 1866 and 1870.[7] Yet the warfare of the
Plains Indians – nomadic horse-mounted hunters – finally caught the attention
of Eastern readers. Just at the time when the plight of Native Americans in
Florida and the Southeast was prominent news, Davis dismantles both the popular
location and the characterization of the Plains Indian. The people Dickinson
called "Jobese" were probably a small northern branch of powerful Tequesta
Indians, whose numbers would dwindle in the early eighteenth century under
attacks by Lower Creek tribes pushing southward under pressure from British
expansion in South Carolina. Eventually, all the remaining tribes in Florida
would be termed Seminoles, the "Wild People," those who held aloof from
whites. Following their defeat in the brutal Seminole War in 1842, Seminoles
who refused to move into the swamps of the Florida interior endured the infamous westward march to Oklahoma. After the Civil War, despite their loyalty
to the Union, Seminoles were forced to confess to war guilt, cede two million
acres to the government at 15 cents an acre (land which Congress then bestowed
on the railroads) and resettle on a 200,000-acre tract for which they paid 50
cents an acre to the US Government.[8] It is estimated that a population of Native
Americans which totaled one million before contact with Europeans fell to
approximately 237,000 by the census of 1900, a decline of nearly 75 percent;
the pre-colonial population of 150,000 Southeastern tribal people was reduced
by 90 percent. By the time that Davis wrote "Faded Leaf" in 1873, the Tequesta
and Ais were extinct.[9]

Dickinson's colonial narrative reflects an optimistic Quaker testimony of a
merciful God who operates through providential nature; the Bible is useless:
"Being all stripped as naked as we were born, and endeavoring to hide our
nakedness; these cannibals took the [Bibles] and tearing out the leaves would
give each of us a leaf to cover us; ... instantly another of them would snatch

away what the other gave us, smiting and deriding us withal." Nonetheless, explains Dickinson, "It pleased God to order it so that we went on shore, as though there had been a lane made through the breakers."[10] Unlike Cotton Mather's appropriation of Hanna Dustin's tale of captivity, *God's Protecting Providence* is never a cautionary exhortation.

Davis, however, sees Dickinson's pamphlet itself as a fetish for a death-like narrative of history. At first she finds the thin coffee-colored pages of his ragged pamphlet "like rotting leaves in the fall . . . grown clammy to the touch . . . from the grasp of so many dead years," and she expects to read another expansionist history, "some 'Report of the Condition of the Principalities of New Netherland, or New Sweden, for the Use of the Lord's High Proprietors thereof' (for of such precious dead dust this library is full)." What she is seeking in such stories of conquest is historical subjectivity: "If only to find human interest in them, one would rather they had been devoured by inhuman cannibals than not." Initially, Dickinson's party "seemed to me to be only part of that endless caravan of ghosts that has been crossing the world since the beginning; they never can be anything but ghosts to us."[11]

Within Dickinson's expansionist narrative, however, Davis's narrator suddenly finds "wrapped in the weighty sentences and backed by the gravest and most ponderous testimony, the story of a baby." The "father's book" was "scribbled over with the name John . . . in a cramped, childish hand." Through the act of writing, childlike and inept though it may be, another version of history announces itself.[12] In her version, Davis addresses the "sweet-tempered, gracious women," warm in their snow-covered homes in contemporary Philadelphia, "with their children close about their knees," and intends "to bring this little live baby back . . . out of the buried years, where it has been hidden with dead people" and "give it a . . . home among us." In this sentimental interpretation, Davis will revise the ur narrative of colonization. Yet home for Davis and Dickinson was Philadelphia, not a Quaker utopia but "a most savage country" and "to this savage country our baby was bound."[13]

In Davis's tale, it was the men's rigidity and prejudice that quickly imperiled the travelers:

The captain held all the power and the Quaker all the money. . . . The captain, Kirle, debarred from fighting by cowardice, and the Quaker Dickinson [*sic*], forbidden by principle, appear to have set out upon their perilous journey, resolved to defend themselves by suspicion, pure and simple. They looked for treachery behind every bush and billow; the only chance of safety lay, they maintained, in holding every white man to be an assassin and every red man a cannibal.

Furthermore, Dickinson ignored the informative, aesthetic, and redemptive power of nature. He was so obsessed with pirates and savages that he would not "spare time to his jealous eyes" to enjoy the beauty of the white-sailed fleet "scudding over the rolling green plain" or permit his sickly baby to prosper from the vitality of the sea air, but keeps him smothered, below decks, "in the finest of linens and the softest of paduasoy." In Davis's view, the shared ineptitude and racist paranoia of Dickinson and Capt. Kirle caused the calamitous wreck: "It is curious to observe how these early Christians met the Indians with the same weapons of distrust and fraud which have proved so effective with us in civilizing them since." As "the good Quaker" prays that God's wrathful punishment will rain upon these "pagan robbers," he orders his slaves to bury his money on the beach, "quite blind to the poetic justice of the burial, as the money had been made on land stolen from the savages." Unlike Dickinson, Davis's narrator is a cultural relativist who observes that because of the famine, "in all probability these cannibals returned thanks to whatever God they had for this windfall of food and clothes devoutly as our forefathers were doing at the other end of the country for the homes which they had taken by force."[14]

In contrast to Dickinson's interpretative paradigm of "God's Protecting Providence," Davis shapes the historical narrative through sentimentality: the travelers' survival is evidence of the redemptive powers of Indian motherhood and female community. Yet because Davis represents history *through* but not solely *as* a psychological dilemma, the political context – power that is white, masculine, and wealthy – endures as a real presence. "Faded Leaf" remains in the public realm; the rescue of Mary and the baby underscores the capacity of sympathy to change the reader's views of Indians. Thus, unlike Dickinson's vivid descriptions of physical hardships inevitably ameliorated by a beneficent God, Davis returns to the vocabulary of feelings to portray Anglo-Indian contact. If Dickinson's poignant version invokes the inexorable traumas to establish God's redemptive presence, Davis's story centers on Mary and the baby, whose perils are exacerbated by the blind egotism of Jonathan. It is the melodrama of maternal plight that prompts observations on colonialism and misogyny, as "Faded Leaf" invokes the insurgent politics of sentimental sympathy. Davis's revision of Dickinson's tale recalls Lydia Maria Child's short story "Adventure in the Woods" in which an old Indian "squaw" finds two lost settler children and returns them to their desperate parents who have displaced the Indians on their own land – in effect an anti-captivity narrative.[15]

According to Davis, Jonathan's racism and expansionist hunger continually make his family vulnerable. Despite the sexual contract of domesticity, rather than offer sanctuary patriarchy puts a wife at risk. Comparing the dangerous sea voyage from the male and female perspective, Davis's narrator notes that the sailors had "chosen a life of peril," John enjoyed a "tough courage," and the old prophet had the comfort of access to the Divine word. Mary Dickinson, by contrast, "was only a gentle, commonplace woman . . . whose highest ambition was to take care of her snug little house, and all of whose brighter thoughts of romance or passion began and ended in this staid Quaker and the baby that was a part of them both."[16] Unlike the Promethean egotism of Jonathan's quest, domestic life, inscribed in the language of physical passion, represents Mary's image of fulfilled desire. In a story of female adventure, Mary has no power to affect the course of the journey but rather she collaborates in images of her own confinement.

Unique in Davis's writings is "Faded Leaf's" focus on a baby rather than a wife as a totem both for maternal martyrdom and imminent female community. It is through the primal trope of food and orality that Davis represents the "bonds of womanhood," as Mary finds refuge in the enduring sensibility of female dependence which contrasts with Jonathan's obsessive fear of cannibalism. While the white woman forges a community with the Indian women through the hungry baby and finds food and friendship in the tribal community, Jonathan remains "sure of the worst designs on the part of the cannibal, from a strange glance which he fixed upon the baby as he drove them before him to his village." As soon as the shipwrecked travelers reach the Jobese village, the Cassekey takes them to the wigwam of his wife, who puts aside her own child to suckle the Dickinson baby. In Dickinson's text, Mary tries to resist this gesture, but in Davis's version, the baby, who had been "born tired into the world, and had gone moaning its weak life out ever since," now "thus warmed and fed, stretched its little arms and legs out on the savage breast comfortably and fell into a happy sleep, while its mother sat apart and looked on."[17]

By feeding the white child with her own milk (also a recurrent gesture in slave narratives), the lactating Indian mother appears closer to nature, tied to pre-industrial life, while the arid and alienated white mother, feeling intense loss over her one area of power, observes the rebirth of her child, an image of regeneration which the reader understands through the conduit of the white female gaze. Because the Jobese's maternal act rejuvenates the white family, on the imagistic level it participates in the defeat of the view of the Indian as defiant. Thus, Mary's role as witness to a performance which preempts Jonathan's masculine duty to engage in violence on her behalf serves to co-opt the Indian and the white female at the same time.[18] This moment recalls "The Tenas Klootchman" by the Mohawk author E. Pauline Johnson (1861–1913), in which an Indian woman whose daughter has died rescues and adopts an orphaned child – a similar gesture of redemptive motherhood – which is effectively witnessed by an outsider-narrator who is a white woman and with whom the Indian, Maarda, shares her story.[19] As Richard Slotkin has observed, the cultural litmus test of nineteenth-century Indians is how they respond to whites.[20]

The sentimental metaphor of orality – hunger, nursing, famine, provision – shapes Davis's critique of Romantic male egoism, and, in turn, defines Jonathan's racism. Davis describes the emaciation and hunger of the travelers and the Indians alike, observing that Jonathan Dickinson, trapped in "his suspicious bigotry," was convinced that every warming fire "has death in the pot,"[21] that is, the Jobese intend to cook and consume him and his party. Davis uses the metaphor of cannibalism, a trope with long colonialist associations, to expose Jonathan's stereotypical assumptions about Indian danger. Louis Montrose has described Amerigo Vespucci's sixteenth-century personification of America as a nude female Indian performing cannibalistic fellatio, an oral fantasy of female insatiability and male dismemberment which forged a powerful conjunction of the savage and the feminine.[22] Involving tribes ranging from New England, the Great Lakes, the Plains and the Southwest, captivity narratives from the seventeenth through the nineteenth centuries recorded incidents of cannibalism but rarely was it interpreted in tribal terms as a ritual which bonded victor and vanquished, capturing the courage and strength of the enemy.[23] Women's captivity narratives virtually never recorded incidents of ritualized cannibalistic slaughter, although they did include accounts of captives eating human flesh to avoid death from starvation.[24]

Indicative of the relationship between domination and the denial of connection, Davis's Jonathan defends himself from what he takes to be the alien otherness of the Jobese. Repudiating the maternal gestures and locked in his racial stereotypes, he persists, for example, in denying the Indians' generosity. Because Mary, as a woman, does not have to forego dependency, she may forge relationships with the other Indian women and children, connections that appear to deny the role of race.[25] In "Faded Leaf" white women, children, and Indians forge a sympathetic community in which all but the white men partake. Davis arrives at this sentimental unity through the eradication of difference and the cultural assimilation of the Indians. While Jonathan insists on his role as the agent of his own desire and destiny and while he persists in the dangerous myth of endangered white independence and power, the narrator, identified with Mary, sees the Jobese chief as "this friend in the wilderness."[26]

When the chief understands that Jonathan, still suspecting treachery, is resolved to lead his party northward, he retrieves the long boat from the wreck, along with barrels of butter, sugar, wine, and chocolate, which he presents to Jonathan. Themes of female vulnerability and communalism shape Davis's version of the journey north. With Barrow, Mary, the baby, and two sick members of the crew traveling by canoe, and the rest of the members of the party walking on foot, they begin the long trek, suffering from extreme cold, sand-flies, and mosquitoes. Soon they encounter the Ais ("Jece") Indians, the "fiercer savages of whom the chief had warned them" and again the travelers pretend they are Spaniards. Davis's narrator sardonically observes that "By this time, one would suppose, even Dickinson's [*sic*] dull eyes would have seen the fatal idiocy of the lie." Interestingly, it is when she pictures Indian brutality that Davis quotes Dickinson directly, " 'They rushed upon us, rending the few Cloathes from us that we had; they took all from my Wife, even tearing her Hair out, to get at the Lace, wherewith it was knotted.' " Davis continues to read through Dickinson to stress aspects of this attack which endanger Mary and the baby, who is also stripped of his clothes "while one savage filed its mouth with sand." Yet while the purported sexual danger of the Indians undermines community, the Ais chief's wife also comes to Mary's rescue, "protects her from the sight of all" (that is, covers her nudity), and cleans out the baby's mouth, "whereon the mass of savages fell back, muttering and angry."[27] Even in a fierce tribe, a woman has the authority to nurture and protect orality.

As in Child's "Adventure in the Woods," in "Faded Leaf" the reformative power of gender triumphs over the dangerous essentialism of race. The Ais woman brings "poor naked" Mary to her own wigwam, and shows her how to cover herself with deerskins. Davis observes that the Ais were also suffering from famine and had little to share but scarce fish and palmetto-berries: "their emaciated and hunger-bitten faces gave fiercer light to their gloomy treacherous eyes." Speaking from the point of view of one whose duty it is to provide food, the narrator observes that nothing could have been more unwelcome to the tribe than this hungry "crowd of whites." Even so, by the second day, the chief "looked pleasantly" upon Mary and the baby, and instead of fish entrails and the filthy water in which the fish had been cooked, he brings Mary clams and shows her how to roast them; the native male enters the domestic sphere. The Ais women soon realize that Mary has no breast milk and, like the Jobese, they pass her baby around to nurse, "putting away their own children that they might give it food."[28] The redemptive power of mother and child and the profound maternal identification of Mary and the Indian women not only deprive Jonathan of power, and hence, of masculinity, but again de-emphasize the difference between the whites and the Indians.

Nonetheless, by focusing on lactation, food, and famine, "Faded Leaf" participates in what Lora Romero calls a transformation of Native Americans into vanishing Americans by "incorporating the racial other as an earlier and now irretrievably lost version of the self."[29] The famine suggests the inevitable demise of the Indians; the feeding of the white infant alludes to the ultimate survival of the white race. After the baby is nursed by the Indian women, whose own children are dying of famine, Davis notes, "The child, that, when it had been wrapped in fine flannel and embroidery had been always nigh to death, began to grow fat and rosy, to crow and laugh as it had never done before, and kick its little legs sturdily about under a bit of raw skin covering."[30] The restoration of social equilibrium atrophies native activity in domesticity and involves the colonization of the Indian woman's body and the white son's assumed right to possess her breast. The appropriation of the Indian woman's breast similarly constructs a dominant subject position for the presumably white reader of the *Atlantic*; through the discourse of sentimentality, the female reader becomes complicit in this objectification. Davis, I suggest, hints at the link between the narrative of the feminization of power and racial genocide, the geopolitics of the conflation of the body and the state. As Romero astutely points out, such "micro" narratives of individuals usually appear oblivious to the politics of the nineteenth-century "macro" narrative of modernization, which involved the massive destruction of populations.

Expansionism, as Amy Kaplan suggests, locates the colony as the site for recuperating a primitive corporeal virility. In "Faded Leaf," this recuperation is achieved through a feminized view of the Indians and an Indianized view of Mary. In Kaplan's theory, any feminized view of colonial people makes it hard to represent them as subjects taking action on their own accord.[31] Yet

Davis's conflation of race and gender is somewhat more complicated. In neither Dickinson's nor Davis's version does Mary rage against her predicament, nor does she attempt any act of survival on her own behalf. Davis's maternal figure, however, powerfully aware of the extensiveness of the famine and the arrogant role of her husband, challenges Annette Kolodny's view that westering women accepted the "disappearance of the primal wild" with equanimity.[32] For Davis, the domestic images of nurturance and community function as the ethical core of nationhood. Yet, by reconstructing a domestic and Indian utopia in the wilderness, Davis imposes a cultural view that reflects Mary's dream of domesticity and Davis's fantasy of racial harmony. At a time of racial genocide, "Faded Leaf" perpetuates a representation of America which dates back to the earliest engravings of explorers: an image of the immanent nation as a voluptuous Indian woman.[33] But rather than invoke this popular trope in order to legitimize possession, Davis dialogically inscribes this sentimental figure in an anti-imperialist voice – ambivalent though it may be.

In "Faded Leaf" Davis's representation of nature contests the traditional trope of a journey as a ritualized passage toward power, understanding, and growth. Her images of Florida's scorched beaches and humid swamps subvert Mary's regressive fantasy of pre-Oedipal nurturance and intimacy, as well as Jonathan's masculine dream of patriarchal authority in the wilderness. She sees the parched land, with dead palmetto trees, as hostile to their expansionist enterprise: "It was a bleak, chilly afternoon as they toiled mile after mile along the beach, the Quaker woman far behind the others with her baby in her arms, carrying it, as she thought, to its death."[34] In effect, the mother and child enter the wilderness alone, figuratively behind the group of men. Mary's exodus marks the end of Romantic exuberance; and when a woman undertakes a pilgrimage, she makes it not alone but in the company of a child. Mary is a dwarfed and abandoned female figure who never aspires to transcendence.

Davis's representation of nature instead suggests a Darwinian struggle for survival in the most bleak landscape of her œuvre, a landscape which insists that nature will frustrate economic enterprise. The image of the abandoned woman on the barren beach mocks what critic David Miller terms the conservative "aesthetic desiderata" of the picturesque: unity, hierarchy, and collective continuity with the past.[35] Unlike the picturesque, which promised the harmony of nature's parts in the presence of human associations – a facsimile of social and political harmony – the reemergence of the primal swamp on the flight from the Ais Indians suggests the political and psychic degeneration of the travelers' endeavor: "Once a tidal wave swept down into a vast marsh where they had built their fire, and air and ground slowly darkened with the swarming living creatures, whirring, creeping about them through the night, and uttering gloomy, dissonant cries."[36] The swamp, which resists the civilizing campfire, displaces the patriarchal urge to control or suppress a "female," "savage," or pre-civilized nature, traditionally the source of heretical and potentially anarchic meaning. Nature, once the fruitful mother, turns into the withholding mother who threatens the hero with annihilation if he tries to establish his independence.[37] Thus, unlike the popular visual images of distant prospects of vastness and light of the Hudson River school, controlled by the gaze of a viewer at the pictorial edge, Davis's travelers move through mysterious wet and dark swamps, by tradition dangerous and infected female spaces which challenge the sentimental quest for purity and the flight from death. In "Faded Leaf," nature is no longer a place to recover childhood in the absence of history. Instead, nature condemns rather than redeems the present, undercutting Lydia Sigourney's vision of women's reluctant acquiescence to westering pictured in the tragic felling of trees (see "The Western Emigrant"[38]) or Thoreau's vision of transcendental progress which subsumed the wilderness in an optimistic vision of unity. Davis finds no enduring regeneration in pastoralism – either for the individual or the state.

As Davis feminizes the wilderness, and thereby renders nature valuable, vulnerable, and menacing (all at the same time), so too does she feminize the Native American Indian – man and woman. By identifying the Native American both with nature and with a female culture of nurturance and community, Davis's story of captivity offered the postbellum reader, whose country was engaged in brutal Indian slaughter and expulsion, an image of national identity which incorporates the Native American Indian at a most fundamental ideological level.[39] Unlike captivity narratives of adaptation to Indian life, such as Mary Jemison's, Susannah Johnson's, and Frances Kelly's, or of militant resistance to Indian violence, such as Hanna Dustin's, "Faded Leaf" fuses Mary's subject position as both colonial and colonizer. Through the sentimental vocabulary of gender, Davis positions the Indian as redemptive and hence, culturally valuable. Thus in "Faded Leaf," sentiment's insurgent voice parries with its complicitous voice in a complex story of difference and assimilation.

By consolidating the wilderness and the Native American as mutually engendered "sites" of exploration, exploitation, and conquest, Davis inscribes rather than effaces a narrative of cultural destruction. As the baby, now full of milk, kicks its legs under a bit of raw deerskin, the narrator comments, "Mother Nature had taken the child home, that was all, and was breathing new lusty life into it, out of the bare ground and open sky, the sun and wind, and the breasts of these her children."[40] Davis's domesticated image of mother earth/mother Indian recalls Thoreau's rejection of that common metaphor when he climbed Ktaadn mountain: "Perhaps I most fully realized that this was primeval, untamed and forever untameable *Nature*. . . . Nature was here something savage and awful . . . not [man's] Mother Earth that we have heard of, not for him to tread on or be buried in. . . . It was a place for heathenism and superstitious rite, – to be inhabited by men nearer of kin to the rocks and to wild animals than we."[41] Where Thoreau embraces a gendered image of nature as a witch (unworthy to tread on) in order to free himself from civilization, Davis pictures maternal primitivism as a return to the sanctuary of domesticity and community. Thus she challenges the mid-century view of the relationship between nature, nationalism, and the Native

American, typified in Tocqueville's "honest citizens" who announce that "This world here belongs to us. . . . God, in refusing the first inhabitants the capacity to become civilised, has destined them in advance to inevitable destruction. The true owners of this continent are those who know how to take advantage of its riches."[42] In feminizing the Native American, Davis, by contrast, confronts the tenet of Manifest Destiny which constructs the Indian as degenerate in order to view expansion as providential. As she parodies Dickinson's image of himself as a member of the chosen people of superior race, an identity which served to disguise his economic goals, she points to the contradiction of an expanding democratic society that denied democracy to those who lived on its newly conquered lands.

"Faded Leaf" is a palimpsest, a revisionist captivity narrative which engages in an ambivalent dialogue with the genre's traditional conclusions about nature, nurture, and nationalism. By the 1860s and 1870s the captivity narrative had reemerged as a tremendously popular genre; Edward Ellis's *Seth Jones's or the Captives of the Frontier* (1860), for example, quickly sold 400,000 copies.[43] Yet the captivity narrative's recurrent motifs of confinement, separation, contamination, adaptation for survival, the break-up of a family, ambivalence about adoption, and female survival and adventure were tropes inherited from the domestic novel. Interestingly, these are the same literary strategies which shape the slave narrative. In contrast to such popular masculine texts, in "Faded Leaf," two female voices, that of Mary's passive endurance and the narrator's articulate cynicism, put forward a decentered female subjectivity that refuses to be forged in opposition to the Native American man.

By repudiating Dickinson's popular text, Davis revokes Mary's symbolic function as the innocent victim of barbarous savagery – a trope also found in dime novel stories of Indian captivity, abuse, and rape in the 1870s, which strengthened the white male hero at the expense of a frail, childlike, and sexually vulnerable female captive. "Faded Leaf" calls into question familiar portraits of female victims who were viewed by Francis Parkman and George Bancroft as sacrificial "bit players" in the drama of conquest and progress.[44] In contrast to tales of rape in such captivity narratives as those of Caroline Harris and Clarissa Plummer of the 1830s, as well as popular contemporary tales of Moccasin Bill (1873) which titillated white audiences and played upon postwar fears of miscegenation, Davis refuses to portray Indian men as sexually dangerous. Of the two thousand captivity narratives which documented tens of thousands of white and Mexican captives, few directly address the issue of sexuality.[45] Recent scholarship has documented some instances of Indian rape, gang rape, and enslavement of white women, but it has found it difficult to establish just how common such acts were.[46] Anglo women were reticent about discussing sexual violation and Eastern tribal men generally showed little sexual interest in their female captives due, apparently, to ritualized practices of sexual abstinence in times of war, lack of interest in white women, and incest taboos in case a white woman was to be adopted into the tribe.[47]

Davis's title itself, "A Faded Leaf of History," is a self-deprecating comment on the ancient text which her narrator has discovered. Seen through the experience of the baby, the tale culminates in the travelers' final passage northward. If in Cooper's tales the Indian is the occasion for moral growth of the white men, here it is the baby who transforms "savage or slave or beast" who "were his friends alike, his laugh and outstretched hands were ready for them all." Through his totemizing power as sentimental innocent, the baby transforms the Indians, the slaves, and the local animals into one homogenized and safe "other." Reiterating the conflation of gender and race, the narrator, speaking for the first time as a mother, observes, "It makes a mother's heart ache even now to read how these coarse, famished men, often fighting like wild animals with each other, staggering under weakness and bodily pain, carried the heavy baby, never complaining of its weight, thinking, it may be, of some child of their own whom they would never see or touch again." Contact with the baby, rather than the experience of captivity and wilderness, transforms all men: "a gentler, kindlier spirit seemed to come from the presence of the baby and its mother to the crew; so that, while at first they had cursed and fought their way along, they grew at the last helpful and tender with each other."[48] In other words, the baby makes the men act like women.

Nonetheless, in the end, the discourse of sentiment and the ideology it espouses cannot thwart the corrupt inevitability of patriarchy and imperialism, pictured in the figure of the unredeemed father whose beliefs will triumph in the construction of American nationhood. The lost party is finally tracked by a Spanish scout from St Augustine, who has heard of the infant in the shipwrecked party; hence, it is "through the baby that deliverance came to them at last." Recalling that all the men along the way have been willing to give their life for the baby, the narrator discovers that she can now "understand better the mystery of that Divine Childhood that was once in the world." In April, 1697 the family sails into the raw settlement town of Philadelphia in an arrival which suggests the restoration of patriarchy and the inevitability of civilization. Reminiscent of mid-century paintings of conquest in which Indian wigwams abut houses under construction, the Dickinsons find that many settlers are still living in caves, but the village's "one or two streets of mud-huts and curious low stone houses" will soon frame and contain the wilderness.[49]

In Philadelphia, according to Davis, Jonathan Dickinson "closed his righteous gates thereafter on aught that was alien or savage" and became a power in the new principality, remembered mainly for his "strict rule as mayor, his stately equipages and vast estates." Mary, able to lactate once she is back in civilization, is restored to her previous domestic status and her limited capacity to act; in her new home she "nursed her baby, and clothed him in soft fooleries again." Yet the narrator refuses to investigate what happened to the baby, and decides to atrophy him in eternal infancy. Insisting on his divine role, she concludes: "I will not believe that he ever grew to be a man, or died. He will always be to us simply a . . . laughing baby, sent by his Master to the desolate places of the earth with the old message of Divine love and universal brotherhood to his children."[50] The images of maternalism and childlike natives and the anticipation of white civilization eclipse the narrative of the Indian; nonetheless, Davis refuses to let the baby become a civilized adult, complicitous with the reign of his powerful father.

Gayatri Spivak has suggested that "the discourse of man is in the metaphor of woman."[51] In rewriting Dickinson's popular captivity narrative, Davis appropriated a central masculine paradigm of contemporary expansion in order to question both its public and private ideologies. At the same time, she reiterated the convention which romanticized colonial space; Indian land is still a utopian site which projects the fantasies and needs of colonizers. This invented landscape permits fulfillment of a desire to possess land and people, which become one. Like other Euro-American women, Davis presumed, in Carroll Smith-Rosenberg's astute phrase, "the right to write" the story of conquest, and thus, inevitably, she too appropriated the right to "represent a white America, . . . assum[ing] the dominant male discourses of imperialism and social order."[52]

The white captive presumes the role of mediator between native and white civilization; as a female she presumes an affiliation with both worlds. Yet even though "Faded Leaf" ends in a utopian moment of redemptive Christianity, a metaphor which allows for a humanist belief in the realization of progress, it represents the narrative of colonial captivity and conquest in relation to patterns of history which Davis views as ongoing. The autobiographical nature of the captivity narrative allowed Davis a form that made the private world public, at the same time that it positioned white men as agents of history which they fail to understand. In this story of colonization, Davis has again told a sentimental story of involuntary enclosure. Like her earlier stories, "A Faded Leaf of History" describes how a female subject – whether slave, woman writer, or abandoned mother – attempts to fantasize community. Thus, the power of Davis's story derives from her reworking of the heroic conventions of the captivity narrative in terms of her assumption that women reside both inside and outside public history. By rescripting the captivity narrative as a story of female/Native American dispossession, Davis questions the legitimacy of the narrative perspective of the form itself. Through a parody of the genre, Davis repudiates the activities which prompt it; "A Faded Leaf of History" interrogates the captivity narrative's very act of claiming historicity.

NOTES

1 A version of this material appears in *Parlor Radical: Rebecca Harding Davis and the Origins of American Social Realism* (Pittsburgh: University of Pittsburgh Press, 1996).

2 James Fenimore Cooper, "American and European Scenery Compared," in *Home Book of the Picturesque* (New York: G. P. Putnam, 1851), 52, 56–8.

3 Evangeline Walker Andrews, "Introduction," in Jonathan Dickinson, *Jonathan Dickinson's Journal or God's Protecting Providence* (New Haven: Yale University Press,

1945), 18. All quotations from Dickinson are from this edition, which strictly follows the text of the 1699 first edition. Richard VanDerBeets suggests that there were twenty-one editions, including translations into Dutch and German. VanDerBeets, "The Indian Captivity Narrative as Ritual," *American Literature* 43 (1972): 548.

4   Rebecca Harding Davis, "A Faded Leaf of History," *Atlantic Monthly* 31 (1873): 44–52. Citations to the story are from *A Rebecca Harding Davis Reader*, ed. Jean Pfaelzer (Pittsburgh: University of Pittsburgh Press, 1995), abbreviated as *RHDR*; the story is also reprinted in Kilcup, *NCAWW*, 233–41.

5   Robert F. Berkhofer, *The White Man's Indian: Images of the American Indian from Columbus to the Present* (New York: Alfred A. Knopf, 1978), 95–106.

6   Berkhofer suggests that the post-Civil War policy of the Federal government was to have Native Americans enter the polis as individuals rather than as tribes. *The White Man's Indian*, 155.

7   Richard Slotkin, *The Fatal Environment: The Myth of the Frontier in the Age of Industrialization, 1800–1890* (New York: Atheneum, 1985), 304.

8   Wilcomb Washburn, *The Indian in America* (New York: Harper and Row, 1975), 201. See also Angie Debo, *A History of the Indians of the United States* (Norman: University of Oklahoma Press, 1970), 151.

9   These statistics are drawn from *The Harvard Encyclopedia of American Ethnic Groups* (Cambridge, MA: Harvard University Press, 1980), 59, 69; and *The World Book Encyclopedia* (Chicago: World Book Inc., 1991), 191.

10 Dickinson, *Jonathan Dickinson's Journal*, 44, 42.

11 *RHDR*, 362.

12 In discussing the "legibility" of paternal power in the antebellum period Lora Romero observes, "Although *the* book is usually associated with the reign of the father, in the antebellum period *books* seem to be associated with the reign of the mother." Figures such as Thoreau, argues Romero, are anxious about both the multiplicity of female texts and women's assumption of educational duties formerly administered by the father. Romero, "Vanishing Americans: Gender, Empire, and New Historicism," in *The Culture of Sentiment: Race, Gender, and Sentimentality in 19th Century America*, ed. Shirley Samuels (New York: Oxford University Press, 1992), 122.

13 *RHDR*, 363.

14 Ibid., 363–4, 364, 365, 365, 366.

15 See *NCAWW*, 65–8.

16 *RHDR*, 367.

17 Ibid., 366, 367–8.

18 Amy Kaplan discusses the role of a female witness in novels of empire as a strategy for displacing the masculine necessity to engage directly in violent acts. In Kaplan's view, in the novels of empire, men "recover their primal virility in a relation of difference in contrast to the native men around them" (unlike Davis's baby who is saved in an act of theatricalized chivalry). "Romancing the Empire: The Embodiment of American Masculinity in the Popular Historical Novel of the 1890s," *American Literary History* 2 (1990): 676.

19 See *NCAWW*, 504–8.

20 Slotkin, *The Fatal Environment*, 102–3.

21 *RHDR*, 368.

22 Louis Montrose, "The Work of Gender in the Discourse of Discovery," *Representations* 33 (1991): 5.

23 VanDerBeets, "The Indian Captivity Narrative as Ritual," 550–1.

24 Kathryn Zabelle Derounian-Stodola and James Arthur Levernier, *The Indian Captivity Narrative, 1550–1900* (New York: Twayne Publishers, 1993), 126–7.

25 Drucilla Cornell and Adam Thurschwell observe that this sort of explanation traces social and institutional forms of power to individual psychological motivations. "Feminism, Negativity, and Intersubjectivity," in *Feminism as Critique: On the Politics of Gender*, ed. Seyla Benhabib and Drucilla Cornell (Minneapolis: University of Minnesota Press, 1987), 157. However, as Jane Flax reminds us, the family is constituted by three types of social relations: production, reproduction, and psychodynamics. "The Family in Contemporary Feminist Thought," in *The Family in Political Thought*, ed. Jean Bethke Elshtain (Amherst: University of Massachusetts Press, 1982), 223.

26 *RHDR*, 368.

27 Ibid., 368, 369.

28 Ibid., 369.

29 Romero, "Vanishing Americans," 119.

30 *RHDR*, 369.

31 Kaplan, "Romancing the Empire," 664, 674.

32 Annette Kolodny, *The Land Before Her: Fantasy and Experience of the American Frontiers, 1630–1860* (Chapel Hill: University of North Carolina Press, 1984), 8.

33 See, for example, Carroll Smith-Rosenberg, "Subject Female: Authorizing American Identity," *American Literary History* 5 (1993): 482.

34 *RHDR*, 366.

35 David Miller, *Dark Eden: The Swamp in American Culture* (New York: Cambridge University Press, 1989), 10.

36 *RHDR*, 370.

37 See Miller, *Dark Eden*, 8. Miller observes that the "Good" mother who bestows sustenance turns into the "Terrible" mother who threatens annihilation if the hero tries to establish his independence by going beyond the "objective reality" of nature (*Dark Eden*, 103). Yet this trope only applies to male characters' relationship to nature.

38 *NCAWW*, 44–5.

39 Carroll Smith-Rosenberg has observed that many nineteenth-century white women who contested "with white men for a liberal humanist subjectivity [also] joined with them in espousing Europe's imperial venture, and in so doing, denied subjectivity to women of color." "Subject Female," 486.

40 *RHDR*, 369.

41 Henry David Thoreau, *The Maine Woods* (New York: Harper and Row, 1987), 93–5.

42 Alexis de Tocqueville, *Journey to America*, trans. George Lawrence, ed. J. P. Mayer (Garden City, NY: Doubleday Anchor, 1971), 354.

43 Richard VanDerBeets, "A Surfeit of Style: The Indian Captivity Narrative as Penny Dreadful," *Research Studies* 39 (1971): 305.

44 See June Namias, *White Captives: Gender and Ethnicity on the American Frontier* (Chapel Hill: University of North Carolina Press, 1993), 67, 15.

45 Derounian-Stodola and Levernier, *The Indian Captivity Narrative*, 2.

46 Namias, *White Captives*, 97–122; Lonnie J. White, "White Women Captives of Southern Plains Indians, 1866–1875," *Journal of the West* 8 (1969): 327–54; Stanley B. Kimball, "The Captivity Narrative on Mormon Trails, 1846–65," *Dialogue* 18 (1984): 82–8; Derounian-Stodola and Levernier, *The Indian Captivity Narrative*, 127.

47 Derounian-Stodola and Levernier, *The Indian Captivity Narrative*, 3–5.

48 *RHDR*, 370, 371.

49 Ibid., 373.

50 Ibid., 373.

51 Gayatri Spivak, "Displacement and the Discourse of Woman," in *Displacement: Derrida and After*, ed. Mark Krupnick (Bloomington: Indiana University Press, 1983), 169.

52 Smith-Rosenberg, "Subject Female," 486.

7

Crippled Girls and Lame Old Women: Sentimental Spectacles of Sympathy in Nineteenth-Century American Women's Writing

ROSEMARIE GARLAND THOMSON

The Cripple, the Lame, the Blind, the Halt, the Mute, the Deaf – figures we today term physically disabled – appear with some frequency in the fiction of nineteenth-century American women writers. Indeed, such figures are often fundamental to the thematic preoccupations and rhetorical purposes of sentimentalism, the literary convention that informs much women's writing of this period. Replete with a rich traditional array of multiple significations, the physically disabled figure provides a pliable and congenial vehicle for attending to reform, feeling, religion, domesticity, and the body – the overlapping primary arenas of concern that characterize sentimentalism.

Sentimentalism is most usefully seen as the primary discourse of nineteenth-century femininity. It is the essential element in a doctrine of feminine difference manifest in practices and values that both limited and expanded women's place in a rapidly modernizing culture. Sentimentalism is the affective and relational component of domesticity. Consequently, sentimentalism is best seen within the context of domesticity, that larger ideology and set of practices that structured women's place and roles in the nineteenth century.[1]

Domesticity held that the home was the site of differentiation where women enacted a femininity that was antithetical and complementary to masculinity as well as competitive with it. Whereas women had previously been cast as lesser forms of men, domesticity in its broadest sense redefined women as fundamentally different from and opposed to men.[2] The strength of this belief was that it empowered women by offering them a potentially separate but equal, even superior, rendering of themselves. Its limitations, however, were the inevitable restrictions of segregation and differentiation in a society that privileges men in its unequal distribution of wealth, power, and status. In other words, women were both trapped and valorized by the notion of domesticity and its script for femininity.

Nevertheless, the celebrants of domesticity eagerly seized its logic and locations in order to forge a vital version of womanhood to both meet and challenge the demands of a rapidly changing social order. Although the idea of domesticity shifted considerably over the century, it was fundamentally a division of labor that assigned women to the privatized realm of the home, which became the site and source of feeling, religion, morality, childrearing, purity, and order. In contrast, domesticity assigned men to the public world of politics, economic production, money, and other activities outside the home. Imagined at once as sheltered and fragile but morally and spiritually privileged, women were both confined and enabled by domesticity.

While these supposedly opposing realms of the masculine and feminine were in fact complexly entangled in practice, their ideological distinction often emerged clearly in women's writing and public activities, much of which centered on a didactic, reform agenda that was seen as primarily feminine.[3] Humanitarian reform emerged as Christian dogma shifted its view of human fate from determinism to perfectibility in the nineteenth century, launching Americans into what John L. Thomas calls "a huge rescue operation" aimed at obliterating sin, suffering, and secular wrongs.[4] This massive movement was seen through a religious lens as salvation and through a secular one as progress. Such social reform was the national equivalent of individualism's doctrine of self-reliance and self-improvement, thus implicating women in the very program that governed the masculine-dominated marketplace they criticized and from which they were excluded.[5]

Nevertheless, domesticity's image of women as moral exemplars and givers of care fueled and shaped the century's urgent, pervasive reform movements. Although never exclusively a female movement, reform flourished as a female enterprise because it conformed to domesticity's script. The feminized project of moral reform was informed by Christianity, emanated from the home, was mobilized by feeling, and enhanced the status of its practitioners. As male power shifted from religious to economic in an expanding market economy, religion was left to women, providing them with the rationale to enter into the public realm in order to reform it according to the moral mission with which they saw themselves charged.[6] Animated by feeling and the values associated with the home, the feminine assignment of moral suasion provided status and agency to women of the emergent middle class who were increasingly excluded from economic production and required to act as domestic ornaments and consumers who testified to their husbands' or fathers' social positions in a supposedly egalitarian order that was in fact becoming more economically stratified.[7]

Reform thus became domesticity's conduit through which women might leave the confines of the home while still remaining firmly within the prescribed domestic role. Barred traditionally from access to the public realm, women were nevertheless imagined by domestic ideology as being responsible for and best suited to purging it of corruption. Under the banner of domesticity, many middle-class women marched into the public world, authorized by religion and a supposedly natural feminine moral sense to enact humanitarian reform. Abolitionist writers such as Harriet Beecher Stowe, who claimed that God wrote *Uncle Tom's Cabin*; feminists like Lucretia Mott and Elizabeth Cady Stanton, who organized the Seneca Falls Women's Rights Convention; and reformers such as Jane Addams, who founded settlement houses for the poor, enlisted domesticity in the name of public humanitarian progress. Women lectured, wrote, protested, commanded, and organized in the name of reform. They mounted campaigns for such varied causes as abolition, temperance, suffrage, education, dress reform, and sanitation, as well as against such vices as prostitution, lynching, prisons, poverty, and obscenity.[8]

Almost all reform issues involved controlling the body or altering its material situation. Reform focused on bodily excesses like drinking and licentiousness, health and cleanliness, eating and dressing practices, bodily deprivations caused by poverty or bad living conditions, and the enslavement of the body. Much anxiety centered on bodily appearance and functioning in a society based on the principles of self-governance and social mobility. An unstable social order, and even anarchy, become constant threats in a democratic order that licenses individual freedoms and neither formalizes nor clearly marks status, hierarchy, and authority. Within this shifting, indecipherable social order, controlling one's body and behavior are the necessary individual corollaries to the national premise of self-governance. Without rigorous systems of external authority and order, such as an aristocracy, the newly democratized nation needed its citizens both to internalize bodily regulation and to display social status. Shorn of the clear and stable markers of social position provided by an aristocracy, the index of identity provided by the actions and appearance of the body becomes fraught with confusion and anxiety.[9] Deciphering and governing the individual body thus became an obsession of nineteenth-century Americans and was carried out in the context of myriad reform programs dressed as progress, self-improvement, or morality.

Not only did reform movements focus on controlling the body, they mobilized the female-centered work of caring for and regulating the body, expanding it from the private home to the larger world. The body itself – especially its excesses, frailties, limitations, and recalcitrance – has traditionally been seen within patriarchy as the province of women. The rhetoric and activism of reform allowed women to appropriate their authority as the traditional representatives of the carnal, transforming it from a social stigma to a religious and social calling. Whereas women had been cast previously as perpetrators or victims of an ungovernable carnality, as subject to their own frail, sensual, vulnerable, and venal bodies, under nineteenth-century domesticity they accepted a mandate to police and extirpate from the social body this very condition. Replete with its exigencies and liabilities, the territory of the body and its association with women was where reform was played out.

Literature became a major tool of reform as literacy and print culture expanded. This was especially so for women because the literary rhetoric of reform offered one means of negotiating domesticity's inherent contradiction that women were responsible for national morality but restricted from morality's larger public arenas. Through writing, women's voices could move freely in the public world while their bodies could remain at home.[10] By entering the public realm in the interests of reform legitimated by domesticity, women both challenged and conformed to the accepted script of femininity. So while much women's reform fiction argues for its cause, it also promotes a larger, more powerful role in the society for women as the agents of that reform. For example, Harriet Beecher Stowe's *Uncle Tom's Cabin*, the prototypical and most successful reform novel of the nineteenth century, simultaneously denounces slavery and glorifies feminine domestic ideology. Stowe was thus able resolutely to present herself as a dutiful, unambitious mother and minister's wife while at the same time actually being one of the century's most influential public figures.

If reforming and rescuing the social body was the civic enactment of domesticity, sentimentality was its strategy, and women's writing was its public site. The term sentimentality expresses the moral component of domesticity. Capturing the essence of the relation women were to have with others, sentimentality describes the dual prescription of emotional connection and moral responsibility that was fundamental to domestic femininity. The inextricable elements of the sentimental imperative that Joanne Dobson calls "[c]onnection, commitment, community"[11] were distinguished from the often individualistic, masculine notions of service in that their medium was emotional and physical connection. This valorization of feeling was of course limited to the domain of emotions gendered as female and positive, such as love, pity, and joy. But the primary emotion of sentimentality was sympathy, the affective bond that enables one to share another's feelings. Feeling with another intensifies the permitted sentiments while focusing women upon others rather than the self. Women's writing became an arena where sympathy could be both manifest and mobilized toward achieving reform and empowering women.

Sympathy is an effective rhetorical strategy in women's writing because it combines and embodies the fundamental elements of the feminine script. If women are to exist for others, sympathy connects women to those they are required to serve. If women are to be religious, sympathy aligns them with the saints and Jesus. If women are to be passive and subservient, sympathy keeps them meek. If women are to remain in the domestic realm, sympathy prepares them for such tasks as tending to bodily needs. If women are to be moral, sympathy catalyzes their interest in reform. Thus, sympathy acts as both bond and incentive, as repression and liberation. Cast as the quintessential feminine emotion, sympathy entails an attachment to others that facilitates female subordination to male interests by requiring women to deny their own concerns and serve others. Yet women manipulated sympathy's demand to focus on their masters by turning it upon the world outside the husband, children, and home. Sympathy became the sentiment that legitimated their entrance into and appropriation of the public sphere.

What ignites sympathy most effectively is suffering. Suffering arouses the feminine charge of care giving and moral responsibility. Suffering demands alleviation. Sympathy licenses a moral mandate to assuage suffering, a mandate that confers both status and agency on the sympathizer. In other words, to rescue or palliate someone who is suffering empowers the redeemer. Moreover, suffering is manifest in the body, that fraught signifier of identity so carefully controlled and watched in democratic society and so closely aligned with the female sphere. America was anxiously distrustful about how and whether the body revealed the truth about its bearer. However, the suffering body that manifests the marks of its misery was an unambiguous, stable sign. Culturally bound to the realm of women, the body that testified to its own suffering could function as an anchor for interpretation and provide a clarity of mission for middle-class women seeking authority and influence in the wider world through reform work.

Take for example two prototypical stories in which disabled figures occupy similar narrative positions to one another and serve corresponding aims. These two stories trace a narrative pattern replicated in much women's fiction, in which resonant disabled figures enable the authors both to challenge and confirm the dominant ideology that governed women's lives in nineteenth-century America. First is Mary Mapes Dodge's "Sunday Afternoon in a Poor-House," published in 1876; second is Sarah Orne Jewett's longer narrative, "The Town Poor," which appeared in 1890. Both stories participate in the Christian social reform impulse characteristic of much women's writing of the period and employ the sentimentality which frequently informs such rhetoric. Both implement as well the conventional narrative strategy, featured earlier in Harriet Beecher Stowe's *Uncle Tom's Cabin* and even more directly in Rebecca Harding Davis's "Life in the Iron Mills," in which the middle-class reader or her materially comfortable fictional stand-in is conducted on a kind of tour of the site that the story would inspire her to change. This excursion represents a witnessing on the part of the main characters and the reader. Dodge's account, for example, figures this inspection as the narrator's impulsive poorhouse visit, which is cast repeatedly in terms of "explorations" and "revelations." These introductory narrative encounters occur between representatives of two socially estranged groups who are both identified with and differentiated from one another in the story; for Dodge and Jewett, these two groups are middle-class women and the poor. Although "Sunday Afternoon in a Poor-House" begins and ends with, as well as emanates from, the perspective of the middle-class narrator's "I," that focus is quickly eclipsed by the vivid scenes of physical destitution her gaze registers and her voice details. By pointing only to the "Poor," both Dodge's and Jewett's stories' titles replicate the relationship the narratives establish between the obscured viewer and the highlighted object of her scrutiny.

What cements this relationship is sentiment: the suffering on the part of the spectacle generates sympathy on the part of the spectator. Indeed, Dodge's spare plot consists entirely of this sentiment-charged encounter between spectator and spectacle. The narrator and her friend intuitively abandon for the day their "pleasant conditions" where they are "surrounded by luxury" in order to seek "extreme opposites" in the poorhouse trip. Their "glorious day" and "blue sky" are soon blotted out by the "revelations [they see] in those rows of pauper faces." At first, the spectacle of the poor is "easy" to endure for the inmates are praying and being ministered to by a sermon assuring them that "Jesus loves you." Descending further into the Infernoesque poorhouse, however, the narrator confronts a grim series of worsening tableaux, through which she hurriedly moves, "for there was too much to be seen."[12] Constituting a kind of trial for the narrator, the spectacles emerge in graphic physical detail, each a "poor creature," one "tortured," another "lean[ing] on a crutch," yet another "ugly and faded and wretched," and another a "half-witted creature" with a "poor helpless face" suggestive of "a monkey." Filled with "a vague dread that [she] might see something which it would not be pleasant to discover," the narrator nevertheless delineates the dreaded unpleasantness with relentless specificity.[13]

The narrative strategy here is one of witness. The narrator and reader witness the body which indexes the suffering to which they respond emotionally and then move to ameliorate. Economic exclusion is embodied here as visible physical disability. The suffering of poverty must be visually apprehensible to the spectator for sentiment and revelation to occur. Thus, the visible disability functions as the mark of a whole range of exclusions: poverty, physical misery, expulsion from the work force, social rejection, mental instability. The visual semantics of these exclusions are the "poor helpless face," the "crutch," the hands "badly swollen at the knuckles," the "aimless look" on the face of the "idiot," the body "doubled up with rheumatism." In contrast to this narrative of witness that exposes bodily particularity is the narrator's disembodied voice. If the inmates are all body, the narrator is all agency. The narrator's emotion bridges this gap as she emerges from the poorhouse overcome by "a choking sense of human misery."[14] Identification with the inmates' suffering bodies has quelled the narrator's voice; their bodies have thus disclosed her previously unnarrated and invulnerable body. Although momentarily aligned with their bodily limitations, the narrator quickly retreats from that identification by escaping to her home.

Despite the urgency of what is witnessed, the reader remains uninstructed and the story's mission unelaborated at the close of the tour. Departing into a day now cold and cloudy, the friend is "filled with grand philanthropic ideas." The narrator, on the other hand, tersely delivers the story's final line: "Let us walk fast. There'll be a bright fire at home; and they'll all be sitting round it, waiting for us."[15] This idealized image of domesticity contrasts starkly with the institutional despair from which the narrator is fleeing. Such an ending implies that the spectacle of the assuredly miserable poor and disabled bodies is sufficient to activate the reader's philanthropic agency, especially if the narrator does not express a commitment. In fact, the reader's intervention becomes all the more necessary since the narrator – like many others, the story implies – flees the depressing and miserable scene without helping. Furthermore, the inmates are clearly incapable of acting in their own behalf. The narrator condemns herself in order to create a mandate for the reader to act since the narrator and her friend probably will not. In the name of sympathy for the suffering other, that quintessentially female appeal, the story rhetorically recruits the reader in its program of reform and delivering succor. Middle-class domesticity, the story suggests, is not where the suffering body is found, but rather is the empowered space from which the suffering body can be assuaged.

Sympathy with the visible suffering of others not only corresponds with the feminine ideal, but it harmonizes with the middle-class notion of self that emerged during the mid-nineteenth century along with industrialization, urbanization, and the consolidation of class differences. In an effort to distinguish itself from other economic and ethnic groups, the predominately white bourgeoisie cultivated manners, practices, and other class markers that it defined as respectable and genteel. Middle-class status became a matter of performance, composed primarily of what Karen Halttunen calls the "sentimental demand for a transparent display of feeling."[16] Pity, compassion, sincerity, and other supposedly elevated feelings were seen as the sensitive, civilized responses of bourgeois subjects to those with less status and power. For women, domesticity's moral mandate and religious affiliation combined with this middle-class form of *noblesse oblige* to intensify the fusion of femininity with sympathy.

The performance of bourgeois respectability dictated that the relationship between the middle and the lower classes was one of stewardship, rather than crass authoritarianism. Sympathy rather than domination best suited this notion, even though both could be mobilized for similar outcomes. Figures such as the paternalistic slave master or the benevolent industrialist testify to the interdependence of class identity and suggest that the subjugation of the working classes could amount to a form of oppression that appeared as fondness rather than antipathy.[17] The pathetic and impotent confirmed the bourgeoisie's status by arousing their finest sentiments. As the increasingly empowered middle class imagined itself capable of capitalizing the world, it began to see itself as responsible for the world as well, a stewardship that launched humanitarian and reform movements.[18]

Continuing the development of the dynamic that we see in Dodge's story between the middle-class rescuer and her suffering beneficiary, Sarah Orne Jewett's "The Town Poor" articulates more fully the relationship between spectator and spectacle that constitutes these narratives of witness. As in Dodge's story, the revelatory tour structures the narrative, and economic exclusion is figured as physical disability in the story's attempt to mobilize the middle-class spectator, the "[c]omfortable Mrs. Trimble,"[19] whose sojourn into the realm of material vulnerability the reader joins. The more complex plot here relates the spontaneous visit of Mrs. Trimble and her companion, Rebecca, to the farm where the now indigent Bray "girls," former friends of both women, are lodged by order of the indifferent city fathers in a kind of protowelfare system. Identification and differentiation among the characters are more enmeshed in Jewett's story than in Dodge's. Of the same community, Mrs. Trimble and the Bray sisters are all elderly women whose economic umbilical cord has been severed by the deaths of the men to whom they were attached. The widowed Mrs. Trimble, however, was left with "a good farm" and had become "an active business woman" who "looked after her own affairs" while the Bray sisters' father "didn't lay by" for them.[20] The past similarities among these women have been transformed in the present into a gulf of difference for which none of the women is directly responsible.

The Brays' material vulnerability, their tenuous position in a male-dominated economic order, is figured as a bodily difference that operates as the undeniable index of social position and status. Whereas Mrs. Trimble moves freely through the community in a horse and wagon, one Bray sister is nearly blind and the other has a "lame wrist." Recalling the inmates of Dodge's poorhouse, the Bray sisters too are "the unwelcome inmates" of "a starved-lookin' place." Although not yet an "inmate," Mrs. Trimble's companion, Rebecca, is also "lame-footed," positioning her midway in the female hierarchy between the secure, still able-bodied widow and the destitute disabled sisters. Witnessing such cautionary figures of female helplessness whose bodies have shifted them into the realm of the vulnerable, Mrs. Trimble responds with a combination of "tender feeling," "tears," and "shame."[21]

As their tour of the Bray sisters' grim attic room and equally bleak spectacle of their lives ends, Mrs. Trimble is filled with resolve. In contrast to Dodge's laconic narrator who flees the poorhouse to the secure middle-class home, Mrs. Trimble coaches the reader in a soliloquy of self-reprimand: "I consider myself to blame, . . . I make no reproaches, an' I take it all on my own shoulders; but I'm goin' to stir about me, I tell you! I shall begin early to-morrow."[22] The story ends as Mrs. Trimble and Rebecca ride off together in the wagon, fervently planning their rescue of the Bray "girls."

The narrative frame of both "Sunday Afternoon in a Poor-House" and "The Town Poor" ultimately centers the stories on the issue of middle-class women's agency, mobilized by the sentiment generated by the sympathetic spectacle of poverty and legitimated by the seemingly undeniable truth of the body. As with reform fiction in general, the reader's point of view is aligned with the spectator/reporter who is presented as having the power to affect the social changes the genre urges. What Dodge's and Jewett's stories illustrate is that the rhetoric of reform embedded in the narrative of witness demands an asymmetrical relationship between the agent of reform and the object. The poor must be incapable of acting on their own behalf, and the reformer must be able to act for them. In other words, the genre requires a victim and a rescuer. The rescuer must be able to identify with the victim enough to respond, but the two positions must be differentiated enough to guarantee a fixed impotence in the victim and a stable capability in the rescuer. If the poor can alter their own circumstances, the rescuer becomes redundant. The disability functions as an absolute yet threatening assurance of the differing positions of the victim and the rescuer. Furthermore, for reform to ensue the reader must imagine herself unequivocally in the position of the rescuer at the moment of the appeal, even as her vulnerability to becoming the victim herself intensifies her response.

Jewett's "The Town Poor" reveals more complexly than Dodge's story some of the cultural narratives that construct disability. For example, a paradox in the way that culture mobilizes disability for its own ends emerges in Jewett's story as the "lame" Rebecca and Mrs. Trimble enthusiastically discuss their plans to rescue the Bray "girls." The Bray sisters' misery, figured as disability, becomes a series of problems that Mrs. Trimble and Rebecca intend to solve by recruiting the community, finding work for the sisters, finding them a new home, and consulting a doctor to "do somethin'" to correct the women's disabilities. We see here that in addition to catalyzing the middle-class spectator/rescuer figure, disability also operates as a problem for the rescuer to solve, an obstacle to be eliminated, a challenge to be met. In this way, disability is transformed from an attribute of the disabled person to a project that morally enables the rescuer. To the rescuers, disability becomes an occasion where their own narratives of progress, improvement, or heroic deliverance can be enacted. Such framing of disability, especially accompanied by today's faith in technology, creates what Paul Longmore calls the "cure or kill" approach to permanent physical disability.[23] If the disabled body cannot be normalized, if it does not respond to being improved, if it refuses to register the success of the rescuer's moral effort, the disabled body becomes intolerable, a witness to the human inability to perfect the world. By thwarting the narrative of heroic redemption, the permanently disabled body testifies to the impotence of its failed rescuer, a reminder that the body is ultimately not fully under the control of the human will. The disabled body thus moves from opportunity to rebuke if it will not be remediated. This aspect of the relationship between the disabled and the nondisabled has led to such contemporary practices as aborting disabled fetuses, emphasizing elimination rather than accommodation of disability, and the sometimes excessive surgical procedures that normalize disabilities.

Rebecca Harding Davis's story, "Blind Tom," suggests this cultural intolerance of the irreparable body, the body that refuses to be reformed. The story is based on the actual life of the musically prodigious slave boy, Thomas Greene Bethune, who was displayed widely by his master in the mid-nineteenth century. Congenitally blind, deformed, and autistic, Tom was also a musical genius. Such a combination of traits rendered him an immensely popular curiosity in an era when the exhibition of freaks and exotics was widespread. Like his fellow freaks, Tom is "an agreeable monster"[24] whose purpose is to prompt astonished contemplation in his audiences. Despite the story's title, Tom is not the protagonist of his narrative, but rather – like most disabled figures – he is an occasion for the edification of his spectators, whether they view his exhibition or read his story. Similar to Dodge's tour through the poorhouse, Davis employs the narrative of witness, teaching her readers a lesson by taking them along to Tom's performances. In "Blind Tom," Davis enlists Tom's body as a spectacle of suffering in the service of an abolition-ist argument framed in the language of the Christian mission to perfect the world.

Davis's account of Tom's startling performances centers on the disjunction between Tom's remarkable ability to generate beautiful music and what she insists is his degenerate body. This discordance operates in the story as a figure for the Christian opposition of body and soul: Tom's is a "beautiful caged spirit . . . struggl[ing] for breath under [a] brutal form and idiotic brain." Race and disability merge as Davis details the "foul bestial prison" of Tom's body.[25] The "idiotic" Tom is "of the lowest negro type . . . coal-black, with protruding heels, the ape-like jaw, blubber-lips constantly open, the sightless eyes closed, and the head thrown far back on the shoulders." While playing, he is "like an ape clawing for food." Davis invokes and intertwines here racist and ablist discourses of the deviant body in her Christian rhetoric. Black and disabled, Tom is the vehicle Davis uses to figure the transcendent spirit trapped in the corrupt body, a concept fundamental to Christianity. Because sentimental conventions dictate that Tom must suffer in order to motivate the reader to act, Davis must narrate "a weary despair . . . on the distorted face" which ostensibly witnesses Tom's awareness of his own degeneracy.[26]

Davis thus recruits the essential, permanent quality of Tom's physical disability to fulfill her rhetorical mandate that Tom's body be irredeemable and his soul saved. Tom's is the body that will not be improved and cannot be normalized. As such, it generates repulsion, the other side of sentimental sympathy. A lost cause, Tom's body condemns him in the end. Davis concludes that, "You cannot help Tom," but that in "your own kitchen" and "back-alley" are "spirits as beautiful, caged in forms as bestial" as Tom's.[27] Since Tom's irremediable bodily prison excludes him from being part of the national redemptive project, Davis ends her story by advocating that the reader, the "you" to whom so much women's reform writing is directed, "set free" the others, whose bodily cages may be less restricting. In the end, the story suggests that the permanently disabled are intransigent enough obstacles to progress that the rhetoric of reformation must logically shift to a rhetoric of elimination. The American ideology of self-reliance combined with the Protestant work ethic have always engendered an anxious suspicion that disabled people – as well as the poor – may be malingerers, as the current debates over welfare reform indicate. When this combines with the American belief in improvement, progress, and perfection, permanently disabled people often are imagined as failures of will or testimonies that the body will not always be rehabilitated. When thwarted, compassion can transform into frustration or defeat, and this imagined resistance by the body to being healed or improved sometimes creates hostility toward disabled people who "take more than their share" of resources or even legitimates such political programs as "mercy" killing of those whose bodies remind collective America that the will is not always the master of the body.

Davis's story suggests, as well, that the disabled figure serves as an effective literary signifier in the project of Christian reform. Within Christian tradition, the disabled figure is associated with Christ, both as the New Testament's "least of these" and as a human manifestation of the suffering body of Jesus with which he redeems humankind.[28] For example, Davis imagines Tom's music as saying, "Bless me, even me, also, O my Father!" Davis invokes the equation of disability with suffering as she insists that Tom's music expresses "all the pain and pathos in the world."[29] As such, the disabled figure recalls those at the bottom of the social strata that the new Christian order wishes to elevate in its reversal of political hierarchy from Jewish to Christian narrated in the New Testament. Much women's reform fiction implicitly advocates a similar reversal of power and priorities so that a feminine domestic value system replaces the masculine marketplace system. For example, Stowe sees abolition as an inherently feminine enterprise that she pits against slavery as marketplace practice. The Christian injunction to respond to disability with compassion rather than revulsion casts the disabled body as a magnet to which the cluster of sentiments associated with femininity could attach themselves. Thus, the body imagined as suffering, frail, needy, rejected, home-bound, and chosen of God operates as an exceedingly appropriate vehicle of rhetorical appeal to emerge from women's culture. For women, this figure is at once the cultural script of the female self and the image of the Other whom they must redeem to fulfill their female destiny.

The pathetic sufferer whose body testifies to its own misery is thus the most effective rhetorical vehicle with which the feminine reform movement might solicit both fine sentiments and a humanitarian impulse, as well as confirm itself as sympathetic. Because the physically disabled figure most closely fits the stereotypical script of the pathetic sufferer, such figures appear often within this complex matrix of domesticity, sentimentality, reform, and women's writing. Always invested with a surplus of meaning, these disabled figures in nineteenth-century women's writing range from the brief rhetorical occasion, to the essential but minor instrumental character, to the central narrative figure. Whatever the nature of the disability itself or the function of the character who bears it, these always visible physical traits refer to the undeniable yet inscrutable authority of the body in order to operate as a semantics of the social or spiritual order that the fictions manifest. The "crippled" body serves as a text within a text through which many women writers advance a particular rhetorical project, register its ambivalences, and testify to its contradictions.

A rhetorical figure's effectiveness depends upon its capacity to invoke the arguments or sentiments that will persuade the reader. If a figure is to exemplify suffering within a Christian, domestic context intended to motivate a reader toward reform, then that suffering must be visibly perceptible so that it can be represented. Therefore, the bodies that authors use to represent suffering must be highly visibly marked to unequivocally evoke the response. Disability operates as the manifestation of suffering, a seemingly undeniable sign that makes what is internal and unnarratable into something external and narratable. In this way the visibly disabled body operates as the spectacle of suffering rather than the reality of suffering which is less representable.[30] In other words, disability acts as the stigmata of suffering. Consequently, reform fiction's witness narrative deploys disabled bodies for their effect, for what they elicit from the reader, rather than to correlate in any way with the actual lives or situations of disabled people. The disabled figure operates in this way as an exhibition, a visual spectacle of suffering on the narrative tour that informs the plot of such fiction as "The Town Poor" and "Sunday Afternoon in a Poor-House." But while this spectacle of suffering acts as a figure of otherness to activate the middle-class women readers and narrators, it is at the same time a hyperbolic yet haunting version of the feminine self, of women, excluded from the dominant sites of power and influence supposedly because of the frailty and deviance of their bodies.

This confluence of the disabled figure and the feminine self is most apparent in Elizabeth Stuart Phelps's story, "The Tenth of January." In it Phelps employs a disabled figure as a spectacle of sympathy similarly to Jewett, Dodge, and Davis in their pleas for the impoverished. The important difference is that the disabled figure is the main character. In contrast to Davis's Tom, Phelps's Sene Martyn is a true protagonist rather than simply an occasion for another rhetorical goal. With this centering of the disabled figure, the dichotomy between heroine and victim that informs Dodge's and Jewett's stories collapses and the reader must fully identify with the disabled figure as the heroine. Phelps's story is particularly interesting because the disabled figure not only operates as the vividly embodied presence that argues for improvement of factory conditions, but also as a touchstone for several other protests, including a critique of women's social position in general.

Originally published in 1868, "The Tenth of January" revises Rebecca Harding Davis's 1861 story, "Life in the Iron Mills," which Phelps acknowledged later as the inspiration for much of her writing.[31] Both stories introduce a sympathetic "hunchbacked" mill girl who is rejected by men because of her appearance so that the stories can expose exploitation and terrible working conditions in the mills. But where Davis focuses her story on a heroic male iron worker whose tale of victimization is merely enhanced by a sympathetic but ineffectual disabled woman figure, Phelps relocates her version of Davis's disabled woman at the center of her story, making her its noble heroine. In essence, in "The Tenth of January's" Sene Martyn, Phelps infuses the pathetic Deb from "Life in the Iron Mills" with the exemplary qualities Davis confers upon her hero, Hugh Wolfe. And like Davis's story, a privatized plea on behalf of the woman rejected because of her appearance is embedded in the call for reform of the public exploitation of mill workers.

A fictionalized account of the actual collapse near the writer's home of the Pemberton Mill in Lawrence, Massachusetts, on January 10, 1860, Phelps's story fuses the veracity of journalistic form with the conventions of sentimental writing, gaining authority and immediacy from the story's factual origin and invoking the ardor of Christian reform with its fictional elements. As America industrialized in the first third of the nineteenth century, the burgeoning textile factories in Massachusetts began employing poor farm girls who seized the jobs as opportunity even though they were paid half as much as men workers. Although the mills provided dormitories, supervision, community, and the appearance of an improved life, working conditions soon became abusive and exploitation was rampant.[32] As the terrible conditions and situations such as the Pemberton

Mill accident illustrate, the new machine culture fueled by capitalist interests simply did not accommodate human needs, rhythms, or scale. Phelps figures the disastrous human toll with the bodily stigmata of her heroine to create the conventional spectacle of suffering that is sentimentalism's chief reform tool.[33]

A hybrid of sentimentalism and realism, "The Tenth of January" freely sculpts its heroine to support its social critique while enlisting the power and truth value of the moving story of hundreds of young girls singing hymns as they burned in the collapsed mill, first undermined by faulty construction and then set ablaze by a rescuer's lamp carelessly tumbled amid the cotton thread. The story begins with generic fidelity to the witness narrative, conducting its readers on a tour of the mill town. "The time to see Lawrence," we are told, "is when the mills open or close." Addressing the reader as "you" and aligning our viewpoint with hers, the narrative voice, which is never embodied in the story, points out the "common dinginess," "restlessness," and "despair" on the "[f]actory faces," some of which are "old before [their] time," or anxious over "many mouths to feed at home."[34] To maximize a sense of the real, the reader is brought to the corner of Essex Street in Lawrence at four o'clock on a Saturday afternoon at the end of November, 1859, to witness a detailed display of Phelps's heroine, Sene.

The narrative directs the gazes of the readers and characters relentlessly upon the particulars of Sene's body and face as it reveals her history. Even Sene herself is haunted by her own image in the mirror as she recalls seeing as a child "the ghastly twisted thing that looked back at her." We see the "faded scarlet hood" under which she hides her shameful body and her "sickly," "pallid face" which "would have been womanly" had it not been disqualified from that description by a large "white scar." Instead of being "womanly," Sene's face shows "a certain wiry nervous strength" that makes her noble in the suffering such unsexing causes her. The spectacle of Sene's rejected, deviant body visually structures the plot. At every opportunity, the story returns to the "scarred mouth" and the "rounded and bent" shoulders of this "little crippled girl" victimized by her now dead, drunken mother.[35] At one point, our gaze moves uncomfortably between Sene's and that of Dick Cross, the man she loves, when she views "the look of his face" at the same time that "he for the first time saw what she was, her cape having fallen off in the full lamplight." In several particularly dramatic moments, Phelps replays the mirror scene in which Sene sees herself as others see her, as "a humpbacked white creature with distorted face and wide eyes." After learning that Dick pities her rather than loves her, she strips behind her locked door and torments herself by staring at her own image before the mirror and assuming the normative, evaluating male gaze that condemns her body as ugly and unacceptable. In this anxious ritual of female self-evaluation and self-alienation shared under patriarchy by all women, Sene objectifies her own viewed body, shrinking "at the first sight of herself" but nevertheless vowing "resolutely" to "see the worst of it . . . letting the cruel light gloat over her shoulders, letting the sickly shadows grow purple on her face." Reduced to tears by the image of her own rejected, repulsive body, Sene cries out, "Why did a good God make such faces?"[36] This painful scene divides the female reader's gaze between objectification and identification, swathing her in a conflicting welter of compassion and revulsion.

But Phelps insists on justice in this story of dual protest against women's treatment in the cotton mills and the marriage mills. She unequivocally pries female virtue away from beauty here by counterpointing Sene with a beautiful, much sought-after foil, Del, who has good looks but no character, indeed who is a "pretty, shallow thing . . . [a] worthless bewildering thing!" With Sene and Del, the story documents the injustices of a female economy of appearance in which Del gets the men and Sene endures harassment by small children crying "Humpback! humpback!" and gawking strangers who comment loudly, "Look at that girl! I'd kill myself if I looked like that." The good-hearted but foolish Dick Cross — whose name suggests he is both the burden Sene must bear and the site of her suffering — falls prey to the transient world of appearances by falling in love at the sight of the beautiful, Circe-like Del, who views him as just another suitor in her thoughtless quest for a husband who might let her have "a parlor and a door-bell." In the climactic scene of the mill collapse toward which the narrative relentlessly marches, justice finally triumphs. As the fire permits rescuing only one more girl from the disaster, the wounded, trapped Sene bids Del go, blessing her union with the waiting Dick and forgiving them both. Watching Dick as he bears Del to safety in his arms, quite forgetting Sene, the now condemned girl becomes the chosen of God, if not man, to be a "lamb for the burnt-offering." Assuring her distraught old father outside that she doesn't "mind it very much," Sene sings hymns beside "the form of the Son of God" until hers is the last voice silenced by the fire.[37]

In this final spectacle of suffering the problem of the disabled, devalued body is effaced in the narrative by the fire and in the story's governing ideology by the Christian dismissal of the body and elevation of the soul. The realm in which Sene will get a man who loves her for herself is heaven. Since Sene's body is the site/sight of her oppression, her disembodiment provides her only fulfillment as a woman. Freed from being a bodily spectacle of suffering, she transforms into a voice of suffering-as-redemption, singing "triumphantly, — 'To die no more, no more, no more!' "[38] Sene's suffering is not pathetic but ennobling; indeed, it repeats the suffering of Christ. As her name, "Martyn," suggests, Sene is a Christ-like martyr, whose cross to bear is not only the faithless Dick Cross, but her corrupt body as well. As with Davis's Tom, the permanence of Sene's disability, its irremediable quality, disqualifies it from the progress narrative that redeems the suffering sentimentalism equates with disability. Instead, the disabled body thwarts rescue and must be severed from soul in order for redemption to occur. As with Tom, whom "[you] cannot help," Sene's disabled body becomes an obstacle to the course of Christian progress. The disabled body thus becomes a problem that must be eliminated in sentimental discourse's final solution.

Phelps's merging of the disabled figure, the woman outside the economy of marriage, the heroine, and Christ in the character of Sene suggests the entanglement of identification and differentiation that middle-class women had with the figures on whose behalf they launched reform movements in the nineteenth century. Proscribed from self-interest by rigid gender roles, their only legitimate avenue to self-promotion was to advocate for others with whom they identified. Spectacles themselves in an order that measured a man's success by the actions and appearance of the women attached to him, the middle-class women who spearheaded reform movements as well as wrote and read its literature were accustomed to the anxieties and vulnerabilities of the evaluative gaze. Perhaps, then, it is middle-class women's familiarity with being spectacles that suggested the convention in their own reform writing.

The disabled figures that Dodge, Jewett, Davis, and Phelps employ in their stories help reveal the double purpose of much nineteenth-century women's fiction. Imagined historically as an essential property of the body, physical disability operates as a particularly resonant trope to satisfy the demands of this feminized rendering of reform fiction. While this writing's explicit mission is didactic or aimed toward reform, it often places beneath the moral or spiritual message an implicit, usually anxious and conflicted subtext concerning women's own sociopolitical roles and relationships. In such fiction, disabled figures prove especially adept both in conveying a lesson and in exploring the fraught issues surrounding female identity. Because the care of the body has also been the task of women, people with disabilities and their needs have traditionally been associated with women. Women and the disabled are ideologically linked as well through the persistent framing of the female body as defective, as in Aristotle's rendering of women as mutilated males.[39] Consequently, an ambivalent identification between women and disabled figures inhabits much of this fiction.

Women's writing thus sentimentalized disability, as well as other forms of embodied Otherness, in nineteenth-century bourgeois culture. The brutish Other, the Savage, and the Monster become the sympathetic Other as middle-class hegemony solidifies. As the disabled figure is domesticated, it shifts from monster to cripple. Shakespeare's Richard III becomes Dickens's Tiny Tim; Caliban becomes a Teddy Bear. Feminine sympathy thus served to solidify the ascendancy of the middle class as stewards of the pathetic. Such a move promoted as well the image of the genteel entrepreneurial self at the same time that it garnered status for women and improved the social body.

As women's writing manifested the dramatic social and material changes that took place in America during the nineteenth century, it appropriated and significantly shaped the social construction of disability. The disabled body was deployed to witness suffering so that the disability came to visibly mark the anguish that the characters and readers themselves were then to witness. Such spectacles of suffering served the rhetorical purpose of eliciting sentiments and igniting efforts that ennobled the middle-class participants in the economy of humanitarian fiction that dominated women's writing. In short, nineteenth-century women's writing consolidated the cultural figure of the physically disabled person into a sentimental spectacle of sympathy, the predominant image of disability that prevails in the twentieth century.

NOTES

1 On domesticity, see Gillian Brown, *Domestic Individualism: Imagining Self in Nineteenth-Century America* (Berkeley: University of California Press, 1990); Mary P. Ryan, *Empire of the Mother: American Writing About Domesticity, 1830–1860* (New York: Institute for Research in History and The Hawthorne Press, 1982); Barbara Welter, "The Cult of True Womanhood: 1820–60," *American Quarterly* 18 (1966): 151–74. On sentimentality see, Joanne Dobson, "The American Renaissance Re-envisioned," in *The (Other) American Traditions: Nineteenth-Century Women Writers*, ed. Joyce W. Warren (New Brunswick: Rutgers University Press, 1993), 164–82; Philip Fisher, *Hard Facts: Setting and Form in the American Novel* (New York: Oxford University Press, 1985); Shirley Samuels, ed., *The Culture of Sentiment: Race, Gender, and Sentimentality in Nineteenth-Century America* (New York: Oxford University Press, 1992); Jane P. Tompkins, *Sensational Designs: The Cultural Work of American Fiction, 1790–1860* (New York: Oxford University Press, 1985).

2 Nancy F. Cott, *The Bonds of Womanhood: "Woman's Sphere" in New England, 1780–1835* (New Haven: Yale University Press, 1977); Thomas Walter Laqueur, *Making Sex: Body and Gender from the Greeks to Freud* (Cambridge, MA: Harvard University Press, 1990); Nancy Tuana, *The Less Noble Sex: Scientific, Religious, and Philosophical Conceptions of Women's Nature* (Bloomington: Indiana University Press, 1993).

3 Nina Baym, *Woman's Fiction: A Guide to Novels by and About Women in America, 1820–1870* (Ithaca: Cornell University Press, 1978); Mary Kelley, *Private Woman, Public Stage: Literary Domesticity in Nineteenth-Century America* (New York: Oxford University Press, 1984).

4 John L. Thomas, "Romantic Reform in America, 1815–1865," *American Quarterly* 17 (1965): 662.

5 Rosemarie Garland Thomson, "Benevolent Maternalism and Physically Disabled Figures: Dilemmas of Female Embodiment in Stowe, Davis, and Phelps," *American Literature* 68 (1996): 555–86; Thomas L. Haskell, "Capitalism and the Origins of the Humanitarian Sensibility, Part 1," *American History Review* 90 (1985): 339–61 and "Capitalism and the Origins of the Humanitarian Sensibility, Part 2," *American History Review* 90 (1985): 547–66; and Brown, *Domestic Individualism*.

6 Ann Douglas, *The Feminization of American Culture* (New York: Knopf, 1977); Carroll Smith-Rosenberg, *Disorderly Conduct: Visions of Gender in Victorian America* (New York: Oxford University Press, 1985); Lori D. Ginzberg, *Women and the Work of Benevolence: Women, Morality, and Class in the Nineteenth-Century United States* (New Haven: Yale University Press, 1990); see also Barbara McCaskill, "'To Labor . . . and Fight on the Side of God': Spirit, Class, and Nineteenth-Century African American Women's Literature," chapter 9 in this volume.

7 Stuart Blumin, *The Emergence of the Middle Class: Social Experience in the American City, 1760–1900* (Cambridge: Cambridge University Press, 1989); Thorstein Veblen, *The Theory of the Leisure Class* (1899; reprint, Boston: Houghton Mifflin, 1973).

8   Many of the texts in Karen L. Kilcup's *Nineteenth-Century American Women Writers: An Anthology* deal with reform issues. For some examples, see Lydia Sigourney's "Drinking Song" on temperance; Sigourney's "Indian Names," Lydia Maria Child's "Adventure in the Woods," Sarah Winnemucca's "First meeting of Piutes and whites," and Zitkala-Ša's "The School Days of an Indian Girl" on Native American issues; Margaret Fuller's Woman in the Nineteenth Century and Frances Harper's "John and Jacob – a Dialogue on Women's Rights" on women's rights; Lucy Larcom's "Weaving" and Harper's Aunt Chloe poems on abolition; Fanny Fern's "A Word on the Other Side" on anti-prostitution; Betsey Chamberlain's "A New Society" and Fern's "Soliloquy of a Housemaid" on the situation of the working classes; Celia Thaxter's "Woman's Heartlessness" on ecology; Child's "General Maxims for Health" and Fern's "Fashionable Invalidism" on health and sanitary issues; Child's "The Education of Daughters" and Anna Julia Cooper's "The Higher Education of Women" on education; and Ida Wells-Barnett's "History of Some Cases of Rape" on lynching.

9   Karen Halttunen, *Confidence Men and Painted Women: A Study of Middle-Class Culture in America, 1830–1870* (New Haven: Yale University Press, 1982); G. J. *Barker-Benfield, Horrors of the Half-Known Life: Male Attitudes Toward Women and Sexuality in Nineteenth-Century America* (New York: Harper and Row, 1976).

10   See Kelley, *Private Woman, Public Stage.*

11   Dobson, "The American Renaissance Reenvisioned," 167.

12   *NCAWW*, 243, 244.

13   Ibid., 244, 245, 246.

14   Ibid., 245, 246.

15   Ibid., 246.

16   Halttunen, *Confidence Men and Painted Women*, 193.

17   Keith Thomas, *Man and the Natural World* (New York: Pantheon, 1983); Yi-Fu Tuan, *Dominance and Affection: The Making of Pets* (New Haven: Yale University Press, 1984).

18   See Haskell, "Capitalism and the Origins of the Humanitarian Sensibility, Part 1" and "Capitalism and the Origins of the Humanitarian Sensibility, Part 2."

19   *NCAWW*, 386.

20   Ibid., 384, 386.

21   Ibid., 385, 387, 386, 385, 389, 388.

22   Ibid., 390.

23   Personal conversation, January 1997.

24   *NCAWW*, 230.

25   Jean Pfaelzer, "The Common Stories of Rebecca Harding Davis: An Introduction," in *A Rebecca Harding Davis Reader*, ed. Jean Pfaelzer (Pittsburgh: University of Pennsylvania Press, 1995); see especially xxv–xxvii.

26   *NCAWW*, 233, 231, 228, 232, 233.

27   Ibid., 233.

28   Nancy Eiesland, *The Disabled God: Toward a Liberatory Theology of Disability* (Nashville: Abington Press, 1994); Julius Rubin, *Religious Melancholy and the Protestant Experience* (New York: Oxford University Press, 1994); Robert A. Orsi, "'Mildred, Is It Fun to be a Cripple?' The Culture of Suffering in Mid-Twentieth Century Catholicism," *South Atlantic Quarterly* 93 (1994): 547–90; Charles Kokaska et al., "Disabled People in the Bible," *Rehabilitation Literature* 45 (1984): 20–1.

29   *NCAWW*, 233.

30   In *The Body in Pain: The Making and Unmaking of the World* (New York: Oxford University Press, 1985), Elaine Scarry argues that pain as a form of suffering is not narratable because it is not manifest in the body. Disability operates as pain's opposite in that it is visibly manifest in the body and therefore can be employed as the representation of suffering, even though it may not actually entail suffering.

31   Elizabeth Stuart Phelps, "Stories that Stay," *Century Magazine* 59 (November 1910): 120.

32   Benita Eisler, *The Lowell Offering: Writings by New England Mill Women (1840–1845)* (New York: J. P. Lippincott, 1977), 13–33.

33   With its blends of journalistic style, sentimentality, and grim detail, Phelps's story illustrates the connection between sentimentalism and regional realism that Joanne Dobson finds.

34   *NCAWW*, 316.

35   Ibid., 318, 317, 318, 319. The subplot of the drunken mother who causes Sene's disabilities adds the argument for temperance reform to the rhetoric of class and sex exploitation that inform the story.

36   Ibid., 320, 321, 324.

37   Ibid., 322, 318, 319–20, 322, 332, 333.

38   Ibid., 333.

39   Barbara Hillyer, *Feminism and Disability* (Norman: University of Oklahoma Press, 1993); Tuana, *The Less Noble Sex*.

8

Fracturing Gender: Woman's Economic Independence

Joyce W. Warren

In Charlotte Perkins Gilman's short story "If I Were a Man" (1914) the female protagonist is magically turned into her husband. As she walks to work, she puts her hands in her pockets and feels money. Gilman writes: "All at once, with a deep rushing sense of power and pride, she felt what she had never felt before in all her life – the possession of money, of her own earned money – hers to give or withhold, not to beg for, tease for, wheedle for – hers."[1] In this sudden realization by her character of the "power and pride" that comes with the possession of one's own money, Gilman articulates the key to her analysis of the situation of women. As she wrote in her autobiography, "the basic need of economic independence seemed to me of far more importance than the ballot."[2]

In thus asserting the necessity of economic independence for women, Gilman broke with the cultural assumptions that had dominated the nineteenth-century attitude toward women, an attitude that cut across the lines of class and race. In this essay I will be dealing with four women writers whose outspoken advocacy of economic independence for women set them apart from their society: Fanny Fern (1811–72), Frances Watkins Harper (1825–1911), Louisa May Alcott (1832–88), and Charlotte Perkins Gilman (1860–1935). Instead of reifying notions of gender along with their contemporaries, these writers displaced the notions of female dependency which supported male hegemony and substituted new and radical performative acts.[3] Asserting the intersecting identities of race and/or class, they advocated behavior that was at variance with the behavior that their culture had defined as natural to them as women – thus fracturing the concept of gender. Demonstrating that gender identity is constituted by discursive forces, they introduced a new and politically charged discourse which defined women as economically independent. I will look first at the discursive forces that defined gender in nineteenth-century American society and examine the effects of that discourse on women writers; in the last half of the essay I will discuss the works of these four women writers whose assertion of economic independence fractured discursive definitions of gender.

Nineteenth-Century Gender Identity

Although many nineteenth-century women worked for wages, the need to work was usually regarded as an unfortunate (and, it was hoped, temporary) necessity – by the society and by the women themselves.[4] Middle- and upper-class women, the exponents of "true womanhood," were expected to remain in the home, and this image of the proper "sphere" for women established the criterion for American Victorian womanhood. White working-class women aspired to domesticity as the dominant cultural model for women, and Northern middle-class black women (eager to dissociate themselves from the degradation of the enforced labor of slavery) accepted "domestic economy" as an empowering cultural mode.[5]

For most of the nineteenth century, if a woman did have money of her own (through inheritance or through her own labor), legally and by tradition her money belonged to her husband. He could use her money in any way he wished: he could use it to support the family *or* he could spend it on alcohol and other women or lose it through unwise investments. In 1850 James Fenimore Cooper wrote the novel *The Ways of the Hour* in opposition to proposed laws that would give a married woman control of her property. Cooper reflected the opinion of many of his contemporaries when he asserted that the laws of nature and of God intended woman to be dependent upon man. If she possessed any money of her own, Cooper wrote, she should "reverently pour it into her husband's lap."[6] Married women retained this *feme covert* status throughout most of the nineteenth century, and even when state laws were changed giving married women control of their property, tradition and social pressure made women slow to take advantage of their rights.

Tradition and the law took women's money away from them; tradition and religious opinion erected obstacles against their earning any money of their own. Theologians such as Horace Bushnell and John Todd warned of the dangers of women's "unsexing" themselves by pursuing "masculine" activities.[7] The Rev. Jesse Peck expressed the general opinion of the age regarding women's employment when he declared in the *Ladies' Repository* of August 1853 that woman's sphere was exclusively domestic. Women, he said, were not suited for the "rude antagonisms and fierce collisions" of public and professional life.[8]

The ubiquitous nature of the assumption that women should remain in the home is apparent in the fact that Ralph Waldo Emerson gave the same advice to a women's rights convention in Boston in 1855. Woman, he said, was the "Angel in the parlor"; her proper function was to "embellish trifles." Asserting that a true woman would not wish to act for herself, Emerson concluded that if a woman wanted to get anything done, her best recourse was to rely on a good

man: "Woman should find in man her guardian."[9] Aside from Emerson's effron-
tery in making such a speech to a women's rights convention, the reality, of
course, was that many women (lesbians or others who were single by choice)
would not want to take Emerson's advice, and many other women could not
take his advice even if they wanted to: they did not have a "good man" to rely
on. As Sarah Orne Jewett's "The Town Poor" (1890) makes clear, husbands and
fathers died or became ill; and, as we see in Fanny Fern's *Rose Clark* (1856) and
Pauline Hopkins's "Bro'r Abr'm Jimson's Wedding," not all men were "good."

Not only did society frown on women's entrance into the marketplace, there
were few opportunities for women workers, and the pay was considerably lower
than it was for men. The seamstress, the mill-worker, the domestic worker, the
orphan, the widow, the wife or daughter of a man who either could not work or
who dissipated his family's money – all of these women, black and white, and of
every class, found themselves with few options: if a woman had sufficient education and the correct manners, she could find a post as a teacher, a governess, or
a paid or unpaid companion. Otherwise, her choices included prostitution, work
at subsistence wages, or humble dependency as an unpaid servant in the home of
a relative. Betsey Chamberlain's 1841 utopian sketch in the *Lowell Offering*, "A
New Society," looks forward to the day twenty years thence when two-thirds
of the population of the United States would advocate equal wages and equal
opportunities for men and women. However, as such works as Elizabeth Stuart
Phelps's "The Tenth of January" (1868), Lucy Larcom's *An Idyl of Work* (1875),
or Fanny Fern's "Soliloquy of a Housemaid" (1852) demonstrate, a woman's earning power remained at a low level, and her "opportunities" included being able
to work from 6:30 a.m. to 6:30 p.m. six days a week as a "machine" in an airless
factory, or even longer hours as a "dray-horse" in somebody else's home.

If traditional American society provided little help for working women,
working-class organizations were equally discriminatory. Organized labor functioned primarily to protect the interests of working-class men. The trade unions,
for the most part, refused to admit women and restricted women to the lowest-
paying jobs. The short-lived National Labor Union in 1868 and the Knights of
Labor in 1878 came out in favor of "equal pay for equal work,"[10] and women
organized their own unions, but the craft unions kept women shut out. The
leader of the New York Working Women's Society in 1898 pointed out that
because of the unions' refusal to admit women, there were forty thousand working women in New York City whose wages were so low that in order to survive
they had to resort to charity "or worse."[11] In 1900 women petitioned the American Federation of Labor, complaining that they were being kept out of the trade
unions, but the A.F. of L. leaders justified the exclusion on the grounds that
women did not enter the workforce "permanently."[12]

As Meredith Tax points out in *The Rising of the Women* (1980), the principal
allies of working-class women were not working-class men, but other women:
middle-class reformers, settlement house workers, feminists, and socialist housewives.[13] Mary Kenney, a Chicago wage-earner who had determined early that

women needed to organize to protect themselves, pursued an independent course attempting to organize women workers in the 1880s; her main support came from Jane Addams at Hull House.[14] In 1892 Kenney was appointed by Samuel Gompers as a woman organizer for the A.F. of L., but despite her many successes, she was fired from the job after six months, the executive board having concluded that it did not want to spend the money on organizing women. Kenney provides an important comment on the problems inherent in society's definition of women; she found that not only did men view women as dependent, but women themselves accepted this definition. Recognizing the need to redefine gender, she wrote in 1893: "If our mothers would teach us self-reliance and independence, that it is our duty to wholly depend upon ourselves, we would then feel the necessity of organization. . . . [But women] feel that an institution [a union] which has for its platform protection, is for men only[,] and the only protection they expect is the protection given them by men, not realizing that it is their duty to protect themselves."[15]

Not only did organized labor discriminate against women, but American Marxists did not help the cause of women either. Ironically, the Marxists adopted the same values as bourgeois society with respect to women, idealizing woman in her domestic role. As Mari Jo Buhle points out in *Women and American Socialism, 1870–1920* (1981), the Marxists used "scientific" principles to reaffirm woman's traditional role.[16] Commenting on the devastation of the proletarian family by the exploitation of labor, Marx and Engels in *The Communist Manifesto* (1848) stressed the importance of "family ties."[17] As Buhle notes, the German American Socialists, influenced by Marx and by their own romantic view of woman, did not support women's rights (women's right to labor or to vote) and saw it as their duty to "protect woman's domestic role."[18] American Socialist Adolf Douai wrote in 1878 that "one of the most beautiful aims of Socialism was the restoration of family unity," and European Socialist Ferdinand Lassalle praised the "coziness" and "poetry of domestic life."[19]

Although organized labor and Marxist Socialists did not encourage women's economic independence, there were socialist and reformist movements that explicitly advocated it. One such movement was inspired by Edward Bellamy's utopian novel, *Looking Backward*, published in 1888. Bellamy portrayed a future society in which women were economically independent; as one character comments, "That any person should be dependent for the means of support upon another would be shocking." Bellamy's book was a bestseller and provided a catalyst for women activists who founded a collectivist movement based on the ideas of political and economic equality outlined by Bellamy.[20] Other cooperative movements that were led by women also advocated women's economic independence. Such groups included those of Melusina Pierce in the late 1860s; Mary Livermore and Helen Campbell in the 1880s; and Marie Howland from 1874 to 1885. However, the ideas of these reformers were often utopian and did not gain a large following. In addition, some of them were made unpopular by their inclusion of free-love principles.[21]

The question of women's sexual purity was in fact the most difficult issue for women to deal with. Even so liberal a man as Robert Bonner, the editor of the *New York Ledger*, who was sympathetic to women's issues, was unable to separate women's economic independence from ideas of sexual promiscuity and antimaternal feelings. "Transplant" woman from the home to the marketplace, he wrote in an editorial in 1859, and she becomes a "monster, a *man-woman*." "The so-called 'strong-minded women' of the day," said Bonner, are women "with their own 'independent' platform, self-condemned as infidels, as contemners of marriage and its obligations, as the advocates of the 'largest liberty' in the indulgence of the passions."[22]

This, then, was the most difficult problem for nineteenth-century women: their culture associated women's independence, particularly economic independence, with sexual promiscuity and immorality. At the same time, however, their culture insisted upon female purity. Even to get oneself talked about was dangerous for a woman. For this reason, it was risky for a woman to advocate women's economic independence. Just as the term "communist" was damning in the 1950s, and the associations given to the word "liberal" in the 1988 presidential campaign put liberals on the defensive, so negative associations with the concept of women's economic independence forced nineteenth-century women either to deny any interest in the idea or to defend themselves against its pejorative associations. For the most part, American women writers in the nineteenth century either agreed with or did not try to resist this discursive construction of gender. The price was too high. It was not only that they would be labeled unfeminine or unwomanly, but also that they would be labeled immoral.

Many nineteenth-century American women writers began writing as a "respectable" means of earning an income (e.g., Sigourney, Hale, Fern, Alcott, Freeman), and many novels portrayed a heroine who, finding herself in straitened circumstances, was able to earn her own living. In most novels, however, the heroine's work was regarded as a stop-gap measure, necessary only to fill the years between childhood and marriage. Once the heroine found a man, she gladly gave up her job, and with it her independence, for what most readers would have agreed was her proper profession: wifehood and motherhood. This is the story in some of the most popular mid-nineteenth-century novels by women: Susan Warner's *The Wide, Wide World* (1850) and *Queechy* (1852), Maria Cummins's *The Lamplighter* (1854), and Augusta Evans Wilson's *St. Elmo* (1866).

Ironically, most women writers did not advocate economic independence for women even when they themselves were economically independent. Although they had in their personal lives often adopted the role of principal breadwinner for their families, in their fiction they continued to portray domesticity as the only acceptable goal for women. It is possible that they did not believe it themselves but were astute enough to know that if they wanted to get their books published, and if they wanted to sell their books, they could not risk seeming to advocate what the public regarded as immoral or improper for women. Not only would such writing jeopardize their reputations as respectable women, it would jeopardize their sales. Moreover, the two were connected: publishers for the most part would not publish, and the public would not buy, books by a woman who was regarded as immoral.

In order to understand just how important it was for nineteenth-century women writers to conform to public standards of morality and feminine propriety, one only has to look at what happened to the careers of women who did transgress the code of convention. The best-known example is that of Kate Chopin, who had established a successful career as a writer of short stories. After the 1899 publication of her novel, *The Awakening*, which contained the sympathetic portrayal of a woman whose search for personal autonomy led her to commit adultery and leave her husband and children, editors would no longer buy Chopin's stories, and her career ended. Chopin never published in her lifetime an even more radical work like "The Storm," which legitimized female sexual pleasure. Lydia Maria Child's career as a popular writer was similarly ended by the publication of a work that was considered radical and improper for a woman to write. Child was the author of two successful novels and the founder of the first children's periodical, the *Juvenile Miscellany*. In 1833, however, she published the pamphlet *An Appeal in Favor of That Class of Americans Called Africans*, one of the first antislavery books in the United States. After the publication of this "radical" text, people would no longer buy her books or subscribe to her children's magazine. That women writers deliberately modified their writing to conform to social prescriptions of femininity is apparent in the career of Caroline Kirkland. After the criticism she received for her outspoken and unconventional satire in *A New Home, Who'll Follow?* (1839), Kirkland toned down her writing and even went out of her way to establish her propriety by criticizing other women writers whom she regarded as imprudent. When her husband died in 1846, she was able to support herself and her children by her writing and editing, but she deliberately suppressed her private voice and, as she said, always wrote within the "restraints" of a "lady."[23]

It is clear, then, that women writers who transgressed the conventional code of behavior for "respectable" women risked losing the ability to earn a living from their writing. In any case, whether out of fear or conviction (and my guess is that it was a little of both), most women writers reiterated the dominant discourse. If a writer did introduce the idea of economics into an occasional work, the situation was particularized in that work. For example, Rose Terry Cooke's "How Celia Changed Her Mind" (1891) portrays an "old maid" who finds that the independence of "single blessedness" is preferable to marriage to a tight-fisted widower, and Constance Fenimore Woolson's "Miss Grief" (1880) illustrates the contrast between a less talented but financially successful male writer and a woman writer who cannot make a living from her superior but unmarketable writing. For the most part, however, women writers did not take a sustained stand in defense of woman's economic autonomy; even when they themselves were economically independent, they did not publicly advocate such a role for women.[24]

Although most women writers reified conventional notions of gender, there were a few who had struggled to support themselves and who publicly asserted the need for women's economic independence. Their realization derived in part from a recognition of the plurality of gender identity: fracturing gender revealed its intersections with other identities, such as those of race and class. Generalizations about gender became impossible when one considered women's differences. Although middle-class men like Emerson might comfortably assert the ideal of male protection of women, women writers who themselves had to work recognized the fatuousness of ideas like Emerson's: the fact was that men could not be counted on to protect women, particularly women whom they regarded as their racial or social inferiors. In fact, such women were fair game for sexual and economic exploitation by men. By pointing out the different treatment that women received when they did not have money, and/or were racially vulnerable, women writers – for example, Fanny Fern in *Ruth Hall* (1855), E. D. E. N. Southworth in *The Hidden Hand* (1859), Harriet Wilson in *Our Nig* (1859), and Rebecca Harding Davis in *Margret Howth* (1861) – called attention to the fallacies inherent in the myth of the male protection of women. Moreover, by demonstrating that many women needed to work but that job opportunities were severely limited, they called attention to the gender and race of American individualism: white male Americans could hope to better themselves by self-reliance and seek the American Dream, but women (and non-white men) were left out of the equation. As the nuns recognize in Alice Dunbar-Nelson's story "Sister Josepha" (1899), there is no future for the racially mixed, poor, friendless young woman if she leaves the convent; economics, race, and gender combine to hamstring her.

The construction of women as financially dependent ensured the maintenance of patriarchal capitalism, and the association of female independence with immorality was an insidious way of preventing women from attempting to change the status quo. In fact, the woman who was able to assert publicly the need for women's economic independence often already had a blighted reputation or for some reason was regarded by her society as ineligible for inclusion in the ranks of true womanhood. The writers whom I discuss more specifically below were among the few nineteenth-century American women writers who advocated economic independence as a lifelong goal for women, married or single. The fear of the loss of reputation which inhibited the writing of most women for the most part did not apply to them: two had already had their reputations tarnished; the African American woman was disqualified from the expectations of white society because of her race; and the other white woman refused to sign her name to her unconventional writings.

Woman's Economic Independence

In 1851, Fanny Fern, born Sara Payson Willis, left her abusive second husband, who retaliated by spreading scandalous stories portraying her as sexually promiscuous.[25] Her father and father-in-law refused monetary assistance in an

attempt to force her to return to her husband. This was the same economic lever-
age that her husband had used against her; he had forced himself on her sexually, and in order to gain control, had refused to give her money for herself and
her children. When she left her husband, her father-in-law demanded that she turn
her children over to him and his wife. When she refused, he rewrote his will,
stipulating that her children would inherit nothing from him unless their mother
gave them up to him. At the time that her father-in-law wrote this will, Fern
was destitute and working as a seamstress for fifty cents a week; she knew that
if she did not acquire money of her own, she would have to give up her children.

This experience had several important effects on Fern. First, she learned that
women had no autonomy as long as they were financially dependent: her father,
father-in-law, and husband had used their economic power to gain control over
her. Second, in her desperate drive to keep her children while under the shadow
of her second husband's spurious allegations, she found herself liberated from
the need to adhere to middle-class notions of propriety in her writing. She was
not afraid to say in public what she believed in private – including her belief in
economic independence for women – because her reputation was already tarnished; in a sense she had nothing to lose.[26]

For Fern, the shift from protected middle-class wife to working-class single
mother also had the effect of fracturing the concept of the universality of gender identity. The man who is a protector of women in his own class is often,
Fern noted in the *Olive Branch* on May 29, 1852, a "highwayman" in relation
to working-class women: he takes advantage of them *because* they are "alone and
unprotected." Consequently, characteristics that had seemed to be essential to
middle-class womanhood – dependency, delicacy, ingenuousness – were suicidal
for the working-class woman, whose survival depended on her independence,
strength, and knowledge of the world. It was this recognition of the fluidity of
gender identity that enabled Fern to assert her own definition of gender.

Fern became the first American woman newspaper columnist and the most
highly paid newspaper writer of her time. Her autobiographical novel *Ruth Hall*
(1855) was a female success story, portraying a woman who realized the American
Dream. Yet not one of the conventional critics recognized the novel as a success
story; instead, they savagely attacked Fern because of her satirical treatment of
her male relatives and her "egotistical" portrayal of an assertive, independent
woman. The novel, which ends with the heroine's acquisition of ten thousand
dollars in bank stocks instead of the more conventional acquisition of a husband,
provides an unusual example of female economic independence.

Fern reiterated this message in her newspaper articles. In 1861 she noted in
the *New York Ledger* the economic double standard which condemned women
for attempting to make themselves financially independent:

There are few people who speak approbatively of a woman who has a
smart business talent or capability. No matter how isolated or destitute
her condition, the majority would consider it more "feminine" would she

unobtrusively gather up her thimble, and, retiring into some out-of-the-way place gradually scoop out her coffin with it, than to develop that smart turn for business which would lift her at once out of her troubles, and which, in a man so situated, would be applauded as exceedingly praiseworthy.[27]

On July 16, 1870, Fern wrote in the *New York Ledger*: "Why shouldn't women work *for pay*? does anybody object when women *marry for pay*? – without love, without respect, nay, with even aversion? . . . How much more to be honored is she who, hewing out her own path, through prejudice and narrowness and even insult, earns honorably and honestly her own independence." Her most succinct observation on the subject concluded, "I want all women to render themselves independent of marriage as a mere means of support" (*New York Ledger*, June 26, 1869).

Conventional critics were shocked by Fern's independent stance in thus redefining gender and labeled her work "vulgar," "monstrous," and "abominable"; they condemned Fern as "unfeminine," "immodest," and "indecorous." Moreover, it was not only conservative critics who criticized Fern. Reviewing *Ruth Hall* in the suffragette journal *The Una* in 1855, Caroline Dall condemned Fern for her "unwomanly" behavior and declared that she would not allow her children to read Fern's children's book lest they be "taught to take bitter views of men and things, to question the motives of their fellow-men." Not only was Fern criticized by literary critics, but her private life suffered as well. "Respectable" people refused to be introduced to her, and her third husband's relatives treated her as if she were a pariah and attempted to break up her marriage.[28]

How did Fern deal with this criticism? It was painful for her as a private woman. She wrote in the *Ledger* many years later: "How I *did* cry if an editor reviewed *me* personally, instead of my book" (November 26, 1864). But professionally, Fern responded to criticism by satirizing her critics; she made it seem ridiculous for anyone to think that a woman could not be independent. Women, she wrote in the *Ledger* in 1857, should not be intimidated by the criticism of "conservative old ladies of both sexes."[29] Moreover, Fern commented, once a woman has become successful, she need not worry about her critics: "*Take* your rights, my sisters; don't beg for them! Never mind what objectors say or think. Success will soon stop their mouths" (*New York Ledger*, July 16, 1870).

Another woman writer who asserted explicitly the need for economic independence for women was Frances Ellen Watkins Harper. Although many African American women had to work, black middle-class men in the nineteenth century adopted the white ideal of true womanhood; an important measure of success for a black man, as for a white man, was the extent to which he could afford to keep his women in the home.[30] Given the importance of self-esteem for African American men emerging from the emasculating effects of slavery, it is not surprising that black middle-class men and women were willing to adopt the dominant culture's binary of aggressive maleness versus dependent femininity.

Harper, who was a middle-class, educated free black woman, devoted her life to writing and activism, working, as she said, to elevate her race; but she refused to buy into the dominant culture's notion that the way to assert men's independence was to enforce the dependence of women.

In certain respects, it was more acceptable for black women to assert their financial independence because, although they were subject to white society's standards of true womanhood, they were also outside of white society. Moreover, nineteenth-century African American women had access to an alternative standard for womanhood that conflicted with the dependent status required of white women: the free black woman who worked for her own money was socially superior to the slave woman. Consequently, for black women the ability to earn one's own money had a positive association that did not exist for white women. For example, in Harriet Jacobs's *Incidents in the Life of a Slave Girl* (1861), Linda Brent has as a role model her grandmother, a free black woman who runs her own business and is highly regarded in the community. The existence of this alternative tradition of womanhood in the black community had the effect of fracturing gender identity.

In "Fancy Etchings" (1873) Harper asserted the need for self-reliance among women, and as one of the characters says in her 1893 novel *Iola Leroy*, "We should teach our boys to be manly and self-respecting, *and* our girls to be useful and self-reliant." Harper believed that this self-reliance would lead to woman's ability to become financially independent. As Iola Leroy asserts, "Every woman ought to know how to earn her own living. . . . Every woman should have some skill or art which would insure her at least a comfortable support."[31] Economic independence, however, was dependent upon legal equality between men and women, noted Harper. In her 1866 speech "We Are All Bound Up Together" Harper described how after her husband's death their farm was taken from her, even though it was her means of livelihood. "[J]ustice is not fulfilled," she said, "so long as woman is unequal before the law."[32]

All of her life, even during her marriage and as the mother of a young child, Harper worked: she wrote and lectured and taught and organized.[33] She published nine books and numerous poems, essays, and stories in magazines. She donated her own money to the antislavery cause. She organized and practiced an economic boycott of slave-produced goods; she worked actively with the Underground Railroad; she traveled to Canada to meet with and help fugitives. After the Civil War she became active in the Women's Suffrage movement. As she said of the self-reliant protagonist of her "The Two Offers" (1859), a story that points out the folly for women of attempting to find happiness in marriage alone: "Too self reliant to depend on the charity of relatives, she endeavored to support herself by her own exertions, and she had succeeded. Her path for a while was marked with struggle and trial, but instead of useless repining she met them bravely, and her life became not a thing of ease and indulgence, but of conquest, victory, and accomplishments. . . . She had a high and holy mission on the battle-field of existence."[34] The same can be said of Harper herself.

Expressing attitudes that paralleled Harper's, Louisa May Alcott was one of the few mainstream nineteenth-century American women writers who articulated the need for work as a lifelong means of independence for women. She wrote of herself in 1872, "Work is and always has been my salvation."[35] In her juvenile fiction, Alcott did not usually link her heroine's work to financial independence; work could mean simply becoming involved in useful and productive activity. Rose Campbell in *Rose in Bloom* (1876) says to her male cousin: "It is as much a right and a duty for women to do something with their lives as for men. . . . Would *you* be contented to be told to enjoy yourself for a little while, then marry and do nothing till you die?"[36] In this novel the heroine is an heiress, and she uses her money for philanthropic enterprises, such as providing housing for working women and health care for orphans. However, the other young woman in the novel, Phebe, works for a living. Phebe gives up her career when she marries, but Jo March in *Little Women* (1868) continues to write after her marriage, although she will no longer write thriller fiction.

Alcott's popular fiction written for children contains suggestions of her belief in women's independence, but it was in her pseudonymous and unconventional fiction for adults that Alcott gave full expression to her belief in autonomy for women. The thriller stories that were published anonymously focus almost wholly on the theme of female power. The subtitle of the most well known of these stories, "Behind a Mask," is "A Woman's Power." Jean Muir, the female protagonist, orchestrates her own ascendance to power through the acquisition of wealth. "I am tired of pity," she says; "Power is sweet, and I will use it."[37] Similar assertions appear in such pseudonymous fiction as "Pauline's Passion and Punishment," "A Pair of Eyes," and "Taming a Tartar." This bold assertion of female power never appears so explicitly in the fiction to which Alcott signed her name.

Implicit in Alcott's focus on the search for power is the realization that the ability to possess money is in itself a source of power for women. Alcott herself exulted in her own power of independence. Her capacity to earn a living from her writing made her father call her an "arsenal of powers" – which was particularly significant considering the lifelong power struggle between Alcott and her father.[38] Alcott wrote in her journal: "I want to realize my dream of supporting the family and being perfectly independent."[39] In her fiction Alcott was not able to reconcile traditional notions of marriage and motherhood with women's need for independence. She felt that in a society that did not grant equal power to women, marriage was enslaving. The satirical "Transcendental Wild Oats" (1873), in which Alcott portrays her heroic mother as the "beast of burden" in her father's idealistic scheme, reveals Alcott's sense of the inequality of the marriage relationship.

Her fear of the effacing power of marriage for women is particularly apparent in her novel *Moods*, first published in 1864, then revised in 1882. The protagonist Sylvia fears that she is losing her individuality after marriage. Her husband's possessiveness frightens her, and the man whom she really loves turns out to be just as possessive as her husband. When Sylvia asks a wise spinster, Faith Dane, which man she should go to, Faith tells her "neither," warning her that her lover "unconsciously absorbs into himself the personality of others."[40] Alcott tells her readers of the secret unhappiness of women, which she indicates is more widespread than is publicly admitted. Because of her own "household grief," Sylvia "found herself detecting various phases of her own experience in others. She had joined that sad sisterhood of disappointed women; a larger class than many deem it to be, though there are few of us who have not seen members of it." Such women include "unhappy wives," "mistaken lovers," women who make "a long penance of their lives for the sins of others," and gifted women who cannot fulfill their talents.[41] A woman can escape becoming a part of that "sad sisterhood," Alcott suggests, if she does not marry. In 1868 Alcott wrote an article for the *New York Ledger* entitled "Happy Women," in which she described the happy lives of women who had not married. Her message is similar to that of Frances Harper in "The Two Offers." Young girls, Alcott said, were so afraid to be old maids that they often rushed into marriage without realizing that the "loss of liberty, happiness, and self-respect" was a high price to pay. One of the women she described was a writer, "A," who is probably Alcott herself. Having seen much of the "tragedy of modern married life," she chose not to marry but found happiness because necessity taught her "the worth of work."[42]

Thus it is work, and the economic independence that comes with it, that brings women happiness. In her adult novel *Work* (1872) Alcott explicitly develops the connection between economic independence and female autonomy. Unable to reconcile independence with marriage, Alcott solves the problem in this novel by killing off the husband of the heroine. As a widow, the protagonist is able to resume her independent work, and she forms a business with other women. The novel ends with a vision of female independence and unity. The novel *An Old-Fashioned Girl* (1870) also looks toward a visionary future of working women living together and supporting themselves.

Alcott knew that the portrayal of woman as power seeker was not socially acceptable – particularly in a married woman, but even in an unmarried woman. In a revealing interview, Alcott once commented that the reason she did not write "lurid" material (she did not acknowledge that she wrote it anonymously) was because she did not want to forfeit the approval of the patriarchy: "To have had Mr. Emerson for an intellectual god all one's life is to be invested with a chain armor of propriety. . . . And what would my own good father think of me if I set folks to doing the things that I have a longing to see my people do?"[43] Alcott's publishers attempted to persuade her to sign her name to her thriller fiction, but she adamantly refused. There were only two occasions when Alcott did agree to sign her name to her mystery stories, and it is significant that in those two cases the stories, although "lurid," did *not* involve a power-seeking woman as did most of her mystery fiction.[44] Clearly, it was not simply because of the "luridness" of the material that Alcott refused to acknowledge her thriller fiction.

When protected by her anonymity, Alcott redefined female gender to include the power that comes with economic independence. The heroine could assert her power, challenging the annihilating male will; in this context Alcott portrayed the female power seeker as autonomous, shrewd, and unregenerate. But unlike Fern, she did not have nothing to lose. In the fiction to which she signed her name, she was more circumspect, and her heroines kept within the bounds of normative behavior. Privately and anonymously, Alcott established new and radical performative acts constituting gender identity for women, but she was not willing to risk her own reputation by publicizing her redefinition of woman. Instead she looked toward a visionary future.

In contrast to Alcott's more divided stance, Charlotte Perkins Gilman uncategorically stated her belief in the need for economic independence for women. It is significant that like Fern's, Gilman's reputation was already blighted when she spoke out for this cause. She had left her husband, and that in itself was unconventional; but her principal crime came later when she gave up her daughter to her husband. Although she did so for her daughter's benefit, she was pilloried as an unnatural mother, and the scandal caused her a great deal of pain. But it also put her in the position of having nothing to lose by speaking out.

In "The Yellow Wallpaper" (1892) Gilman portrays a woman who goes mad because her husband, her doctor, and society as a whole insist that the cure for her depression is the total suppression of her individuality. She must not think for herself, and she must not "do" anything. Intellectual stimulation and productive activity are forbidden. Reduced to childlike dependence, she goes insane. The story describes the rest cure of S. Weir Mitchell that Gilman had herself undergone, and the conclusion provides an indication of what Gilman believed would have been the result for herself if she had remained in a marriage that was so destructive of the self. Instead of accepting the definition of womanhood that destroys her protagonist, Gilman fractured the concept of gender to redefine womanhood. Having learned from her own experience the stultifying effect of passive nonactivity, Gilman in her life and in her work asserted woman's need for independence.

Whereas Alcott had difficulty envisioning a married woman's economic independence, Gilman was able to imagine, in both her fiction and nonfiction, a future which contained a realistic process by which it might be realized. In her short stories, Gilman portrays the solution to women's dilemma: the woman needs to find something practical to do that will enable her to earn money of her own. As long as she is dependent, she cannot realize autonomy in her own life. This is the theme of stories like "Making a Change" (1911), "An Honest Woman" (1911), "Turned" (1911), and "The Widow's Might" (1911). In her novels *What Diantha Did* (1912) and *Benigna Machiavelli* (1914) the protagonist asserts her independence. Diantha establishes her own business and refuses to marry unless her husband will recognize her right to continue her business.

Gilman's most complete statement of her ideas is contained in *Women and Economics*, published in 1898. For Gilman, the crucial concern was not women's political freedom. She began her book-length essay with the assertion that human beings are affected more by "economic conditions" than by any other force. In language reminiscent of Marx (although she was not a Marxist), Gilman pointed out that women's labor "is the property of another." Like Marx, she emphasized a historical imperative. For Gilman, however, this was not a class issue, but a gendered social issue. Progress, she said, would come only when "both men and women stand equal in economic relations."[45]

How did Gilman reconcile women's work with marriage and motherhood? Unlike Fern who ridiculed her critics into silence or Alcott who could only look toward a visionary future, Gilman proposed a practical change in living arrangements. In *Women and Economics* Gilman developed a plan in which families and individuals would live in kitchenless apartments or kitchenless suburban houses constructed around a central food-supply building. The food would be centrally prepared by professional nutritionists and served in community dining rooms. The dwellings would be cleaned professionally, and each complex would provide professional childcare services in nurseries within the building complex.[46] Thus freed of housework, cooking, and constant childcare, women would be able to have meaningful and fulfilling employment outside the home, from which they would derive financial remuneration that would enable them to be economically independent in the marriage relation. Moreover, said Gilman, her plan would enhance traditional values like marriage, motherhood, and the home; women would be better wives and mothers because of it.[47] On the one hand, such an assertion was Gilman's way of placating critics by demonstrating that the goal of her plan was not to destroy the institution of marriage. At the same time, however, it offered a radical redefinition of gender identity: in Gilman's discourse the terms wife and mother no longer connote the discursive construction of the dependent "angel in the parlor."

In their recognition, over a hundred years ago, of the necessity of economic independence for women, Fern, Harper, Alcott, and Gilman took a stand on an issue that still has not been resolved. A passage from a letter written by a liberal congressman from Wisconsin suggests just how problematic this issue has been and continues to be. On August 15, 1954, Tom Amlie wrote to his son Tom who was having problems with his wife Polly, who apparently wanted to finish college and get a good job. Amlie wrote: "This determination on Polly's part to be in control took the form of an attitude of self indulgence. Polly told me that she considered her own career to be as important as your career. There is no use in going into the absurdity of this statement."[48] The author of this letter was no timid conservative. He was a radical lawyer whose support of "production for use" as opposed to the profit motive in capitalism in the 1930s had prevented him from realizing a successful political career. He was too radical for either political party, but his radicalism apparently did not include looking at women as autonomous beings. A sad footnote to the 1954 letter is a letter from his own wife ten years earlier, begging him to let her have a regular allowance and not make her have to plead for money for household expenses. Like the nineteenth-century woman who had to "beg, tease, or wheedle" for her money, Mrs. Amlie describes her own humiliation: "I have *no* feeling of independence. I must ask you every other day for a few dollars."

Amlie's letter to his son was written over forty years ago. What are men advising their sons to do today? How much has the advice changed? And even if the advice has changed in view of the economic necessity of two-paycheck families, what about practical concerns? Today most of us would agree that women have the right to independent employment. Women – married and single, white women and women of color, lesbian women and heterosexual women, middle-class women and working-class women – today women are working. But many, particularly those whose finances do not permit expensive childcare and house-cleaning services, must rely on a hodgepodge of inadequate arrangements. The results are sometimes destructive to children and to women themselves. Women have been told they can work, and many of them have to work. But little has been done to make the prospect easier. Gilman wrote of her plan in *Women and Economics*: "If there should be built and opened in any of our large cities to-day a commodious apartment house [with professional cooking, cleaning, and day-care services for working] women with families, it would be filled at once."[49] I suspect that this is even more true today. The principal opposition to such a plan for kitchenless apartments on a wide scale would probably come from the manufacturers of kitchen appliances. As the "nannygate" scandals of 1993 showed us,[50] the question of how to reconcile outside employment with marriage and a family continues to be a problem for working women; women have been left on their own to solve the problem as best they can.

Fern, Harper, Alcott, and Gilman were radical spokespersons for an idea that still has not been realized. They deconstructed the substantive appearance of gender, revealing that gender identity in their culture had been discursively produced. Refusing to reify cultural notions of identity, they fractured the concept of gender to assert the economics of independence.

NOTES

1   Charlotte Perkins Gilman, "If I Were a Man," in *The Charlotte Perkins Gilman Reader*, ed. Ann J. Lane (New York: Pantheon Books, 1980), 33–4.
2   Charlotte Perkins Gilman, *The Living of Charlotte Perkins Gilman* (1935; reprint, New York: Arno Press, 1972), 131.
3   See Judith Butler, *Gender Trouble* (New York: Routledge, 1990), e.g., 24–5.
4   Alice Kessler-Harris writes, "Though many women were drawn into the labor force for a while, most managed to drift in and out of it in response to family needs. Up until 1900 less than 20 percent of all women over fourteen were in the paid labor force at any one time. . . . Up until the 1960s, though many women worked for wages at some point in their lives, especially as young adults, the normal expectation was for women to be unpaid housewives." *Women Have Always Worked* (Old Westbury: Feminist Press, 1981), 17–18.

5   See Carla L. Peterson, "'Doers of the Word': Theorizing African-American Women Writers in the Antebellum North," in *The (Other) American Traditions: Nineteenth-Century Women Writers*, ed. Joyce W. Warren (New Brunswick: Rutgers University Press, 1996), 190.

6   James Fenimore Cooper, *Complete Works*, Leatherstocking edn, 32 vols (New York: Putnam, 1893?), 24: 179–83, 364, 431, 436–8.

7   See Fanny Fern's response to Bushnell and Todd in the *New York Ledger* (November 6, 1869).

8   Rev. Jesse Peck, "The True Woman," *Ladies' Repository* (August 1853), 337.

9   Ralph Waldo Emerson, *Complete Works*, ed. Edward W. Emerson, 12 vols (Boston: Houghton Mifflin, 1903–4), 11: 403–26.

10 Philip S. Foner, *History of the Labor Movement in the United States*, 6 vols (New York: International Publishers, 1955), 2: 61–6.

11 Ibid., 2: 367.

12 Ibid., 2: 364–6.

13 Meredith Tax, *The Rising of the Women: Feminist Solidarity and Class Conflict, 1880–1917* (New York: Monthly Review Press, 1980), 20. Tax calls this alliance the "united front of women" and points out that it was particularly successful in the Illinois Woman's Alliance in Chicago in 1888 (21, 65–89).

14 Ibid., 60–1.

15 Ibid., 63, 58.

16 Mari Jo Buhle, *Women and American Socialism, 1870–1920* (Urbana: University of Illinois Press, 1981), 9.

17 Karl Marx and Frederick Engels, *The Communist Manifesto* (New York: Labor News, 1961), 40.

18 Mari Jo Buhle, *Women and American Socialism*, 3–12.

19 Ibid., 9–11. The issue of women and Marxism in the United States came to a head in 1872 with the ouster of New York's Section 12 from the party because of its focus on women's rights. Obtaining the go-ahead from Marx, Friedrich Sorge ousted the offending group, he said, in order to purge the party of middle-class "reformers" who were concerned with "women's emancipation and the right to vote." Friedrich Sorge, *Labor Movement in the United States: A History of the American Working Class from Colonial Times to 1890*, ed. Philip S. Foner and Brewster Chamberlin (Westport, CT: Greenwood Press, 1977), 158–9.

20 Edward Bellamy, *Looking Backward* (New York: New American Library, 1960), 176, 180. For a discussion of women's involvement in the Nationalist movement which derived from Bellamy's novel, see Buhle, *Women and American Socialism*, 75–82.

21 As Dolores Hayden points out, Gilman objected to such communal efforts for two reasons: she felt that cooperative attempts would not work, and she objected to projects that included free-love principles. Hayden, "Charlotte Perkins Gilman and the Kitchenless House," *Radical History Review* 21 (1979): 225–47. See also Hayden, *The Grand Domestic Revolution: A History of Feminist Designs for American Houses, Neighborhoods, and Cities* (Cambridge, MA: MIT Press, 1981).

22 Robert Bonner, "Woman's True Sphere," *New York Ledger*, May 14, 1859.

23 For a discussion of the relationship between Kirkland's self-suppression and her success in the marketplace, see Sandra A. Zagarell, "Introduction," in Caroline Kirkland, *A New Home, Who'll Follow?*, ed. Sandra A. Zagarell (New Brunswick:

Rutgers University Press, 1990), xvii–xx. For Child's career, see Carolyn Karcher, *The First Woman in the Republic: A Cultural Biography of Lydia Maria Child* (Durham: University of North Carolina Press, 1994).

24   Nowhere is this paradox more evident than in the example of one of the most influential "career women" of the nineteenth century, Sarah Josepha Hale, the editor of *Godey's Lady's Book*. Left a widow with five children in 1822, Hale supported herself for the remainder of her life, but in her columns she glorified women's domestic role. Although she supported women's education, she emphasized that women should be educated, not for their own improvement, but in order to become better wives and mothers.

25   For information about the life of Fanny Fern, see my biography, *Fanny Fern: An Independent Woman* (New Brunswick: Rutgers University Press, 1992).

26   I discuss the background of Fern's nothing-to-lose mindset and the effect it had on her writing in "Uncommon Discourse: Fanny Fern and the *New York Ledger*," in *Periodical Literature in Nineteenth-Century America*, ed. Kenneth M. Price and Susan Belasco Smith (Charlottesville: University Press of Virginia, 1995), 51–68.

27   Fanny Fern, "A Bit of Injustice," *New York Ledger* (June 8, 1861), in *Ruth Hall and Other Writings*, ed. Joyce W. Warren (New Brunswick: Rutgers University Press, 1986), 318. The dates of articles from the *New York Ledger* that have not been reprinted will be given in the text.

28   See Warren, *Fanny Fern*, e.g., 124–30, 179–94, for Fern's treatment by the critics and by people in her personal life.

29   Warren, ed., *Ruth Hall*, 295.

30   For a discussion of the way in which African American middle-class men sought to privatize their women by adopting the values of the dominant culture, see James Oliver Horton, "Freedom's Yoke: Gender Conventions among Antebellum Free Blacks," *Feminist Studies* 12 (1986): 69–72.

31   Frances E. Watkins Harper, *Iola Leroy, or Shadows Uplifted* (1893; New York: Oxford University Press, 1988), 253, 205, 210.

32   Frances Smith Foster, ed., *A Brighter Coming Day: A Frances Ellen Watkins Harper Reader* (New York: Feminist Press, 1990), 217; Kilcup, *NCAWW*, 156.

33   On Harper's life, see Foster, "Introduction," in Foster, ed., *A Brighter Coming Day*, 3–40.

34   Frances Watkins Harper, "The Two Offers," in Foster, ed., *A Brighter Coming Day*, 107, 114.

35   Martha Saxton, *Louisa May Alcott: A Modern Biography* (New York: Farrar, Straus, and Giroux, 1977), 353.

36   Louisa May Alcott, *Rose in Bloom* (1876; reprint, Boston: Roberts Brothers, 1880), 11.

37   Louisa May Alcott, *Behind a Mask: The Unknown Thrillers of Louisa May Alcott*, ed. Madeleine B. Stern (New York: Quill, 1975), 206.

38   A. Bronson Alcott, *The Letters of A. Bronson Alcott*, ed. Richard L. Herrnstadt (Ames: Iowa State University Press, 1969), 397.

39   *Louisa May Alcott, Her Life, Letters, and Journals*, ed. Ednah D. Cheney (Boston: Roberts Brothers, 1891), 193.

40   Louisa May Alcott, *Moods*, ed. Sarah Elbert (New Brunswick: Rutgers University Press, 1991), 180.

41   Ibid., 190.

42 Louisa May Alcott, "Happy Women," in *Alternative Alcott*, ed. Elaine Showalter (New Brunswick: Rutgers University Press, 1992), 203–6.

43 Cited in LaSalle Corbell Pickett, "Louisa Alcott's 'Natural Ambition' for the 'Lurid Style,'" in *Critical Essays on Louisa May Alcott*, ed. Madeleine B. Stern (Boston: G. K. Hall, 1984), 42.

44 The two thriller stories that were originally published under Alcott's name were "The Mysterious Key *and* What It Opened" (1867), reprinted in *Behind a Mask*, ed. Stern; and "The Skeleton in the Closet" (1867), reprinted in *Plots and Counterplots: More Unknown Thrillers of Louisa May Alcott*, ed. Madeleine Stern (New York: William Morrow and Company, 1976). Not only are the heroines of these stories not power seekers, they are wholly *selfless*.

45 Charlotte Perkins Gilman, *Women and Economics: A Study of the Economic Relation Between Men and Women as a Factor in Social Evolution*, ed. Carl Degler (New York: Harper and Row, 1966), 2–3, 7, 138, 340.

46 Gilman, *Women and Economics*, 241–5. Edward Bellamy proposes a similar arrangement in *Looking Backward*.

47 Ibid., 289–90, 312–15.

48 Thomas Amlie papers, Wisconsin Historical Society.

49 Gilman, *Women and Economics*, 242.

50 In his attempt to appoint a woman attorney general, President Clinton found it difficult to find a professional woman who had legal childcare arrangements (his first two appointments were rejected because the appointee had hired an illegal alien and/or had failed to make social security payments for her nanny). Clinton finally solved the problem by appointing Janet Reno, a single woman with no children. The case highlighted the problems encountered by working women with children in the United States today.

9

"To Labor . . . and Fight on the Side of God": Spirit, Class, and Nineteenth-Century African American Women's Literature

BARBARA McCASKILL

I

It is something, yes, all, for us to stand
Clasping by faith our Saviour's hand;
To learn to labor, live and fight
On the side of God and changeless light.[1]
Frances E. W. Harper

Mystic. Evangelist. Missionary. Willing worker. Church mother. Healer. Prodigal-returned. Visionary-departed. Prophet. Preacher. Saint. Behind such auspicious, hagiographic titles stand nineteenth-century African American women who were laborers and fighters – and orators and writers. Pauline Elizabeth Hopkins. Frances Ellen Watkins Harper. Anna Julia Cooper. Sojourner Truth. Their names bear witness to a battle-scarred grace, like a pair of starched white ushers' gloves reposed on a sere black Bible, or rows of stained-glass windows comforting weary pine planks. Such women as these defined their faith not only as a miraculous fire that invited prayerful thoughts and thoughtful souls to Zion but as a flame that invigorated earthly lives. Their short fiction, poetry, memoirs, and speeches describe a Christianity that is relevant, immediate, politicized. In their creative productions, the sacred intersects with the secular subjects of class divisions, class consciousness, and illusions of classlessness among their African American contemporaries.

For nineteenth-century evangelical African American women, to champion Christians as both laborers and fighters meant to challenge deeply rooted assumptions about black women's involvement in sacred and secular history. As laborers, nineteenth-century African American women had become flash-frozen in the collective national consciousness in the form of slaves and servants generally, and laundresses, cooks, seamstresses, nannies, prisoners, and prostitutes in particular. (An exception might occasionally be made for a teacher, a stenographer, an elocutionist, or a nurse.) As fighters, nineteenth-century African American women had marched shoulder-to-shoulder with African American men in struggles against every facet of cultural and psychological domination. Their resistance had ranged all the way from the violence of armed slave revolts, murders, and suicides, to sabotage, forgery, expatriation, lies, protest, prayers, and flight.

Unfortunately, when the nineteenth century is memorialized, African America's women of the spirit have been likely to be remembered less as laborers, fighters, orators, or writers than as itinerant, irrational hysterics, or Bible-thumping, hallelujah-strutting exhibitionists, notwithstanding the intelligent power and authority of a voice like that of "Old Elizabeth." Or perhaps they have been remembered as deferential – and silenced – handmaids to the trinity of God, to His corps of Heavenly Hosts (Hostesses having been consigned to heavenly hearths and cradles), and to His corporeal, masculine ministers pining about the sinful, erring world. Our late twentieth-century memories have obscured the more complex, divergent dynamic in which African American women lived, spoke, and wrote. Before the Civil War, every abolitionist worth his or her salt routinized a catechism that held African American women (both enslaved and free) as despised, neglected, and martyred on the cross of the very same Christianity that they – among all Christians – worshipped the most ardently and practiced with an arduous rigor. What antislavery supporter had not memorized the autobiographical fulminations of Douglass, self-christened the "American Slave," against the "women-whipping, cradle-plundering, partial and hypocritical Christianity"[2] of America's self-styled "democratic" slaveocracy? In antislavery fiction such as William Wells Brown's *Clotel* (1853), Christianity fronted an economy that exchanged its morals for the currency of a black woman's body on the Southern auction block. What reader had not moaned at the tragedy of Brown's mulatto heroine: "[h]er moral character [sold] for two hundred; . . . her Christianity for three hundred; and her chastity and virtue for four hundred dollars more. And this, too, in a city thronged with churches, whose tall spires look like so many signals pointing to heaven, and whose ministers preach that slavery is a God-ordained institution"?[3]

Antebellum antislavery women were probably as inclined as their male counterparts to insert black women's bodies into this lingo of a Christendom descended into moral turpitude, even if, when they did so, they portrayed African American women as autonomous agents of change rather than passive victims. Frances Ellen Watkins Harper's "The Slave Mother" (1854) is a poem that accomplishes this by envisioning a "heroic" woman whose heroism (anticipating that of Sethe in Toni Morrison's *Beloved* [1987]) means murdering her four "precious" children when she realizes the unlikelihood of liberating them from bondage. The "mournful mother" of Harper's poem falls victim to a so-called Christianity whose mercy is more meager – and clemency less colorblind – that that of the pagan eras that preceded it. As the poet warns: "E'en Rome had altars, 'neath whose shade / Might crouch the wan and weary slave. / But Ohio had no sacred fane, / To human rights so consecrated."[4] A similar irony operates in *The Stars and Stripes* (1858), Lydia Maria Child's near-forgotten antislavery melodrama. In this play the "Georgia Fugitive" Ellen Craft plots escape with her husband William, in part because her "Christian" master desires to exercise the planter's *droit du seigneur* and force her into concubinage or *plessage* as his mistress. Adding incest to her catalog of injuries, Ellen reminds her master that she is his daughter by another of his slaves, only for him to "[p]ay no attention to" her counsel. "My poor, poor mother!" mourns Ellen. "I suppose *she* was afraid, too; for I remember she always seemed so modest. Oh, it is a dreadful situation to be in!"[5]

Indeed, throughout the nineteenth century, African American women writers regularly joined literary forces with African American men, with white American women and men, and with Native American, Asian, and Latina/o women and men,[6] in reckoning Christianity among the social ills identified by this fiction-alized Ellen's euphemistic "it." Their awareness of Christianity's complicity in the annihilation and/or subjugation of nonwhite cultures – and their valency with members of other racial and ethnic groups who shared in this awareness – is demonstrated by Jarena Lee's disagreement (although she is restrained because of her dedication to Methodism) with the assumption that "heathen" or reprob-ate Native American culture must be erased in order to prepare the red man's salvation (*Religious Experience and Journal*, 1849). If their criticism did not apply to Christianity as a whole, then certainly it implicated the hypocritical and color-inflected version practiced, as Rebecca Cox Jackson implies in "Dream of Home and Search for Eldress Paulina" (1843), even among the forward-thinking and visionary Shakers. As Anna Julia Cooper wrote in her essay on "The Higher Education of Women," the "key-note," "banner-cry," and "grand modulation" of the nineteenth century's second half was that "[e]ven Christianity is being brought to the bar of humanity and tried by the standard of its ability to alleviate the world's suffering and lighten and brighten its woe."[7] Yet even Cooper's forceful statement grossly oversimplifies – and romanticizes – the matter.

First, African American women exchanged a querulous, victim stance vis-à-vis Christianity for an insouciant one that sprang from the goals of collective and individual sociopolitical empowerment. Second, African American women writers were as likely to abruptly disregard or break as to foster alliances with African American men, and with women and men of other races and ethnicities, when the nature, extent, and effectiveness of religion's role in a multiracial, democratic society was debated. Affected simultaneously by a feminized race and a racialized femininity, "confronted by," as Anna Julia Cooper stated, both "a woman question and a race problem,"[8] African American women writers often registered experiences with God's church above and "Satan's down below"[9] that could not be expressed by the discourse of an essentialized, deracinated Chris-tian identity. Merely because Cooper had theorized that an "earnest well trained Christian young woman, as a teacher, as a home-maker, as wife, mother, or silent influence,"[10] might modify the crass material motives of a cold, impersonal age, it did not necessarily follow that such an earnest young African American woman would unflappably subscribe to the Christian agenda lock, stock, and barrel.

Over time, travels, regions, and religious affiliations, what does seem consistent among these writers is that their literature on Christianity ineluctably interrogates class stratification in African American communities. To our postcolonial world, wary of the dangers of merging church and state, this affiliation between the sacred and secular might appear a curious partnership at best – or, at worst, a powder keg. Yet for four centuries of African Americans, black churches have acted as businesses, treasuries, schools, legislatures, and even garrisons. They have synthesized all classes under the gospel and the cross when no other space has been available and safe for the collective. In part because of this function of black churches as community spaces, in the South the "peculiar institution" either prohibited organized worship among the enslaved, or else it monitored their services with preachers (as with Elizabeth Keckley's Rev. Mr. Burwell and Harriet Jacobs's Rev. Mr. Pike[11]) who were hand-picked by plantation masters and mistresses for their complicity in Southern enslavement. The militant activist African American faithful congregated both on the physical soil of surreptitious groves and in metaphysical spaces of encoded hymns and inspirational lyrics. In the Northern quasi-freedom of cities such as Boston, Rochester, Albany, Hartford, and Philadelphia, in the aisles and balconies of Yankee houses of worship, segregated "nigger" pews drove African American communities to found their own meeting halls. While Cooper might have identified Oberlin, Ann Arbor, and Wellesley as oases of democratic liberalism at the turn of the century, the handfuls of African American women matriculating at these campuses often reported the Christian fellowship of their white peers to be lacking.

Along with historical, cultural, regional, and economic differences, religion – its forms of worship, its points of origin, its rituals and creeds – divided African Americans. Nevertheless, as a consequence of their mutual disenfranchisement, the different classes of African Americans could claim religion as the common ground on which all could stand united.

II

Then why should one worm say to another,
"Keep you down there, while I sit up yonder;
For I am better than thou?"[12]
                                    Maria Stewart

Pauline Elizabeth Hopkins's short story, "Bro'r Abr'm Jimson's Wedding" (1901) satirizes African American class consciousness against the backdrop of the period of race uplift. This era spanned the failure of the Reconstruction in the 1870s to the eve of World War I and the New Negro Movement. Unlike the Progressive Era, "spanning at its broadest," as Elizabeth Ammons writes, the period "from the early 1890s to the middle 1920s,"[13] the era of uplift combined a stronger emphasis on morality, tradition, domesticity, and sexual propriety with a diminished acknowledgment of the deleterious impact of enslavement. Uplift emphasized self-reliance, patriotism, philanthropy, civil rights, political activism, social reform, educational and material attainment, investment and thrift, bourgeois tastes and respectable manners, good citizenship, pan-Africanism, black history and heritage, modernity, urbanization, industrialization, hygiene, temperance, suffrage, culture, ethics, entrepreneurship, coalition-building, and Christian morality and wholesomeness.

This was an era that advanced an elite platoon of literate, representative African American "race" men and women. Byproducts of the pulpit and the schoolroom, this crème de la crème confronted the daily paradox of speaking for the majority yet leading lives quite different from the flock that followed their example — lives consisting of international traveling, public policy-making, institution-building, lecturing, protesting, fundraising, being visible. The signature of this superlative era was inscribed by masculine hands. And the hands of this masculinized, political leadership (fronted by the educator Booker T. Washington and the sociologist/philosopher W. E. B. Du Bois) alternately clasped in fellowship or checked others. Both tutelary leaders, for example, were as one in the understanding that educational attainment and economic development were important to pursue for race progress, even though, in tracking these worthy prey, their courses might well diverge. And to uplift's detractors and offenders, particularly to those who defied its codes of propriety and conduct, both men could be swift to mete out penalties – and severe. In spite of her trenchant analyses of the racist and sexist ideologies underpinning lynching, and in spite of her launching an international campaign to lobby and legislate this and other violent practices out of existence, Ida B. Wells-Barnett found a cold reception with both Washington *and* Du Bois. She was ostracized, as Hazel Carby writes, "for she was a woman who refused to adopt the 'ladylike' attitudes of compromise and silence."[14]

All told, uplift would bleach blackness of its dehumanizing, satanic, objectified, and exotic connotations. Having memorized the litany of uplift virtues and assimilated bourgeois, white, middle-class norms and aspirations and moral and civil codes of conduct, African American people would loom legitimately as peers of and equals to white Americans. Yet, as Carla L. Peterson rightly reminds us, "if this elite's assimilationist ideology was on one level complicitous with the dominant culture, at the same time it sought to subvert this culture, critiquing its failure to uphold its stated ideals and asserting the African American's right to both political freedom and cultural distinctiveness."[15] Uplift's leadership vocally denounced the stereotyping of their race as beasts, demons, "God-breathing machines,"[16] and other creatures of a lesser God, not excepting such marvels as New England's Phillis Wheatley or slaveholding Georgia's "Blind Tom." Additionally, uplift (en)gendered emancipated women and their freeborn female progeny. This era attempted to integrate African American women, made monstrous by lies dichotomizing them as either hypersexed viragos or asexual mammies, within conventional Victorian ideology concerning the "natural" (male-subordinated) functions of femininity and the motherly, nurturing offices of womanhood. During this era, Ida Wells-Barnett would expose the mendacity, brutality, and lawlessness of white American women as well as men – effectively questioning their dualistic racial vision that demonized or exoticized African Americans. In her *A Red Record* (1895), the sequel to her antilynching pamphlet, *Southern Horrors* (1892), she documented cases in which white women had engaged in willful, consensual sex with black men and then falsely accused the men of raping them, and she provided evidence that "the same crime [of rape] committed by white men against Negro women and girls, is never punished by the mob or the law." "[C]olored women," she said, setting the record straight, "have always had far more reason to complain of white men in this respect than ever white women have had of Negroes."[17] Wells-Barnett established that, like enslavement before it, lynching relied upon a white supremacist rhetoric, one that, in the words of Angela Davis, "annulled [the black woman] as woman, that is, as woman in her historical stance of wardship under the entire male hierarchy."[18]

Among late nineteenth-century African American women writers, uplift meant all this. Much more, it meant expanding artistic horizons that in the antebellum era were more often contingent upon the politics and economics of emancipating the enslaved. Their blossoming of expression was characterized by a tremendous accretion of experimentation, introspection, and preliminary exploration of taboo subject matter. In addition, these women writers inaugurated a sustained and self-regulated attempt to fictionalize issues that during abolition had been treated journalistically or polemically, appearing in essays, pamphlets, and/or sermons.

"Bro'r Abr'm Jimson's Wedding" stands as one of many, increasingly daring, precocious attempts by Pauline Hopkins to design, execute, market, and distribute an African American popular literature. Prior to publishing this story in the *Colored American Magazine*, Hopkins had written two novels, *Contending Forces* (1900) and *Hagar's Daughter* (1901–2, serialized). In them, she had paraded plots, settings, characters, and discursive conventions from practically every best-selling literature of the century: domestic fiction, gothic novels, detective stories, melodrama, sentimental fiction, plantation novels, ghost stories, slaves' narratives. In stories such as "Talma Gordon" (1900), Hopkins ambitiously synthesized and renewed the sentimental, gothic, and realist genres. She did not submit her literary productions as intellectual games, or as curiosities calculated to sell more copies of the *Colored American Magazine*, but rather as pragmatic responses to the challenge of her hero Du Bois to uncover examples of African American genius and discover forms of expression that originated from, honored, and delimited an African-centered aesthetic. Her artistic philosophy anticipated Du Bois's famous 1903 description of the "double consciousness" of the African American citizen, who possesses "no true self-consciousness, but only lets him see himself through the revelation of the other world."[19] Hopkins's innovative use of literary genre would facilitate an emergence of an authentic African American self-consciousness. Her achievement would question assumptions of a white American world which purposed to diminish those African Americans who entered its haughty gaze.

An independent American writer, packed off by ambitious parents to schools among privileged white Boston's upper strata, Hopkins probably felt supremely entitled to appropriate the "best" of the British and American canons – and more popular materials – in order to confirm her project of creating an African American popular literary genre. As an Africa-identified African American writer, Hopkins sought subject matters and forms that distilled an Afrocentric ethos and did not merely imitate white American culture in blackface. What richer reservoir existed for Hopkins's imagination than the African American church, where, like a primeval feather laminated in amber, so many sensations and ideograms of African culture beckoned, blatant yet intangible? Heard in gospel song and revival meeting oratory, felt during ring-shout dance, beheld at Easter pageant and Founder's Day ritual, tasted First Sundays in communion, touched in Georgia pine pew and oaken Pennsylvanian baluster, Africans and Africa were nevertheless familiar strangers to many Americans, black and white.

The fashionable church where Brother Jimson's neighbors gather to gossip, woof, keep up with the Joneses, see-and-be-seen, and, at the minister's prompting, worship and pray, shares in the historical tradition of black churches as storehouses of homespun spiritual values. Preserved among the working classes, the innocent, and the poor, these are values, Harper suggests, that the "higher" leaders of uplift have abandoned. In her sardonic descriptions of the church as an item for consumption ("the richest plum in the ecclesiastical pudding") and of churchgoers ("small Vanderbilts and Astors") as consumers, Hopkins holds up classism for our contempt. From the most incidental details she extracts a lode of material meanings: the air wafts past the congregants "laden with rich promise"; the soprano soloist is blessed with a "rich voice"; the altar is carved of "rich wood." Even the organist plays the "richest melody." That this church is a "vault" of acquisitive patrons and wealth-and-liquid-assets wannabees is reinforced by its "star-gemmed ceiling," "deep garnet cushions," "hint of gold" on the altar, and "silvery cadences" of one of its singers.[20] If God is love, then love of money ironically replaces God's love in this setting. Hopkins could have chosen no more appropriate language to organize a story about a May–December romance fueled by desire for property and possessions.

As the story unfolds, her irony is heightened by our awareness as readers that during the workweek the majority of the snooty worshippers are nondescript janitors, maids, bellhops, and laundresses. When they speak, they speak the street: dialect, slang, and malapropisms ("receiptfulness" for "deceitfulness" and so on). Their nest eggs are not inherited legacies but "small competenc[ies]" meticulously assembled over the years as a consequence of "frugal nature[s]."[21] At work among the white folks, even the wealthiest of the black bourgeoisie come dead last in a pecking order where race matters, and, as the story "Talma

Gordon" indicates, merely one drop of African heritage relegates its possessor to a second-class status. This is social realism of the order of Charles Chesnutt's stories on the aristocratic "Blue Vein Society," which were published throughout the 1890s in the *Atlantic Monthly* and other highbrow American periodicals. In fact, with a plot that reunites a fat, frowzy Mrs. Jimson with her reprobate husband who favors a slim and slick new bride, "Bro'r Abr'm Jimson's Wedding" bears more than passing resemblance to Chesnutt's fictions of African American manners, such as "The Wife of His Youth" and "Uncle Wellington's Wives."

Apart from this connection to another black writer, what demonstrates the author's command of an African American aesthetic? The key to Hopkins's aesthetic lies in how she satirically deploys Christianity in order to shift the values of the African American upper classes from something more than their present obsessions with "broadcloth, biled shirts, and money." (Her subtitle, after all, is "A Christmas Story.")[22] Hopkins works in the tradition of the *griots* or oral storytellers of West Africa who employ parable, double entendre, and indirection to point out a group's deficiencies. Yet she also African Americanizes the process by using as her template both the written tradition of scripture and the oral one of conjure.

If we read Brother Jimson's wedding ceremony as a story-within-a-story, we can uncover many irreverent inversions of New Testament theology. Where the Nativity centered upon a lowly stable and manger, Hopkins's story-within-a-story cheekily unfolds in the dictiest, most pretentious of religious institutions. Where the birth of Christ was connected to three immortal visitations,[23] Jimson's wedding revolves around three very mortal African American women: Chocolate Caramel Johnson, his nubile bride; Sis'r Maria Nash, Chocolate's aunt and Jimson's previous flame; and (plain) Jane, Jimson's long-abandoned, lawful wife. Brother Jimson's wedding falls on Christmas morning, "when the heart of the whole Christian world feeds its faith and hope." Yet these principles of faith and hope are obscured by the blatant materialism and exclusivity of the well-heeled guests, the groaning refreshment table, the "world-renowned" preacher come to sanctify the union, and the "many and costly" presents. Where the nativity story emphasizes humility, charity, sacrifice, and innocence, Jimson's wedding day coalesces ambition, competition, peroration, social climbing, opportunism, and greed. "The bride's trousseau," we are told, "was a present from the groom and included a white satin wedding gown and a costly gold watch. The town house was refurnished, and a trip to New York was in contemplation." After reading from the very first gospel (St Matthew), Jimson's preacher leads a hymn that celebrates Christ as "the Great," "the First," "the Prince," and "the Lord, Messiah, King,"[24] suggesting that a rhetoric of aristocracy and privilege intertwines even Christ in the commerce of this church. The theme of this day is not the Christmas theme of unconditional love, but of narcissism and contingent love that brings neglect and disunion.

Abandoned by the Striver's Row[25] of uplift are secrets as hidden and apparent as the African American aesthetic itself. In keeping with her system of satirical oppositions, Hopkins reassigns uplift values from Christianity to conjure. Conjure, goophering, or hoodoo is associated with Southern African American folk culture. Arising as a dynamic creolization of Western and Central African religious belief and practice, Christian iconography, ritual, and scripture, and the personal and collective resistance of blacks to white supremacist domination, it encompasses spells, charms, homeopathic remedies, oral tales, and magical practices. It has been spoken and told from generation to generation in the stories of Brer Rabbit, High John the Conqueror, Jack, and other tricksters who outfox their foes with wit, cunning, patience, humor, a little bit of luck, and a lot of intuitive knowledge of human nature. Because it stands in opposition to "the theology of Nation," Zora Neale Hurston writes, "believers conceal their faith. . . . Nobody can say where it begins or ends."[26] Conjure or hoodoo thus embodies the soul of the elusive African American aesthetic that artists like Hopkins aspired to lay claim to, describe, and institutionalize. It manifests itself explicitly in her story when Sister Nash accuses Brother Jimson of having "goophered" Caramel, and when Jane accuses Caramel of "hoodooin' hones' men from their wives."[27]

Yet in many nonfictional Northern, "pianorer playin'" uplift circles, conjure had been dismissed as rot. Thanks to misappropriations of it by such revisionist, proslavery novelists as Thomas Nelson Page and Thomas Dixon, conjure had sunk lowest in the esteem of those loftiest classes of blacks who needed its epistemologies the most. An oral tradition, it was, to some blacks, an impediment and shame in an age when youth competed to study with the Talented Tenth[28] at Tuskegee and to read the valedictories of the Ivy League. Many of the black elite perhaps considered conjure to be pagan and satanic. This view was a vestige of the times when slaveholders feared that it might incite violence and revolt, or when they worried that its indigenous African rituals and signs would awaken the chattel to a nationalistic fervor, thus reversing the "seasoning" process that was meant to disunify and cow the slaves. To suppress independence and assertiveness among the enslaved, in many cases, Christianity had been offered as an antidote to conjure – if another choice besides torture and death had been offered at all.

As one who "conceived of her writing as an inspiration to political action, a pattern for encouraging forms of resistance and agitation, and an integral part of the politics of oppression,"[29] Hopkins took issue with this history that superimposed a Eurandrocentric system of beliefs where once an Afrofemcentric one had existed. (In her book-length expression of this vision, the fantasy *Of One Blood. Or, the Hidden Self* [1902–3], the underground, female-governed, Ethiopian city of Telassar, "at variance with the European idea respecting Central Africa," is the source of ancient, Afrofemcentric values sustained and contemporized by the protagonist, an African American psychologist and metaphysician named Reuel Briggs.[30]) By reconstituting the "profane" culture of conjure as the sacred root and marrow of uplift values, "Bro'r Abr'm Jimson's Wedding" joins an African American aesthetic to both literature and life. What the delusional, consumerist Brother Jimson is to Christianity, the insightful, spiritual Sister Nash is to conjure. She knows the value of a dollar, but she tempers this with the conjurer's common-sense wisdom. She says to Jimson, "I've got the faith,"[31] and she means it in that she holds him and the rest of her African American community accountable to inviolable standards of honesty, ethics, kinship, and reciprocity. To her, "Sister" and "Brother" carry expectations of righteousness in thought and action. She sees through Jimson's duplicity and confronts him, for example, for reneging on his promise to bail her son from jail.

A vulgar character, Sister Nash is not so righteous as to be immune from the slapstick moments into which every church member descends at one time or another. Delighting the right-thinking reader, she throws clothes-stick, shovel, broomstick, coal-hod, and stove covers at Jimson's retreating back. Yet in contrast to this farcical interlude, she and her son Andy are the only African American characters revealed to us in the more solemn contexts of their grinding, everyday employments. Coupled with comparisons that allegorize her at turns as Justice, as an avenging Judgment Day angel, and as the wise Queen of Sheba, this earthy side represents Sister Nash as the conduit of an authentic, archetypal moral system. While every "sho sho" and "thrub thrub" of her washboard bleaches the white folks' dirty laundry, Sister Nash's message to the black bourgeoisie is that "a nigger's boun' to be a nigger. . . . You kin skin him, but he's a nigger still." When his attempted bigamy is bared back for the whole congregation to see, Brother Jimson affirms this axiom by behaving like some Sambo, "face . . . ashen, teeth chattering, hair standing on end,"[32] who has been hauled before Ole Massa on a mighty bad offense. Yet defendant, judge, and jury are really very much the same: They are members of the African American elite and its aspirants, who cannot escape themselves. The more snobbish and superior they are, the faster they become more like the coarse, rural, ridiculous black proletariat they are running from and the crude, urban, ridiculous white mobocracy (like Bridget McCarthy) that they run to. Instead of attempting to distance itself by checkbook and ballot from the rest of the race, this elite class, Hopkins suggests, must return to the collective advancement and self-respect that uplift purists – or conjurers, for that matter – intend.

"Bro'r Abr'm Jimson's Wedding" finally might be read as an allegory of the artistic motives of Hopkins and other nineteenth-century African American women writers. The importance to this story of triads – for example, the tale is divided into three sections; Andy and Chocolate Caramel argue three weeks before her wedding; it is on a Wednesday, the third day of the business week, that Brother Jimson argues with Sister Nash; and Jimson's three lovers converge on the day he makes his matrimonial vows – holds one key to this interpretation. "Three," as Zora Neale Hurston writes, "is the holy number and the call to preach always comes three times. It is never answered until the third time. The man flees from the call, but is finally brought to accept it."[33] In Hopkins's case, she and her fellow African American women writers have been "called," as it were, to write a literature of and for their race. The "marriage" of their pens to page means loss and gain, departure and arrival, separation and union, completion and renewal. For the sake of their art, they might be required to surrender social approval, dreams of husband and home, or perhaps even personal freedom or fiscal stability. Yet like the unwilling Chocolate Caramel, what the women writers give away in wealth and prestige they gain in integrity and insight. They can awaken their race to the knowledge that to face and then move beyond a deleterious Southern past (allegorized in the wedding scene by Ma Jane) is *really* to begin the march toward upbuilding. They might lose singularity, but they gain the awareness that writing, as Elizabeth Ammons states, "is corporate – . . . a collaborative act in which the otherwise lost voices of the past find expression [and in which voices establish] communion across generations, a link between the living and the dead."[34] Out of conjure and Christianity, Southern folk and Northern Brahmins, oral and written, visible and unseen, Hopkins and other African American women writers will collectively create an art, like Sister Maria's "lightning speech," that energizes and inspires generations.

III

God is Love,
Love is God;
There is no God but Love
And Work is His Prophet![35]
     W. E. B. Du Bois

In a 1902 series for the *Colored American Magazine* entitled "Famous Women of the Negro Race," Hopkins memorialized one "literary worker" named Frances Ellen Watkins Harper. A poet, novelist, and lecturer whose "literary labors" spanned most of the nineteenth century, Harper epitomized the merger of intellect and sweat that characterized a race woman of the age. She refused to hide behind the petticoats of respectability and breeding in order to escape exposure to the suffering and the poor. In one of her "Aunt Jane" sketches from the *A. M. E. Christian Recorder* (1873), she vocalized this humanitarian creed: "I hardly know what I shall succeed in doing, but I want to be a living loving force, not a mere intellectual force, eager and excited only for my own welfare; but a moral and spiritual force. A woman who can and will do something for a woman, especially for our own women because they will need me the most."[36] Born free, yet orphaned after three years, Harper dedicated the prime of her life to advocating the relief of paupers, the suffrage of women, the liberty of the enslaved, and the education of freedmen and freedwomen. By marrying, teaching, preaching, and practicing piety, wisdom, temperance, and restraint, she challenged the myths of promiscuity and careless motherhood into which mainstream culture would normally circumscribe her and her peers. In her "Aunt Chloe" poems (1872), Harper, like Hopkins, links issues of class to those of religion and race. Yet her project, like that of Hopkins, is not only to inspire African American audiences to inoculate themselves with the wisdom and power of their collective cultural pasts, but also to organize and unveil to the entire American nation an immediate agenda for reunion and social reform.

What had marked British and American abolitionist poetry as well as prose was an abiding scorn at the United States for having abandoned its Revolutionary goals of defeating autocracy, giving voice to the aspirations of ordinary men and women, and making one nation out of many. Instead of a democracy, transatlantic abolitionists contended, antebellum America featured a plantation oligarchy; instead of unity, secession. Like their counterparts, the pre-Revolutionary white laborers and farmers who were classed out of the gentrified electorate, the enslaved were excluded from elections, land, citizenship, and humanity. Thus, abolitionists had formalized the position that England, America's former tyrant, was more humane and democratic than its old colony. After all, John Bull had freed his slaves in the Caribbean in 1833; and, upon the enactment of the Fugitive Slave Act of 1850, his country had become an asylum for American fugitives fleeing legalized remandment. Authored in England by firsthand witnesses to and objects of this irony, William Wells Brown's *Clotel* and William and Ellen Craft's *Running a Thousand Miles for Freedom* (1860) had summed up America's hypocrisy, the latter quoting these lines from the English poet Cowper: "Slaves cannot breathe in England: if their lungs / Receive our air, that moment they are free; / They touch our country, and their shackles fall."[37] Similarly, on a tour of England with her Northern employer, Harriet Jacobs stated, "During all that time, I never saw the slightest symptom of prejudice against color. I entirely forgot it, till the time came for us to return to America."[38]

For the first time since Independence, the America of Reconstruction – black and white together – is positioned in Harper's poetry to respond to its English rival without hypocrisy. The Americans in her poetry are ready to make real their dashed Revolutionary vision of a diverse, democratic republic. Such revitalized ideals demand a different genre to express them. So we find that the Aunt Chloe poems are to some extent poetical equivalents of what the critic Frances Smith Foster has described as "progress-report autobiographies." From slave narratives like those of Old Elizabeth (1863) and Primus in Lydia Sigourney's *Sketch of Connecticut* (1824), to postbellum narratives such as those of Elizabeth Keckley (1868) and Susie King Taylor (1902), to contemporary, late twentieth-century first-person and ghost-written memoirs, this "progress-report" genre, Foster writes, combines and then transforms the testimonial qualities of St Augustine's *Confessions's* – and Franklin's *Autobiography's* – portrait of the self-made man. What characterizes the "progress reports" across generations and genders are: (1) the goal of inspiring African Americans to achieve; (2) the author's faith in an improved and brighter future in spite of limited or contingent success; (3) individualism: i.e., a will and a commitment to make a better life even if it means leaving home or departing from convention; (4) a bold determination to critique the faults of the race so that those flaws may be excised or corrected; and (5) both pride in one's blackness and respect of and cooperation with other

races. Central to these autobiographies, writes Foster, are that they "specifically propose to inspire black people toward increased participation in American
society and to assure them and others that their dreams of life, liberty, and the
pursuit of happiness were obtainable within the theory, if not the practice, of
the United States Constitution."[39]

The Aunt Chloe poems brilliantly testify to the accuracy of Foster's model.
Just as *Uncle Tom's Cabin* (1852) inspired Harper's poem on the famous crossing-
the-ice scene of the fictional Eliza Harris ("Eliza Harris," 1853) as well as her
"To Mrs. Harriet Beecher Stowe" (1854) and "Eva's Farewell" (1854), so, too, is
Stowe's novel a probable source, at least for the narrator's name, of the Aunt
Chloe series. According to Christina Zwarg, Stowe holds up Aunt Chloe (Uncle
Tom's wife) as both a failed subversion and an empowered transformation of
the nurturing, pious, capitalist ideal of white femininity. Zwarg writes, "By
entering Tom's 'cabin' [and Aunt Chloe's 'kitchen' in the big house] we enter
into a curious and undecided space where rules of the larger patriarchal world
are sometimes subverted and traditional notions of self and authority fall into
question even as they are assumed."[40] In contrast, Harper's Aunt Chloe is not at
all focused on conforming to patriarchal versions of whiteness or womanhood.
Harper's Aunt Chloe is at once a revision of Stowe's mammy character[41] and a
revisitation to African American women's roles in post-Reconstruction communities. "Learning to Read" at the "rising" age of sixty, she implies that no enter-
prising African American permits age, naysayers, an impoverished, enslaved
childhood, or any other factors for that matter, to hold back the dawn of mental
and material development. Lincoln has been shot, the Reconstruction has floun-
dered, the promised repatriations (forty acres and a mule) have not materialized,
and the white-sheeted Ku Klux Klansmen ride. Yet, "everything will pass
away," Aunt Chloe assures her readers, just as Uncle Jacob had assured her in
"The Deliverance" that "I feel right and certain, / Slavery's bound to pass away."
Aunt Chloe encourages her fellow former slaves to defy whatever laws stand
between them and success: she relishes, for example, the stories from slavery
days of men like Uncle Caldwell and Mr. Turner's Ben, men – not slaves – who
defied their master's proprietary claims and titles on their persons by "stealing"
in order to read "by hook or crook." At the same time, Aunt Chloe also points
out the weaknesses among her race, in "The Deliverance" hurling a series of
rebukes at African American men who have sold their votes to the carpetbaggers
and anti-Reconstructionists in exchange for food and money. Finally, her "Aunt
Chloe's Politics" is a recitation of the era's dual politics of building intraracial
pride and broadening interracial coalitions: "When we want to school our children, / If the money isn't there / Whether black or white have took it / The loss
we all must share."[42]

Where the church is corrupt, narrow-minded, and snobbish in Hopkins's
story,[43] in the Aunt Chloe poems it figures as a utopian, collaborative site.
The church unifies African Americans, diverts their attention from material
attainment to spiritual and intellectual enlightenment, and focuses them upon

achievement for the sake of collective good. "Since freedom blessed our race /
We all ought to come together / And build a meeting place"[44] is the command of
"Church Building." This poem dimensionalizes the project of racial unity: it is
a lateral one that allies the genders, and a vertical one that blurs class boundaries
up and down the social scale. Attesting to gender unity is the fact that even
though Chloe is speaking, she credits her advice to a now-deceased male community member, Uncle Jacob. His "uncle" to her "aunt," Jacob and Chloe both
occupy the same stature as respected community elders and impervious reposit-
ories of experience and mother-wit.

"We are all bound up together," Harper had said, meaning black and white,
men and women, laborer and professional, rich and poor, "in one great bundle of
humanity, and society cannot trample on the weakest and feeblest of its members without receiving the curse in its own soul."[45] Towards this paradisaical
classlessness among her race, "Church Building" unites the entire African American
community under the assumption that all are cooperative servants of God. In
contrast to the spiritual and physical isolation of Alice Dunbar-Nelson's Sister
Josepha in a white-dominated church community,[46] Harper's black church offers
a means of collective empowerment. The first three stanzas model African Americans as one army of spiritual/uplift laborers who have "pinched, and scraped, and
spared / A little here and there." In the last three stanzas, Uncle Jacob's admonition to "meet me / Right in the promised land"[47] reminds Harper's African
American Christian readers of the same eternal Savior whom they all aspire to
rejoin. The African American community is referred to in the first person plural
– "we," "our" – as if to emphasize its necessary singularity of purpose: to build
a spiritual community on earth that mirrors the heaven to which Uncle Jacob
has already ascended. When Uncle Jacob in the sixth stanza calls his neighbors
"Children," he points toward an aspect of the African American sermon tradition that rhetorically unites the congregants, the preacher, and their God as one
familial and "communal voice" that is "raised," as Dolan Hubbard writes, "in
opposition to the reality that the dominant culture chose to make the arbitrary
sign of skin color into an ontological distinction. The ostracized community
seeks closure first on the social and secular and second on the spiritual and sacred
levels. Taking their cue from the preacher, the people break free from economic,
psychological, and spatial immobility."[48] Thus, attention to Uncle Jacob's proposed unity of thought and action teases out the ironic connotations of the
terms "Brothers" and "Sisters" in "Bro'r Abr'm Jimson's Wedding," where an
individualistic, capitalistic, short-sighted mindset rules – and ruins – the day.
That Uncle Jacob is individualized only heightens Harper's theme of union. A
mystical, Christ-like figure with a supernatural gift of speech, he embodies the
divine Creator who focuses the attention of all striving classes on sharing one
goal of salvation, faith, and peace.

Envisioning a better future for men and women of all classes, "Church Building" skillfully puns on the spiritual's familiar lines, "We are climbing Jacob's
ladder. / We are climbing Jacob's ladder. / We are climbing Jacob's ladder. /

Soldiers of the Lord." Not only does Harper intend the song's traditional theme of soldiering on towards spiritual redemption; she uses language ambiguously to imply that earthly "church" or "meeting place" and heavenly "promised land" stand for post-Emancipation African Americans' "moiling / And toiling" and accession to all vocations and professions. His eyes "bright and young" as he says his last goodbyes, Uncle Jacob allegorizes the spirit of the Reconstruction generations of African Americans.[49] The "city" to which he hopes to gain admission recalls the "city upon a hill" or New Jerusalem that the Puritan communities of Massachusetts fled Europe's tyranny to create. Enslavement, Civil War, border wars, the genocide of Native Americans, pauperism, and other social troubles may have whittled national conviction in the construction of this Eden to a tentative "hope." Harper centers African Americans in the Reconstruction, emblematized by Uncle Jacob, as architects of a democracy that will perfect freedom, tolerance, equality, and love – or at least, in the face of disappointments, persevere to attain them.

It is noteworthy that, at the midpoint of "Church Building," Harper should turn our ears to Uncle Jacob's "trumpet" voice and "mighty" tongue. As a poet, she herself is a trumpet voice and mighty tongue, one whom Hopkins once described as making "noble deeds" that spoke in "trumpet tones" on her behalf;[50] her process of creating "Church Building" is analogous to the divine event of the creation of the universe. After all, the Bible says, before God gave form to heaven and earth, there was the Word. Harper has constructed a poem about creating a people: a racial community that really believes and practices the religion it espouses. One of the race of people recognized in this poem, Uncle Jacob, reminds us with his voice and tongue of his genesis in the poet's imagination; at the same time, he stands for Harper's divine co-creator, God. This Chinese box of creations-within-creations at the middle of the poem comprises a mandala-like structure very similar to the story-within-a-story plot of Hopkins's "Bro'r Abr'm Jimson's Wedding." This mandala-inspired design of meanings is feminine in its circularity and proliferation, and non-Western by virtue of its associations with the earliest, original expressive cultures of humanity.[51] We might view this connection, as we did in a similar fashion with Hopkins, as a cue that Harper intends to speak broadly to the position of nineteenth-century African American women.

Divine truth in Harper's canon, as in Hopkins's, manifests itself in threes. First, by masking her polished speech and book knowledge with the dialect and experiential wisdom of Aunt Chloe's poems, Harper conjoins the roles and standpoints of the intellectual and "everyday" classes of African American womanhood. Her technique demonstrates that more unites these counterparts of black femininity than might divide them: both classes endure the same kinds of stereotyping; both have shared the history of enslavement; both are excluded from the vote and demonized by lynching; both experience sexism and racism. Let us not forget that Aunt Chloe, for all of her backwardness in "book-learning," possesses an evolved religious consciousness that Harper holds up to readers of all classes as the standard to which their own souls should strive. Second, by superimposing the unrefined Aunt Chloe where the urbane poet would ordinarily speak, these poems bring from abstract to concrete Harper's "Aunt Jane" axiom that blacks should never "place the culture of the intellect before the development of your soul."[52] Finally, to blend the voices of the evangelistic, humanitarian Harper and her evangelistic, humanitarian Aunt Chloe means to unify all African American women, of whatever class or situation, as especial participants in community service and Christian stewardship.

* * *

Anne Dalke proposes that "[R]eligious conviction, far from limiting the self-expression of black women writers, emphatically gave them literary voice."[53] The origin of African American women's writing in both spiritual autobiography and slave narrative traditions ensured that a religious dimension would prevail in their canon no matter how secularized their literary themes became. Yet among nineteenth-century African American women writers, the high road to heaven could not be undertaken without getting down and dirty on class. Spirit led to class. Class, once reckoned with, did not necessarily arouse contention and strife. Instead, its pathways often pointed nineteenth-century African Americans and African American women writers towards enlightened spiritual progress and progressive social advancement in a vexed material world.

Notes

1   Frances Ellen Watkins Harper, "Nothing and Something," in *A Brighter Coming Day: A Frances Ellen Watkins Harper Reader*, ed. Frances Smith Foster (New York: The Feminist Press, 1990), 251–2.

2   Frederick Douglass, *The Narrative of the Life of Frederick Douglass, An American Slave. Written by Himself*, in *Frederick Douglass: Autobiographies* (New York: Literary Classics of the United States, 1994), 97.

3   William Wells Brown, *Clotel; Or, The President's Daughter: A Narrative of Slave Life in the United States*, ed. William Edward Farrison (New York: Carol Publishing Group, 1969), 67.

4   Foster, ed., *A Brighter Coming Day*, 58–60.

5   Lydia Maria Child, *The Stars and Stripes: A Melodrama*, in *The Liberty Bell* (Boston: American Antislavery Society, 1858), 143.

6   As an example of the nexus of nineteenth-century Native American culture, Latino culture, and racial bigotry, see John Rollins Ridge's fictional response to the Supreme Court's displacement of the Georgia Cherokees and the disenfranchisement of Mexicans in California. Ridge is treated in Timothy Powell's "Theorizing Beyond the Binary: Cultural Complexity in the First Native American Novel," in *Beyond the Binary: American Identity and Multiculturalism*, ed. Timothy Powell (New Brunswick: Rutgers University Press, 1998).

7   Anna Julia Cooper, "The Higher Education of Women," in *Black Women in Nineteenth-Century American Life: Their Words, Their Thoughts, Their Feelings*, ed. Bert

James Loewenberg and Ruth Bogin (University Park, PA: Pennsylvania State University Press, 1976), 322; Kilcup, *NCAWW*, 451. See also Karen Baker-Fletcher's book-length discussion of Cooper's Christianity in *A Singing Something: Womanist Reflections on Anna Julia Cooper* (New York: Crossroad Publishing Company, 1994).

8   Anna Julia Cooper, "The Status of Women in America," in *Words of Fire: An Anthology of African-American Feminist Thought*, ed. Beverly Guy-Sheftall (New York: The New Press, 1995), 45.

9   Harriet Jacobs establishes this dichotomy between heavenly and earthly churches. Remarking on slave masters like her own Dr Flint who give mere lip service to Christian principles, she writes, "No wonder the slaves sing, – 'Ole Satan's church is here below; / Up to God's free church I hope to go.'" See her *Incidents in the Life of a Slave Girl. Written by Herself*, ed. Jean Fagan Yellin (Cambridge, MA: Harvard University Press, 1987), 75. Anne Dalke compares the religious suppression that characterizes white Christianity in Jacobs's narrative to the expansive, liberatory black Christianity of Rebecca Cox Jackson's journals (1830–64) in "Spirit Matters: Re-Possessing the African-American Women's Literary Tradition," *Legacy* 12 (1995): 1–16.

10   Cooper, "Higher Education," in *Black Women in Nineteenth-Century American Life*, ed. Loewenberg and Bogin, 328; *NCAWW*, 458.

11   See Jacobs, *Incidents*, 68–70; and Elizabeth Keckley, *Behind the Scenes. Or, Thirty Years a Slave, and Four Years in the White House* (New York: G. W. Carleton, 1868), 32–9.

12   Maria W. Stewart, *Religion and the Pure Principles of Morality, the Sure Foundation on Which We Must Build*, in *Black Women in Nineteenth-Century American Life*, ed. Loewenberg and Bogin, 186.

13   Elizabeth Ammons, *Conflicting Stories: American Women Writers at the Turn of the Twentieth Century* (New York: Oxford University Press, 1991), 5.

14   Hazel V. Carby, *Reconstructing Womanhood: The Emergence of the Afro-American Woman Novelist* (New York: Oxford University Press, 1987), 108.

15   Carla L. Peterson, "'Doers of the Word': Theorizing African-American Women Writers in the Antebellum North," in *The (Other) American Traditions: Nineteenth-Century Women Writers*, ed. Joyce W. Warren (New Brunswick: Rutgers University Press, 1993), 187.

16   "These God-breathing machines are no more, in the sight of their masters, than the cotton they plant, or the horses they tend." Jacobs, *Incidents*, 8.

17   *NCAWW*, 524.

18   Angela Davis, "Reflections on the Black Woman's Role in the Community of Slaves," in *Words of Fire*, ed. Guy-Sheftall, 205.

19   W. E. B. Du Bois, *The Souls of Black Folk*, in *W. E. B. Du Bois: Writings* (New York: Literary Classics of the United States, 1986), 384.

20   *NCAWW*, 469.

21   Ibid., 475, 469.

22   Ibid.

23   These were the angel Gabriel's announcement to Zacharias of the birth of John the Baptist (Luke 1: 11–22), the Annunciation (Luke 1: 28–38), and the appearance of the angelic host to the shepherds (Luke 2: 8–14).

24   *NCAWW*, 476, 471, 476.

25   So named because of its inhabitants' single-minded struggles for financial security, celebrity, and elite social status, Striver's Row identifies the "tree-lined blocks" of

private homes and apartments in Harlem, fronting "138th and 139th Streets between Seventh and Eighth Avenues." This neighborhood became synonymous among 1920s African Americans with upward mobility, social ease, prestige, rags-to-riches stories, and affluence. Its residents included professionals, entertainers, socialites, artists, and entrepreneurs: for example, the musician and composer Eubie Blake. See Jervis Anderson's *This Was Harlem: A Cultural Portrait, 1900–1950* (New York: Farrar, Straus, and Giroux, 1981), 339–40.

26 Zora Neale Hurston, *Mules and Men*, in *Zora Neale Hurston: Folklore, Memoirs, and Other Writings* (New York: Literary Classics of the United States, 1995), 178.

27 *NCAWW*, 475, 477.

28 This was Du Bois's term for the "best and most capable" echelons of college and university graduates, trained primarily in the liberal arts, who would diligently inspire and educate the majority of their race and, as "leaders of thought and missionaries of culture," lead their peers from ex-enslavement into modernity (*Writings*, 847, 861). In his essay entitled "The Talented Tenth," anthologized in his *The Negro Problem* (1903), Du Bois did not propose this group to disparage or replace Booker T. Washington's model of industrial education and manual education, as has been widely held, but rather to undergird it with an artistic and cultural component. He wrote: "I would not deny, or for a moment seem to deny, the paramount necessity of teaching the Negro to work, and to work steadily and skillfully; or seem to depreciate in the slightest degree the important part industrial schools must play in the accomplishment of these ends, but I *do* say, and insist upon it, that it is industrialism drunk with its vision of success, to imagine that its own work can be accomplished without providing for the training of broadly cultured men and women to teach its own teachers, and to teach the teachers of the public schools" (*Writings*, 855).

29 Hazel V. Carby, "'On the Threshold of Woman's Era': Lynching, Empire, and Sexuality in Black Feminist Theory," *Critical Inquiry* 12 (1985): 310.

30 Pauline Elizabeth Hopkins, *The Magazine Novels of Pauline Elizabeth Hopkins*, introd. Hazel V. Carby (New York: Oxford University Press, 1988), 565. On the one hand, the number of women characters is minimal in this novel, and its protagonist is male. On the other, the novel's male protagonist, Reuel Briggs, cultivates the traits of sensitivity, nurturance, unselfishness, charity, and emotion that characteristically have been regarded as feminine in the sociocultural context of late nineteenth-century British and American literature and life. In the tradition of the Byronic or Romantic hero, even his appearance is one of melancholy femininity. My graduate student Heather Mitchell has suggested an interpretation that resolves this incongruity between Hopkins's pursuit of an Afrofemcentric vision and her selection of a male, albeit feminized, hero. In a June 2, 1995 electronic mail correspondence, Mitchell proposes that Reuel stands for Hopkins herself and other outspoken, activist, Afrocentric African American women: "It has been suggested that Hopkins's retirement from writing in 1905, one year after *Of One Blood* ended serialization, was a consequence of growing frustration with the political and social climate for blacks and women. It might be, then, that the fact that women are essentially absent in *Of One Blood* except for the tragic Dianthe, who is continually used, mesmerized, and robbed of her identity, reflects an increasing belief on the part of Hopkins that there was no place [in political and intellectual leadership] for the black woman. Indeed, if one reads Reuel Briggs as Hopkins's voice in the novel, Hopkins could be suggesting that the only identity for a woman is that of a man."

Through a comparison of *Of One Blood* with its predecessor, Hopkins's novel *Contending Forces: A Romance Illustrative of Negro Life North and South* (1900), Elizabeth Ammons undertakes a similar interpretation in her *Conflicting Stories*. She writes: "Whatever guarded optimism Hopkins might have felt about the future of the African American woman artist at the time she wrote *Contending Forces* was gone by the time she wrote *Of One Blood*. Grounding the black woman's story in unrequited heterosexual desire, violent sexual violation by white America, and erasure of her empowering African heritage, Hopkins tells in her 'fairy tale,' her wildly unbeliev-able fiction (if looked at in conventional western realistic terms), the awful truth about the African American woman's reality at the beginning of the twentieth cen-tury. In *Of One Blood* the black American woman artist *has* a past. What she does not have is ownership of that past, or a future" (84).

The technique of projecting feminine qualities onto a male character in order to comment on barriers to women's politics or creativity would not be monopolized by nineteenth-century African American women writers. Hugh Wolfe, the hero of Rebecca Harding Davis's "Life in the Iron Mills" (1861), possesses traditionally feminine traits – and even carves a statue of a woman – to convey one of Davis's pet literary themes: the suppression of the female artist.

31   *NCAWW*, 474.

32   Ibid., 475, 477.

33   Hurston, "Conversions and Visions," in *Folklore, Memoirs*, 847.

34   Elizabeth Ammons, "Introduction," in *Short Fiction by Black Women, 1900–1920* (New York: Oxford University Press, 1991), 12.

35   Du Bois, "The Damnation of Women," in *Writings*, 952.

36   Frances Ellen Watkins Harper, "Fancy Etchings," *A. M. E. Christian Recorder* (Feb-ruary 20, 1873).

37   William and Ellen Craft, *Running a Thousand Miles for Freedom* (London: William Tweedie, 1860), title page.

38   Jacobs, *Incidents*, 185.

39   Frances Smith Foster, "African American Progress-Report Autobiographies," in *Redefining American Literary History*, ed. A. LaVonne Brown Ruoff and Jerry W. Ward, Jr (New York: Modern Language Association, 1990), 274.

40   Christina Zwarg, "Fathering and Blackface in *Uncle Tom's Cabin*," in Harriet Beecher Stowe, *Uncle Tom's Cabin; Or, Life Among the Lowly*, ed. Elizabeth Ammons (New York: Norton, 1994), 571.

41   Frances Smith Foster, *Written By Herself: Literary Production by African American Women, 1746–1892* (Bloomington: Indiana University Press, 1993), 151. Similarly, Carla Peterson cites the first-person narration of the Aunt Chloe poems and their use of black dialect and idiomatic expression as a rejection of the notion that "black language, thought, and action must inevitably be framed by a white perspective," as well as of the stereotypical hierarchization of white language as " 'matured' " and "the black dialect as 'infantile,' 'chaotic,' and in need of containment." "According to [John Edgar] Wideman," writes Peterson, "the task facing twentieth-century black writers has been 'to escape [this] literary frame which *a priori* devalues black speech.' I would argue that such a freeing is exactly what Harper accomplishes in her Aunt Chloe cycle as she deconstructs the binary opposition of white literary frame and black dialect and invents a black idiom that exists on its own terms, unframed by the language of the dominant culture." See her *"Doers of the Word":*

African-American Women Speakers and Writers in the North (1830–1880) (New York: Oxford University Press, 1995), 212–13.

42   *NCAWW*, 166.

43   The ambivalent and complex portraits of churches and church members appear elsewhere in stories of pastors and parishes by nineteenth-century white American women, including Harriet Beecher Stowe's "Laughin' in Meetin'" (1891), Rebecca Harding Davis's "A Faded Leaf of History" (1873), or Rose Terry Cooke's "Miss Beulah's Bonnet" (1881); see *NCAWW*, 138–42, 233–41, 180–91.

44   *NCAWW*, 168.

45   From a speech of Harper's delivered at the Eleventh National Woman's Rights Convention, New York City, May 1866. Reprinted in Foster, ed., *A Brighter Coming Day*, 217; *NCAWW*, 156.

46   See Alice Dunbar-Nelson, "Sister Josepha" (1899), in *NCAWW*, 566–70.

47   *NCAWW*, 168.

48   Dolan Hubbard, *The Sermon and the African American Literary Imagination* (Columbia: University of Missouri Press, 1994), 7.

49   *NCAWW*, 168.

50   Pauline Elizabeth Hopkins, "Famous Women of the Negro Race – Literary Workers," *Colored American Magazine* (January–February 1902): 366.

51   Pierre Daco, *The Mammoth Book of Dreams* (New York: Carroll and Graf, 1995), 125. Other African American women writers have experimented with the mandala as a symbol of creativity, transformation, and a collective artistic and expressive consciousness. See, for example, my discussion of Zora Neale Hurston's evocation of the quartered circle in "The Folklore of the Coasts in Black Women's Fiction of the Harlem Renaissance," *CLA Journal* 39 (1996): 291–3.

52   Harper, "Fancy Etchings."

53   Dalke, "Spirit Matters," 2.

10

"Essays of Invention": Transformations of Advice in Nineteenth-Century American Women's Writing

KAREN L. KILCUP

In a letter of summer 1883 to her friend Mrs. Howard J. Sweetser, Emily Dickinson wrote, "Your sweet beneficence of Bulbs I return as Flowers, with a bit of the swarthy Cake baked only in Domingo." Dickinson enclosed the following recipe:

Black Cake –

2 pounds Flour –
2 Sugar –
2 Butter –
19 Eggs –
5 pounds Raisins –
1$\frac{1}{2}$ Currants –
1$\frac{1}{2}$ Citron –
$\frac{1}{2}$ pint Brandy –
$\frac{1}{2}$ Molasses –
2 Nutmegs –
5 teaspoons
Cloves – Mace – Cinnamon –
2 teaspoons Soda –

Beat Butter and Sugar together –
Add Eggs without beating – and beat the mixture again – Bake 2$\frac{1}{2}$ or three hours, in Cake pans, or 5 to 6 hours in Milk pan, if full – [1]

If Emily Dickinson were not Emily Dickinson, we would probably dismiss the letter and recipe as a mere "domestic" exchange, however clever. But given the identity of the writer, we must be tempted to reread this communication in a more "purely" "aesthetic" context. The opening letter is frankly metaphorical. The poet's transformation of "Bulbs" into "Flowers" suggests the generative power explored more explicitly in poems like "I send two sunsets," "I'll tell you how the sun rose," "We play at paste," "I cannot dance upon my toes," "South winds jostle them," and "A route of evanescence," while the "swarthy Cake" intimates the exotic and unique ("*only* in Domingo") nature of that power.[2] In this context, beauty is synaesthetic, it crosses over the senses, as the flowers invoke sight and smell, and the cake conjures taste and smell. More than a sensual experience, the "recipe" transcends its quotidian antecedents and seeks to attain the status of poetry. Highlighting surplus in its form as well as its content – one would have to be very hungry indeed to consume such a weighty cake, with its nineteen eggs and two pounds of butter – the text invokes Dickinson's characteristic poetic strategies of capitalization, line breaks, and dashes, along with her familiar substantive concern (and love for) excess that appears in more familiar poems like "Your riches taught me poverty" and "One of the ones that Midas touched."[3]

This glance at the continuities between Dickinson's letters, her "domestic writing," and her poetry suggests the need for a more generous conception of the larger genre of writing to which the "recipe" and texts like it belong. In a broader context, one goal of an enlarged critical vision of nineteenth-century American literature might be to understand better the relationship of diverse popular and "everyday" forms of writing to other, more canonical forms. Ostensibly a "private" mode when addressed to a female audience, "advice writing," to take one example of the popular literature of which cookbook writing could be considered a subgenre, often had larger ambitions. Not only did the "codes" in advice writing provide "an instrument of inclusion and socialization," representing "standards by which to assess entire social classes, ethnic groups, and cultures (often justifying their subordination). . . . "[4] Advice writing could also work across class and ethnic lines, it could embody subtle or not-so-subtle critiques of American culture, and it could articulate the writer's perception of "America" just as strongly as Emerson's "The American Scholar" or Margaret Fuller's "American Literature." To take a larger view implies the recognition that "conduct books for women must be viewed as just one among many forgotten kinds of information which are . . . woven into the fabric of literature."[5]

This essay explores the premise that "advice" writing, and its close relation, writing about "behavior," occurs on a continuum whose extremities are conformity and resistance to actual or perceived cultural norms. In exploring the complexities of individual works on this continuum I will suggest that such writing readily translates into another dimension via the mediation of genre, and that short fiction by many nineteenth-century American women also encodes advice and similarly belongs on this continuum. Because advice writing is tempered by an understanding of what constitutes "respectability," I will touch upon the relationship of "advice writing," broadly construed, to the project of constraining or reconstructing class situation. As John Kasson has pointed out, advice writing "sought to respond to democratic aspirations while curbing their egalitarian 'excesses.'" I am arguing that advice writing is potentially more subversive than Kasson and other historians acknowledge: that is, we cannot always take the writer literally at her word.[6] What sometimes seems to be a conservative attempt by women writers to recuperate women (and by extension, working people and immigrants) into standards of behavior formulated by white middle-class culture often reveals itself as a coded affirmation of a different, and more complex set of "American" values, sometimes in a movement toward a national (rather than simply local) identity. Finally, I will suggest that we can see the relationship between popular advice writing and more canonical forms of prose writing as a circulatory one, in which writers often cross the generic boundaries with which we have confined them; from this perspective, "advice writing" often possesses aesthetic ambitions, while "fiction" incorporates a body of practical advice that negotiates norms of respectability.[7]

"Delicious-made dishes": Advising Americans

Carolyn Karcher reminds us that advice writing emerged in a society of "increasing geographical mobility [that] was carrying young wives away from the mothers and grandmothers on whom they had traditionally relied for guidance in running a household and bringing up children."[8] Although these remarks focus on the particular genre of Lydia Maria Child's domestic writing, "advice writing" over the course of the century was addressed to rich and poor, male and female, black and white;[9] and it included such subcategories as cookbook writing, etiquette writing, medical manuals, and domestic economies. Many such texts were initially aimed at the affluent, but conduct manuals came to encompass a larger and increasingly urban audience, "an audience of aspiring men and women who hoped to fulfill the promise of the allegedly open society of Jacksonian America, either by entering the ranks of the middle class from below or by rising within those ranks to higher and higher levels of gentility." Offering advice on "manners, morals, personal appearance, mental development, and work habits," and instructing readers "where to live, what to eat, how to entertain themselves, and when and whom to marry," such texts were astonishingly popular.[10] Although those before 1800 tended to be reprints or plagiarisms of French and British editions, by the early decades of the nineteenth century, Americans were more often creating their own standards.[11] From the early nineteenth century, advice volumes responded to the increasing complexity of US society, for such changes as universal suffrage for white men, the dissipation of religious authority into many denominations rather than a few, the potential disorderliness of cities filled with increasing numbers of immigrants, the movement west of many individuals (and hence their remoteness from traditional centers of authority), and the transition from a home-based to a factory-based economic system all contributed to the development of an ideology of home as a locus for social cohesion and stability. To create this idealized and emotionalized home as haven, and to fashion herself as its similarly idealized center, the housewife required guidance.[12]

The epitome of American women's advice writing is Lydia Maria Child's bestselling *The Frugal Housewife* (1829). An early biographer of Child's observed that the book "proved so suited to the wants of the public that it has since attained its fortieth edition"; it sold so well that after its first issue it went to a second edition in three months. Child's purpose for herself was to be "a useful writer," and she believed that "ideally, books (and authors) should educate minds and morals. Literature was important because it nurtured Christian virtues and democratic ideals."[13] The volume begins with Child's characteristic forthrightness: "The true economy of housekeeping is simply the art of gathering up all the fragments, so that nothing be lost. I mean fragments of *time*, as well as *materials*. Nothing should be thrown away so long as it is possible to make any use of it, however trifling that use may be; and whatever be the size of a family, every member should be employed either in earning or saving money."[14] Assuming a stern intimacy with the reader, much as a grandmother or great-aunt might employ, Child depicts the forms that such economy might assume: children making fans from turkey feathers, elderly people knitting stockings, everyone saving string.

Conforming to the standard of Franklinian frugality ("a penny saved is a penny earned"), Child nevertheless marks off her resistance to the function of ordinary advice writing when she asserts that "books of this kind have usually been written for the wealthy: I have written for the poor." Her frustration with the customary tone and content of such texts emerges in her own review of another contemporary text: "the economy, the benevolence, all the duties inculcated, presuppose great wealth, high station, and fashionable habits. We should indeed tremble for the twenty four *Disunited States* of this Republic, if we thought such books would become necessary here."[15] While in this class consciousness she clearly resists the sentimentalization of the home that many of her contemporaries evince,[16] from one perspective her own book offers a conservative message, teaching readers not to overreach their means, counseling "self-denial, in proportion to the narrowness of your income." Yet Child's work seeks not to reinforce norms of respectability – though that respectability might be a valuable, if sometimes frivolous, commodity, as her remarks on the education of daughters suggest – but to counsel financially pressed housewives like herself on the best use of their resources.[17] One of Child's contemporaries, Catharine Maria Sedgwick, would point to an American dream of class transcendence when she affirmed, "It is not here as in the old world, where one man is born with a silver spoon, and another with a pewter one, in his mouth. You may all handle silver spoons, if you will. That is, you may all rise to places of respectability."[18] Recognizing from her own experience the difficulty of achieving this transcendence, Child reinvents respectability to include hardworking persons of all classes, asking, "Is he [the lad who conceals his manual labor] one whit more respectable than the industrious lad who sweeps stores, or carries bottles . . . ?"[19]

Although one of her expressed goals is to write for the poor, Child's writing pursues another purpose, to educate readers how to be better Americans: "To what are the increasing beggary and discouraged exertions of the present period owing? A multitude of causes have no doubt tended to increase the evil; but the root of the whole matter is the extravagance of all classes of people. We never shall be prosperous till we make pride and vanity yield to the dictates of honesty and prudence! We never shall be free from embarrassment until we cease to be ashamed of industry and economy." In speaking to and of a broader "we," Child sought to foster the creation of a community of self-sufficient and proud Americans whose foundation was the empowering concept of Republican Motherhood that reached its fruition in the mid-nineteenth century.[20] If she invokes again the values represented by Ben Franklin, at the same time Child resists both sex role stereotypes and the construction of the domestic, "mundane" realm of feathers and fans as purely private, for the private had public and political potential. Implicitly speaking to women readers, Child implies that being better women means being, and making, better American citizens; hence, she asserts that a "false and wicked parade" of living beyond one's income is "wrong – morally wrong, so far as the individual is concerned; and injurious beyond calculation to the interests of our country."[21] Respectability and the class consciousness that it suggests yield to considerations of national as well as individual self-sufficiency, happiness, and self-confidence. In keeping with her goal of addressing women who faced financial challenge and hardship, she defies the middle-class standards of "true womanhood" that specified respectable women's nonparticipation in economic matters, a defiance that ensured the criticism of reviewers like powerful Sarah Josepha Hale. In some sense, Child appeared to be advocating the (problematic) economic independence that Joyce Warren explores elsewhere in this volume. Furthermore, her "indecorous" attention to practical matters relating to animal body parts, coupled with a plain and even "rude" style, engendered vicious attacks from at least one self-appointed guardian of social class, Nathaniel Parker Willis.[22] By frankly addressing a disadvantaged group of readers in an accessible style, she resisted norms of substantive and lexical purity also determined by elite standards, creating her own blunt, "everywoman" aesthetic.

Addressing a more affluent and urbanized audience with the leisure to concern themselves with matters of decorum,[23] Eliza Leslie's *The Behavior Book* (1835) also gained its author a national audience. On one level, the chapter entitled "Incorrect Words" enters the realm of socially conservative literature, for, in sharp contrast to the linguistic freedom embodied by Child's text, its aim appears to be one of solidifying social distinctions via conformity to a linguistic "standard" not readily achieved by those without education and the resources necessary to obtain it. As John Kasson points out, "Manners provided yet another way of avoiding talking about the dirty secret of class in America."[24] The fussy advice that the essay offers might seem to be readily assimilable only to socially elite females whose primary concern is not to appear foolish or ignorant to their peers: "Pincushions are pincushions and not pin-balls, unless they are of a globular shape. If in the form of hearts, diamonds, &c., they are not balls." Such advice aims at the homogenization of regional differences, as when Leslie admonishes, "Even if you are a provincial New-Yorker, give up calling the door-step or porch by the ancient Dutch name of 'stoop,' (stoep,) and do not talk of going out on the stoop, or sitting on the stoop." The class consolidation that frames the essay resonates in remarks like "The word 'mayhap' (instead of perhaps) is a positive vulgarism. It is of English origin, but is only used in England by very low people – and by English writers, never."[25] Such lexical norms reinforce distinctions of "high" and "low" culture as they promulgate an ethic of respectability. English travelers of Leslie's time and later were quick to notice not only the wide variations in American speech but also its wide divergence from the elite dialect of the mother tongue, while "American men and women anxious to testify to their country's 'refinement' . . . maintain[ed] that there were no real differences between 'educated speech' in the United States and in the mother country."[26]

In spite of the resonance of a reading in which "Incorrect Words" seeks to establish and perpetuate the "refinement" of educated American speakers, Leslie's text is also amenable to an ironic reading, especially when we contextualize it within the circumstances of her own life and her larger work. Like many nineteenth-century women writers, her family suffered a financial reverse when her father died, leaving the sixteen-year-old Leslie and her mother to support the family of five children. Perhaps it was this change of fortunes, along with her education at the Philadelphia cooking school of a Mrs. Goodfellow, that formed an important foundation for her later writing, including *Pencil Sketches* (1833), whose subject is "American social life, its pretensions, absurdities, and even insanities."[27] In this context it is possible to read "Incorrect Words" as a text that strongly resists the hierarchization of social class by parodying its excesses. That is, the hardship of Leslie's younger years and her accomplished social satire writing intimate an "echo text" or concealed message beneath the essay's sternly comfortable exterior: "Every one who sees much of the world must observe with pain and surprise various unaccountable instances of improper and incorrect words that sometimes disfigure the phraseology of females who have gone through a course of fashionable education, and mixed in what is really genteel society."[28] "Fashionable education" and "*really* genteel society" are not necessarily coterminous, and "pain" seems to be an excessive response to "improper" and "incorrect" *words*. What, Leslie's essay invites us to ask, is "really" respectable?

Beyond specific examples of textual excess, the incipient irony in "Incorrect Words" resides in a larger accumulation of basically petty and often humorous details that ultimately form the structural pattern of the essay. For example, one admonition about food preferences suggests subtextual amusement on the part of the author: "it is wrong to talk of *loving* any thing that is eatable. They may *like* terrapins, oysters, chicken-salad, or ice-cream; but they need not *love* terrapins or oysters, or *love* chicken-salad." In a move that conjoins literal "taste" with tasteful speech, Leslie may be engaging in a doubly "aesthetic" enterprise, satirizing the pretentious behavior of her subjects. The linguistic excess that appears here has a structural counterpart in the numerous anecdotes and adjurations that seem to pile one on top of another with no particular organization or direction; they include the laconic paragraph that warns, "The word 'slump,' or 'slumped,' has too coarse a sound for a lady."[29] Finally, the essay's cumulative humor, from the story of the two officers who receive more sweetening than they might like, to the narrative of the "ugly" boy whipped by his mother, is typical of American women's skill in developing humor over a longer and more diffuse narrative space than their male counterparts.[30] As a whole, the essay reflects indirectly on the development of a diverse American cultural identity that requires skill in its negotiation. Because of today's differing standards of behavior, present-day readers clearly need to be cautious in the attribution of such pettiness, excess, or humor – to Leslie or to any writer in this genre. But the biographical context for Leslie's work, along with these textual markers, suggest at least its openness to a reading that attributes resistance as well as conformity to "Incorrect Words."

After the Civil War, the already vigorous demand for advice writing intensified, as "new etiquette books for grown-ups streamed from the press at the rate of five or six a year between 1870 and 1917." Such widely distributed magazines as the *Atlantic* and *Lippincott's* incorporated advice as regular features, and by the end of the century, even the daily press had entered the field.[31] As the century progressed, Americans also became increasingly concerned with their relationship to food (and to "appetite" more broadly construed), voraciously consuming books not only on *how* to eat but also *what* to eat.[32] Catherine Owen's *Culture and Cooking; Or, Art in the Kitchen* (1881) reflects a later development of one form of advice writing that remains attentive to matters of class as it was reflected in the constitution of its audience. At least as much as their counterparts on etiquette, cookbooks establish a relationship with their readers; "even the root of *recipe* – the Latin *recipere* – implies an exchange, a giver and a taker. Like a story, a recipe needs a recommendation, a context, a point, a reason to be."[33] In this context, Owen challenges the reader to understand that respectability is constructed by an ostensibly cosmopolitan attitude toward food often marked by national difference. On one level, this cosmopolitanism clearly signals an audience with the means and desire to travel internationally as well as nationally; indeed, one etiquette writer lauded "that wide experience which is gained by travel and association with broad and cultivated minds."[34] But where Catharine Sedgwick's scornful discussion in *Letters from Abroad to Kindred at Home* (1841) critiques norms of dress ("taste") for older English women, Owen offers a critique of her own countrypeople in the guise of writing on an ostensibly private, local, quotidian, domestic (and hence female) subject, food:

Many people have strong prejudices against certain things which they have never even tasted, or which they do frequently take and like as a part of something else, without knowing it. How common it is to hear and see untraveled people declare that they dislike garlic, and could not touch anything with it in. Yet those very people will take Worcestershire sauce, in which garlic is actually predominant, with everything they eat; and think none but English pickles eatable, which owe much of their excellence to the introduction of a *soupçon* of garlic. Therefore I beg those who actually only know garlic from hearsay abuse of it, or from its presence on the breath of some inveterate garlic eater, to give it a fair trial when it appears in a recipe.[35]

The prejudice that Owen describes extends not only to food, but to the people associated with particular foods; she tells the humorous story of an ignorant Englishman who is constantly suspicious that French cooks are serving him frog for chicken, and horse for beef. On the other hand, she locates such prejudices close to home as well, for she points out that "Americans think the hare and rabbits, of which the English make such good use, very mean food indeed, and if they are unprejudiced enough to try them, from the fact that they are never well cooked, they dislike them, which prejudice the English reciprocate by looking on squirrels as being as little fit for food as a rat." Finally, she concludes with a statement that resonates far beyond the "narrow" confines of domestic writing: "The moral of all of which is, that for our comfort's sake, and the general good we should avoid unreasonable prejudices against unfamiliar food. We of course have a right to our honest dislikes; but to condemn things because we have heard them despised, is prejudice."[36] Although the degree of her self-consciousness is something that contemporary readers might argue, Owen provides indirect advice on proper behavior that offered at least the potential to heal divisions within American culture itself, in particular, the divisions of race, ethnicity, and class that increasingly threatened social fragmentation and disruption at this time in US history.[37] Far from representing mere "domestic" writing, Owen's essays contend with national attitudes and perspectives.

Recalling both Franklin's maxim to "waste not, want not" and Child's frugal housewife, Owen's "Warming Over" also resists the "merely" domestic with its implication that cooking is an art form, an attitude announced in her larger title, *Culture and Cooking in the Kitchen*.[38] Her account of a prototypically American, "democratic" dish, hash, reconstructs class in a delicious account of making cheap food not only respectable but also elegant. In influencing her readers' literal "taste," she is also interrogating the meaning of "aesthetic" matters, for the name of hash "stinks in the nostrils of those unhappy ones whose home is the boarding-house." Language and interpretation are central issues for Owen, as she points out the "dignified" reinvention of "our hash, in its best form" to "*mince*," now an "elegant little *entrée*." Translated both literally and figuratively, hash is stripped of its lower-class associations; in effect, Owen erases class difference. The reinvented dish can then be enjoyed by a re-educated public palate: "In England and America there is great prejudice against warmed-over food, but on the continent one eats it half the time in some of the most delicious-made dishes without suspecting it."[39] Having to eat warmed-over food implies one's participation in a disadvantaged group that cannot afford to have it "fresh" at every meal, yet Owen wittily implies that this distinction is a false one, since continentals – *truly* cosmopolitan people – can so readily convert the distasteful into the delectable.[40]

The humor of Owen's description underlines her emphasis on the newly defined "aesthetic" and the lexical (signified by a relentless and emphatic pun) as a leveling medium: "With us and our transatlantic cousins [the English] the warming over is so artlessly done, that the *hard* fact too often stares at us from the watery expanse in which it reposes. . . ."[41] By artful cookery that itself helps to reinvent language, class differences based primarily on superficial appearances and expectations are readily obliterated. In some sense, Owen takes up Child's democratic project when she states clearly in her first chapter, 'You see by my speaking of rag carpets and dainty meals in one breath, that I do not consider good things to be the privilege of the rich alone."[42] Fostering this erasure of difference is the generic complexity of *Culture and Cooking* itself: part behavior book, part travel writing, part cookbook, part humorous essay, and part sketch, the volume parallels the fluid forms of many more "traditional" "fictions."

"A study of becomingness": Intermediate Texts

Frances Harper's "Fancy Etchings" (1873) translates advice writing into a complex combination of sketch, parable, sermon, and oral "literature."[43] Using this intermediate form to critique the treatment of the working poor, Harper is also responding to a wide range of traditional advice writing about dress and fashion. Although published slightly later than Harper's sketch, both Marion Harland's *Eve's Daughters* (1881) and Mrs. John Sherwood's *Manners and Social Usages* (1884) continue their precursors' emphasis on proper attire. Harland, for example, castigates an "excessive" concern for dress but affirms the necessity and propriety of a more modest concern: "A study of becomingness, of harmony of fabrics and colors – a knowledge of the prevailing modes and the ability to adapt these to the wishes and means of wearers – are as reasonable, in their way, as the endeavor to be so far acquainted with the general principles of music and painting as to be competent to discern between the good and bad of each art. Because a worthy thing is abused there is no need of casting wholesale opprobrium upon it." Harland's translation of dress into a "Fine Art" belies the social hierarchy that it encodes, a hierarchy that Sherwood's chapter, "Costly Thy Habit," makes explicit: "one can always tell a real lady from an imitation one by her style of dress. . . . There should be harmony and fitness, and suitability as to age and times and seasons."[44]

As Harland's and Sherwood's admonitions suggest, Harper wrote "Fancy Etchings" at a time when American consumer habits were rapidly gaining momentum; women's participation was a defining feature of this trend.[45] An important marker of this consumerism was the popularity of the fashion plates that began to appear in magazines like *Godey's Lady's Book* in the early 1830s. In spite of editor Sarah Josepha Hale's criticism of "the display of fashion as a symbol of extravagance and European luxury," and the simultaneous presence of articles by dress reformers in the magazine, the success of *Godey's* was due in no small measure to its acceptance of readers' desires for these fashion plates.[46] Depicting a domestic scene between Aunt Jane and her two nieces, Jenny and Annie, Harper transforms the commonplace of women's attention to their clothing into a social and moral lesson. This moral lesson transcends the customary warnings by contemporary advice writers about the frivolity of fashion, however, to address the matter of economic distinctions between women. Jenny seems particularly concerned with outward appearances, observing to her sister and aunt that "I hear that [New Paradose] is a dressy place, and of course I don't want to appear odd"; she plans to visit her impoverished dressmaker, whom she values principally because her work represents a bargain and Jenny can take advantage of her. In contrast to contemporaries who sought to maintain social disparities via a rigid code of middle-class behavior centered on a specious "sincerity,"[47] Harper's sketch argues explicitly for more honest self-assessment and a resistance to these norms, as Aunt Jane calls her niece to responsible behavior: "Jenny, I think one of the great lessons we women have to learn is to know how to treat each other better. We fail, I think, in fully comprehending our relations to society, and the reflex influence of that ignorance upon its purity and progress, and evil may be wrought by want of thought as well as want of heart."[48]

Creating a community of women, Harper, like Child before her, translates the domestic to the national, in the process offering a gentle sermon that exceeds the notion of correct "behavior": "The Bible says, 'blessed is he that considereth the poor,' and how many unavailing regrets this consideration might save us. . . . We help to keep up their poverty by our exactions, and their depression by our social pride, and we save for ourselves by taking advantage of their wants." Jenny seeks a superficial form of respectability, Harper implies, via her concern for dress; such a standard of conformity perpetuates false social distinctions, especially among women. Aunt Jane reminds Jenny and Annie that it is not the male "tradesman" who suffers in the satisfaction of their desires for new clothing, but the vulnerable women who have no other means of support. Urging resistance explicitly (Aunt Jane tells the girls, "non-conformity is a social heresy that people are slow to tolerate, and so I learned to stand alone"), Harper's "behavior" writing transcends narrowly national and merely superficial forms of propriety to assert, "The Bible has not only the highest code of morals, but also the best rule of manners,"[49] as she develops what we might call an "aesthetics of character" over an "aesthetics of dress." At the same time that such advice about behavior encoded resistance to artificial social standards, especially those related to class distinction, it exemplified the strong reform impulse of Victorian society, as well as its sense of "striving" for self-improvement.[50] Yet Harper's sketch intimates another kind of striving that, as Joyce Warren's and Barbara McCaskill's essays above underscore, was personally important to her: the improvement of the lives and status of African Americans. The class distinction explored in "Fancy Etchings" also serves as a metaphor for the racial hierarchy that Harper spent her life battling to overturn; a subtext of the sketch – published in an African American church-affiliated periodical – is that middle-class black women should not participate in the same kind of social stratification that had for so long and so severely disadvantaged them.

Appearing a number of years before the publication of Mary Frances Armstrong's advice text for black Americans,[51] Harper's groundbreaking work has a precursor in "The White Dress, or, Village Aristocracy" (1840), written for the "factory girls'" newspaper, the *Lowell Offering*. This sketch may have been written in response to the consumption of magazines like *Godey's* by working-class women, who were consciously excluded from representation in its pages: "Even though the ideology of domesticity was not alien to working women, *Godey's Lady's Book* was designed as a magazine for ladies and claimed the respectability of its audience."[52] Like Harper's "Fancy Etchings," "The White Dress" critiques class-based standards of respectability signified by fashion, as its subtitle and epigraph (which cites "great gentlefolks" opposed to "common country people") make readily apparent from the outset. Tongue planted firmly in cheek, as we eventually learn, the narrator describes certain families as "*the aristocracy*," and the next lower class as "good, but no better than their neighbors. . . . a little richer than the common people, for they *expended more*."[53] An important marker of social distinction in Clairbury village is the fashion consciousness of its young ladies. When a local merchant brings home six dress patterns for these girls, and the young store clerk gives away an unclaimed pattern to a black girl who arrives in church wearing the same dress as her white counterparts, the social order is effectively undone.

The author makes plain her resistance to the norms of fashion (and the respectability that it supposedly generates) with a number of strategies. One is to pass explicit judgment on the Misses Crawsons, "three very pretty and amiable girls, only a little foolish for an American farmer's daughters, about fashion, style, and *exclusiveism* (I did not find that word in Webster, but manufactured it for the occasion)." Exclusivity represents a specious value in a democratic "American" society; deliciously highlighting her own verbal inventiveness, the author invents an audacious pun for a factory girl author: "manufactured." Another strategy that underscores her resistance to social stratification is the emphatic use of italics throughout the text for many words related to status. The author also signifies her approval of egalitarianism in her depiction in the opening paragraph of the "aristocratic" Governor as "a good plain farmer," elevated in title only; she undoes social distinction further in her description of (black) Ruth Mingo: "the most genteel and elegantly formed female in the country of any color; and withal a good and virtuous girl." Finally, the tricksterism of the store clerk parallels that of the author herself. When Ruth arrives in church "dressed in a white gown, of the exact pattern, quality, and fashion of the five fashionable young ladies, who had passed up the aisle, a few minutes before," the false respectability and spurious exclusivity attained by the white women is comically obvious, and the use of language like "common" and "uncommon" is finally and radically revised: "*white* girls were *common* girls in Clairbury, and *black* girls were *uncommon*."[54]

Like Harper's intermediate text, "The White Dress" balances strategies of didacticism with those of aesthetics. Not only is the story explicitly *about* "beauty" (in the sense of fashion), it investigates the beauty of language and the imbrication of "common" language with "uncommon." From this perspective, the author-narrator coins the ostensibly awkward word "exclusiveism" as an antidote to the "correct words" found in Webster's dictionary (as well as to those recommended in Eliza Leslie's "Incorrect Words"); the majority of the story is told in plain, everyday language. At the same time, the form of the title and subtitle, and the use of an epigraph, bespeak a well-read and sophisticated author who delights in overturning the expectations that she institutes with these stylistic conventions. Finally, her first-person interpolation suggests the continuity between this "sketch" and an oral narrative, as the writer confounds the boundary between "storytelling" and autobiography. She crosses another boundary as well, for just as Harper encodes racial inequality in a tale of class differentiation, the author of "The White Dress" highlights the class hierarchy in American culture via racial difference, drawing on traditional affiliations of whiteness with purity (and conversely, of colorful dress with prostitutes)[55] to affirm the purity of Ruth (as we have seen, "a good and virtuous girl") in spite of her race. Ironically, it is the white *middle* class here, not the "aristocracy," who seek to enforce social distinctions, who desire conformity and uniformity, while resistance comes from "below": Aunt Ruth ("the nurse of all the babies 'round about'") and her daughters ("the best *help* in the country"),[56] as well as from the working author herself. Like Harper reinventing respectability, the author of "The White Dress" implicitly responds to the gentility and false distinctions embodied in the fashion plates of *Godey's*.

"As though you was somebody": Placing Women, Women's Places

Fanny Fern regarded much advice writing with suspicion, calling it "moral molasses" and observing, "The most thorough emetic I know is in the shape of 'Guide to Young Wives,' and kindred books."[57] Yet from the perspective outlined above, if advice writing often attempts to shape behavior according to acceptable and conventional norms, it sometimes exceeds this project of social normalization and critiques standard notions of respectability. Moreover, it elaborates an explicit investment in and sometimes a discussion of aesthetic norms related to language, structure, and genre that we more typically assign to "mainstream" "literary" works of fiction. Indicating the circulatory relationship between popular and elite forms of writing, such advice about behavior occurs not only in actual advice texts and "intermediate" texts like those discussed above, but in more canonical literary forms; because it is coded as fiction, it potentially offers even more radical alternatives to the norm. That is, women writers as a group engage in a larger form of generic resistance to aesthetic standards that segregate "advice" writing from "imaginative" writing. In the pages that remain, I will sketch several translations of the former into fictional forms.

The issues of proper dress, respectability, and economic status that are the central concerns of "Fancy Etchings" and "The White Dress" reappear in Rose Terry Cooke's "Miss Beulah's Bonnet," where the protagonist lacks the proper clothing to attend church. By honoring her commitments to church missions and to her niece who is about to be married, she cannot afford to replace a bonnet damaged by her mischievous nephew. When the church fathers take her to task for her absence and demand an explanation, they cannot fathom her reply that she has no bonnet: "The two men looked at each other in blank amazement, and shook their heads. Here was a pitfall. Was it proper, dignified, possible, to investigate this truly feminine tangle? They were dying to enter into particulars, but ashamed to do so: nothing was left but retreat."[58] To a certain degree Cooke is responding, like Harper and "The White Dress" author, to contemporary warnings about the frivolity of fashion that paradoxically parallel the intricate advice about its permutations. Although Miss Beulah is resistant to fashion's dictates, she is concerned about the appropriateness of her attire, seeking the "suitability as to age and times and seasons" urged by Sherwood.[59] There remains a residue of feminine vanity, however, in Miss Beulah's insistence that her niece straighten a bow that is, like her own desire in this connection, imperceptibly off center. From this perspective, Miss Beulah represents both a quirky model of conformity to female-authored social norms relating to dress and an image of resistance to male-centered social institutions (represented by the church deacons).[60]

Yet Cooke reserves her more severe criticism for the gossip that ensues as a result of Miss Beulah's absence from church. Patricia Meyer Spacks locates gossip on a continuum, with one end representing "distilled malice" in which the gossiper "plays with reputations, circulating truths and half-truths and falsehoods about the activities, sometimes about the motives and feelings, of others." At the other end of the continuum lies "serious" gossip, "which exists only as a function of intimacy. It takes place in private, at leisure, in a context of trust, usually among no more than two or three people."[61] Reflecting the first of these poles, the sewing circle gossip forces Miss Beers to defend Miss Beulah's character when she discovers that "the scorn and jeers and unfounded stories, [had] come on like a tidal wave to overwhelm her friend's character." In a scene that echoes the sermonlike qualities of Harper's sketch, Miss Beers explains the reason for Miss Beulah's absence from church:

"And here everybody's ben a-talkin' bad about her, while she's ben a real home-made kind of a saint. I know she don't look it; but she doos it, and that's a sight better. I don't b'lieve there's one woman in forty could ha' had the grit and the perseverance to do what she done, and hold her tongue about it too. I know I couldn't for one."

"She shouldn't ha' let her good be evil spoken of," said Mrs. Morse with an air of authority.

"I dono as anybody had oughter have spoken evil of her good," was Miss Beers's dry answer; and Mrs. Morse said no more.[62]

Like Sarah Orne Jewett and María Amparo Ruiz de Burton,[63] Cooke critiques women's judgmental attitudes and willingness to gossip, offering in the person of Miss Beulah a standard for one kind of proper behavior: reticence about private matters and self-abnegation in the face of economic hardship.

Cooke's criticism responds directly to contemporary advice writing about gossip; Harland's *Eve's Daughters* contains an entire chapter on the subject, which she allies with Spacks's negative pole, citing "the unwritten stories of blasted reputations, thwarted lives, and broken hearts" created by gossip. Significantly, she regards it as the "favorite pastime of their [educated young women's] inferiors," and she admonishes, "if gossip must make mince-meat – seasoned with the malice without which it would be insipid – of her neighbors' characters, teach her by firm but polite measures that you will lend neither tray, chopping-knife, nor condiments."[64] As the activity of social "inferiors," however, gossip possesses a potentially subversive element: "Gossip as a phenomenon raises questions about boundaries, authority, distance, the nature of knowledge; it demands answers quite at odds with what we assume about our culture's dominant values."[65] In this light, we can read "Miss Beulah's Bonnet" not merely as a transcription of gossip (which in this instance is *not* socially subversive), but as a form of gossip itself, with the narrator establishing an affirmative relation of intimacy with the reader in order to critique the social hierarchy and conformity that dress – never mind fashion – encodes and perpetuates. At the narrative level, then, gossip represents a form of transgression, of resistance to male-authored norms about what kinds of stories can be told and what they ultimately mean: here, Cooke suggests the moral power of economically challenged women like the silently suffering Miss Beulah who, in the words of Mrs. Deacon Morse, cannot simply "get another" bonnet when the first one is destroyed.[66]

If gossip represented one subject with which late nineteenth-century American women writers (of both "advice" and "fiction") concerned themselves, marriage was another, even more important. Marion Harland urges young women to "Choose as the partner of your heart, your home, your life a good, sound, clean-hearted man, who loves you and wins your love by the development of tastes congenial with yours; a man whom, as a friend, you could esteem and admire were he the husband of another. *That* is a test that would shake a mere fancy into thin air." Her emphasis upon the romantic element in marriage is

epitomized in a stern declaration: "A loveless marriage is an unchaste union."[67]
We see the white middle-class values that are embedded here interrogated and
revised in Laura Jacobson's "The Wooing of Rachel Schlipsky" (1896). Jacobson's
Rachel suffers from false pride and foolish expectations that almost prevent her
from attaining a marriage that promises to be both happy and financially secure.
When her mother reveals that hardworking Elias Schwarz wishes to marry her,
Rachel reveals her foolishness and her mother is incensed, for Rachel has already
declined offers from several suitors, one, as her mother so pointedly observes,
"because he had red hair and his eyes vatered." But "Rachel gave her pretty head
a toss but answered nothing to this tirade. She was not so indifferent as her
mother supposed, but she had a vain little head. Her idea of supreme happiness
was to have numberless suitors sighing like furnaces in eager rivalry for her
affection." When she learns from the matchmaker Moses Klebstock that her
prospective husband has ostensibly betrayed her, she bursts out: "'When I get
married it ain't going to be to a man who looks like a bean pole and can't say
seven words in an hour. I could have had lots better than him and I wouldn't
take them.'"[68] Rachel dreams of a "higher," more romantic, and more "mainstream" "American" standard than either her mother or the matchmaker possess.

Part of Rachel's bias against Elias is clearly his status as an immigrant: he
speaks poorly and seems to retain older, European values, echoed in Rachel's
mental soliloquy when she enters his store: "People said he was a splendid son
to his aged, mother, and that he had more book learning than most of her
acquaintances, even if he couldn't talk much or dance well. Well, what did she
care, she wouldn't have him on any account anyway. But people should see how
crazy he was about her before many days, and he [should] not marry that girl
in Newark."[69] The Jewish community values standards of behavior that include
respect for one's mother,[70] respect in which we see Rachel herself is sorely lacking. Ultimately conforming to this standard, Rachel overcomes her "artificial"
behavior and ends up taking the advice of her mother and the matchmaker,
as Jacobson gives readers a revised edition of an American love story. In this
sense, to be a "proper" (and "respectable") American does not necessarily mean
devaluing one's history and one's ethnicity; to the contrary, it may mean that
honoring that past more fully makes one more of an American. When Elias asks
her, "'Rachel, could you not like me a little bit?'" we learn that "the girl, moved
by a new emotion, forgetting the gossips, forgetting her anger, forgetting even
Klebstock, forgetting all but the present question, looked shyly at her lover who
joyfully drew her behind the barrel out of sight of the customers and kissed her
rapturously. Quickly she slipped out at the side door, forgetting her syrup; but
with greater sweetness in her heart than the pitcher could have held."[71] Proper
behavior here means following one's heart, but first following one's traditions, as
Jacobson provides an exemplary tale of conformity to community norms, but
resistance to larger "American" ideals of happiness and respectability founded in
the "ideal" of romantic marriage that Harland articulates. Ironically, by adopting
the standards of her community, Rachel ensures a healthy economic future for

herself and security from poverty for her mother. As Diane Lichtenstein observes of Jewish women's writing more broadly, "Many [Jewish women] used their writing to explore, justify, and demonstrate the premise that dual national loyalties were possible."[72] Central to understanding "The Wooing of Rachel Schlipsky" is an acknowledgment of its publication in the *American Jewess*, a magazine edited and published by a Jewish woman and aimed at Jewish women. Written in a larger cultural context of advice writing aimed at making foreigners more "American" and homogeneous, Jacobson's story treads a middle ground that enables her heroine to retain both identities.

If Jacobson offers an affirmative vision of marriage, Cooke provides us with a grim form of advice in "How Celia Changed Her Mind" that entirely subverts the white middle-class notion of romantic marriage. It is not just fear of the social stigma of being an "old maid" but falsely idealistic notions about matrimony that impel the protagonist Celia to marry, late in life, one of the most notorious pennypinchers in the village, the aptly named Deacon Flint. Similarly, Celia enables young Rosabel Stearns to marry her suitor Amos and to move West. Cooke makes her own advice about conformity to social norms (and to a large body of middle-class advice literature) clear-cut and biting: not only does Celia suffer for "four wretched years" under the regime of Deacon Flint, but Rosabel pays even more sternly for her romantic visions, for soon after her father rescues her from a deplorable state of poverty in the west, she dies in childbirth. Celia learns this lesson vividly, for her acceptance of social pressures to marry engenders unhappiness for herself and disaster for her young counterpart. Rosa's failed romantic vision of marriage displaces Celia's superficial understanding of the respectability that women gain: "A woman that's married is somebody; she's got a place in the world; she ain't everybody's tag; folks don't say, 'Oh, it's nobody but that old maid Celye Barnes; it's 'Mis' Price,' and 'Mis' Simms' . . . as though you was somebody."[73] Both Rosa and Celia would have done well to heed Child's much earlier advice, advice that diverged widely from the social norms (as well as the literary ones embodied by most advice books of her day), against "teaching girls to exaggerate the importance of getting married; and of course to place an undue importance upon the polite attentions of gentlemen."[74]

In both "The Wooing of Rachel Schlipsky" and "How Celia Changed Her Mind," reading romantic fiction generates obstacles for young women protagonists. Rachel "believed that her pretty face ought to win her a very rich husband; she had read so much of such happenings." Similarly, both Amos and Rosabel read cheap romances; when Rosa's father forbids her to see Amos, we learn that "he had read too many dime novels to doubt that her tyrannical father would intercept their letters, and drive them both to madness and despair. That well-meaning but rather dull divine never would have thought of such a thing; he was a puffy, absent-minded, fat little man, with a weak, squeaky voice, and a sudden temper that blazed up; like a bunch of dry weeds at a passing spark, and went out at once in flattest ashes." Rosabel, on the other hand, announces her marriage to her father in the most dramatic novelistic fashion: "There was a

scene of wild commotion at the parsonage next day, when Rosa's letter, modeled
on that of the last novel heroine she had become acquainted with, was found on
her bureau, as per novel aforesaid."[75] Though with different aims and ambitions,
the advice that both Cooke and Jacobson give their readers is that marriage is an
economic institution, and the behavior that they seek to engender will enable
women to look to their own needs first. Realism, not romance, is what young
women need to read when thinking about love, as Celia's pragmatic and clear-
minded rejection of one "do-nothing" suitor in her youth suggests:[76]

> Marry *you?* I wonder you've got the sass to ask any decent girl to marry ye,
> Alfred Hatch! What be you good for, anyway? I don't know what under
> the canopy the Lord spares you for, – only He doos let the tares grow
> amongst the wheat, Scripter says, and I'm free to suppose He knows why,
> but I don't. No, *sir*! Ef you was the last man in the livin' universe I
> wouldn't tech ye with the tongs. If you'd got a speck of grit into you,
> you'd be ashamed to ask a woman to take ye in and support ye, for that's
> what it comes to. You go 'long! I can make my hands save my head so
> long as I hev the use of 'em, and I haven't no call to set up a private
> poor-house![77]

Celia's actions here are the ones that Cooke regards as proper, reflecting a sense
of personal integrity and self-care. When women act according to individual
norms of behavior rather than relying upon spurious social "standards" that
serve only to limit their lives, she suggests, they can shape and transform those
lives. Naming themselves in contradiction to externally imposed identities, they
can create a realm where being "respectable" and being an "old maid," as in
Celia's case, are not mutually exclusive but coterminous. At the same time, as
we see also in Jacobson's story, this independence must be contextualized within
a pragmatic and rational understanding of the economic bases of American gender relations and of American culture more broadly.

Negotiating between conformity and resistance to social norms, nineteenth-
century American women writers not only translated advice writing into fictional
forms of advocacy, they also wrote artfully in genres such as advice, cookbook,
and behavior that have yet to gain canonical currency. In closing it is perhaps
most appropriate to return to the aesthetics of advice with which this essay
began, and specifically to the "taste" of the cookbook author, Catherine Owen.
"Sauces" dedicates itself to the artistry of cooking and of writing; saucily revising
Talleyrand at the opening, this chapter relies on metaphor to convey its message
and tone. Imagining food as a volume of its own, Owen notes "how often the
[American] white sauce is like *bookbinder's paste.*" Style is as critical in cooking
as it is in other creative forms; "the espagnole once made, with no two meats is
it served alike in flavor, and in this matter of flavor the *artist* appears." Within
this metaphorical context, the passage about variations in flavoring that follows
transforms itself into a meditation on all forms of composition, concluding with

a sly witticism about the interrelationship of "flavor," "taste," "consumption," and "value": "A pickled walnut chopped, or a gherkin or two, go admirably with mutton or pork chops. In short, this is just where imagination and brains will tell in cooking, and little *essays of invention* may be *tried with profit.*"[78] Readers today profit from renewed attention to the tasteful essays of invention written by such imaginative foremothers, as well as to more careful scrutiny of the investment of writers working in canonical forms with the concerns and techniques of their "domestic" counterparts.

NOTES

1 Kilcup, *NCAWW*, 223.
2 Ibid., 207, 208, 213, 209, 221. If Dickinson represents herself as an inhabitant of "Domingo" here, she is claiming an identity with an excluded, racialized "other." Yet her views on race in American society are generally problematic for contemporary readers. See, for example, Betsy Erkkila, *The Wicked Sisters: Women Poets, Literary History, and Discord* (New York: Oxford University Press, 1992), 46, 47, 50.
3 *NCAWW*, 216, 220–1.
4 John F. Kasson, *Rudeness and Civility: Manners in Nineteenth-Century Urban America* (New York: Hill and Wang, 1990), 43, 7.
5 Nancy Armstrong and Leonard Tennenhouse, "Introduction," in *The Ideology of Conduct: Essays on Literature and the History of Sexuality* (New York: Methuen, 1987), 23. Armstrong and Tennenhouse have remarked that "despite remarkable parallels between the literature of conduct and the conduct of literature, literary histories rarely if ever contain references to the literature of conduct, and even more rarely are conduct books for women allowed to contribute to our notion of cultural history" (3). Although their collection works to ameliorate this problem, it focuses on European texts. The situation that they describe has changed very little in the last ten years; see, for example, Armstrong's essay, "The Rise of the Domestic Woman" (96–141). We cannot readily generalize from English texts to American ones because of the very different cultural situations in each country, especially the circumstances relating to class.
6 Kasson, *Rudeness and Civility*, 6.
7 One could reasonably claim that in some sense *all* literature offers "advice" – even critical work like this article, which offers advice on how to read – but the women's writing on which I am focusing responds, with varying degrees of directness, to explicit advice offered in the nonfiction genre addressed specifically to women.
8 Carolyn Karcher, *The First Woman in the Republic, A Cultural Biography of Lydia Maria Child* (Durham: Duke University Press, 1994), 127.
9 On the diverse readership of advice writing, see Kasson, *Rudeness and Civility*, 45, 53–7. Kasson focuses on urban readers (70–1 and passim).
10 Karen Halttunen, *Confidence Men and Painted Women: A Study of Middle-Class Culture in America, 1830–1870* (New Haven: Yale University Press, 1982), xv, 1. On popularity, see Arthur M. Schlesinger, *Learning How to Behave: A Historical Study of American Etiquette Books* (New York: Macmillan, 1946), 18.

11   Schlesinger, *Learning How to Behave*, 1–14; Kasson, *Rudeness and Civility*, 12, 47–53.
12   Glenna Matthews, *"Just a Housewife": The Rise and Fall of Domesticity in America*
      (New York: Oxford University Press, 1987), 10, 11, 34. Matthews also points out
      that advice books were not merely for women; the investment of men in the ideo-
      logy of home required men's respectful attitude toward, and sometimes participation
      in, the tasks of the domestic sphere (26, 35).
13   Susan Coolidge, "Lydia Maria Child," *Our Famous Women. An Authorized Record of
      the Lives and Deeds of Distinguished American Women of Our Times* (Hartford: A. D.
      Worthington, 1885), 232. Karcher observes that Child earned over $2000 from
      sales in the first two years (*The First Woman*, 127). See also T. W. Higginson,
      "Lydia Maria Child," *Eminent Women of the Age; Being Narratives of the Lives and
      Deeds of the Most Prominent Women of the Present Generation* (Hartford: S. M. Betts,
      1872), 38–65. On Child's desire for usefulness, see Bruce Mills, *Cultural Reforma-
      tions: Lydia Maria Child and the Literature of Reform* (Athens: University of Georgia
      Press, 1994), 5.
14   *NCAWW*, 68.
15   Ibid., 69; [Lydia Maria Child], "Domestic Duties," *Massachusetts Weekly Journal*
      (December 17, 1828), 3. Karcher discusses Child's divergence from the normal
      practice of writing for the wealthy (*The First Woman*, 127–9); Kasson discusses
      advice writers' opposition to decadence (*Rudeness and Civility*, 63).
16   On this sentimentalization, see Glenna Matthews, *"Just a Housewife,"* 9.
17   Karcher observes that "the impetus that generated *The Frugal Housewife* was prac-
      tical rather than ideological." It was also written for a largely rural audience, which
      accounted for its decline in popularity in the urbanizing 1840s (*The First Woman*,
      130, 131). Like Karcher, Matthews highlights the volume's origins in Child's own
      state of financial hardship; she also enables us to see Child's resistance to cultural
      (and literary) norms when she points out that the early "exponents [of domesticity]
      usually made a series of invidious assumptions about women of other classes, regions
      [than New England], and ethnic origins, to say nothing of other colors" (*"Just a
      Housewife,"* 23, 33). These assumptions included the availability of domestic help
      for their readers.
18   Catharine Maria Sedgwick, *Morals of Manners; or, Hints for our young people* (New
      York: Wiley and Putnam, 1846), 61.
19   *NCAWW*, 75.
20   Ibid., 69; Matthews, *"Just a Housewife,"* 21, 26, 45; on Republican Motherhood, see
      also Linda Kerber, "The Republican Mother: Women and the Enlightenment – An
      American Perspective," *American Quarterly* 28 (1976): 187–205; Rosemarie Zagarri,
      "Manners, Morals, and the Republican Mother," *American Quarterly* 44 (1992):
      192–215; and Jan Lewis, "The Republican Wife: Virtue and Seduction in the Early
      Republic," *William and Mary Quarterly*, 3rd series, 44 (1987): 696–721.
21   *NCAWW*, 69. By 1841, Catharine Beecher would claim that "American democracy
      rose or fell on the efforts of its female members" (cited in Matthews, *"Just a
      Housewife,"* 46). See also Kathryn Kish Sklar, *Catharine Beecher: A Study in American
      Domesticity* (New York: Norton, 1976), 161.
22   [Sarah Josepha Hale], review of *"The Frugal Housewife. By the Author of Hobomuk,"*
      Ladies' Magazine 3 (January 1830): 42–3; Nathaniel Parker Willis, review of *The
      Frugal Housewife*, "Editor's Table," *American Monthly Magazine* 1 (January 1830):
      721–2. See Karcher's important discussion of these reviews, where she observes that

Child refined her language for the second edition (*The First Woman*, 133–5). Ann Douglas also notes the response of Sarah Josepha Hale to Child's book, but she assumes that Child's text was written for "ladies," not the economically challenged women whom Child identifies as her audience. Douglas, *The Feminization of American Culture* (New York: Discus-Avon, 1977), 65–6. Kasson points to the norm that "middle-class girls and women were to think of money as little as possible" (*Rudeness and Civility*, 68).

23 Matthews discusses the increasing leisure that accrued to some early nineteenth-century American women along with urbanization (*"Just a Housewife,"* 11).

24 Kasson, *Rudeness and Civility*, 67.

25 *NCAWW*, 22, 23, 24.

26 Jack Larkin, *The Reshaping of Everyday Life 1790–1840* (New York: HarperPerennial, 1989), 153.

27 Judith Fetterley, "Introduction," in Eliza Leslie, *Provisions: A Reader from 19th-Century American Women* (Bloomington: Indiana University Press, 1985), 72. Fetterley cites Alice B. Haven's memorial essay which recollected the writer's kindness to the needy (71).

28 *NCAWW*, 21.

29 Ibid., 23.

30 Nancy Walker, *A Very Serious Thing: Women's Humor and American Culture* (Minneapolis: University of Minneapolis Press, 1988), xii.

31 Schlesinger, *Learning How to Behave*, 31, 32.

32 Kasson, *Rudeness and Civility* 188–9, 204–7.

33 Susan J. Leonardi, "Recipes for Reading: Summer Pasta, Lobster à la Riseholme, and Key Lime Pie," *PMLA* 104 (1989): 340.

34 Mrs. John Sherwood, *Manners and Social Usages* (1884; New York: Harper and Brothers, 1887), 3–4. Many texts by nineteenth-century American women writers that are about travel also fit into the present discussion; such texts in *NCAWW* include Harriet Beecher Stowe's *Sunny Memories of Foreign Lands* ("Letter I Sea Travel," 132–8), Catharine Maria Sedgwick's *Letters from Abroad to Kindred at Home* ("An American in London," 33–6), and Marietta Holley's send-up of the middle-class rage for travel in "A Pleasure Exertion" (294–9).

35 *NCAWW*, 301.

36 Ibid., 302.

37 According to Thomas Schlereth, 1882 was "a new peak" in nineteenth-century immigration, with 788,992 people entering the United States. Thomas J. Schlereth, *Victorian America, Transformations in Everyday Life* (New York: HarperPerennial, 1991), 8–12. Given Owen's perspective, it is ironic that much advice writing actually served to reinforce prejudices; for example, Sherwood refers directly to the menace of immigration in relation to the relative "freedom allowed in the manners of our young women – a freedom which, as our New World fills up with people of foreign birth, cannot but lead to social disturbances" (*Manners and Social Usages*, 5). In addition to the cultural conflict engendered by increasing immigration, the bitter Indian wars that were taking place on internal borderlands and labor union unrest also shattered utopian visions of a "united" America.

38 Schlesinger observes that "etiquette conceived as an art acquired an aura that had been lacking when it was viewed more prosaically as a species of unofficial law," but he does not include cookbook writing in this brief discussion (*Learning How to*

Behave, 35). See Marion Harland, *Eve's Daughters, or, Common Sense for Maid, Wife, and Mother* (New York: Charles Scribners and Sons, 1881), 321. I am relying primarily on Sherwood and Harland as representatives of later advice writing because of their wide popularity and their contemporaneity with many of the texts in my discussion.

39 *NCAWW*, 300.

40 Both Kasson and Halttunen discuss the tension between appearance and reality in their account of nineteenth-century middle-class selfhood. See Kasson, *Rudeness and Civility*, 30–1; Halttunen, *Confidence Men and Painted Women*, 1–56 and passim.

41 *NCAWW*, 300.

42 Catherine Owen, "A Few Preliminary Remarks," *Culture and Cooking: Or, Art in the Kitchen*, in *Catherine Owen's New Cook Book* (New York: Cassell Publishing, 1885), 3.

43 The specific "Fancy Etchings" discussed below represents one of a series of such sketches that Harper did for the *A. M. E. Christian Recorder*.

44 Harland, *Eve's Daughters*, 343; Sherwood, *Manners and Social Usages*, 167.

45 Schlereth, *Victorian America*, 141ff.

46 In spite of this nod to consumerism (and, they thought, hedonism) – or perhaps because of it – *Godey's* editors before the Civil War attempted to appropriate the fashion plate into a strategy of improving female literacy and offering "maternal instruction and public virtue." Isabelle Lehuu, "Sentimental Figures: Reading *Godey's Lady's Book* in Antebellum America," in *The Culture of Sentiment: Race, Gender, and Sentimentality in Nineteenth-Century America*, ed. Shirley Samuels (New York: Oxford University Press, 1992), 76, 83.

47 On advice manuals' warnings against the excesses of fashion, and on the standard of sincerity as a middle-class norm, see Halttunen, *Confidence Men and Painted Women*, 63–4; 193–4.

48 *NCAWW*, 170, 171.

49 Ibid., 171, 170, 171.

50 Schlereth, *Victorian America*, 243–69.

51 Mary Frances Armstrong, *On Habits and Manners* (Hampton, VA: Normal School Press, 1888).

52 Lehuu, "Sentimental Figures," 82. Lehuu claims the working women's participation in gender norms over class ones; I am investigating the interaction of these norms and the writers' resistance to the *Godey's* set.

53 *NCAWW*, 92.

54 Ibid., 92, 93.

55 Kasson, *Rudeness and Civility*, 176.

56 *NCAWW*, 92.

57 Sara P. Willis [Parton], *Fresh Leaves* (New York: Mason Brothers, 1857), 210.

58 *NCAWW*, 190.

59 Sherwood, *Manners and Social Usages*, 167.

60 Martha Wolfenstein's story, "Genendel the Pious," offers another variation on this theme of religious observance: if respectability means conformity to certain standards, then Genendel never meets them, for at first she attends synagogue twice a day, which is too much ("This, as everyone knows, is not even proper for a woman; but still Genendel did it" [*NCAWW*, 561]), and then, when she gains economic means, not at all. We should observe that, like Miss Beulah, Genendel is the object

of gossip (561–2), and that it is this gossip that provokes an investigation by her rabbi (562–3). At another level Cooke critiques the limitations of the heroine's behavior in relation to her male nephew, as Judith Fetterley's article elsewhere in this volume suggests.

61 Patricia Meyer Spacks, *Gossip* (New York: Knopf, 1985), 4, 5.

62 *NCAWW*, 190.

63 See "The Passing of Sister Barsett" (391–7) and "The Arrival," "The Little Black Girl," and "The Mysterious Black Boxes" (256–63) in *NCAWW*. Jewett's and Ruiz de Burton's pieces are very differently inflected and, like "Miss Beulah's Bonnet" and Wolfenstein's "Genendel the Pious," indicate complex attitudes toward gossip.

64 Harland, *Eve's Daughters*, 365, 364, 377; see also her *Common Sense in the Household, A Manual of Practical Housewifery* (1871; reprint, New York: Scribner's, 1880), where she advises, "It is time sensible women ceased, in this respect, to imitate the fashion of the class they censure, and put down the bootless tattle with a strong will" (367).

65 Spacks, *Gossip*, 12.

66 *NCAWW*, 190.

67 Harland, *Eve's Daughters*, 399, 403. Kasson notes that by the end of the eighteenth century, "romantic love assumed new importance on entering marriage" (*Rudeness and Civility*, 18).

68 *NCAWW*, 479, 482.

69 Ibid., 484.

70 Diane Lichtenstein, *Writing Their Nations: The Tradition of Nineteenth-Century American Jewish Women Writers* (Bloomington: Indiana University Press, 1992), 23–35.

71 *NCAWW*, 485.

72 Lichtenstein, *Writing Their Nations*, 8.

73 *NCAWW*, 202, 192.

74 Lydia Maria Child, "Education of Daughters," *NCAWW*, 71; see Karcher, *The First Woman*, 130. Interestingly, much like her precursor, Harland criticizes an excessive emphasis on marriage while she seeks to make young women useful in their marriages. Nevertheless, in somewhat ambiguous (and ambivalent) terms, Harland also discusses the status of the "old maid" (*Eve's Daughters*, 322–30; 285–86).

75 *NCAWW*, "The Wooing of Rachel Schlipsky," 479; "How Celia Changed Her Mind," 196, 197.

76 The term "do-nothing" comes from Harriet Beecher Stowe's depiction of Sam Lawson, a character who appears in her novel *Oldtown Folks* (1869) and in a series of related sketches like "Laughin' in Meetin'" (*NCAWW*, 138–42).

77 *NCAWW*, 193–4.

78 Ibid., 301, emphasis added.

11

Inventing a Feminist Discourse: Rhetoric and Resistance in Margaret Fuller's *Woman in the Nineteenth Century*

ANNETTE KOLODNY

I

When Margaret Fuller's *Woman in the Nineteenth Century* first appeared in the winter of 1845, few readers were prepared to accept her uncompromising proposition that "inward and outward freedom for woman as for man shall be acknowledged as a right, not yielded as a concession."[1] Elaborating arguments she had first encountered in Mary Wollstonecraft's *Vindication of the Rights of Woman* (London, 1792), Fuller insisted that because "not one man, in the million, . . . not in the hundred million, can rise above the belief that woman was made for *man*," woman would have to "lay aside all thought, such as she habitually cherished, of being taught and led by men" (*W*, 25, 107).[2] Incorporating the platform logic of women's rights and antislavery activists like Angelina Grimké and Abigail Kelley Foster,[3] Fuller tersely observed that "those who think the physical circumstances of woman would make a part in the affairs of national government unsuitable, are by no means those who think it impossible for the negresses to endure field work, even during pregnancy, or the sempstresses to go through their killing labors" (*W*, 24). And, risking the charge of employing "language . . . offensive to delicacy,"[4] Fuller wrote graphically about women's sexual bondage in marriage, condemned male sexual license, and insisted upon society's moral obligations even to the "degraded" prostitute, comparing the prostitute's economic exchange of her body with "the dower of a worldly marriage" (*W*, 133, 132).

To read Fuller today is to be impressed anew with the sheer revolutionary daring of her attempt both to question existing gender hierarchies and to disrupt accepted sexual practices. Unfortunately, the potential impact of her arguments was long ago obscured amid the reluctance of critics seriously to analyze the even greater daring of her rhetorical strategies. As a result, when the second wave of feminist theorists in the United States began to call for a pluralistic discourse that was both collaborative and noncoercive, they showed no awareness that Fuller had earlier responded to the same challenge. In an article published in 1979, for example, Sally Miller Gearhart expressed her fear that in the "attempt to change others," "any intent to persuade is an act of violence," and she called for "the womanization of rhetoric" as an antidote.[5] Three years later, in 1982, Jean Bethke Elshtain wondered "what sort of language, public and private, do feminists propose that women speak?" And she further asked "what models for emancipatory speech are available?"[6] By the end of the 1980s, Elshtain's questions still had not been answered, prompting Marianne Hirsch and Evelyn Fox Keller to observe that "feminists in the late 1980s have become exceedingly accomplished at articulating theoretical positions on the basis of disagreement and opposition. . . . But with this mastery of disputation, has come a corresponding difficulty in treating other positions with sympathy and respect. The task of clearing space for multiple agendas representing conflicting interests," concluded Hirsch and Keller in 1990, "therefore poses a major challenge."[7] That none of these scholars – and not a single author included in the collection edited by Hirsch and Keller, *Conflicts in Feminism* – looked to Fuller as a potential source for (at least some) solutions, demonstrates how damaging the continuing critical response to Fuller's experimental method has been for feminism.

To be sure, most of the early reactions to *Woman in the Nineteenth Century* were predictable. The Boston-based social reformer Orestes Augustus Brownson opened his review by naming Fuller "the chieftainess" of the transcendentalist "sect," thereby confirming his growing disaffection from the religious radicalism of the New England transcendentalists and revealing, also, his continuing jealousy that Fuller had been chosen – instead of him – to edit their journal, *The Dial*. Brownson's main objections, however, were theological. Writing in his own *Brownson's Quarterly Review* for April 1845, Brownson explained: "She says man is not the head of the woman. We, on the authority of the Holy Ghost, say he is."[8] Brownson's view was echoed by the book critic for the Charleston, South Carolina, *Southern Quarterly Review*, who flatly rejected Fuller's claim of woman's "perfect equality with man," declaring "this cannot be."[9] An unsigned series of articles that ran weekly throughout March 1845 in New York City's *Broadway Journal* challenged "the radical error of Miss Fuller's reasoning" as "directly opposed to the law of nature, of experience and revelation." "The restraints which Miss Fuller complains of as hindering women," this reviewer continued, "are the restraints which Nature has imposed." Charles F. Briggs, the ambitious young editor responsible for the series, then damned the entire book by characterizing it as "not sufficiently plain and direct," its materials only "loosely arranged."[10]

Even those less hostile to Fuller's views could not accord her work unalloyed praise. In a generally laudatory notice for the same *Broadway Journal*, Fuller's friend and the well-established feminist writer, Lydia Maria Child, tacitly agreed with her colleague Briggs by observing that while Fuller's style was often

"vigorous and significant," the book as a whole "is sometimes rough in construction, and its meaning is not always sufficiently clear." Similarly, the reviewer for
the *Christian Examiner* complained that "the book lacks method sadly." For him,
it read more like "a collection of clever sayings and bright intimations, than a
logical treatise."[11]

But it was Brownson who offered the most influential rationale for dismiss-
ing *Woman in the Nineteenth Century*. Complaining "we do not know what is its
design," Brownson joined other reviewers in emphasizing discomfort with the
book's organization. Unlike the others, however, Brownson exploited Fuller's
local reputation as an eloquent conversationalist in order to justify his view of
the text's structural flaws. "The book before us . . . is no book, but a long talk,"
Brownson maintained. "It has neither beginning, middle, nor end, and may be
read backwards as well as forwards, and from the centre outwards each way,
without affecting the continuity of the thought or the succession of ideas. We
see no reason why it should stop where it does, or why the lady might not keep
on talking in the same strain till doomsday, unless prevented by want of breath."
Although Brownson found it necessary to devote seven full pages to refuting
Fuller's arguments, his opening remarks had already effectively characterized
the book for his own and subsequent generations: "As talk, it is very well, and
proves that the lady has great talkative powers, and that, in this respect at least,
she is a genuine woman."[12]

Brownson's accusation that Fuller had produced only written proof of un-
restricted female volubility was (as he knew) one to which Fuller was acutely
sensitive. Her most recent biographer, Charles Capper, reminds us that, only
weeks after accepting the editorship of *The Dial* in 1840, Fuller confided to
her private journal a recurrent concern regarding, in Capper's words, "the gap
between her conversational talents and her writing abilities" (*MF*, 339). After
noting that her uncommon education had given her "an undue advantage in
conversation with men" – who were often surprised by such learning in a woman
– Fuller expressed her abiding anxiety that "then these gentlemen are surprised
that I write no better because I talk so well." "But," as she herself acknowledged, "I have served a long apprenticeship to the one, none to the other"
(quoted in *MF*, 339).

Because Fuller corresponded with a wide circle and freely shared her journals
with several of her closest friends – including transcendentalism's intellectual
leader, the disaffected Unitarian minister, Ralph Waldo Emerson – her doubts
about her writing were well known. In fact, Emerson himself contributed to
the view of Fuller as a better speaker than writer when he composed his memoir
of Fuller after her death in 1850. "In her writing she was prone to spin her
sentences without a sure guidance, and beyond the sympathy of her reader,"
Emerson recalled. "But in discourse, she was quick, conscious of power, in perfect tune with her company."[13]

Twentieth-century appraisals have tended to follow either Brownson or
Emerson, or both. Vernon L. Parrington set the tone in 1927 when, following

Brownson – who had stated that Fuller "has little artistic skill" – he portrayed Fuller as "in no sense an artist, scarcely a competent craftsman." In 1982 David M. Robinson again raised the question of Fuller's ability to control her text's "design" when he acknowledged that while she "did in fact achieve a good many high moments stylistically," she was nonetheless "often guilty of digression and obscurity." Just two years later, in his reading of *Woman in the Nineteenth Century*, William J. Scheick gave yet another nod toward Brownson when he noted that "*Woman* shares with other Transcendental works an acknowledgment of its oral heritage."[14]

Not even the renewed interest in Fuller that accompanied the second wave of feminist activism in the United States in the late 1960s succeeded in challenging the dominant view of *Woman in the Nineteenth Century* as devoid of system, method, or "design."[15] With the exception of Marie Urbanski's 1980 study, which reads the text "within the sermon framework," relatively few scholars troubled themselves to examine *Woman in the Nineteenth Century* (in Urbanski's words) "as a literary work from the standpoint of form, tone, and use of rhetorical devices." Instead, as Robinson has observed, even into the 1980s, Fuller scholarship remained "heavily biographical, reflecting the general sense that Fuller's life and example far outweigh her work in importance."[16] Indeed, until the appearance of Mary Kelley's 1994 *The Portable Margaret Fuller*, with its reprinting of the complete original 1845 edition, this trend went largely unchallenged, thus allowing earlier authoritative editions of *Woman in the Nineteenth Century* to go out of print and leaving only the posthumous 1855 edition, ineptly cut and repunctuated by Fuller's brother, Arthur B. Fuller.[17]

The problem with this cumulative critical consensus is that it commits us to believing that the only woman invited as an intellectual equal into the Transcendental Club of Emerson, Frederic Henry Hedge, George Ripley, Bronson Alcott, and the other reform-minded Harvard-trained intellectuals of the day – and urged by these same men to take up the editorship of *The Dial* – was somehow incompetent. That a person generally reputed to have been among the best read and the best educated of her generation – responsible for first translating and introducing Goethe and Schiller to American audiences – could not control "the succession of ideas." That the critic and journalist who won praise from her contemporary and fellow New York journalist, Edgar Allan Poe, for a "style [which] . . . is one of the very best with which I am acquainted," could not write clearly.[18] That the child who delighted in the descriptions of Congressional debates in her father's letters from Washington, and the woman who would "ready myself to sleep" by poring over the debates transcribed in the *Congressional Record*,[19] could not design an argument. That an individual trained in both classical and contemporary rhetoric, who had taken the initiative to form a rhetoric class for senior girls at the Greene Street School in Providence, Rhode Island, could not compose a "logical treatise." And, further, this consensus asks us to accept Fuller's anxieties about her writing skills as authoritative critical judgments when, in truth, *every* woman author of the period – British and American

– larded her letters, journals, and published book prefaces with apologies for her ineptitude with the pen. Fuller was hardly the only woman of her era to complain that in "fulfilling all my duties" to family and society she had lost the precious time required for concentrated writing "and a literary existence."[20]

Rather than repeat critical judgments that have served to suppress the truly radical nature of Fuller's text, and rather than accept a consensus so loaded with implausible conjectures, it is time to probe Fuller's rhetorical intentions and to measure her book against these. For if we take seriously Fuller's injunction to her female readers that they set aside the habit "of being taught and led by men" (*W*, 107), then we understand that Fuller wanted not only to put forward a radical critique of all "arbitrary barriers" to women's free development (*W*, 158). Additionally, as a *woman* speaking for women, she needed to put forward a treatise that would not simply replicate the strategies that might have been employed by any of her well-intentioned male contemporaries. After all, as she stated repeatedly in *Woman in the Nineteenth Century*, the time had come for women to give over merely following male models and, instead, find "out what is fit for themselves" (*W*, 51).

In the arena of public oratory, Fuller knew that a few brave women were already beginning to explore just such possibilities. From her own observations and from the reports she had read about the powerful female antislavery lecturers of her day, Fuller concluded that women like Angelina Grimké and Abigail Kelley Foster, "women who speak in public, if they have a moral power . . . invariably subdue the prejudices of their hearers" (*W*, 98). A letter from one of her many (male) correspondents, quoted approvingly in *Woman in the Nineteenth Century*, suggests that Fuller also agreed that the female antislavery speakers were better able to reach their audiences than were their male peers. As her correspondent phrased it, the women brought "the subject more into home relations" than did the men because the men, by contrast, "speak through, and mostly from intellect, . . . which creates [combat] and is combative" (quoted in *W*, 99). It was precisely that "combativeness" that Fuller sought to avoid, even as she attempted – through what her contemporaries called "the affluence of her illustrations"[21] – to bring her subject "more into home relations." The result was the text that Brownson would aptly characterize – albeit for all the wrong reasons – as "a long talk."

II

Scholars have repeatedly recognized a connection between Fuller's teaching at the Greene Street School, her subsequent formalized "conversations" for adult women in the Boston area, and the development of her original essay, "The Great Lawsuit: Man *versus* Men. Woman *versus* Women," which appeared in the July 1843 issue of *The Dial* and was then expanded into *Woman in the Nineteenth Century*.[22] Most studies see Fuller's eighteen months at the Greene Street School as an interlude during which "she practiced on the schoolgirls of Providence a progressive style of teaching that she would later apply to the prominent women of Boston."[23] Other studies suggest that, both during the Greene Street period and throughout the Boston conversations, Fuller "was developing her own formative attitudes" towards women's issues which would then find expression in her essay and book.[24] Even more important, in my view, is the considerable evidence that, beginning with her decision to use Richard Whately's *Elements of Rhetoric*[25] in a course for the senior girls at Greene Street and continuing through her readings in Plato's dialogues to prepare herself for her first Boston conversation series, Fuller was consciously trying to fashion a set of rhetorical strategies appropriate to the emerging feminist consciousness of her era.

Fuller had never anticipated a career in teaching. Through her early twenties, she had continued to read widely among the European romantics, preparing to become a professional writer, and publishing three early pieces of literary criticism in the June, August, and December 1835 issues of the liberal Unitarian journal, *Western Messenger* (see *MF*, 146–50). But with the unexpected death of her father in the autumn of 1835, the twenty-five-year-old Fuller found herself suddenly responsible for her own support as well as that of her widowed mother and her six younger siblings. During the winter of 1836–7, she taught briefly in Bronson Alcott's Temple School in Boston, but then left – both because the work kept her from her own reading and writing and, more importantly, because local disapproval of some of Alcott's experimental teaching methods was causing the school to fail, and Alcott could no longer pay her salary. When Hiram Fuller (no relation to Margaret) offered her a position at his newly established Greene Street School in Providence, Rhode Island, Fuller could not refuse. Hiram Fuller was offering the munificent annual salary of one thousand dollars and the promise of a teaching schedule light enough to permit her to continue with her own intellectual pursuits.

By the time she took up her duties, however, her schedule proved heavier than anticipated and, by July 1837, Fuller was writing her brother, Arthur, that she was responsible for lessons "in composition, elocution, history, three classes in Latin, . . . two classes in Natural philosophy, and one in Ethics" (*Letters*, 1: 289–90). She would later add a class in French, a class in English literature for the senior girls, and, for the same group, she also took it upon herself to develop a course in rhetoric. Consistent with conventional nineteenth-century gender role expectations, the boys at Greene Street were being trained both in rhetoric and elocution and, twice monthly, they were expected to speak – or *declaim* – before the rest of the school. While Fuller had no intention of training her senior girls for this kind of public declamation, she did want to employ the study of rhetoric to overcome the restraints of feminine modesty and provide each student practical tools with which to communicate clearly "what was in her mind."[26]

In a letter dated December 20, 1837, a nineteen-year-old from rural Massachusetts, newly enrolled in the Greene Street School, reported to her parents that "[Miss Fuller] formed a class in rhetoric to-day, which I have joined, and which *with her*, I think will be made very useful and interesting. We are to recite once a week in Whately's Rhetoric." But the weekly recitations in this class were not to replicate the rote memorization that characterized the boys' training. Instead, they were to involve a sharing of ideas through "pleasant conversation." Fuller was trying to develop in her charges both intellectual discipline and independence of mind: "One of the girls asked her if she should get the lesson by heart. 'No,' said she, 'I never wish a lesson learned by heart, as that phrase is commonly understood. . . . I wish *you* to get your lessons by *mind*.' She said she wished no one to remain in the class unless she was willing to give her mind and soul to the study, unless she was willing to communicate what was in her mind, . . . that we should let no false modesty restrain us." Fuller intended the students' exchanges to be "social and pleasant," but as this young correspondent well understood, there was no question that she and the others would be "exerting ourselves."[27]

A month later, writing to her parents on January 18, 1838, this same student again highlighted the conversational nature of the rhetoric class: "I am studying Whately's Rhetoric, which I like very much because we have such pleasant conversation. The lessons are long and hard, and require a good deal of study. In connection with that study, we write definitions of words, which, though difficult, is very useful. The first we wrote were definitions of Logic, Rhetoric, and Philosophy, as these words were suggested by the conversation."[28] Whately's goal for the "School-boy" for whom his text was intended – like Fuller's goal for each of her senior girls – was to qualify him for "uttering his own sentiments" in a natural manner (*ER*, 257). In order to develop facility in the rhetorical strategies he was recommending, Whately suggested that students become accustomed to "rational *conversation*" (*ER*, 222). Clearly, Fuller had taken this to heart, utilizing conversation as a method for generating calls for definition and accuracy in the group's shared pursuit of the meaning of words and ideas. In good Whatelian fashion, in other words, Fuller was insisting upon clarity and lucidity in expression and, at the same time, teaching her charges to inquire together into topics of mutual interest.

Although as a student at Miss Prescott's School in 1824 Fuller had been assigned another widely read text – Hugh Blair's *Lectures on Rhetoric and Belles Lettres* (London, 1783) – when it came to her own class, she preferred Whately. First published in England in 1828 and then issued in a Boston edition in 1832, Whately's *Elements of Rhetoric* originally had been composed as a manual for divinity students while Whately (who was later to become archbishop of Dublin) served as the principal of St Alban's Hall in Oxford. As an introductory manual, it was "designed principally for the instruction of [the] *unpracticed*" (*ER*, iv) – which is clearly what attracted Fuller.

Unlike his influential predecessor, Blair – who defined rhetoric as a science concerned both with rules for composition and with rules for the critical appraisal of literature – Whately omitted literary considerations altogether and treated rhetoric not as a science but rather as a set of procedures for "*Argumentative*

Composition, generally, and exclusively" (*ER*, 5). Burdened neither by theories of human understanding nor by analyses of what constitutes truth in argument, Whately's *Elements of Rhetoric*, as he announced in his Introduction, was an *"instrumental"* text (*ER*, 4). It concentrated on the systematic application of specific rules and procedures for developing and organizing an argument. As long as the central function of logic was not ignored, moreover, Whately expected his "rules" to be applied neither rigidly nor inflexibly. "Instead," as Ray E. McKerrow has pointed out, Whately's rules functioned more as guides which "may be abandoned whenever greater advantage results from a different approach."[29]

Having been educated by her father in the classical rhetorical tradition, and having resisted the assignment of Blair at Miss Prescott's school because she preferred "Cicero's oratory" (*MF*, 75), Fuller should have found Whately relatively elementary. And yet, in January 1838, Fuller wrote to a friend that she was not only reading and teaching Whately's *Rhetoric* but also "thinking it over with great profit to myself" (*Letters*, 1: 322–3). It was part of a larger pattern of activity that marked Fuller's eighteen months in Providence.

On August 9, 1837, just two months after her arrival, Fuller defied gender proprieties by attending the otherwise all-male state Whig caucus – not because she had any interest in the issues, but because she wanted to hear the two main speakers, State Representative John Whipple and Rhode Island's most popular orator, Congressman Tristam Burges, former Brown University professor of oratory. As a woman, she had difficulty gaining entrance; and news of her attendance later horrified Hiram Fuller, Greene Street's circumspect principal. Disturbed by neither, Fuller recorded in her journal acute observations of the speakers' style, "manner," and oratorical devices (see *MF*, 213). For the same purpose, she took every opportunity for brief visits to Boston and Cambridge, attending a variety of lectures, including some by her friend Emerson. And in the spring of 1838 she herself participated in a series of debates at Providence's Coliseum Club on the subject of the "progress of Society" (see *MF*, 242–3). The rhetoric class for senior girls and her study of Whately were thus part of an increased engagement in the practical application of rhetorical principles and in what Capper has called "her by now well-ingrained fascination with public oratory" (*MF*, 213).

Despite the generous salary, the pleasures she experienced in teaching were not enough to sustain Fuller. The heavier schedule had taken its toll on her health, and she repeatedly complained to correspondents of insufficient time and energy for work on her translation of Johann Peter Eckermann's *Conversations with Goethe in the Last Years of his Life* (see *MF*, 253). She also missed the more sophisticated intellectual activity of Boston and Cambridge. Accordingly, in December 1838, after three terms at the Greene Street School, Fuller resigned her position and rejoined her family in their current home in Jamaica Plain, a suburb of Boston. "I do not wish to teach again at all," she wrote a friend. And yet, in that same December 1838 letter, she confided that she was "not without my dreams and hopes as to the education of women" (*Letters*, 1: 354).

Fuller's encounters with the poorly prepared senior girls at Greene Street had reinforced her sense of the inadequate educational opportunities for women. At the same time, the practical strategies she had gleaned from Whately, combined with her continuing fascination with all forms of public discourse, now prompted her to consider some means by which "to systemize thought and give a precision in which our sex are so deficient" (*Letters*, 2: 87). Her plan, as she described it in an August 1839 letter to Sophia Ripley, was to organize a series of weekly meetings for "well-educated and thinking women" which would forge intellectual community ("supplying a point of union" in Fuller's words) and, as well, "answer the great questions. What were we born to do? How shall we do it?" (*Letters*, 2: 86–7). Alluding to the pedagogy she had employed in the rhetoric class for senior girls, Fuller declared her "confidence" in her project because "in former instances I have been able to make it easy and even pleasant to twenty five out of thirty to bear their part, to question, to define, to state and examine their opinions" (*Letters*, 2: 88). As she had at Greene Street, Fuller would ask her conversation participants to throw off "the garb of modesty" in order to "openly state their impressions and consent to learn by blundering" (*Letters*, 2: 87–8).

"Of course," as Capper emphasizes, "these were not 'conversations' in the ordinary sense. The ideal of a conversation as a critical intellectual method derived from Plato," whose Socratic dialogues Fuller had been recently rereading, and from the "great Romantic talkers" like Mme de Stael, Coleridge, and Goethe (*MF*, 296). Closer to home, Fuller had witnessed Bronson Alcott's efforts to utilize conversational dialogues as a teaching tool at his Temple School (later adapting some of his techniques for her Greene Street classes). And, more recently, as Fuller was aware, "Alcott . . . had launched a series of moderately successful traveling conversations in various towns in eastern Massachusetts" (*MF*, 296). The conversation thus became for Fuller both a mode of feminist activism and a modest source of income.

Beginning in November 1839 and continuing through May 1844, each fall and spring Fuller conducted a series of conversations on different subjects, ranging widely from mythology through philosophy and the arts. Elizabeth Palmer Peabody's Boston bookstore was sometimes the site; at other times George and Sophia Ripley offered their front parlor. For a fee of ten dollars (later raised to twenty) for each three-month series, Boston area women found a forum for the investigation and exchange of ideas. Although few series enrolled more than twenty-five, the participants changed often enough that, by 1844, Fuller had counted in her conversations most of Boston's female writers and activists, as well as the wives and daughters of the area's most prominent men. Some participants came from as far away as Providence and New York.

With one exception, no detailed record remains of these conversations.[30] That exception is young Caroline Healey Dall's transcription of ten conversations that she attended, beginning in March 1841, on "The Mythology of the Greeks and its Expression in Art" – the only series to which Fuller admitted men. Because the men included well-known personages like Emerson, who tended to dominate discussion, the Dall transcription cannot stand as an accurate index to Fuller's strategies when only women were present. For, with the first conversation on March 1, a pattern emerged which only occasionally gave way in subsequent meetings: the ten males take up far more of the verbal space than do the twelve women present. The results were frequent digressions into areas interesting only to one or another of the men. After the second week's meeting, in a typical observation, Dall recorded that "Emerson pursued his own train of thought. He seemed to forget that we had come together to pursue Margaret's."[31]

If Dall's chronicle portrays Fuller as often arch in her attempts to restrain a loquacious male, sometimes irritated, occasionally impatient, and even capable of sharp retort, her chronicle also suggests features of Fuller's behavior that may have surfaced more prominently when only women were present. To elicit greater participation from everyone in the group, Fuller understated her own expertise on a subject. To maintain focus and continuity, she habitually recapitulated the main ideas of a discussion at the end of the evening's conversation and, again, at the beginning of the next. Fuller's ready wit and sense of humor are also apparent. And, perhaps most important to Fuller, she never found herself "haranguing too much" – an early fear that she had expressed in her August 1839 letter to Sophia Ripley (*Letters*, 2: 88). Instead, despite the men's tangents and interruptions, Dall's transcription shows us a Fuller determined to enact the role she had first proposed for herself in these conversations: "truly a teacher and a guide" (*Letters*, 2: 97). As Fuller had explained at the first meeting of the initial series, she was not there "to *teach* anything," but "to call . . . out the thought of others" (quoted in *MF*, 296).

The magnetic intensity of Fuller's personal presence, upon which so many of her contemporaries commented, no doubt contributed substantially to the success of the Boston conversations. Additionally, her easy familiarity with literature and philosophy in several languages, along with her reading and teaching in formal rhetoric, now came together to enable her to awaken the enthusiasms of the conversation participants. From the platform orators she admired, she had learned something of the "manner" of public presentation and even an occasional argumentative strategy. From Whately she had imbibed the importance of "the skilful arrangement" of thought (*ER*, 28). And from Plato, especially in his early dialogues, she had taken the courage to raise questions for which there might not be sure answers. "I have been reading Plato all week," she informed Emerson as one series began, "hop[ing] to be tuned up thereby" (*Letters*, 2: 104). Her vast education supplied the ground upon which she would "open a subject" and offer "as good a general statement as I know how to make" (*Letters*, 2: 88). But her study of rhetoric had supplied her with the practical tools for "select[ing] a branch of the subject and lead[ing] others to give their thoughts upon it" (*Letters*, 2: 88).

Those same strengths came together once more, as Fuller prepared her first formal "*Argumentative Composition*." Her long apprenticeship in initiating what Whately had called "rational *conversation*" prompted her to try a bold experiment, however. Instead of relegating the conversation to an exclusively oral exercise, Fuller would simulate its components in a written treatise. In so doing, she chose her rhetorical devices carefully, emulating the female antislavery lecturers by bringing her "subject more into home relations" and by eschewing "combativeness."

III

While Fuller had first encountered the dialogue as a pedagogical device at Alcott's Temple School, it was not until she began using Whately at Greene Street that she found the means to convert dialogue into a full-fledged conversation aimed at probing received wisdom and arriving at collective reassessments. And while Fuller's letters indicate that she consulted Plato throughout the years of the Boston conversations, characteristic Whatelian recommendations – like understating one's own command of a subject, recapitulating complex arguments, and the judicious use of humor – are clearly evident in Dall's account of the spring 1841 conversation series. Not surprisingly, echoes of Whately's phrasings can also be detected in both the *Dial* essay and in *Woman in the Nineteenth Century*, suggesting that as Fuller attempted her first *"Argumentative Composition,"* Whately continued as an influence.[32] *Elements of Rhetoric* was not only the rhetoric manual Fuller knew most intimately, however. In addition, as Fuller was aware (and Whately readily acknowledged), it was a highly derivative work, offering a compressed compendium of rhetorical practice from Aristotle, Cicero, and Quintillian through George Campbell's *Philosophy of Rhetoric* (London and Edinburgh, 1776) and Hugh Blair's *Lectures on Rhetoric and Belles Lettres* (Dublin, 1789), with copious quotations from and references to each. As such, to read Fuller's text against Whately's allows us easily to measure what Fuller was prepared to accept – and, no less important, what she felt bound to reject – from the entire rhetorical tradition then available to her.

More to the point, Whately's "System of Rules" (*ER*, 15) was specifically designed for Fuller's present purpose. Her goal, after all, as she began the *Dial* essay, was to prompt readers to their own independent discovery of a "truth" to which Fuller was herself already deeply committed. And for Whately, as for most eighteenth- and nineteenth-century rhetoricians, "the process of *conveying truth* to others" constituted the very heart of "the Rhetorical process" (*ER*, 23). The divinity students for whom Whately's text was originally intended, we recall, were being instructed in the practical strategies for leading their prospective parishioners to the revealed truths of Christianity.

Fuller, of course, had a different truth to convey. Defining men and women as "the two halves of one thought" in the preface to *Woman in the Nineteenth Century*, she then explained: "I believe that the development of the one cannot be effected without that of the other. My highest wish is that this truth should be distinctly and rationally apprehended, and the conditions of life and freedom recognized as the same for the daughters and the sons" (*W*, vi). In urging readers toward their own rational apprehension of this truth, Fuller sought to replicate the rhetorical situation in which she was experiencing her greatest success: the weekly meetings in which women "have time, patience, mutual reverence and fearlessness eno' to get at one another's thoughts" (*Letters*, 2: 118).

In order to mimic the polyphony of conversation, Fuller's treatise on women's rights introduced a variety of voices – her own, the autobiographical Miranda's, her anonymous correspondent's, and even the wholly fictive "irritated trader" determined to maintain authority over his wife (*W*, 18–19). The spontaneity of conversation was captured in Fuller's direct addresses, as when she suddenly changed course by informing the reader that she had already "brought forward" enough on a subject to satisfy her point (*W*, 49). To suggest the give and take of contested positions, Fuller offered a panoply of conflicting views of women by including lengthy selections from a variety of authors – a speech by John Quincy Adams (*W*, 128–30), a poem by the young transcendentalist, William Ellery Channing (*W*, 177–9), and a passage from the French essayist, Suzanne Necker (*W*, 147), among others – even where she did not wholly agree with the point of view expressed. Even more important, following a loose historical chronology, she catalogued "signs of the times" (*W*, 26), a survey of mythological as well as historical events and personages, each variously interpreted as evidence of the obstacles to women's advancement *and* as harbingers of what might yet be achieved. And in order to invite her reader to participate actively in the ongoing epistemic inquiry, Fuller enunciated the commitment not to enroll "ourselves at once on either side" but, rather, to "look upon the subject from the best point of view" (*W*, 20). Her model, she reassured her readers, was the eminent Unitarian minister, the late Dr William Ellery Channing, who, in Fuller's estimation, "always furnished a platform on which opposing parties could stand, and look at one another under the influence of his mildness and enlightened candor" (*W*, 101).

With these last two statements, Fuller signaled that she was intent on conducting what Whately termed "a process of Investigation" (*ER*, 24). By and large, her arguments would appeal to those who had not yet formed a hardened opinion, "but are merely desirous of ascertaining *what* is the truth in respect of the case before them" (*ER*, 24). Fuller was thus enacting what Whately called "Instruction" – a word with which she felt especially comfortable – but a species of instruction that at once preserved Fuller's preferred role as a facilitator and a guide, even as it acknowledged that she had a particular "truth" to convey. The rhetor was "conducting a process of Investigation" relative to readers only, explained Whately, "though not to himself" (*ER*, 24–5).

Whately's "process of Investigation" was also wholly consistent with Fuller's characteristically romantic notion of "truth" as a process of unfolding revelation, a notion that had been reinforced by her experience with the conversation series. Through the conversations, she had refined the art of carrying on a critical inquiry by means of shared discussion, and she had taught other women to participate actively in the dialectical testing of ideas. In effect, the conversations represented the conceptual model for her treatise's rhetorical design. But, as he had in the past, Whately would provide a source for formal strategies and lead her to "the skilful arrangement of them" (*ER*, 28).

All editions of Whately's *Elements of Rhetoric* are organized into four parts: 1 "Of the Address to the Understanding, with a View to Produce Conviction (Including Instruction)"; 2 "Of the Address to the Will, or Persuasion"; 3 "Of Style"; and 4 "Of Elocution, or Delivery." Because it deals exclusively with oral presentation, part 4 includes a number of items adapted by Fuller for both the Greene Street School and the Boston conversations; but its imprint is not detected in either "The Great Lawsuit" or *Woman in the Nineteenth Century*. For reasons to be explored shortly, part 2 had only limited influence as well. Much of parts 1 and 3, by contrast, helps us to understand why Fuller constructed her treatise as she did.

From part 1 of Whately, Fuller took the kinds of arguments most appropriate to "conducting a process of Investigation," and she followed his advice as to their "various use and order" (*ER*, 70). Her central syllogism, for example, derived from Whately's tactics for shifting the burden of proof to one's opponent when responding to the "Presumption in favour of every *existing* institution" (*ER*, 76). In the face of "a Presumption against every Change," Whately advised, the rebuttal is "true, but . . . every *Restriction* is in itself an evil; and therefore there is a Presumption in favor of its removal" (*ER*, 80). In "The Great Lawsuit" and in *Woman in the Nineteenth Century*, Fuller acknowledged at the outset that popular opinion was against her, "society at large not [being] prepared for the demands" she is about to make (*W*, 18). Following Whately, her response is to weave into her discourse a syllogism that appeals to patriotic motives and, at the same time, shifts the burden of proof by challenging imposed restrictions: because the United States has been founded on the belief that "all men are born free and equal," Fuller predicts that it "is surely destined to elucidate a great moral law" for all humanity (*W*, 15). But slavery and restrictions on women run counter to this founding proposition. Therefore, concluded Fuller, for the nation to attain its destined greatness, it must free slaves and remove all restrictions on women. As Whately had taught her, she now had the opposition on the defensive.

In the second chapter of part 1, entitled "Of Arguments," Whately catalogued the kinds of strategies that would prove most conducive to "conducting a process of Investigation." He recommends the use of testimony and cross-examination of adversaries, recommendations that Fuller followed in her introduction of Miranda's first-person narrative and in her own dialogue with "the irritated trader" intent on maintaining his white male privileges. Whately recommends the argument from analogy, to which Fuller repeatedly resorted in her insistence on the parallels between white women's status and that of slaves. And he urges the efficacy of drawing a conclusion from a single instance and then inferring from that a conclusion "respecting the whole Class" (*ER*, 53). Fuller obviously found this an appealing device, using it regularly. She offered the vignette of the father who would not educate his daughter, for example, in order to illustrate an instance of the male who does not always act in women's best interest. Fuller then drew from this the general rule undergirding her entire thesis: because men see only their own needs and "do *not* look at both sides, . . . women must leave off asking them and being influenced by them" (*W*, 108). In recommending this argument from example, moreover, Whately allowed for the "real or invented" (*ER*, 67), as long as the "case [had] . . . intrinsic probability" (*ER*, 65). Fuller, of course, included both, incorporating her knowledge of Greek and Roman mythology, stories from German folk ballads, and the real-life biography of the Polish heroine, Emily Plater.

Finally, Whately stressed the value of combining different kinds of arguments, each "singly perhaps of little weight," into the "progressive approach" (*ER*, 49). This gave Fuller license to include the many different kinds of arguments that might mark any spirited conversation, confident that together they would "produce jointly, and by their coincidence, a degree of probability far exceeding the sum of their several forces, taken separately" (*ER*, 49). The key to success here, continued Whately, was the order in which the different arguments were "considered, and . . . their *progressive* tendency to establish a certain conclusion" (*ER*, 49).

How to achieve that order was then the focus of the third chapter of part 1. Here again Whately drew a distinction between "convey[ing] *instruction* to those who are ready to receive it" and "*compel{ling}* the assent, or silenc[ing] the objections, of an opponent" (*ER*, 70). Since Fuller's object was the former, she followed Whately's view that the argument from cause to effect would give the greatest "*satisfaction to a candid mind*" (*ER*, 70), and she took seriously his hint that arguments "from Cause to Effect . . . have usually the precedence" in the organization of a treatise because they help to prepare "the way for the reception of other arguments" (*ER*, 83–4). In fact, Fuller devoted the first twenty-five pages of the printed book (almost one-sixth of the text) to laying the groundwork for her first major cause-to-effect proposition: because men can only think of women as "made *for man*" (*W*, 25), and because men are bound by habit and convention in this regard, they can never adequately speak for woman nor act in her best interests. Not until near the end of the book did she introduce, as a kind of corollary, the more controversial cause-to-effect argument regarding the male's historical abuse of his privileges over the female. The consequence of this unhappy history, Fuller asserted, was that the male now found himself "a temporal master" rather than a "spiritual sire," "a king without a queen . . . his habits and his will corrupted by the past" (*W*, 156). Of course, Fuller was here following Whately's view that a "Conclusion . . . likely to . . . offend the prejudices of the hearers" be kept "out of sight, as much as possible . . . till the principles from which it is to be deduced shall have been clearly established" (*ER*, 89).

In short, Fuller adopted most of the advice offered by Whately in part 1. In the *Dial* essay, the "refutation of Objections" was placed as Whately had recommended, "nearer the beginning than the end" (*ER*, 92); and this remained so in the essay's expansion. Fuller worked to "avoid an appearance of abruptness" by carefully laying out her basic premises before "enter[ing] on the main argument" (*ER*, 112). And her conclusion – in both the essay and the book – was the recapitulation called for by Whately.

Similarly, Whately's part 3, "Of Style," also reads as a kind of rhetorical road map to Fuller's text. From the first chapter on perspicuity or clarity in language usage, she seems to have adopted Whately's advice on the relative proportion of Saxon and Latinate words. And, even more important, she embraced his view that "the same sentiment and argument" could be offered "in many different forms of expression" in order to expand "the sense to be conveyed" and thereby detain "the mind upon it" (*ER*, 171). In fact, Fuller circled around the same points and sentiments throughout her book, each time attempting a different analogy or illustration that would arrest attention and, as had the women anti-slavery orators, thus bring the "subject more into home relations."

From the second chapter of part 3, "Of Energy," Fuller incorporated advice that she hoped would "stimulate attention, . . . excite the Imagination, and . . . arouse the Feelings" (*ER*, 183–4). For example, her direct comments to the reader were often framed as questions: "You ask, what use will she make of liberty, when she has so long been sustained and restrained?" (*W*, 158). Here Fuller followed Whately's observation that a direct interrogative "calls the hearer's attention more forcibly to some important point, by a personal appeal to each individual" (*ER*, 241). In order to avoid what Whately called "a tedious dragging effect," Fuller generally constructed her "complex sentences of any considerable length" along Whately's model, with the longer clauses preceding and the shorter phrases concluding the sentence (*ER*, 233). Her habitual penchant for Latinate syntax was somewhat tempered thereby.

The type and structure of individual sentences, however, was not the only focus of Whately's part 3. Patterns of organization exerted their impact on stimulating attention and thus were also a component of "Style." Especially important to Fuller as she expanded her essay into the book was Whately's stress on "the energetic effect of Conciseness" (*ER*, 212), a stylistic effect for which she was not widely known. Because she had been criticized by some for "not making my meaning sufficiently clear" in the essay, she now "tried to illustrate it in various ways," expanding the text by almost a third in that effort (*W*, 154). Conscious of the possibility that the additional material might strike some readers as only "much repetition" (*W*, 154), Fuller eagerly followed Whately's advice for creating at least "the *effect* of brevity" (*ER*, 216). To accomplish this, Whately instructed the rhetor "first to expand the sense, sufficiently to be clearly understood, and then to contract it into the most compendious and striking form" (*ER*, 215). This "addition of a compressed and pithy expression of the sentiment" – even after expansion and repetition – Whately promised "will produce the *effect* of brevity" (*ER*, 216). In *Woman in the Nineteenth Century*, Fuller explained the form of her new closing peroration by paraphrasing Whately's justification for "the insertion of such an abridged repetition" (*ER*, 216). And she acknowledged that the authority for this rhetorical strategy was a manual written for future ministers: "In the earlier tract, I was told, I did not make my meaning sufficiently clear. In this I have consequently tried to illustrate it in various ways, and may have been guilty of much repetition. Yet, as I am anxious to leave no room for doubt, I shall venture to retrace, once more, the scope of my design in points, as was done in old-fashioned sermons" (*W*, 154). What followed was a brief compendium of pithy closing statements, including the bold pronouncement for which, at the time, Fuller was most ridiculed: "But if you ask me what offices they may fill; I reply – any. I do not care what case you put; let them be sea-captains, if you will" (*W*, 159).[33]

Unquestionably the most influential section for Fuller came in the second chapter of part 3, where Whately endorsed "the *Suggestive* style" (*ER*, 221). Functioning by means of "slight *hints*" and "notices of the principles" rather than the particulars (*ER*, 222), the suggestive style not only coincided with the advertised intention of the *Dial* to discuss "principles" rather than advocate particular "measures" (see *MF*, 348). Of greater significance for Fuller, it also closely approximated the use of conversation as a collaborative device to prompt instruction. It "shall put the hearer's mind into the same *train of thought* as the speaker's," explained Whately, "and suggest to him more than is actually expressed" (*ER*, 221).

Whately himself made the comparison explicit when he recommended "rational *conversation*" as "a very useful exercise" for developing this particular stylistic technique. After all, Whately went on, "in conversation, a man naturally tries first one and then another mode of conveying his thoughts" (*ER*, 222). Child and others may have judged the effect "rough in construction," but in fact this *was* Fuller's method. Moving from one type of argument to another, surveying history and mythology for analogies and examples, introducing the authority of Miranda's personal testimony in one place, the authority of the Declaration of Independence in another, Fuller was determined to try out as many means as possible for conveying her ideas. "When I meet people I can adapt myself to them," Fuller had written to fellow member of the Transcendental Club, William Henry Channing, in 1840, "but when I write, it is into another world" (*Letters*, 2: 125). The suggestive style was thus her solution, because it gave her permission to adapt herself to an imagined variety of readers much as she had always adapted herself to different partners in conversation.

Although Whately refrained from "lay[ing] down precise rules for the Suggestive kind of writing I am speaking of" (*ER*, 222), the image he chose to represent that style resonated in Fuller's closing declaration. According to Whately, the suggestive style might best be compared "to a good map, which marks distinctly the great outlines, setting down the principal rivers, towns, mountains, &c., leaving the imagination to supply the villages, hillocks, and streamlets" (*ER*, 221n). By the time she completed her book, Fuller was confident that she had "now . . . designated in outline, if not in fulness, the stream which is ever flowing from the heights of my thought" (*W*, 154). Her text did sketch the central questions and "the great outlines." And, as Fuller herself explained, her purpose had never been to "deal with 'atrocious instances'" nor to "demand . . . partial redress in some one matter, but [to] go to the root of the whole. If principles could be established," she was sure, "particulars would adjust themselves aright" (*W*, 22).

If Fuller's adherence to the suggestive style was risky in its rejection of both explicit program and the drama of "atrocious instances," her boldest gamble was her decision to dispense with almost everything in Whately's part 2, "Of the Address to the Will, or Persuasion." To be sure, she did not reject it all. Having taught part 2 at Greene Street,[34] she appreciated the impact of an occasionally "gentle and conciliatory manner" (*ER*, 151), and she did her best to dwell on areas of mutual agreement in order not to alienate reluctant readers. She was also well aware of the value of "attentively studying and meditating on the history of some extraordinary Personage – by contemplating and dwelling on his actions and sufferings – his virtues and his wisdom – and by calling on the Imagination to present a vivid picture" (*ER*, 124). As she had done for her pupils at Greene Street, Fuller offered the "extraordinary" lives of exemplary women, from the Polish patriot, Countess Emily Plater, to Cassandra, "the inspired child," emblem of the intuitively gifted woman whom none yet understand (*W*, 93).

That said, Fuller did not embrace the strategies that Whately claimed would call out "passion, sentiment, or emotion" for the purpose of persuasion (*ER*, 125). She did not expend any effort at establishing her own good character, a tactic which, according to Whately, can often "persuade more powerfully than . . . the strongest Arguments" (*ER*, 128). She did not affect the suppression of her own strong feelings on the subject but, instead, declared at the outset that "the subject makes me feel too much" (*W*, 22). She did not paint in lurid detail the oppressions of women and then call upon her readers "to consider how they would feel were such and such an injury done to themselves" (*ER*, 140). She never openly ridiculed her opponents. She did not deliberately organize her material so as to lead her reader from the calm "to the impassioned" (*ER*, 142). And she never exhorted her readers "to adopt the conduct recommended" (*ER*, 131). In short, Fuller did not follow Whately in what he termed "the design laid against [the reader's] feelings" (*ER*, 136). This was where Fuller resisted being "taught and led by men" (*W*, 107).

In Whately's rhetoric, persuasion is "the art of influencing the *Will*," and to accomplish that, "two things are requisite": The rhetor's arguments must make "the proposed *Object* . . . appear desirable," and "the *Means* suggested should be proved . . . conducive to the attainment of that object" (*ER*, 117). Fuller attempted only a version of the first, advocating full equality for women as the central condition for the improvement of humankind in general and the fulfillment of national destiny in particular. But, preferring principles to particulars, she detailed no program or "means" to achieve her ends, and there was no specific "conduct recommended."

Even so, her unwillingness to propose specific remedies does not entirely account for Fuller's decision to reject strategies for "influencing the *Will*." Rather, her decision was due to Whately's insistence that persuasion could never rest on logical argument but instead depended on "*Exhortation*, i.e. the excitement of men" (*ER*, 118). To be effective, in other words, persuasion played not just to the emotions or the feelings, but to the passions. On this point, Whately was unequivocal: "there can be no Persuasion without an address to the Passions" (*ER*, 119). In delineating the strategies for persuasion, however, Whately's imagery suddenly turned suggestively sexual and, at the same time, swerved toward the very combativeness that Fuller had worked so hard to avoid. Clearly, persuasion entailed a quality of relationship between rhetor and audience unlike that in any other section of Whately's manual.[35]

Techniques for obliquely arousing an audience, for example, are introduced through the following "homely illustration": "A moderate charge of powder will have more effect in splitting a rock, if we begin by deep boring, and introducing the charge into the very heart of it, than ten times the quantity, exploded on the surface" (*ER*, 132n). In a lengthy note emphasizing the importance of arrangement, Whately recommended that the "statements and arguments should first be clearly and calmly laid down and developed" and then be succeeded by "the impassioned appeal." "The former of these two parts may be compared to the back of a sabre," Whately elaborated, "the latter to its edge. The former should be firm and weighty; the latter keen." The violence latent in that comparison was then rendered explicit at the end of the paragraph where Whately described a properly arranged appeal to the emotions as "an excellent sword" whose "blows would take effect" (*ER*, 142n). Above all else, however, persuasion functioned through an organizational structure that purposefully "raise[d] the feelings gradually to the highest pitch" or, as Whately clarified, "what Rhetoricians call the Climax" (*ER*, 138).

Given Fuller's belief in man and woman as "two halves of one thought" (*W*, vi), and given the rhetorical goals articulated throughout her treatise, she had no choice but to reject the tactics of persuasion. Having identified the containment of male sexual aggression as necessary to full equality between the sexes, Fuller would not play upon "the excitement of men" in constructing her arguments. Having condemned the "love of petty power" that derived from women's enforced "ignorance and foolish vanity" (*W*, 50), Fuller could hardly employ that same power to argue for the rights of women. In her view, after all, the covertly sexual manipulations of persuasion were identical to those she had named as the only available "arms of the servile: cunning, blandishment, and unreasonable emotion" (*W*, 157). Furthermore, unlike the "Address to the Understanding" in part 1, persuasion undermined the collaborative conversation that Fuller had pursued since Greene Street, and it altogether annihilated even the illusion of an unfolding epistemic inquiry. As Whately defined it (and he was hardly alone in this), persuasion emerged as a species of coercion meant to compel the audience members' "resigning themselves" to the feelings evoked

(*ER*, 142n). And persuasion accomplishes this end by overriding the audience's independent will. Indeed, that is its purpose: "When the metal is heated, it may easily be moulded into the desired form" (*ER*, 143).

But molding an audience into some predetermined form had never been Fuller's purpose. Instead, in inventing a discourse appropriate to feminism, Fuller rejected alike the authoritarianism of coercion and the manipulative strategies of the disempowered, endeavoring instead to create a collaborative process of asser- tion and response in which multiple voices could – and did – find a place. She required of her readers, in Stanley Fish's words, "a searching and rigorous scru- tiny of everything they believe and live by" in regard to gender arrangements.[36] But she also required a wholly *voluntary* attentiveness to these matters, in return for which she neither demanded specific remedy nor imposed any single course of action. As she made plain in her preface, Fuller asked of her male readers no less than "a noble and earnest attention," and she solicited from her female readers the independence of mind "to search their own experience and intuitions" in order to identify the problem and invent its solutions (*W*, vi).

Certainly, in conveying her "truth," Fuller's purpose was to initiate a new consensus. But in contrast to the liberal individualism of Emerson's "self- reliance,"[37] Fuller was attempting to forge an ongoing collective search for a social philosophy of *female* "self dependence . . . and fulness of being" (*W*, 84). The consensus that Fuller sought, in other words, was to emerge from the dialectical conversation that her text had set in motion but purposefully not brought to "climax" (or closure). Little wonder that Brownson saw "no reason why it should stop where it does." But then this was precisely Fuller's aim. "And so the stream flows on," predicted Fuller: "thought urging action, and action leading to the evolution of still better thought" (*W*, 158).

IV

By rejecting persuasion as a tactic for feminist discourse, Fuller dispensed with those organizing principles that had come to be associated with most public advocacy in her day. As a result, despite the chronological arrangement of her "signs of the times," and despite Fuller's demonstrated command of formal logic and her employment of both inductive and deductive modes of reasoning, she had opened herself to the charge that she was aimlessly amassing miscellaneous evidence, merely "collect[ing] . . . clever sayings and bright intimations." In other words, because Fuller did not *order* her treatise in the conventional man- ner, critics like Brownson – and others after him – simply dismissed the whole as the byproduct of stereotypically uncontrolled female talkativeness transferred to the printed page.

Her refusal to build to a conclusive "climax" and thereby bring her treatise to definitive closure served Fuller's purpose in two ways, however. First, without damage to either the structure or the intent of her thesis, Fuller was able simply to add to the *Dial* essay in order to turn it into *Woman in the Nineteenth Century*.

As Urbanski has pointed out, while Fuller "occasionally . . . changed a few words to clarify or modify the meaning of a sentence" and made some other minor alterations, she left the original essay essentially intact and appended to it the bulk of her new material. With contemporary references and "more trenchant social criticism," as Urbanski notes, these additions contained some of "the most daring subject matter in the book."[38] Here were frank discussions of sexual matters, including male sexual appetite and the rehabilitation of prostitutes, as well as Fuller's famous remark about allowing women to be sea captains. While her informing arguments remained the same, the new examples added "energy" to what Whately had called the *suggestive style* by giving readers contemporary — rather than historical or metaphorical — referents to ponder.

Second, the lack of closure also opened the way for still further recastings. From another letter that Fuller sent to William Henry Channing in November 1844, we know this to have been her intention. In the midst of expanding the *Dial* essay into *Woman in the Nineteenth Century* — and finding it "spinning out beneath my hand" (*Letters*, 3: 241) — Fuller told Channing that she was now bent on revising the book draft before sending it on for his reading and advice. Certain that the manuscript would "be much better" after these revisions, Fuller not only confirmed the considered crafting that was going into her work but indicated as well that she saw no necessary end to this process. "I should hope to be able to make it constantly better while I live," Fuller told Channing, and she expressed her expectation for "subsequent editions" (*Letters*, 3: 242).

But the few years that remained to Fuller afforded no time for any new editions, and she never even witnessed the practical impact of her work on the organized women's rights movement. With a platform deeply indebted to the ideas promulgated by *Woman in the Nineteenth Century*, the first women's rights convention in the United States convened in Seneca Falls, New York, in July 1848, while Fuller was covering the political upheavals in Italy for Horace Greeley's *New York Tribune*. By the time the first national convention opened in Worcester, Massachusetts, in October 1850, she was already dead. Returning from Italy in May, Fuller had been drowned in a shipwreck off Fire Island.

Although Fuller's loss to the women's movement at this crucial juncture was profound, her conversational strategies proved revolutionary and enduring. With many of her former students arranging similar activities of their own, women's conversation groups proliferated. Elizabeth Cady Stanton, a founder of the Seneca Falls Convention, had attended a Fuller series in Boston one winter and later initiated a series in upstate New York — as Stanton put it, in conscious "imitation of Margaret Fuller's Conversationals." Without question, "conversationals" functioned for the first wave of United States feminists in much the same way that the consciousness-raising groups of the late 1960s and early 1970s functioned for the second wave: as a galvanizing force and, as Fuller had phrased it, "supplying a point of union." "In calling forth the opinions of her sex," wrote the editors of the *History of Woman Suffrage* in the 1880s, "Miss Fuller was the precursor of the Women's Rights agitation of the last thirty-three years."[39]

The text in which those same conversational strategies were employed for *written* argument, however, continued to be regarded, in Dall's words, as "a complete, scholarly exposition" that provided much-needed intellectual grist for the movement's political aims. Like most other antislavery and women's rights activists, Dall credited Fuller with "the first clear, uncompromising, scholarly demand for the civil rights of her sex."[40] But she never suggested that *Woman in the Nineteenth Century* might also be read as a source book of techniques for a feminist public discourse.

Understandably, the women who led the nineteenth-century movement pursued the forms of public advocacy that they had been taught in coeducational academies and female seminaries. But, as Fuller had so well understood, that was the problem. From personal experience she knew that, even at the best of these establishments, women were given "young men as teachers, who only teach what has been taught themselves at college." And even where "women are . . . at the head of these institutions," still Fuller objected that they were not generally "thinking women, capable to organize a new whole for the wants of the time" (*W*, 83). She herself had complained about being assigned Blair at Miss Prescott's School, and when she taught at Greene Street, the best Fuller could offer her senior girls was Whately. Within this delimiting educational context and absent Fuller's continued recreation of her text as the ongoing conversation she hoped for, the general critical response that her treatise "lack[ed] method sadly" effectively discredited the book as a rhetorical model that women should seriously consider.

United States feminists have thus been caught in bifurcated discourses. The inclusive, collaborative, and searchingly open-ended discussions that sustained the conversationals in the nineteenth century and the consciousness-raising groups of the twentieth were only haphazardly translated into corresponding experiments in *written* forms of public argument, especially in the academy. Admittedly, feminist scholarship throughout the 1980s was diligent in scrutinizing its own premises and foundational arguments. And that scholarship also moved toward the inclusion of an ever-widening variety of voices and "feminisms." Additionally, the renewed insistence in the 1990s that the writer identify a subject position certainly echoes Fuller's closing remark that she argued from the ground of maturity, "stand[ing] in the sunny noon of life" (*W*, 163), neither naive from inexperience nor cynical from disappointments. Those innovations notwithstanding, even the boldest of feminist scholars for the most part continue to adapt themselves to the discourse behaviors of their chosen disciplines, eager to be persuasive in the ways that term is commonly understood.

But that practice has never been wholly satisfactory, and Gearhart and Elshtain have hardly been alone in their quest to locate discourse models appropriate to feminist ideals. Gearhart recommended "transactional" communication techniques, while Elshtain approved Jürgen Habermas's "concept of an ideal speech situation" as a precedent for "creating a feminist discourse that rejects domination."[41] Each alternative incorporates much that Fuller attempted,[42] of course (though Fuller is never mentioned by transactional theorists or by Habermas), but neither specifically invokes that conversation through which women can "organize a new whole for the wants of the time" (*W*, 83). Hirsch and Keller recommended no specific rhetorical strategies, but they invoked Fuller's spirit – if not her name – when they encouraged contributors to *Conflicts in Feminism* to engage in "dialogue and conversation among opposing factions." Even here, however, "each of [their] authors expresse[d] increasing frustration at the way the disagreements lead to oppositional politics."[43] While Fuller provides no sure formula for resolving such oppositions, she does offer a play of strategies that ensures ongoing exchange and eschews overheated terminations.

To return to the quality of *that* conversation, Fuller must be read on her own terms, and *Woman in the Nineteenth Century* must be accepted as an intentional experiment in a feminist discourse that refused premature closure. To put it another way, if we seriously re-engage the conversation that Fuller began in 1843 with the publication of "The Great Lawsuit," then we come to understand that that conversation *cannot* be brought to closure – not until, that is, "inward and outward freedom for woman as much as for man shall be acknowledged as a right, not yielded as a concession."

NOTES

A Beer Memorial Trust research grant from Rensselaer Polytechnic Institute in 1987–8 supported the initial research for this essay, and a 1993–4 sabbatical from the University of Arizona allowed its completion. As the research progressed, Joel Myerson was endlessly generous in supplying good advice and vital bibliographical material, including copies of crucial books and articles. At different stages, three outstanding scholars read drafts of the essay-in-progress and sent me back to the drawing board with a better understanding of rhetorical theory and new insights into Fuller: George D. Gopen, S. Michael Halloran, and Carolyn Karcher. Finally, this essay greatly benefited from the devotion, intelligence, and initiative of my research assistant, Ruthe Thompson. My heartfelt thanks to all.

1 S. Margaret Fuller, *Woman in the Nineteenth Century* (1845; reprint, Columbia, SC: University of South Carolina Press, 1980), 26; hereafter cited in text as *W*.

2 In addition to the all-important influence of Wollstonecraft, Fuller was also aware of a growing body of United States literature on women's rights, including Charles Brockden Brown's *Alcuin: A Dialogue* (1798; reprint, New Haven: Yale University Press, 1935), the first book by an American to reject the concept of *separate spheres*; Sarah Moore Grimké's *Letters on the Equality of the Sexes and the Condition of Woman; Addressed to Mary Parker, President of the Boston Female Anti-Slavery Society* (Boston: I. Knapp, 1838), the first book by an American to argue for the legal emancipation of *all* women, both black and white; and Sophia Dana Ripley's essay on married women's rights, "Woman," published by Fuller in *The Dial* 1 (1841): 362–7.

3 Both are specifically mentioned by Fuller, *W*, 98.

4 This charge was leveled in a number of critical reviews, but the phrasing here appeared in a letter from Elizabeth Peabody to her daughter, Sophia Peabody

Hawthorne, and was included in Julian Hawthorne's *Nathaniel Hawthorne and His Wife* (Boston: Houghton Mifflin, 1884), excerpted in Julian Hawthorne, "Margaret Fuller and Hawthorne," *Critical Essays on Margaret Fuller*, ed. Joel Myerson (Boston: G. K. Hall, 1980), 115.

5 Sally Miller Gearhart, "The Womanization of Rhetoric," *Women's Studies International Quarterly* 2 (1979): 195.

6 Jean Bethke Elshtain, "Feminist Discourse and Its Discontents: Language, Power, and Meaning," *Signs* 7 (1982): 605, 606.

7 Marianne Hirsch and Evelyn Fox Keller, "Practicing Conflict in Feminist Theory," in *Conflicts in Feminism*, ed. Marianne Hirsch and Evelyn Fox Keller (New York: Routledge, 1990), 370.

8 Orestes A. Brownson, "Miss Fuller and Reformers," review of *Woman in the Nineteenth Century*, by Margaret Fuller, *Brownson's Quarterly Review* 7 (1845), reprinted in Myerson, ed., *Critical Essays on Margaret Fuller*, 19, 8. For a discussion of Brownson's expectations regarding editorship of *The Dial*, see Charles Capper, *Margaret Fuller, An American Romantic Life* (New York: Oxford University Press, 1992), 1: 333–4; hereafter cited in text as *MF*.

9 A. G. M. (anonymous), "The Condition of Woman," *Southern Quarterly Review* 10 (1845): 148.

10 Charles F. Briggs, review of *Woman in the Nineteenth Century*, *Broadway Journal* 1 (1845), reprinted in Myerson, ed., *Critical Essays on Margaret Fuller*, 9, 12, 11, 13.

11 Lydia Maria Child, "Woman in the 19th Century," *Broadway Journal* 1 (1845), reprinted in Myerson, ed., *Critical Essays on Margaret Fuller*, 7; Frederic Dan Huntington, review of *Woman in the Nineteenth Century*, *Christian Examiner* 38 (1845), reprinted in ibid., 26.

12 Brownson, "Miss Fuller and Reformers," 19.

13 *Memoirs of Margaret Fuller Ossoli*, ed. Ralph Waldo Emerson, William Henry Channing, and James Freeman Clarke (1852; reprint, Boston: Brown, Taggard and Chase, 1860), 1: 337.

14 Brownson, "Miss Fuller and Reformers," 19; Vernon L. Parrington, *Main Currents in American Thought: The Romantic Revolution in America 1800–1860* (New York: Harcourt, Brace and Co., 1927), 2: 418; David M. Robinson, "Margaret Fuller and the Transcendental Ethos: *Woman in the Nineteenth Century*," *PMLA* 97 (1982): 84; William J. Scheick, "The Angelic Artistry of Margaret Fuller's *Woman in the Nineteenth Century*," *Essays in Literature* 11 (1984): 293.

15 Belle Gale Chevigny's *The Woman and the Myth: Margaret Fuller's Life and Writings* (Old Westbury, NY: Feminist Press, 1976) was instrumental in presenting a sympathetic overview of Fuller's life and works; but even Chevigny characterized *Woman in the Nineteenth Century* as "lack[ing] . . . systematic analysis" (222).

16 Marie Mitchell Olesen Urbanski, *Margaret Fuller's "Woman in the Nineteenth Century": A Literary Study of Form and Content, of Sources and Influence* (Westport, CT: Greenwood Press, 1980), 128; Robinson, "Margaret Fuller and the Transcendental Ethos," 83.

17 In 1993 the only edition still in print was published by Norton, with an introduction by Bernard Rosenthal (New York: W. W. Norton, 1971), which reprints Margaret Fuller Ossoli, *Woman in the Nineteenth Century and Kindred Papers Relating to the Sphere, Condition, and Duties, of Woman*, ed. Arthur B. Fuller (Boston: J. P. Jewett, 1855). This edition is particularly troubling because it is prefaced by her

brother's apologetic and sanctimonious assurance that, despite her intellectual pursuits, his sister had never "neglect[ed] the domestic concerns of life" (6). Happily, a selection of Fuller's work that includes a reprinting of the original 1845 edition of *Woman in the Nineteenth Century* in its entirety, with all appendices, is available in Margaret Fuller, *The Portable Margaret Fuller*, ed. Mary Kelley (New York: Penguin, 1994), 228–362.

18   Edgar Allan Poe, "The Literati of New York City. – No. IV Sarah Margaret Fuller," *Godey's Magazine and Lady's Book* 33 (1846), reprinted in Myerson, ed., *Critical Essays on Margaret Fuller*, 37.

19   Margaret Fuller to Caroline Sturgis, March 4, 1839, in *The Letters of Margaret Fuller*, ed. Robert N. Hudspeth (Ithaca: Cornell University Press, 1983–4), 2: 59; hereafter cited as *Letters*.

20   Margaret Fuller to Ralph Waldo Emerson, March 1, 1838, *Letters*, 1: 327.

21   Caroline Healey Dall, *Historical Pictures Retouched: A Volume of Miscellanies* (Boston: Walker, Wise, and Co., 1860), 261.

22   (Margaret Fuller), "The Great Lawsuit. Man *versus* Men. Woman *versus* Women," *The Dial* 4 (1843): 1–47.

23   Laraine R. Fergenson, "Margaret Fuller in the Classroom: The Providence Period," in *Studies in the American Renaissance 1987*, ed. Joel Myerson (Charlottesville, VA: University Press of Virginia, 1987), 131.

24   Judith Strong Albert, "Margaret Fuller's Row at the Greene Street School: Early Female Education in Providence, 1837–1839," *Rhode Island History* 42 (1983): 43.

25   Richard Whately, *Elements of Rhetoric . . . From the Third English Edition* (Boston: Hilliard, Gray, and Co., 1832); hereafter cited in text as *ER*. By 1837, when Fuller began teaching at the Greene Street School, Whately's third edition had become one of the standard rhetoric texts assigned in schools and colleges across the United States. The book was well enough known to be featured in an 1838 advertisement for Greene Street (see Albert, "Margaret Fuller's Row," 53), which suggests that it was also the text used for training boys in rhetoric and public declamation.

26   Harriet Hall Johnson, "Margaret Fuller as Known by her Scholars," *Christian Register* (April 21, 1910), reprinted in Myerson, ed., *Critical Essays on Margaret Fuller*, 135.

27   Quoted in ibid., 135, 136, 135.

28   Quoted in ibid., 136.

29   Ray E. McKerrow, "Richard Whately's Theory of Rhetoric," in *Explorations in Rhetoric: Studies in Honor of Douglas Ehninger*, ed. Ray E. McKerrow (Glenview, IL: Scott, Foresman, 1982), 146.

30   While Elizabeth Palmer Peabody kept summary notes, and while some participants made general statements about the conversations in their journals and letters, only Caroline Healey Dall attempted to record accurately the actual give and take of discussion, noting who said what and incorporating her own candid impressions of the participants and their ideas.

31   Caroline W. Healey, *Margaret Fuller and Her Friends, or Ten Conversations with Margaret Fuller upon the Mythology of the Greeks and its Expression in Art* (Boston: Roberts Brothers, 1895), 46.

32   It is entirely possible that Fuller prevailed upon her friend, the bookstore owner Elizabeth Palmer Peabody, to secure for her from London the revised and expanded sixth edition of Whately's *Elements of Rhetoric* (London: B. Fellowes, 1841); in that event, Fuller worked from a text with additional illustrative material – but its

structure and arguments remained identical to those of the earlier third edition which she had taught at Greene Street. In fact, nothing substantive from the third edition was cut; more examples and an occasional clarification were simply added in the revised sixth edition.

33   Marie Urbanski reminds us (*Margaret Fuller's "Woman in the Nineteenth Century,"* 161–2) that Fuller was later vindicated when a young Boston woman, in the face of her husband's illness, captained a ship around Cape Horn en route to California in the 1850s. As Urbanski points out, this incident "caught the imagination of many people" and elicited respectful responses to Fuller's original remark.

34   In Frank Shuffelton's "Margaret Fuller at Greene Street School: The Journal of Evelina Metcalf," in *Studies in the American Renaissance 1985*, ed. Joel Myerson (Charlottesville, VA: University Press of Virginia, 1985), 38, Metcalf's journal entry for December 12, 1838 records that "our Rhetoric lesson which was on Persuasion to-day was very well recited. It spoke of the province of the orator and the requisites of a perfect orator."

35   While Whately employed occasional martial imagery throughout his text, such images are never brutal, nor are they as concentrated and as elaborate, as those in part 2, *ER*, 117–67.

36   Stanley E. Fish, *Self-Consuming Artifacts* (Berkeley: University of California Press, 1972), 1.

37   See Ralph Waldo Emerson's essay, "Self-Reliance" (*c.*1839–40), in *Selections from Ralph Waldo Emerson*, ed. Stephen E. Whicher (Boston: Houghton Mifflin, 1957), 147–68.

38   Urbanski, *Margaret Fuller's "Woman in the Nineteenth Century,"* 130.

39   Stanton and the *History of Woman Suffrage*, quoted in ibid., 160, 158 respectively.

40   Dall, *Historical Pictures*, 249, 261.

41   Gearhart, "The Womanization of Rhetoric," 199; Elshtain, "Feminist Discourse and Its Discontents," 620, 621.

42   Although Fuller is never cited as a source, recent work in rhetoric and composition theory has reconsidered the meaning of *conversation* as a formal discourse, including most notably Gregory Clark's *Dialogue, Dialectic, and Conversation: A Social Perspective on the Function of Writing* (Carbondale, IL: Southern Illinois University Press, 1990).

43   Hirsch and Keller, "Practicing Conflict," 370, 371.

12

Nineteenth-Century American Women Poets Revisited

CHERYL WALKER

The publication of *Nineteenth-Century American Women Writers: An Anthology* draws attention to the range and variety of nineteenth-century women's writing and reminds us that women published a great deal of poetry during this period. Though Emily Dickinson has been popular since the twenties, most older American women poets were forgotten until the late 1970s when feminist scholars began to bring to light a score of little-known nineteenth-century poets whose works were once again interesting to a new generation of readers. Feminist studies such as Emily Stipes Watts's *The Poetry of American Women from 1632 to 1945* (1977), my own *The Nightingale's Burden: Women Poets and American Culture Before 1900* (1982), and Alicia Ostriker's masterful *Stealing the Language: The Emergence of Women's Poetry in America* (1986)[1] brought new attention to these muted voices, and within a few years Lydia Sigourney, Frances Osgood, and Lucy Larcom were once again making an appearance in college courses and literary anthologies. Around the same time, African American scholarship resurrected and kept attention focused on Frances E. W. Harper, who had been an eloquent abolitionist as well as a poet. New figures emerged in the Schomburg Library of Nineteenth-Century Black Women Writers, published by Oxford University Press in 1988.[2] The work of Helen Hunt Jackson, already well known to Dickinson scholars, and Emma Lazarus, the author of the poem on the Statue of Liberty, began to be looked at in greater detail. Finally, and most recently, the Mohawk poet E. Pauline Johnson and the iconoclasts Rose Terry Cooke and Sarah Morgan Bryan Piatt have returned to view, bringing with them questions about the relation of women poets to romanticism and modernism. It is now possible to say that nineteenth-century American women poets have re-entered the expanded canon. But how should we read their poetry? What does it tell us?

I wish to argue here that there is some value in dividing the century's poets into four primary categories: early nationals, romantics, realists, and moderns. The early nationals, such as Lydia Sigourney, praise moderation, extol duty, appeal to piety, elevate "America," and take seriously questions concerning human rights. Such poets come most directly out of an eighteenth-century context and form the earliest grouping. In contrast, the American romantics, their immediate successors, revel in their emotions and explore extreme psychological states; they defy conventions, even praising sexual excess, and their work is notable for its lack of balance and its dark implications about the human psyche. Romantics luxuriate in the senses and in dreams. Their politics focuses less on broad issues of human rights than on the injustice of oppression as it affects individuals. Rose Terry Cooke's most successful poetry (unlike her realist prose) is best understood as romantic. Realists take up the political challenges of the romantics but devote themselves to portraying the conditions of everyday life. Alice Cary and Lucy Larcom might be classified as realists insofar as they make available the detailed struggles of common people of the working class. And finally we come to the moderns, who are different again, resisting the sentimental (which makes an appearance in both romanticism and realism), refusing comforting resolutions, leaving loose ends, fracturing the linguistic unit or opting for the simple and direct forms of modern speech. Emily Dickinson is surely the modernist *par excellence* but Lizette Woodworth Reese is, in her own way, a modern poet as well.

Having established these categories, however, one is immediately confronted by their inadequacy. Many poets fit under more than one heading. Emily Dickinson, for instance, is both a romantic *and* a modern. Other poets, such as Helen Hunt Jackson, do not fit comfortably under any of these rubrics. Some questions might be raised about the utility of creating such categories in the first place. What does feminism do to literary movements established originally by attention to male writers? If, as Joanne Feit Diehl has shown,[3] Emily Dickinson invokes romanticism only to challenge many of its basic assumptions, can she be called a romantic? Is the sentimental a subset of romanticism, as some have argued, or is it a strategy, employed by women in all categories and throughout the century, to undermine the masculinist separation of intellectual from emotional experience, public from private life? What about writers with roots in communities not governed by European values, such as the African American Frances Harper (born of free black parents) and the Native American E. Pauline Johnson? Should they be forced into traditions that grew out of Euro-American writing and thinking? These are some of the questions we will address in the following pages as we look more closely at a few of the poets represented in *Nineteenth-Century American Women Writers: An Anthology.*

One thing is clear, however. Nineteenth-century American women poets did not function in a world isolated from men or from male literary productions. Though the British poet Felicia Hemans (who preceded Sigourney by some years and in honor of whom Sigourney was called "the American Hemans") might be seen as the foremother of the "nightingale tradition,"[4] all the women poets represented in the collection read poetry by men and were influenced by male as well as female poets. Furthermore, the view we once held that women poets were like Emily Dickinson, restricted in their social contacts, unmarried and reclusive, has been thoroughly revised. Many of the poets in this anthology lived in cities and carried on a bustling social life. Frances Osgood, Alice Cary, and Emma Lazarus, for example, all lived in New York City and were vitally engaged in the intellectual and political movements of their day, meeting the *literati* in salons and operating equally in a world of women dedicated to women's concerns and in the world of patriarchy dominated by male publishers, magazine editors, and patrons. Some women poets such as Alice Cary, Lucy Larcom, and Lizette Woodworth Reese remained unmarried, but others, such as Lydia Sigourney, Frances Osgood, and Sarah Morgan Bryan Piatt, married when they were quite young and struggled thereafter with all the challenges and concerns women usually found in dealing with nineteenth-century conjugal arrangements.

One of the contributions feminist scholars have made to the study of nineteenth-century poetry is their insistence on the importance of historical context. What did it mean to be a woman in this century, a white middle-class woman, a black woman born to free parents, a working-class white woman, a woman living in the West? These questions, which are typically those of race, class, geography, and gender, have helped us to "place" nineteenth-century women poets more accurately. It *does* make a difference that Lucy Larcom had to change her lifestyle completely during her adolescence and go to work in the noisy, tiring Lowell Mills instead of roaming the countryside at will as she had done previously. It *is* important to consider what Emily Dickinson did during the day – washing, cooking, reading, gardening, writing letters – in order to understand the circumstances under which she produced her poems and the extraordinary range of her literary imagination.

Nevertheless, sometimes literary history is useful as well as sociohistorical context. Let us consider the case of Lydia Sigourney, for example. When the possibility of a "women's tradition" in American poetry first began to be explored, the tendency was to privilege those poets who expressed their idiosyncratic "feelings" and their sense of personal identity. Thus, the defiant Frances Osgood was an early heroine of this tradition, applauded in turn by Emily Stipes Watts, myself, Alicia Ostriker, and, somewhat later, Mary DeJong and Joanne Dobson.[5] Since Sigourney was not given to exploring her subjectivity, she was often seen as dull and derivative by comparison to Osgood.

In 1988, as "sentimentalism" was beginning to be reclaimed as a female political and literary strategy, Annie Finch wrote an influential essay that challenged this assessment: "The Sentimental Poetess in the World: Metaphor and Subjectivity in Lydia Sigourney's Nature Poetry." In this essay she argued that Sigourney defied the conventions of romantic poetry, which were premised on a male view of subjectivity and individualism, substituting instead a female "sentimental" ethic based on shared communal values. "Sentimental art takes our common sense, the weapon we most strongly control, and uses it to undermine our sense of individual self," she wrote. According to Finch, the natural world assumes an objective status in this poetry and is not used to carry the poet's emotions and sentiments, as it so often is in romanticism. Finch praises Sigourney for the generosity of her vision and insists that we re-examine our "romantic" assumptions about lyric poetry, concluding: "I hope that before too long it will be possible to see the sentimental tradition as a literary movement in its own right, as a movement having its own roots, its own aesthetics, its own world-view, and its own inheritors."[6]

The terms in which Finch praises Sigourney – her willingness to give object-ive status not only to Nature but also to the poor and oppressed without fore-grounding her own subjectivity – seem to me worth taking seriously, and I too have come to find Sigourney more interesting than I did when I first wrote *The Nightingale's Burden*.[7] Of course, one could argue that there are poems, such as "Meeting of the Susquehanna with the Lackawanna," in which Sigourney is per-fectly willing to impose her own fantasies upon Nature, to metaphorize these rivers and to read them as telling a highly romanticized tale of Indian–white relations. But perhaps to make this point is simply to discover the variety within Sigourney's unusually large opus.

A more important point, it seems to me, is that one need not invoke "senti-mentalism" to explain Sigourney's relatively self-effacing approach to poetry. In fact, Sigourney, who published her first book in 1815, seems to me far too early a poet to be a good candidate for nineteenth-century sentimentalism, which is better understood as a phenomenon of the late 1830s and thereafter. Like William Cullen Bryant, who began publishing at about the same time, she may be read as an "early national" poet with her roots in the eighteenth century. Like Sigourney, Bryant felt that "Poetry lifts us into a sphere where self-interest cannot exist, and where the prejudices that perplex our everyday life can hardly enter. It restores to us our unperverted feelings, and leaves us at liberty to com-pare the issues of life with our unsophisticated notions of good and evil."[8] The domination of the public over the private, of "unsophisticated" (i.e. noncontam-inated) morality over urban forms of pleasure, and of duty over individual ful-fillment: all these are characteristic of literature composed in the early national period. I disagree with Finch that Sigourney always refused to read her own sentiments into Nature. Sometimes she did objectify and fetishize the natural world, just as Bryant did. Both generally resisted the opportunity to develop a subjective presence in the prevailing speaker, however, and thus both may illustrate a pre-romantic attitude toward the role of the artist.

If there is something that distinguishes Sigourney's poetry from that of her male counterparts, I would suggest that it is less likely to be found in aspects of the sentimental (which, it seems to me, Finch essentializes as female) than in the divergent positionality of women poets as compared to men. In "Death of an Infant," for example, Sigourney writes: "There had been a murmuring sound / With which the babe would claim its mother's ear."[9] One could argue that these lines belong to a strain of sentimentalism that makes the deaths of children a standard *topos* in nineteenth-century poetry. But men as well as women wrote poems about the deaths of children. One might look at James Russell Lowell's "On the Death of a Friend's Child," for example. What distinguishes the poems by women is that they offer a density of experience that derives from women's lives, which were often spent caring for children, either one's own or those of other people. Frances Osgood's poems, "Ellen Learning to Walk" and "The Child Playing with a Watch," articulate sentiments inspired by the poet's observations of her own offspring. Such poems are rare in the canons of male poets.[10]

If one of the defining features of sentimentalism is the reversal of the roles usually accorded to reason and emotion, romanticism, rather than the literature of the early national period, would seem to be more in tune with it. In "A Flight of Fancy" Frances Osgood, a romantic poet of considerable interest, creates an allegory in which Fancy (imagined as an "airy coquette") has turned the head of Reason, described as "An old-fashion'd, fidgety, queer-looking wight." As I noted long ago, this poem is an example of one of the principal types of women's poetry in the nineteenth century: the female power fantasy. In typical examples from this genre "the feminine" triumphs over male attempts to constrain and construct her. Here Fancy exploits the potential of a female stereotype to lead Reason on a merry chase. In the end she escapes from her prison cell by finding a way "to get through / The hole in the lock, which she could not undo."[11] In other words, she leaves the structure in place while finding her own individual access to liberation.

It is the emphasis on individualism and subjectivity, of course, that Annie Finch finds incompatible with Lydia Sigourney's feminine practice. And it is certainly true that many women poets had a hard time adopting the arrogant posture of male romantic "authority" (though in "Indian Names" Sigourney makes herself a thoroughly challenging spokesperson for Native American rights). In their classic feminist critique *The Madwoman in the Attic: The Woman Writer and the Nineteenth-Century Literary Imagination*, Sandra Gilbert and Susan Gubar explore the difficulties women writers experienced in trying to assume the dominant and dominating voice of the artist when that voice spoke not just for others but for the self.[12]

Yet some willingness to engage in power play is endemic to romanticism, and female romantics could be just as self-centered, just as power hungry, as their male counterparts. Therefore, one must be careful not to define the feminine as a refusal to deploy power even at the expense of another. Some feminist criticism of Emily Dickinson has fallen into this trap, only to be brought up short by critics such as Mary Loeffelholz, Camille Paglia, and Betsy Erkkila, all of whom have emphasized the level of authorial violence in Dickinson's work.[13] A poem such as "I cannot dance upon my toes" arrogates a good deal of self-aggrandizing power to the female speaker, and women readers for at least a generation now have enjoyed it precisely for this reason.

A lesser-known poet, Rose Terry Cooke, provides an even more surprising example of the way the female power fantasy within romanticism can operate to destabilize feminine stereotypes. Cooke's poem "Fantasia" toys with the sensuality of violence as its disembodied speaker imagines mocking a ship's crew who are in dire straits. The speaker begins as a sea-flower, relatively unthreatening as she watches the surf "[r]ush on the black rocks' side." As a sea-bird (flower and bird being typical nineteenth-century images of the feminine), she emerges as a tease, "Mocking the mariner's cry" and then "Drifting away on the tempest, / A speck on the sullen sky!" Such behavior flies directly in the face of beliefs that women are spiritually superior to men and essentially nurturing. The sea-bird seems to enjoy withholding her favors. Furthermore, in the final stanza, this speaker takes on the role of a sea-wind, and here her darker intentions become even clearer.

> When I am a sea-wind,
> I'll watch for a ship I know,
> Through the sails and rigging
> Merrily I will blow.
> The crew shall be like dead men
> White with horror and woe;
> Then I'll sing like a spirit,
> And let the good ship go.[14]

Even the ending is in doubt. Does this spirit renounce her evil intentions or, in letting the ship go, is she simply leaving it to its own devices, inadequate though they may be? It seems to me significant that a woman poet is here engaging one of the staples of the nineteenth-century male imagination (life at sea) and positioning herself in the role of a subversive spirit willing to watch the men suffer. This poem is a power fantasy whose target may well be literary patriarchy.

Other poems in Cooke's opus, such as "After the Camanches" and the blood-thirsty ballad "Basile Renaud," contain similar elements of sociopathology. Even Cooke's most widely anthologized poem, "Blue-Beard's Closet," tantalizes us by refusing to fulfill our expectations. Instead of taking the famous villain to task, this speaker suggests that "Bluebeard's closet" may be a state of mind rather than the site of patriarchal oppression pure and simple. As I have suggested elsewhere,[15] the poetic voice here is a little salacious, a little mad, as though she were enjoying the opportunity to "play the Bluebeard" herself.

According to the description of sentimentalism that Annie Finch provides, romantic literature of this sort must be at odds with the feminine sentimental. So perhaps she is right to say that sentimentalism represents an independent literary tradition, not subsumable under the standard rubrics of literary history such as romanticism, realism, and modernism. My concern, however, is that by making sentimentalism the dominant mode of women's nineteenth-century literature (prose and poetry), one loses the interplay that clearly went on between male and female poets, the way in which poems by women (such as Frances Osgood's "The Fetter Neath the Flowers") might be seen as responding to or generating poems by men (such as Theodore S. Fay's "Song").[16]

A good example of such interplay is the case of John Greenleaf Whittier, a great supporter of women poets and women's rights, and the "realists" in *Nineteenth-Century American Women Writers: An Anthology*, Alice Cary and Lucy Larcom, who seem to be the most strongly influenced by Whittier. Whittier attended the literary salons of Cary and her poet-sister Phoebe, who addressed him in one poem as "Great master of the poet's art!" Larcom's poem "J. G. W." is also a tribute to his influence. Whittier was an abolitionist, a Quaker, and a man who respected working people. Furthermore, he wrote about women as well as men. In his *Songs of Labor and Other Poems*, he includes a paean of praise to "our farmer girls" whose work, it seems, is valued equally with that of the lumbermen, the drovers, and the shoemakers. "The Yankee Girl" in *Voices of Freedom* sits spinning by her "low cottage door," becoming a heroine when she repulses the rich Southerner who offers marriage and slaves to relieve her of her labors. "Barbara Frietchie" used to be a staple of schoolroom memorization: "'Shoot if thou must, this old gray head / But spare your country's flag,' she said."[17]

It is true that Lucy Larcom and Alice Cary wrote a great many more poems about women than Whittier did. But Larcom's "Weaving," among other works, and the many poems the Cary sisters wrote in celebration of working-class people, clearly owe a good deal to Whittier. Thus, it seems to me useful to look at the way women poets such as these do fit into broader movements in literary history (here "realism"), as well as to reflect on the qualities that distinguish women's poetry from men's.

If one compares the poems of Whittier with those of Lucy Larcom in terms of their purely stylistic qualities, the similarities outweigh the differences. Both employ a variety of stanzaic forms, line lengths, and rhyme schemes. Both use the dramatic monologue as well as dialogue to enliven their portraits of common folk. Both prefer simple rhymes and regular meters over the dramatic effects sometimes achieved by such poets as Walt Whitman, Sarah Morgan Bryan Piatt, Stephen Crane, and Emily Dickinson. A single poem plucked from either's body of work would be very difficult to assign correctly based on stylistic analysis alone.

There are poems that nineteenth-century women do seem to write more often than men, but they are identifiable more through subject matter than style. The female power fantasy, the sanctuary poem (in which a woman fantasizes about retreating to an enclosed, safe space),[18] and the poem about a woman's difficulties with marriage are examples. Indeed, concerning the latter issue, Paula Bennett argues that nineteenth-century women poets offered an extended critique of the domestic ideology often championed and reinforced in the poems of men:

Writing with their poetic mothers in mind (as well as with an eye to the romantic poetry still being produced around them), they [women poets] effect a conscious and deliberately wrought rupture with the tradition high sentimentalism represented. Not only do they reject high sentimentalism as a style, but they reject it as a belief system and a way of knowing, thus turning their backs on the very grounds upon which the earlier generation of women poets empowered themselves.[19]

In Kilcup's collection one could cite Alice Cary's "The Bridal Veil," Lucy Larcom's "The Little Old Girl," and Elizabeth Stuart Phelps (Ward)'s "The Stone Woman of Eastern Point" as examples of poems that challenge domestic ideology with its rhetoric about the glories of being "the angel in the house." Marriage was often a difficult matter for women poets, as biographies of these women illustrate. Celia Thaxter, for example, made her peace with it by spending large amounts of time away from her husband on the island on which she grew up near the coast of New Hampshire. When at the end of Lucy Larcom's "A Little Old Girl" the gossips shake their heads at the romping children, and comment approvingly about Prudence, "What a good wife she will make!," the reader must conclude, first, that marriage is likely to take the energy exhibited by the children and divert it, as Prudence has done, to performing tasks that require the sacrifice of "beauty" and most of the finer feelings. Furthermore, Larcom is critical here of the way older women become complicitous with the system of patriarchal oppression represented by conventional marriage.[20] Rose Terry Cooke's short story, "Mrs. Flint's Married Experience," tells a similar tale.

"Realists," with their attention to the lives of ordinary, working-class people, offered their readers many stories about the blighted hopes of married women. The "modernists" – among whom Paula Bennett lists Elizabeth Stuart Phelps (Ward), at least in "The Stone Woman of Eastern Point" – ask questions instead: "Was it worth living for? Say, / Tell us, thou woman of stone!"[21] Bennett comments: "That there is no sentimentalizing of women's oppression in this poem (no translating it into angelic status) suggests the distance bourgeois women had traveled in 35 years. To Phelps's speaker, the women of the earlier generation have become women of stone."[22]

Paula Bennett has dedicated her recent scholarly energies to resurrecting Sarah Morgan Bryan Piatt, another "modernist," but one who had slipped from view since the turn of the century when Edmund Clarence Stedman claimed that she was the best-known Western "poetess."[23] Though written in 1867, "Giving Back the Flower" is an unusually modern poem: choosing a rough-shod rhythmic pattern over the smooth metrics typically preferred by nineteenth-century poets. It challenges conventional beliefs about romance, marriage, war, and God, and its female speaker is unusually self-possessed and challenging. "The Fancy Ball," in which the speaker insists she will "go as – Myself,"[24] even if her presence will offend or terrorize the company, suggests the affinities between Piatt's independence and Dickinson's. Indeed, a contemporary review of her 1880 volume

Dramatic Persons and Moods grumbles about her work in terms that remind one of Dickinson's critics: "She not only demands an apprehension which is denied to the many, but she demands also that they shall forget the language which is natural to them, and learn the language which is natural to her – a primitive speech, so to speak, because it leaves so much to be supplied by intuition and imagination."[25] These qualities, Paula Bennett argues, are also what make both poets modern.

Of course, there are poets who do not fit easily into any of the primary categories we have so briefly explored. Helen Hunt Jackson was a highly talented lyricist who learned the lessons Thomas Wentworth Higginson tried to teach Emily Dickinson. Her verse is graceful, plangent, and often distinguished by dramatic conclusions, such as the one that lifts the ending of "Poppies on the Wheat." Yet it would be wrong to call her a romantic, a realist, or a modern. More than anything else, she seems to belong among the English Victorians with poets such as Christina Rossetti. Her imagination frequently ran to the kind of allegory we see in "Crossed Threads," where the spider's web is read as a figure for human limitation:

How dare we any human deed arraign;
Attempt to reckon any moment's cost;
Or any pathway trust as safe and plain
Because we see not where the threads have crossed?[26]

A more extended use of allegory may be found in her poem "Acquainted with Grief."

Another American poet whose affinities seem more British than American is Louise Imogen Guiney, who eventually moved to England permanently in 1901. Guiney was strongly influenced by Emily Brontë and Alice Meynell. She immersed herself in historical projects, such as studies of the Cavalier Poets and the seventeenth-century poet Katherine Philips (the "Matchless Orinda"). Some of her most beautiful lyrics have a recognizably late nineteenth-century British sound to them:

When on the marge of evening the last blue light is broken,
And the winds of dreamy odour are loosened from afar,
Or when my lattice opens, before the lark hath spoken,
On dim laburnum-blossoms, and morning's dying star,

I think of thee (O mine the more if other eyes be sleeping!)
Whose greater noonday splendours the many share and see,
While sacred and for ever, some perfect law is keeping
The late, the early twilight, alone and sweet for me.[27]

In such lines as these from "When On the Marge of Evening," one can even hear Swinburne playing in the background.

Like Jackson and Guiney, Frances E. W. Harper is an anomaly in terms of American literary movements. Her poetry was designed to be delivered orally and preserves a strong theatrical vibrancy. Harper gave public performances almost daily when she worked as an abolitionist, and her lectures always created a strong response in her audience. Similarly, "The Slave Mother" uses the techniques of direct address to the audience and repetition of key lines ("He is not hers") that Harper had found effective in her antislavery lectures and later public appearances in support of women's rights, temperance, and justice for African Americans.

Twentieth-century readers have been particularly attracted to the "Aunt Chloe" poems in which Harper uses a folk character ("Aunt Chloe") to address social and political issues of the time. Her flare for narrative and her restraint in the use of dialect suggest comparisons with Paul Laurence Dunbar, whose greater insistence upon dialect has proven problematic for some readers. By contrast, the figure of Aunt Chloe, with her sense of humor and mother-wit, looks forward to Langston Hughes's character "Simple," who is the protagonist of so many of Hughes's subtle and arch short stories.

Rather than force Harper's work into the categories of Euro-American poetry, it seems to me more worthwhile to see it in the context of evangelical rhetoric and what Henry Louis Gates, Jr describes as African American "signifying," a set of practices that includes "'marking,' 'loud-talking,' 'specifying,' 'testifying,' 'calling out' (of one's name), 'sounding,' 'rapping,' and 'playing the dozens.'"[28] Harper was not cut off from European literary texts (her intense and moving poem "Let the Light Enter!" addresses the dying words of Goethe), but her poetic style is better seen as part of an oral rather than a written tradition.

Another poet who makes a less than comfortable fit with Euro-American categories is the Mohawk poet, E. Pauline Johnson. In her case, however, the work is highly "literary" rather than, as one might expect in the case of a Native American, the product of native oral traditions. As Kilcup has suggested, Johnson's poetry combines various literary influences from romanticism, sentimentalism, realism, and modernism.[29] Its roots, like those of most Native American nineteenth-century publications, indicate the hybrid nature of this non-"native" plant. The influence of romanticism is perhaps the first thing one notices in poems such as "Erie Waters":

O! wind so sweet and swift,
O! danger-freighted gift
Bestowed on Erie with her waves that foam and fall and lift,
We laugh in your wild face,
And break into a race
With flying clouds and tossing gulls that weave
And interlace.[30]

Here we find the emphasis upon danger and wildness that belongs to so many women's romantic poems. Even the metrical pattern recalls this tradition: its alternation of short with long lines suggests the ecstasy of an imagined liberation. Rose Terry Cooke's poem "Semele" is another powerful example of the same romantic phenomenon.

The sensual luxuriance of "Marshlands" and the dream motif in "Shadow River, Muskoka" also seem romantic, but one pauses at these lines from the fifth stanza of the latter: "The beauty, strength, and power of the land / Will never stir or bend at my command." This assertion represents almost a direct paraphrase of Annie Finch's definition of the sentimental tradition and its critique of romanticism, except that the speaker then goes on to reject this world: "O! pathless life of mine whose deep ideal / Is more my own than ever was the real."[31] Where are we now? The traditions invoked here do not merge. Similarly, "Low Tide at St. Andrews" and the Indian poems ("The Corn Husker" and "The Indian Corn Planter") bear a strong resemblance to poems in the realist mode: "the grim / Realities of laboring for bread." How does one connect them with Johnson's earlier romanticism? One alternative is to give up on the categories of literary history entirely. Yet, as I have tried to suggest in the course of this essay, I believe that something is lost if one does not explore the way women both entered into the ongoing literary conversation and also revised the direction this conversation took.

How influential were the women poets who appear in Kilcup's anthology? Emily Dickinson, as we all know, has been very influential indeed. Emma Lazarus found a permanent niche because her poem, "The New Colossus," was engraved on the Statue of Liberty. Certain poets have exerted a strong ethnic influence: Frances Harper as an African American and Emma Lazarus as a voice of Jewish resistance. However, as modernism entered in as a disruptive force, most women poets of the nineteenth century were forgotten, even those (such as Sarah Morgan Bryan Piatt) who might have been read as precursors.

Yet the vagaries of literary history are unpredictable. From most points of view, Lizette Woodworth Reese would be an unlikely choice as a twentieth-century influence. She was shy, modest, and wrote "simple" poems that were unconventional mostly because they were so austere, so stripped down, compared to earlier lyric examples. Even Johnson, whose poems also use a certain kind of simplicity to achieve their lyric effects, seems extravagant compared to Reese. Nevertheless, Reese's poems meet most of Ezra Pound's rules for the new poetry of imagism: to use the language of common speech, to create new rhythms, to present a clear image, and to insist upon concentration as the highest virtue. Reese's poems remind one of Sappho's, and Sappho was one of the most powerful influences on the rising generation of modern poets who began writing at the turn of the century. "Bargain" is the kind of poem many early modernists responded to before poetry became the province of the esoteric and the arcane.

A rose will cost you more
Than its gathering;
A song be such a price
You dare not sing.

What must you pay for each,
Else loveliness far amiss?
Yourself nailed to a Tree –
This.[32]

Both Louise Bogan and Sara Teasdale read Lizette Woodworth Reese carefully.
Bogan's poem "The Crows" was written in response to Reese's "Crows," just as
Bogan's "Women" pays homage to Reese's earlier poem with the same title.

Reese's work is just one example of the fact that literary history is always
changing. As one branch of it runs dry, another channel opens. It is especially
important at this time of renewed interest in women's literary productions that
we not lose sight of either the way women supported and influenced one another
or the way women writers reaffirmed as well as challenged the literary ideas of
their male counterparts. If we keep both these views in mind, we will be less
likely to create a critical perspective that loses its momentum because it hasn't
allowed itself to be nourished by the many channels that have fed the literary
imaginations of both men and women throughout our complex history.

NOTES

1   Emily Stipes Watts, *The Poetry of American Women from 1632 to 1945* (Austin:
    University of Texas Press, 1977); Cheryl Walker, *The Nightingale's Burden: Women
    Poets and American Culture Before 1900* (Bloomington: Indiana University Press,
    1982); Alicia Suskin Ostriker, *Stealing the Language: The Emergence of Women's Poetry
    in America* (Boston: Beacon Press, 1986).
2   Joan R. Sherman, ed., *Collected Black Women's Poetry*, 4 vols. The Schomburg Library
    of Nineteenth-Century Black Women Writers (New York: Oxford University Press,
    1988).
3   Joanne Feit Diehl, *Dickinson and the Romantic Imagination* (Princeton: Princeton
    University Press, 1981).
4   I define this tradition in my first book, *The Nightingale's Burden*. Though various
    scholars have quite rightly felt the need to revise my conceptions, which are now
    fifteen years old, the "nightingale tradition," I believe, is still a reasonably useful
    way of contextualizing mainstream white, middle-class women's poetry, especially
    as it achieved prominence in the mid-nineteenth century. In *Masks Outrageous and
    Austere: Culture, Psyche, and Persona in Modern Women Poets* (Bloomington: Indiana
    University Press, 1991), I argue that even some twentieth-century women poets
    might be seen as operating within the general outlines of this tradition.
5   Joanne Dobson, "Sex, Wit, and Sentiment: Frances Osgood and the Poetry of Love,"
    American Literature 65 (1993): 631–50; also *Dickinson and the Strategies of Reticence:
    The Woman Writer in Nineteenth-Century America* (Bloomington: Indiana University
    Press, 1989); Mary G. DeJong, "Her Fair Fame: The Reputation of Frances Sar-
    gent Osgood, Woman Poet," *Studies in the American Renaissance*, ed. Joel Myerson
    (Charlottesville: University Press of Virginia, 1987), 265–83; and DeJong, "Lines
    from a Partly Published Drama: The Romance of Frances Sargent Osgood and

Edgar Allan Poe," *Patrons and Protegees: Gender, Friendship, and Writing in Nineteenth-Century America*, ed. Shirley Marchalonis (New Brunswick: Rutgers University Press, 1988), 31–58.

6 Annie Finch, "The Sentimental Poetess in the World: Metaphor and Subjectivity in Lydia Sigourney's Nature Poetry," *Legacy: A Journal of Nineteenth-Century American Writers* 5 (1988): 5, 13.

7 See my headnote for Sigourney in Walker, ed., *American Women Poets of the Nineteenth Century: An Anthology* (New Brunswick: Rutgers University Press, 1992), 1–2.

8 Quoted in Richard Ruland and Malcolm Bradbury, *From Puritanism to Postmodernism: A History of American Literature* (New York: Viking, 1991), 75.

9 Kilcup, *NCAWW*, 42.

10 Lowell did not write about the deaths of his own four children, perhaps feeling that the topic was too close for him to handle effectively. Hawthorne did write some wonderful journal entries about his daughter, Una, which Robert Peters has turned into verse in a book called *Hawthorne: Poems Adapted from the American Notebooks* (Fairfax, CA: Red Hill Press, 1977); and Longfellow, of course, immortalized "Grave Alice, and laughing Allegra, / And Edith with golden hair" in "The Children's Hour." See *The Complete Poetical Works of Longfellow* (Boston: Houghton Mifflin, 1922), 201.

11 *NCAWW*, 130, 129, 131.

12 Sandra Gilbert and Susan Gubar, *The Madwoman in the Attic: The Woman Writer and the Nineteenth-Century Literary Imagination* (New Haven: Yale University Press, 1979).

13 Mary Loeffelholz, *Dickinson and the Boundaries of Feminist Criticism* (Chicago: University of Chicago Press, 1991); Camille Paglia, *Sexual Personae: Art and Decadence from Nefertiti to Emily Dickinson* (New Haven: Yale University Press, 1990); Betsy Erkkila, *The Wicked Sisters: Women Poets, Literary History, and Discord* (New York: Oxford University Press, 1992). For my comments on these arguments, see Walker, "The Whip Signature: Violence, Feminism, and Women Poets," in *Gender and Genre: Essays on Women's Poetry, Late Romantics to Late Victorians: 1830–1900*, ed. Isobel Armstrong and Virginia Blain (Macmillan, forthcoming).

14 *NCAWW*, 205.

15 See my discussion of this poem in Walker, "In Bluebeard's Closet: Women Who Write with the Wolves," *LIT: Literature Interpretation Theory* 7 (1996): 13–25.

16 See my discussion in *The Nightingale's Burden*, 49.

17 John Greenleaf Whittier, "The Yankee Girl," in *The Complete Poems of John Greenleaf Whittier* (Boston: Houghton Mifflin, [1857]), 46–7; "Barbara Frietchie," 269–70.

18 See *The Nightingale's Burden* for a more complete discussion of the sanctuary poem.

19 Paula Bennett, "'The Descent of the Angel': Interrogating Domestic Ideology in American Women's Poetry, 1858–1890," *American Literature History* 7 (1995): 594.

20 *NCAWW*, 178–9.

21 Ibid., 334.

22 Bennett, "'The Descent of the Angel,'" 605.

23 Stedman cited in *American Women Writers; A Critical Reference Guide*, ed. Lina Mainiero (New York: Frederick Ungar, 1981), 388.

24 *NCAWW*, 285.

25 Anonymous, "Recent Poetry By Women," *Scribner's Monthly* 19 (1880): 635.

26 *NCAWW*, 227.

27 Ibid., 499–500.

28   See Henry Louis Gates, Jr, *Black Literature and Literary Theory* (New York: Methuen, 1984), 86.

29   This observation was originally in the headnote for Johnson in *NCAWW* but was edited out because of length constraints.

30   *NCAWW*, 500.

31   Ibid., 502.

32   Lizette Woodworth Reese, "Bargain," *Pastures* (New York: Farrar and Rinehart, 1929), 32.

Index